Oxford Studies in Philosophy of Mind

Oxford Studies in Philosophy of Mind

Volume 1

Edited by
URIAH KRIEGEL

OXFORD
UNIVERSITY PRESS

OXFORD
UNIVERSITY PRESS

Great Clarendon Street, Oxford, OX2 6DP,
United Kingdom

Oxford University Press is a department of the University of Oxford.
It furthers the University's objective of excellence in research, scholarship,
and education by publishing worldwide. Oxford is a registered trade mark of
Oxford University Press in the UK and in certain other countries

First Edition published in 2021

Impression: 1

Published in the United States of America by Oxford University Press
198 Madison Avenue, New York, NY 10016, United States of America

British Library Cataloguing in Publication Data

Data available

Library of Congress Control Number: 2020948004

ISBN 978-0-19-884585-0

DOI: 10.1093/oso/9780198845850.001.0001

Printed and bound by
CPI Group (UK) Ltd, Croydon, CR0 4YY

Contents

Preface

This is the inaugural volume of *Oxford Studies in Philosophy of Mind*, a new annual publication dedicated to the philosophy of mind. Do we need another philosophy journal? It depends on what "need" means, but *Oxford Studies in Philosophy of Mind* will have certain unique features that separate it from other journals.

First, each volume will combine invited articles and articles selected from submissions. Writing a philosophy paper often involves a familiar tradeoff between rigor and control on the one hand and boldness and innovation on the other. The blind-review process notoriously biases toward the former. The purpose of invited articles is to offer contributors the freedom to fashion their own optimum point for this tradeoff. At the same time, the purpose of allowing submissions to the jorunal is to ensure access to younger scholars, perhaps from lesser-known universities or working in parts of the world of which the English-speaking world, including this journal's editors, may be less aware.

Second, and relatedly, for most of us, when we start reading a philosophy paper, our deepest hope is not that the paper will turn out to be flawless; rather, we hope it will contain some insight that will trigger breakthroughs in our own thinking on the topic, or lure us to start thinking about it if we have not yet. Yet when we wear our referee caps we tend to automatically slide into flaw-detection mode. *Oxford Studies in Philosophy of Mind* will consciously try to skew toward the insightful at the expense of the flawless.

Third, each volume of *Oxford Studies in Philosophy of Mind* will highlight two themes, but will also publish articles outside those themes. The purpose of the highlighted themes is to generate clusters of ideas surrounding a single topic, with the thought that the juxtaposition of perspectives on one issue will intensify interest. At the same time, the openness to submissions from outside these themes will serve two purposes. One is to allow themes that are organically gathering momentum in the philosophy-of-mind community to bubble up to the journal's awareness. The other is to create space for talent and its intellectual idiosyncrasies. Many topics that magnetize much academic activity at one point start out a decade earlier as comparatively isolated spurts of ideas, typically by younger scholars.

Fourth, the philosophy of mind has for at least half a century been torn between a traditional, armchair-led approach and a naturalistic, empirically driven approach. The most prestigious general philosophy journals tend to favor the traditional approach, while journals dedicated to the philosophy of mind, such as *Mind & Language* and *Philosophical Psychology*, tend to favor the naturalistic approach. Meanwhile, the *history* of philosophy of mind gets no play in philosophy-of-mind-dedicated journals, and is published mostly in history-of-philosophy journals. *Oxford Studies in Philosophy of Mind* will publish work from all three sectors: armchair philosophy of mind, empirically driven philosophy of mind, and history of philosophy of mind.

Fifth, as far as invited contributions are concerned, *Oxford Studies in Philosophy of Mind* will observe a strict gender balance, with exactly half of the invitees being women and half men. It does not control, of course, the ultimate delivery of manuscripts by the invitees, nor the quantity and quality of submissions from each gender. (This combination of factors accounts for the unfortunate paucity of chapters by women in the inaugural volume.)

Sixth, the processing of submissions will follow a different procedure. All submissions without exception will receive a verdict within a fortnight, pending *force majeure*. Anonymous referees will come into this process only at this stage, and will be involved even *after* a paper has been accepted for publication. The idea is to treat anonymous input, by carefully selected referees, as a means to improve a paper rather than a way to push authors in directions they are not intrinsically interested in.

Seventh, the journal is paired with an annual conference, hosted by Rice University's School of Humanities, featuring a combination of forthcoming and prospective papers. Just like anonymous review, presentation to a wide audience of specialists can be invaluable in improving a paper; this is one more tool to push articles appearing in *Oxford Studies in Philosophy of Mind* toward excellence.

We hope that these peculiarities of *Oxford Studies in Philosophy of Mind* will result in an exciting publication that will be of interest to all parts of the philosophy-of-mind community and beyond. In this inaugural volume, the two highlighted themes are "the value of consciousness" and "naturalism and physicalism," while four articles concern issues outside these two themes.

The first theme—the value of consciousness—garnered more attention among submissions, and six of the volume's thirteen chapters concern it. It features a long foundational article by a seminal thinker on this topic, Charles Siewert; a defense, by Roger Crisp, of the stark thesis that absolutely all value is grounded in the phenomenology of pleasure and pain; a phe-nomenological analysis of the experience of fulfillment, which Hyunseop Kim takes to ground (when fitting) a meaningful life; an argument, devel-oped by Diane O'Leary, that medicine is better framed not as concerned with fixing the body but rather as targeting improving one's bodily phe-nomenology; and two articles, by Matt Duncan and Chris Ranalli, offering two distinct perspectives on the singular epistemic value of conscious experience (for Duncan, experience *is* knowledge, though knowledge-by-acquaintance rather than propositional knowledge; for Ranalli, experience provides us with an intrinsic epistemic good that goes beyond truth, namely cognitive contact with reality).

Regarding the second theme—naturalism and physicalism—the volume includes an innovative analysis of the essence of naturalism by Lok-Chi Chan, which highlights the role of contingent historical paths in what we consider intuitively as "naturalistically kosher," as well as two important articles on physicalism by Jonathan Schaffer and Karen Bennett: Schaffer leverages the notion of ground to generate a twentieth-century version of functionalism, Bennett develops a new, explanatory argument against dualism.

Three other chapters in the volume bundle somewhat organically around the issue of content: Anil Gomes and Matthew Parrott seek a workable way to draw the line between internalism and externalism about content, Antti Kauppinen offers a novel account of the intentionality of pain, and Adam Pautz tries to generate a total theory of content from the combination of phenomenal intentionality and Lewis's theory of interpretation. The last chapter in the volume is by Peter Adamson and is historical, examining the role of certain dualist arguments in medieval Islamic philosophy.

List of Contributors

Peter Adamson Ludwig-Maximilian University of Munich

Karen Bennett Rutgers University

Lok-Chi Chan National Taiwan University

Roger Crisp St Anne's College, University of Oxford

Matt Duncan Rhode Island College

Anil Gomes Trinity College, University of Oxford

Antti Kauppinen University of Helsinki

Hyunseop Kim Seoul National University

Diane O'Leary Western University

Matthew Parrott St Hilda's College, University of Oxford

Adam Pautz Brown University

Chris Ranalli Vreij Universiteit Amsterdam

Jonathan Schaffer Rutgers University

Charles Siewert Rice University

I
THE VALUE OF CONSCIOUSNESS

1

Consciousness

Value, Concern, Respect

Charles Siewert

1. What Good Does Experience Do Us?

More specifically: does it bring a value of its own to us? Is it good for us in its
own right? I should be clear right off: I'm not asking what good we get just
from having some experience or other (no matter what kind). I am happy to
concede some experiences do us no good at all.[1] But if that's so, you may
think the answer all too obvious. "So you're asking whether there is *some*
experience that's nice to have just in itself? Sure, there is. For example:
tasting chocolate—that's one—or feeling the relief of taking off my shoes,
that's another. Next question!"

But bear with me. What I want is not just to secure acknowledgement that
there is some type of experience intuitively good "in itself" for us to have.
I want to clarify what it means to say experience has this sort of value, and by
doing so lead us to find it—not just in this or that obvious case of sensory
pleasure or relief—but in forms of experience that pervade our lives. I then
want to show how to use this recognition to place experience at the heart of
what makes our lives worth living to us. And this I want to do, without
discounting our desire that we not merely have experience, but that it reveal
to us the world beyond itself and engage us with others. Finally, I want to
show how it can figure fundamentally in our concern and respect for each
other, and in the irreplaceable value we accord a person's life. Carrying out
this agenda fully calls for a more elaborate treatment than I can now provide.
But I do aim here to make enough of a case to merit serious consideration
and inspire discussion.

---

[1] Thus I am in basic agreement with Lee's (2018) position (though he there takes my earlier
work to maintain the contrary view).

Charles Siewert, *Consciousness: Value, Concern, Respect* In: *Oxford Studies in Philosophy of Mind Volume 1*. Edited by:
Uriah Kriegel, Oxford University Press (2021). © Charles Siewert. DOI: 10.1093/oso/9780198845850.003.0001

2. What I Mean by "Experience"

I use the word "experience" to pick out what otherwise might be called a "state of consciousness"—what is sometimes marked by the qualification *subjective* experience. And I will be drawing on a fairly liberal view of what that encompasses. I realize the conception I employ would not be granted by all. However, there just is no standard view of what consciousness is, and what forms it takes, both free of controversy and meaty enough to help us deal extensively with questions about its value. So it won't do to discuss these matters without being upfront about one's starting points, even if I must here offload a detailed defense of mine to other ventures, past and future.

The use I will make of the word "experience" is to be distinguished from others that are common. If someone says something was "an experience" for them, we might ordinarily take them just to mean it was something they were affected by in a way likely to seem remarkable or salient. For example, you may describe either an airplane flight or meeting your in-laws as "an experience" in this sense. But I am using the term "experience" for *states of consciousness*—and I would not put plane trips or in-law encounters in that category. Note, however, that the "salient ways of being affected" sense of "experience" does lead to the other, consciousness sense. For the ways of being affected we typically find salient include what I'd call subjective experiences. For example: your *feeling as you did* when the plane suddenly lost altitude, or when your in-laws asked about your religion. And these feelings are experiences in the "subjective," and not just the "affected-by" sense. What makes that so? I would say: *these* "experiences," these feelings, *coincide* with your feeling them—that is, with your experiencing them. There's a sense in which you "experience" a feeling just in case you feel it, and the feeling itself is nothing apart from experiencing/feeling it. (By contrast: neither the airplane flight nor the in-law encounter *coincides* with someone's experiencing it, in any sense.)

Attention to what you feel when you feel pain, nausea, elation, anxiety, fatigue, giddiness, restlessness, and so on, provides a good place to start in clarifying what a "subjective experience" is. But the category is not confined to states naturally described as "feelings that you feel." For when something *looks* to me located, colored, lit in a certain way, when it *sounds, tastes, smells* somehow to me, or when an object *feels* to me somehow (slippery, bumpy, smooth, rough)—I also *experience* these appearances and feelings in this "coinciding" sense, even if it would be odd to say I "feel" them. For example, how I experience the visual appearance of a word on this page alters, depending on whether I am looking right at it or at the word just next to it. This is not just to say I am differently *affected* by its looking to me as it does: for there's a difference in how I experience the appearance that *coincides* with (and isn't an effect of) its looking to me as it does. This looking, this visual appearing, is also then a "subjective experience."

I follow a widespread practice in saying that states conscious in this sense are states with "phenomenal character." How your feelings *feel to you*, and more generally, how your *experiences* are *experienced* by you—that constitutes their "phenomenal" (or "subjective") character. I will also speak of "phenomenal features" in this context—as features you have just when you experience experiences in this "coinciding" and not just "affected-by" sense. And I take a conscious state/experience just to be an instance of a phenomenal feature.

I also endorse the widespread notion that for a state to be "subjectively experienced" or "phenomenally conscious" is for there to be "something it's like" for one to be in it, in a certain sense. For instance, *my tasting durian fruit* is a subjective experience inasmuch as *there is something it's like for me to taste durian*. What is the relevant, "conscious-marking" sense of this phrase? I regard two points as essential.

(1)   When I wonder, "What would it be like for me to taste durian?," I want to understand what it would be for me to taste it, and to understand this in the way I could claim to acquire through tasting it myself, and could seek to have by trying to imagine tasting it. Thus to say there is "something that it's like for someone" to have a feature in the relevant sense is to say that it is *suitable for you to claim or desire to understand* what it is for them to have it in a way that is *found or sought in "taking up the subject's point of view."* To say the understanding is found or sought through "taking up the subject's point of view" means: it is found in self-attribution of the feature, or sought in imagining having it. Where what it is to have a feature is suited for the type of understanding or curiosity that is, in this sense, "subjective," there is something it's like for its possessor to have it.

(2)   Something is a *phenomenal* feature (a feature whose instances are experiences or conscious states) just in case there is *unconditionally* something it's like for one to have it the sense just explained. Consider: there may sometimes be something it's like for someone or something to *eat* durian— but not *unconditionally*. For there might be a durian-eater for whom there was *nothing that was like*. Maybe this is the case with caterpillars that infest

durian orchards, for example. (That is, maybe *their* ingestion of durian offers nothing for subjective understanding or curiosity to target.) By contrast, there is *always* something it's like for one to *taste* durian—no matter who or what tastes it, or when they do so. That's why *tasting* durian *is* (but *eating* durian is not) a phenomenal feature.

So, there are *features there is unconditionally something it's like for one to have*. This, on my account, means *features whose possession is unconditionally suited for subjective understanding or curiosity*. Those are the *phenomenal* ones—and their instances are conscious states, subjective experiences. By appeal to this conception, we have another way of explaining what's meant by "phenomenal character." Experiences so understood differ in *phenomenal character* just when they differ with respect to what it's like to have them. And that means they differ with respect to what makes their possession suited for a subjective understanding or curiosity. This aligns with the previous account of phenomenal character: for such states differ with respect to what it's like to have them just when they differ in *how they are subjectively experienced*.

I have so far illustrated subjective experience with examples of sensory (e.g., visual) appearances, and of feelings. But I will assume a richer conception of what all subjective character includes or encompasses than this makes clear. So, for example, where visual experience is concerned, I will take it that we subjectively experience not just "color sensations," but visual appearances of *depth and object constancy*, which make it possible for the location of things in our surroundings to become apparent to us: we experience "locational appearances." Moreover, the character of my experience not only makes apparent to me *where things are*, it makes *what* they *are* apparent to me by making them "appear recognizable" to me as of this or that kind. What it's like for something to "look recognizable to me as a hat," for example, differs from what it's like for something (perhaps the same thing) to "look recognizable to me as a basket."[2]

As I see this, something may look recognizable to someone as an F without their being fully competent in using the concept of an F. I do also think, however, that when, on some occasion, I understand a phrase in certain way (as I may in *different* ways understand the expression "He is a man of many hats"), *how I understand the phrase* is not removable from *how*

[2] For more on my conception of "recognitional appearances," see Siewert 2019.

I experience the episode of thought or understanding. (Think of what it's like for you to switch understanding of this and other ambiguous phrases.) There is, on my "inclusive" view, no sense in which we can hold constant what it's like for us to have the experiences of understanding had in thinking, speaking, reading, and listening, while occurrent understanding is itself utterly switched off, or substantially switched around. Conceptual activity is included in the character of our ordinary experience.

I would argue further that what are sometimes termed differences in thought "mode" or "attitude" are inherent to the phenomenal character of cognitive experience. Consider: there is something it's like to "have something to say" in the midst of conversation—and to understand various ways of completing or continuing your part in a dialogue as constituting "saying what you had to say"—even if you did not (as near as you can tell) form a prior intention to say that very thing. For example, think of what it's like for you when you pause to find the right way to express what you have to say, and someone else jumps in with a suggestion. You are in a position to judge (as they are not) whether that was an apt way to finish, to complete what you started to say, so as to constitute *saying what you had to say*, though you have no awareness of a prior intention to say it whose satisfaction dictates this determination. What it is for us to express ourselves in this manner (with or without assistance) is suited for subjective understanding in the sense that implies subjective experience. And this, I maintain, makes *attitude* inherent to the phenomenal character of understanding. For what it is to say (or realize someone else has said) what you had to say about something constitutes a "way of understanding what is said" that also can't be extracted from experience while leaving its character intact. And this isn't just a matter of what you took the words to mean. It's a matter of what you are *doing* with them: whether or not you are *endorsing what is said*, and if you are endorsing it, whether this is *merely agreeing with a proposal*, or whether it constitutes a genuine case of *self-expression*.[3]

Let me mention just one more respect in which mine is a relatively rich or "inclusive" conception of experience. Think of what it's like for you when you have some *affective experience* in connection with a desire's satisfaction or dissatisfaction. For example, you *feel some satisfaction* in my cheerful and prompt compliance with your request to pass the salt. Or you *feel dissatisfied*

---

[3] For more on my conception of the experience of self-expression, the inclusion of understanding in experience, and the issue of "cognitive phenomenology" generally, see Siewert (2020).

that I ignore you. I regard these two categories—of affective satisfaction and dissatisfaction—as diversely manifested in the subjective character of experience, as follows:

Affective Satisfaction: subjectively experiencing or feeling joy, pleasure, delight, or comfort; feeling glad, gratified, relaxed, or relieved; experiencing enjoyment of, or affection for, something or someone.

Affective Dissatisfaction: feeling bothered, annoyed, irritated, uncomfortable, frustrated, distressed, disgruntled, or disturbed; experiencing revulsion, discomfort, or suffering.

To be clear, I would include in subjective experience not only such "affective states" as these, but also experiences of merely imagining or anticipating (dis)satisfaction—and further, affects corresponding to no definite desire whose (dis)satisfaction is experienced, imagined, or anticipated—for example, feeling silly, irritable, gloomy, or lost in romantic infatuation.

To summarize, on my conception, ordinary human experience brings with it a substantial sort of mind. For the right sort of consciousness—experience with the right phenomenal character, a kind that our own experience ordinarily has—entails the possession of highly various *locational, recognitional, conceptual-attitudinal*, and *affective experience*. And having the capacity for this experience suffices for having a mind whose possessor has highly various and complex abilities to perceive its surroundings, to recognize what it's in them, to think about them, and to care what they offer. This is the view of what consciousness is, and what it can bring with it, on which I will draw.

3. What I Mean by "Intrinsic Benefit"

Let me now explain what I mean by saying some experience has for you a "*value of its own*"—or, to put it yet another way—that it has some has "intrinsic value for you." By saying this I mean to say first, that having it *benefits* you (it is better *for you* to have it than lack it)—and second, that this benefit is *not due solely* to its affording you some *other* feature(s) you're better off having than not. This means that there are some phenomenal features it has been or will be more beneficial for you to have rather than lack, and not just for some payoff in what else that brings.

This use of "intrinsic value" is quite detached from the historically prominent use by G.E. Moore (1903). I do not assume that some experience can be beneficial for you "in its own right" only in virtue of its "intrinsic or non-relational" properties, whatever those might be. I probably needn't dwell on this, since ethicists writing in recent decades about intrinsic value tend to shed these Moorean assumptions. But while I certainly don't take my use of "intrinsic value" to break new ground in value theory, there is a set of relatively subtle distinctions in the area I want to investigate, and their lack of standard terminological regimentation suggests I should be very explicit about my meaning here to avoid misunderstanding.

When I say something is "intrinsically valuable (or beneficial) for someone" this does not entail that it is "intrinsically good" in Christine Korsgaard's (1983, p. 171) sense of retaining its "goodness in any and all circumstances". I may be better off with a certain type of experience than without it (though not solely for further goods it affords me), but it doesn't follow that it would make me better off *no matter what*, or *unconditionally*— that is, regardless of what's bundled with it. Nor can what I'm after here exactly be identified with what she refers to as a "final good." For that she takes to be something that is "*valued* for its own sake" (1983, p. 170). But it is not simply built into something's providing you with benefits of its own that you yourself value it for its own sake (or indeed that you value it at all).

Note also that I am now specifically concerned with goods that are *benefits for someone*. And we cannot just *assume* that this is the same as what is good, full stop: what "makes the world a better place," what is "simply a good thing in its own right." So when I say that something is intrinsically beneficial for a person, this doesn't entail that it has what Shelly Kagan (1998, p. 285) calls "intrinsic value" or "value as an end"—for he seems to assume that means it enhances "the value of the world as such." And I want to leave room for the possibility Michael Zimmerman and Ben Bradley (2019, p. 8) describe when they say being healthy might be "good *for* John," even when *his* being healthy is not an intrinsically good thing, full stop—because John, as it happens, is such a noxious blight on the world. Nor should we foreclose on the possibility Gwen Bradford (2015, pp. 6–7) describes by saying someone's achievements might have "intrinsic value," even if they lack value *to the achiever herself*—and, accordingly, do nothing to enhance *her* well-being. So let me be clear: I do not take it for granted that "being intrinsically *beneficial for* someone" entails, or is entailed by, something's being "intrinsically good," period. Initially, I leave their relationship an open question—though I will make some commitments on this front below, in Section 7.

One might be tempted to rephrase what I'm after by saying that some experience has a kind of value for us not "derivative" from other value. But we need to be careful. One might think of non-derived value as what lies at the terminus of a one-way chain of means to ends: other things are good for the sake of affording X, though X is not itself valuable for affording any of these goods—thus its value is in no way derived from them. But that is not what I mean. So let's be clear: a "proprietary" or "intrinsic" benefit as I understand this is not to be construed as one whose value is *wholly non-derivative*. Rather, it's simply a benefit that is *not wholly derivative*.

An example from Shelly Kagan (1998, pp. 284–5) will help illustrate. He observes that we might see a skill at gourmet cooking as something *valuable* "for itself"—but only on the condition that it is also *useful* in producing good food. Similarly, we might regard certain kinds of visual experience as *beneficial* to us in their own right, even though we'd take the benefit to evaporate, if the experience could furnish us no further goods (such as informing us of our surroundings or facilitating action). For suppose the payoffs derived from some experience you had were secured in its absence, but this experiential loss still involved *some* loss of benefit to you. That would seem to indicate the experience had benefits of its own to offer—and it would do so, whether or not they could also survive the additional payoff's complete disappearance. Or suppose this is the case: the further benefits one takes an experience to afford are themselves valued partly because they involve having that very experience. Then again, the experiential benefit would not be *wholly* derivative—even if it could not be retained in the absence of its derived benefits. All that is strictly required for something to provide me with a benefit "of its own" is that the good it gives me not be *exhausted* by whatever further ("derived") benefits it affords. In other words: the good it does me is not *entirely* due to other goods it makes available to me.[4]

---

[4] I deploy basically the same conception in Siewert 1998, pp. 313–15—though hopefully with some improvement here. For clarity, I might also note that while I have here used this (cooking) example from Kagan, my claim is not just the same as his, when he says we should "allow for the possibility that intrinsic value [that is, value 'as an end'] can depend, in part, on instrumental value [value as a means]" (Kagan 1998, p. 285) Partly that's because, again, he does not use "intrinsic value" to mean what I call "intrinsic benefit" to someone, and partly because my point does not require that we always construe the dependence of intrinsic benefits on further goods they make available specifically in *instrumental* terms, as instances of "means to ends."

4. How to Find Intrinsic Benefit in Experience

Once I see the question of the value of experience in the way just explained, I find, through reflection on cases, that there are indeed many forms of experience whose possession I regard as intrinsically beneficial to me. For I consider the sorts of sensory, cognitive, and affective experiences I have had, or anticipate having, and, of these, I discover many that I think it better for me to have or have had—but not just for some further reward, distinct from having them, which I think that brings me. Explaining how I reach this conclusion will show how you might reach it for yourself, and help further clarify the kind of benefit at issue.

One form this reflection can take: there are experiences I deem good for me that arise and pass away but yield me no benefit or detriment beyond themselves, as near as can tell. I open the door and smell the wet earthy freshness of the air after the rain that broke a hot dry spell; I hear the snatch of a tune out of a window as I'm passing by; an amusing thought occurs to me I share with no one and take no further. It's not hard for me to contrast what it's like for me to have these little fortuitous experiences with how I think it likely things might have been without them. Things might well have otherwise been much the same. I confidently judge I was, nonetheless, better off for having them.

We can also highlight subjective experiences that we deem have value of their own for us, not by seeing whether we value them even when nothing else comes of them, but whether we would still value them, were the derived goods they seem to provide taken away. For instance, I consider the case where I take my after-the-rain experience to have had some beneficial result—such as nudging my thoughts away from grim preoccupations. Or the case in which the amusing thought gave me some pleasantry to share later with a friend. Would these experiences still have done me some good even if they hadn't afforded these bonuses? If so, then again, they benefit me in their own right.

Mightn't I broaden the range of cases to embrace experiences which— unlike those just considered—seem unavailable in the absence of their derived benefits? Yes, though it's a bit more complicated. Consider this example. Many times I have gone for a bike ride along the bayou near where I live. Now, I do indeed think it was better for me that things then looked and felt to me as they did (and that I felt as I did), and that I subjectively experienced the thoughts this occasioned, rather than for nothing to have looked or felt to me any way at all then, and to have been experientially void of thought. And I do think there was something *else* for the sake of which it was good *for me to have had* those experiences. For one thing, I assume that normally I need things to appear to me, in vision and touch, if I am to navigate the world as well as I typically do. And I regard this result as a benefit. But I see no readily available means of getting, in the complete absence of such results, *experiences* of the very same character deemed beneficial.

However, I can at least *conceive* of a perfected virtual reality "bike-ride simulator" experience had though stimulation to my brain while I am immobilized. This would indeed omit all the derived benefits I find in the actual bayou ride. Would it entirely kill the good I take the experience to do for me? If I say no, then clearly I should conclude it's not *only* due to its affording me further goods (such as I'd lose in the simulator) that I find it's better for me to have the experiences I had than not. And there will be at least *some* cases like this—even if I put limits on how much merely *virtual* reality I would deem good for me.

It's true that I often would prefer to actually go to a concert, and experience seeing and hearing the performance by flesh and blood musicians in a certain brick and mortar venue in the company of other people, rather than to slip into some virtual reality simulation that duplicated the subjective character of that experience. Still, the latter option might strike me as pretty good, and sometimes, even preferable. (For that matter I might even prefer to just watch the concert on TV.) And I might well judge the perfected virtual cycling experience to be better to have than not, if permanent physical incapacity kept me from the real thing. I might draw similar conclusions from thinking about activities (from skydiving to gourmandise) whose attendant real world hazards I'd just as soon avoid while keeping the subjective experience involved. Such convictions indicate that it can't be entirely for their derived, extra-phenomenal benefits that I think I'm better off with the experiences in question.

But we needn't rely on satisfaction with a bit of merely virtual reality to secure the main point. Here is another way. I don't just think it's better for me to have the cycling experience due to its enabling the journey. I also think it better to take the journey, due to the experience it involves. Here, and wherever this pattern holds, it's evident that the benefits of an experience can't lie *entirely* in something further it gives me, since the benefit had from that further thing is to be understood partly in terms of the benefit of the experience it gives me. This further confirms (and helps clarify) my judgment that it is better for me to have the experience than lack it, but not *solely* due to its provision of some separable pay-offs.

To press the point: I can still see this is so, even where the further benefits are bound to the experience in question by necessity. For example, one benefit of having certain experiences might be the *memories* they afford me. Another might be the *understanding* of what it is like for me to have those types of experiences. And I could get neither without the experience. Consider first the memory case: certain experiences are good for me to look back on. And I could not get *that* benefit in the absence of the experience recalled. However, in such cases I may ask: is it *also* true that I think it better to have *those experience-derived benefits* rather than not, because they involve my having the *experience* I think I'm better off having? In many cases where I would deem recollection of the experience beneficial to me to have, part of what makes the memories good ones is that they are of experiences I was better off for having.

We can recognize analogous points where experience is deemed valuable for the *subjective understanding* of experience it affords. If I want to know what it would be like to smell sandalwood, the experience of smelling it will benefit me by satisfying my curiosity. But it was good to slake *that* curiosity partly because doing so involved having experience good for me to have. So the good the experience did me was not exhausted by the goods I derived from getting things distinct from it. This contrasts evaluatively with a case where the satisfaction of curiosity does seem to be all the good an experience does me—since apart from this benefit I'd have been better off without it. (Suppose I'm curious, not about the smell of sandalwood, but about the smell of death.)

This last point concerns experience with no good of its own to provide, endured just for the sake of its derived benefits. But are there not also cases in which we find the experience beneficial *in spite of its derived detriments*? For example, cases in which we tasted some tainted (or merely unhealthy) food or drink, or fell into some ultimately ill-advised romance. If you think there was *something* good for you about having such experiences (at least "at the time"), though what they brought in their train, distinct from themselves (the nausea, the hangover, the anxiety or depression), only made you worse off, then it seems you must think whatever good they did hold for you came from some value they had for you in themselves. Relatedly, suppose you thought the experience in question did have at least *some* derived benefits (hard-won wisdom?), as well as detriments, though the detriments were decidedly *greater*. Or suppose you are quite unresolved about their relative weight. And yet still you regarded the experience as on the whole "worth it." Then again, you must be according some intrinsic benefit to the experience that tips the final assessment in its favor.

Now for a final way to find proprietary benefits in our experience. Recall the biking trip. I might ask, regarding the further goods brought me by the experience I had, is it at least *conceivable* I could get them *without* the experiences in question? For example, is it conceivable I could navigate on my bike just as adroitly without visual experience, by unconscious perception—in this case, by "blindsight"? If that were the case, would I still regard myself as better off for having the subjective experience than I would be without it? This scenario, however unlikely, is not so hard to conceive of, and once conceived, yields a ready answer to the evaluative question: yes, I would still deem it better for me to have the full-blown cycling experience than negotiate the terrain by unconscious vision. But then, if I suppose all the derived benefits I take some experiences to yield could be had without them, and yet still I would think it better to have the experience as well, then clearly I take the experience to be good for me in its own right, not just for the derived benefits. So here is yet another way to isolate intrinsic benefits.[5]

To review: I've identified five ways in which we can discover that we accord proprietary benefit to our experiences.

(1) There are cases in which experiential benefits accrue in the absence of what we take to be actual derived goods.
(2) We may discover experiential benefits that would remain when the derived goods we think actually present are subtracted.
(3) We can find cases of experience with apparent derived benefits whose value depends for us partly on the benefit of that very experience.
(4) There are experiences we can think had some good to offer us, though either all further value they brought us was negative, or the good had from them was enough to have made them worthwhile in the end, despite its being unclear that their derived benefit outweighed their derived detriment.
(5) We can find cases where we would think ourselves better off for having a given type of subjective experience than not, even when supposing we had the option of getting its derived benefits without it.

---

[5] For more about this fifth way, see my earlier discussion of "selective pheno-ectomy" in Siewert 1998, pp. 322–5. The form of argument is structurally analogous to that Bradford (2015, pp. 94–9) employs to argue that *difficulty* is part of what gives achievements intrinsic value: the value of the process of acquiring their product would be diminished if it became magically near effortless.

Once I have these five ways of discovering the value in my own experience, it is not hard for me to think of many types of experiences I've had or anticipate having, well beyond the examples mentioned, that would return for me similar verdicts. For instance, not just my *leisure* journeys, but even my daily *work commutes* involve experiences with benefits of their own to offer me, discoverable in ways (3) and (5). And during these times, almost invariably my excursions afford me affective and cognitive experiences that I would count myself as better off for having—that would qualify as intrinsic benefits to me by (3) and (5). In fact, now I'd say it's hard for me to think of any but uncommon cases in which my getting somewhere (even around my house) or accomplishing everyday tasks (making breakfast), where the perceptual experience that seems to facilitate my activity isn't revealed as intrinsically beneficial to me by the measures described. So very large stretches of my perceptual history are now included.

Further, in very many—I would say far and away most—contexts, I can find, in some combination of manners (1)–(3) and (5) that I would rather have than not have my experiences of *reading and writing*, and of *speaking and listening*, both in soliloquy and in dialogue, both at work and at home— and not merely for some pay-offs distinct from themselves I took them to provide. And my experiences of communication are only an aspect of a broader experience of association with others—sharing things and doing things together—that swell the great sea of intrinsically beneficial experience by one or more of the measures I've listed.

Admittedly, I can find exceptions: experiences of reading only to get some dreary work done, or to operate some gadget or use some software; tedious conversations whose understanding I'd rather not have subjectively experienced at all, except for whatever derived benefits I find they confer. And there are times when I'd rather be without experience altogether: at three in the morning, tormented by anxious thoughts, I'd clearly be better off asleep. But fortunately such occasions do not dominate my life. And saying this, of course, doesn't require me to claim—incredibly—that I find most of my reading or conversation full of scintillating, profoundly insightful, or delightfully comic remarks. The experience really doesn't have to be nearly *that* good to be worth having in its own right. And good experiences of this sort account for significant portions of my life. To add even more obvious cases: typically, drinking and dining and erotic experiences that don't fall into the "(somewhat) regrettable" category covered by (4); as well as experience of the visual arts generally in all their variety, of beauty and arresting form in nature; and the experience of listening to and making music.

The more I ponder such cases, the more it dawns on me that my life is full of experience to which I accord this kind of value. For there are not many significant blocks of time in my ordinary waking days during which I had *no experience at all* I would take to have proprietary value for me in any of the five ways explained. And that is not because I have lived blessedly free of extended sadness or chronic pain, or because I have only but rarely found myself enduring things out of duty or fear. It's rather that I find on the whole, in spite of everything, relatively small stretches of experience in which I can discern no intrinsic benefit by the measures just articulated. And that realization brings me, in defiance of all my gloomy proclivities, an experience of gratitude for my life, which itself only adds to the total bounty.

I would be surprised if, upon serious reflection, only a few people could draw similar conclusions. That's not to deny that a person is fortunate to be able to draw them. I don't doubt that many around the world and throughout history could not be expected to embrace nearly as wide a range of their experience as I do, having passed so much time in degradation or tedium, laboriously traversing bleak and ugly surroundings, minds numb or exhausted. And an onslaught of depression, or even merely grim moods, can rob us of such appreciation. But I would hope that, even so, many people could still find significant expanses of experience to value in their own right in much the manner indicated.

5. Appreciating Experience—without Swinishness or Solipsism

I now wish to clarify how the sort of positive evaluation just evoked stands quite independent of doctrines prominently associated with according experience intrinsic value. It's good to recognize this, inasmuch as we should not let their vulnerability to doubt obscure or inhibit our full appreciation of experience.

Consider hedonistic views—holding that all the intrinsic benefits experience can afford you derive entirely from *pleasure*. An extreme variant would say that the experiences of pleasure in question are distinctive sensations, separable from—and no more than contingently, causally related to—all the visual, auditory, tactile, olfactory, and gustatory experiences, and all the various affective, cognitive, and imagery experiences I regard myself as better off for having. Such an extreme (I would say *brutal*) hedonism seems to imply that I would suffer no loss in well-being were I paralyzed, blind, deaf, and devoid of all thought and imagination—just so long as I was hooked up to a machine that pumped my brain full of the posited pleasure feelings. The conception of experience involved in this (nightmarish) scenario stands starkly at odds with my own evaluative judgment. Even if pleasure were construed as separable sensation, this wouldn't give me reason to discount the value of the wealth of experience excluded from that category. It would only give me reason to doubt that all intrinsically beneficial experiences are pleasures.

More importantly, though, my valuation of experience presupposes not even a much subtler hedonism (such as we find in Crisp 2006). Notice that the reflections I entertained in the previous section did not invoke notions like *pleasure, enjoyment,* and *feelings of happiness.* It thus seems I can recognize the proprietary value of having the experience I do, even while leaving it open how to interpret and answer questions like: exactly which of the experiences I value constitute pleasures? Which were pleasant? Precisely which did I "enjoy" having? And how are they related to "feeling happy?" I did not base my positive valuation of my experience on answers to such questions for the following reason. I am confident in my judgment that (e.g.) it was better for me that things have looked to me as they have since I woke up this morning, as opposed to never any way at all—and not just for further benefits I take to accrue from this. However, I am *considerably less* confident making judgments about just when I was "feeling pleasure" during this time, or when I "felt happy," or even just what all I then "enjoyed." That is due to my uncertainty about just how to interpret such notions, and just how broadly to apply them, beyond certain paradigms. I don't want to exaggerate this: unquestionably, I found the wine I drank last night delicious, the experience of drinking it was "a pleasure," and a "pleasant experience," something I "enjoyed." And had I not enjoyed it at all, I likely would not have counted tasting it beneficial in its own right. Still, there are many experiences I would count as intrinsically beneficial by the standards described earlier, which I am just not sure I can univocally describe as continually "enjoyed." For all that, it remains possible that only "enjoyed" (or at least "affectively positive") experiences are beneficial to me in their own right.[6] My only point is that I do not always have to first figure out just what belongs in the class of affectively positive or enjoyed experiences, and

---

[6] Thoughtful accounts grounding well-being and/or moral status in affective experience can be found in Shepherd (2018) and Zuk (2019).

just what it means to so classify them, before I can say which I'm better off having.

Another reason I hold back from hedonistic views emerges from the thought that, however we conceive of pleasure, it should be possible for one life to be much poorer than another in *cognitive* experience, while offering the one who lives it at least as much *pleasure* overall. Hedonism would then say that the cognitively poorer life scores at least as high on intrinsic experiential benefits. But I regard this as unacceptable. For suppose I were faced with the prospect of a brain operation that promised to reduce me to the cognitive level of a dim-witted young child. On strictly hedonist assumptions, it seems no concern about what is best for me could rationalize my extremely negative attitude towards this scenario, provided that it *also* supplied me with an untroubled, pleasure-filled existence. For an infantilized life could be at least as *pleasant* as the one I would lead with my cognitive powers intact—hence a life that is hedonically no worse *for me*. Plausibly, it could even be in that respect *better* for me than a life lived in full possession of my faculties. For while the cognitively richer life I would lead has pleasures of its own, these will often enough make company with grown-up discouragement, despair, and anxiety—afflictions of which my fully infantilized self would be spared, luxuriating in a brightly colored playpen full of amusing toys, yummy treats, and kindly caretakers, blissfully unaware of the horrors beyond.

However, I really have no doubt that being permanently infantilized would be a calamity for me. This is just another tweak on the age-old "philosophy of swine" objection to hedonism. Some hedonists, following Mill, would reply to this that there are "higher" pleasures I would miss out on when infantilized, to which a refined hedonism can appeal to account for the superiority of the life for which I just expressed a preference. But, like others (e.g., van der Deijl 2018), I suspect that, once we allow some pleasures are "higher" than others, we admit standards of value other than pleasure, and abandon hedonism in the strict sense. If I'm mistaken about that, my present point would just reduce to this: my valuation of experience easily allows that some pleasures are more worth having than others, even when they aren't greater in quantity.

But even then I'd have trouble with hedonism, since there is another notion usually considered essential to it I would reject—one shared by a non-hedonistic "experientialism" of the sort advanced by van der Deijl (2018)—the idea that "only what affects our experience can alter someone's well-being." I am one of those who believe my well-being would be massively diminished were my actual surroundings and other people to become forever lost to me in the experience of a perfected virtual reality, and that this would remain so, even if the experiences offered were kinds I want for myself, and even if, once in the machine, I'd be none the wiser that I had "plugged in" to it. I recoil from this option of spending the rest of my life in some super VR "feel-good machine" (as opposed to taking my chances with getting experience the old-fashioned way), because I think it would mean forsaking consciousness of the real world, as well as many achievements and relations with others in it. Thus, I think that permanently "plugging in" to anything like Robert Nozick's (1974) notorious "experience machine" would involve a significant sacrifice of my well-being.

For that reason I am not an "experientialist," at least as van der Deijl interprets it. And yet I can and do still consistently believe my life burgeoning with phenomenal features much better for me to have than lack, and not just for the sake of pay-offs in other features. Whether or not I'd also think it might be good for me to spend a weekend in the machine—and whether I think dreams have benefits of their own to confer—I'd still regard a preponderance of "worldly" experience much better for me to have than *only* the "de-worlded" kind—perhaps even if I could arrange to "edit out" a lot of sad and bad real-world experience from the perpetual dream on offer.

I stress this in order to ward off temptations to draw the wrong moral from the experience machine. I think it would be wrong to conclude only "So, subjective experience isn't everything—at most it's just a necessary condition for well-being." This would be to neglect just what I so zealously maintain: how, even if we reject "plugging in," we can recognize forms of experience we have as beneficial to us in their own right. And to see them in this way is to see them *not merely* as necessary preconditions for doing well. For something could be necessary to my well-being (say, an adequate supply of potassium) without being *intrinsically* beneficial to me. Consciousness is not just a necessary condition of doing well, for the forms it takes in me constitute intrinsic benefits that pervade and permeate my life—and do so, even if those benefits would be diminished or lost with permanent confinement to the experience machine.

We are now also well-positioned to warn explicitly against another way of grievously underrating consciousness. Recall that, at the start of this chapter, I declined to say that just any old subjective experience will confer some intrinsic benefit on me. And wisely so, you may think. For what if I were reduced to some *respirating lump of pain*, incapable of experiencing the world around me, unable to tear my thoughts away for a moment from my own incessant, pulsating misery? But—since I grant that experience in such a scenario does me no good at all—someone might say I'm left with the puny point that there is *some* experience that brings me a value of its own. This deflationary attitude would rob us of the appreciation I want to promote. To prevent it, first note that there is obviously *a vast ground* between "all" and "some" (in the sense of "at least one"). And so there is an alternative to both the too-strong claim about *all* consciousness, and the too-feeble "*at least some* consciousness" claim, namely this:

Pervasive Value.   For some subject S, many richly various forms of consciousness that occur commonly or pervasively in S's life are intrinsically beneficial to S.

Clearly this says something far stronger than just there is at least one type of experience S has that benefits S in its own right. However, given the imprecision of "many," "richly various," "commonly," and "pervasively," I need something more than a bare grasp of this thesis to adequately understand the extent to which experience brings a benefit of its own, and even just what it means to say that it does. However, I *can have* what more is needed. I just need to engage in a process of clarifying reflection of the sort expressed in the preceding, supporting an endorsement of the thesis as applied to myself (so that *I am S*). This same process and outcome is of course open to you. If you join me, then together we find that the extent of the intrinsic good experience does us is far from trivial. The effort required need not seem onerous—especially as it can inspire an appreciation of experience that enhances its value for us.

Someone might protest: "All that your exercise of reflection reveals is (at most) a set of convictions about what's valuable in our lives (pervasive forms of experience) and in what way it's valuable (as an intrinsic benefit). But this doesn't speak to whether such convictions are *justified*. Maybe you have *no right* to hold your experience in such regard, or are simply mistaken in doing so. And what if your neighbors won't join your Consciousness Lovers Club, and simply deny they have any such evaluative attitude towards their own experience? Do you have reason to think they are missing something?"

One can be wrong about the value of one's experience, I believe. For example, regarding the "brutal hedonists" earlier imagined, I would think them mistaken about what brings value to their lives—as they might well think I am mistaken about mine. However, I also think one cannot be *argued into* judgments of intrinsic value such as I've expressed. Acquiring them is rather a question of *coming to appreciate* something through being exposed to it in a receptive frame of mind, recognizing it as valuable, "seeing what is good in it." Some experiences we don't really have to *learn* to appreciate—they seem good straight-off, from childhood even. But not all are like this. We come to their appreciation, as part of—and in the way that—we learn to appreciate music or visual art, or performance in any domain of skill, such as athletics (or philosophy for that matter)—or in the way we come to appreciation as a by-product of cognitive development or education, as we often do, I think, in the case of humor.

Thus I believe it would be misguided for you to demand I produce an argument that something is intrinsically beneficial to me, if you cannot recognize such benefits yourself when you properly understand what the "something" is, and what is at issue, through your own reflection. Nor should I be expected to argue you into valuing your own experiences, under such conditions. This is not to say, however, that critical examination has no place here. We should be open to revising our evaluative judgments because they reflect false assumptions, conceptual blind spots, or misunderstandings. And that is partly why we should make the sort of efforts that have lately so absorbed me. Still, mere conceptual clarification cannot by itself yield the evaluations that come only through reflecting seriously on our own experience. Once it does yield these, we are warranted in them, as long as we find no reason to relinquish them, though we persistently explore reasons for doubt, and probe our assumptions. And the more this leaves our judgments in overall harmony with what else we believe, the more we are warranted in making them. You might, however, still complain that this perspective neglects the need for a *unifying* account of what makes experiences contribute to well-being—the sort that hedonism is supposed to deliver. Though I wouldn't be shocked if no such account were available, I do not rule out its possibility. I only deny that I need this to have the right to judge that I am intrinsically better off for having the heterogeneous class of experiences to which I have alluded in my reflections.

6. How Deeply Does Experience Matter to You?

Even if you recognize forms of experience as pervasively and intrinsically beneficial, you might wonder how much this makes them matter. While the *pervasiveness* of what you value may make its significance to you very broad—how *deep* does this go? Perhaps the "great sea" of intrinsically beneficial consciousness I claim to behold is after all rather *shallow*. I want now to speak to this. There is a way of assessing *how much* we value subjective experience in its own right that can deepen recognition of its importance, by showing how to find its intrinsic benefits essential to the value we find in our own continued existence.

You might consider how much intrinsic benefit you accord the forms of consciousness you have by thinking about how you'd regard the prospect of losing these forever. Of course, one way to do this would be to contemplate your own death. You might also consider a future in which you retain basic life functions, but with no experience: a permanent "vegetative" state. Many of us would say that life under such conditions no longer holds for us any intrinsic benefits, even if *some* good would be served by being kept breathing. But even if we rate the evaluative difference between a normal and vegetative existence as *huge*, this doesn't decisively demonstrate the strength of the intrinsic good we take ordinary consciousness to do us. For maybe we deem life without consciousness worthless, *not* because of the enormous intrinsic value we accord it, but because of the enormous value we accord the *other* things we assume we'd lose *along with it*—such as our intelligent interaction with the world and other people. To control for this, we'd need to retain whatever collateral or derived benefits we take consciousness to occasion, while taking consciousness itself away, and see where that leaves us. To do this, I see no way to avoid relying on thought experiment.

We have already opened this door to imagination. Recall way (5) of revealing the benefits you take your experience to have. There I briefly suggested contemplating being temporarily able to maneuver through the world—on a bicycle, for example—just as flexibly and effectively as ever, though nothing is visually apparent to you, and you function by an advanced form of blindsight. Taking this even further, we may, it seems, contemplate what I'll call a "manifest behavioral zombie." This would be *a self-guided human-shaped creature entirely indistinguishable from an ordinary actual human in its manifest behavior—but totally and irrevocably lacking in subjective experience.* "Behavior" here means bodily movements and utterances stripped of psychological or intentional interpretation. What makes such behavior "manifest" is that it's a type one could observe without internal examination of what is behaving.

Philosophy of mind in recent decades has been haunted by the imagined prospect of consciousness-deprived beings that nonetheless outwardly carry on much as ordinary conscious ones such as ourselves. These would be "zombies"—not of the horror movie or voodoo variety, but a metaphysical sort. Most famously perhaps, in the context of debates about consciousness, we have been asked to entertain the possibility that we each have a particle-for-particle twin, in a world physically type identical to our own—even though that entity (like every entity in that world) *has no subjective experience whatsoever—and is incapable of ever having any* (Chalmers 1996). But my interest here is not in this, and the challenge to physicalist views about consciousness it presents. This micro-physically type identical unconscious twin is not the sort of "zombie" I wish us to contemplate. In this context, your "zombie double" can be internally, physically, quite *different* from conscious you.

With this in mind, I ask you to consider the following thought experiment—restating one I introduced in earlier work (Siewert 1998, pp. 319–29; 2014, p. 215). Hopefully, here I will make its salient features clearer, and head off past misunderstandings. What you are to envisage is this: you are told that, given some drastic rewiring or replacement of neural machinery, you will lose subjective experience of any sort forever. Nothing will look anyhow, smell anyhow, sound anyhow to you. You will feel nothing. You will subjectively experience no thought, no understanding. You will experience no satisfaction or frustration in anything ever again. *However*, your altered insides will support bodily responses to the environment (in movements made, in sounds uttered) much the same as those you would have manifested, had you retained normal consciousness.

I don't ask you to believe this scenario comports with psychophysiological truths in our actual world. Maybe there is just no way to engineer such "manifest behavioral zombification" in you or me. Set those concerns aside. It is not even essential that you commit to the "metaphysical" possibility of this scenario. I only ask that you grant it is *intelligible*, and that you can make evaluative judgments predicated on contemplating its realization. The question I ask you then to pose (and that I pose myself) is whether we would find the prospect of its realization nearly as good for us as the ordinary one we anticipate—of continued life as a conscious being. To this end, I evaluate three options.

(a) The conscious future I actually anticipate.
(b) An alternative future of permanent (manifest behavioral) zombification, as described above.
(c) A different future in which my actual body and brain are entirely destroyed, and replaced with a manifest behavioral zombie double that has been lying in wait, ready to be activated on my departure.

Now, when I contemplate the options from the point of view of personal benefit, I have to say: I myself find nothing much to choose between (b) and (c). If my (altered) body's future is utterly experience-deprived, then that seems no better for me than its destruction and replacement (and, clearly, *my* destruction and replacement) by a similar non-conscious being. On the other hand, I view (a)—the normal "consciousness plan"—as *massively* better for me than either (b) or (c). What I take this to show is that, much as before, I find the possession of many of the phenomenal features I ordinarily have intrinsically beneficial to me. Except now this is added: I find the value that having them affords me very great: *so very great as to account for what makes my life intrinsically worth living at all*. Let me explain why I say this.

Think about this: does option (b) "permanent zombification" leave *me* in existence or not? I might intelligibly think it would. For suppose I permanently lose the capacity for experience in the much more ordinary way earlier mentioned—through irreversible brain damage that also leaves me unresponsive to the world in any way indicative of consciousness. It wouldn't be completely beyond the pale to think that, in such a situation, *I* would still exist. "*I* might then be in a permanent vegetative state," I say. And if that's how I view this prospect, it might also seem natural for me to assume, correspondingly, that option (b) would leave me in existence as well.

Recall my strong preference for (a). This implies, first, that I regard having certain phenomenal features as beneficial to me in its own right. For if I thought the only benefits to me they conferred were due to their giving me access to other, non-phenomenal features, I would be just as satisfied with option (b). For (a) is still strongly preferred even if (b) would bring me all of the relevant derived benefits. (It should be clear I do not regard the benefits of the phenomenal features I have as derived entirely from non-phenomenal ones which I'd lose just because my brain has been altered: it's not as if I intrinsically value specific kinds of neurophysiology.) Moreover, it follows that the proprietary value I am according subjective experience is *very great*. For if my choices are reduced to (b) and (c), I basically shrug my shoulders. So I must think the loss of capacity for subjective experience would *drain my continued existence of any benefit to me whatsoever*. Whatever benefits would remain to be garnered from that future existence, they would be no better for me than *posthumous* ones. However, I ordinarily think my continued existence would be *much better* for me than extinction. So the proprietary benefits to be had from experience must be very powerful: it is the prospect of *these* benefits that accounts for the high value I place on my own continued existence.

Now suppose, on the other hand, we *don't* grant that (b) leaves *me* in existence. We say I cease to exist, on both scenarios (b) and (c). That may also seem like a plausible line to take: what emerges from (b) ("zombification") is not a new, experience-free *me*, but a "hollowed-out shell of my former self"—not *me*, but only some uncanny *successor* to me. How should this perspective affect my take on the value of consciousness?

Let me then consider, is the only reason I place such high value on retaining the capacity for consciousness that I judge it to be something I need, if I am to stick around in the world? Is the benefit I get from consciousness entirely due to the fact that it is needed to keep me in existence? This seems absurd. For it's not the case that just "any old consciousness will do," as long as it keeps *me* on the scene. For example, I have no doubt that it would be better for me to feel the cool waters caress my limbs as I glide through the pool, rather than have the feeling of burning hot coals searing my flesh as I writhe in a fiery pit. And that preference stays strong, even if I stipulate that either way, my body will be undamaged and I will emerge just as well provided with non-phenomenal benefits, getting all of those offered in options (b) and (c). So the benefit I take myself to get from subjective experience is not entirely due to its role in keeping me in existence, and the value I get by sticking around also cannot be accounted for in terms of other non-phenomenal benefits, to which I might consider my experience as mere means. Then my existing *with the capacity for subjective experience* (or some forms of it) must have some *benefit of its own* to confer on me.

This is further confirmed when I ask myself simply: is it better for me to have the capacity for experience simply because it's better for me to exist than not, or is it better for me to exist at least partly because *that* way I get to have experience it's good for me to have? The second option is far and away the more intuitive. So I conclude that some forms of experience do have proprietary benefits to confer on me, even on the assumption that I need the capacity for consciousness to continue in existence.

This also puts me in a position to see, once again, that the proprietary good experience has for me is *very strong*. For what accounts for the strength of my preference to remain in existence? It won't just be due to some alleged proprietary good to be had from *sheer existence*. I have seen that this benefit is at least partly due to benefits to be had from consciousness. And I find the mere fact of existence does not in itself bring me any benefit, entirely independently of what *sort* of existence I have: what I am able to experience or what else I am able to be or do. For how good could it be for me to continue to exist, on the condition I was condemned, for all remaining days, to a dreamless sleep from which I could be, but just never was in fact awoken? No good at all, I would say. So, then, the key question is this: is my strong preference for existence to be accounted for by reference to factors that could benefit me independently of having experience? Under our current hypothesis—that my existence requires the capacity for consciousness—these will have to be benefits that could come to me after I cease to exist: posthumous benefits. But whatever benefits of this sort I could hope to garner have been imagined to come to me, via my zombie successor. And even then, still, *I strongly prefer to exist.* Thus there's a sense in which the intrinsic benefits I find in my experience ultimately account for why I find my life so intrinsically worth living. For no benefits I could get independently of having experience, or from the bare fact of existence, can account for why I view it so much intrinsically better for me *to be than not to be.* And this remains so, even if I assume I could not survive without consciousness.

I am not sure how many people would have a different reaction to my scenarios—how many would think they wouldn't stand to lose much, if anything, in the way of intrinsic benefits, by being "zombified" in the way envisaged. Apart from the suicidal, I suspect not many. But I do think it's instructive to consider a style of objection to the strength of my resistance to zombification that might be inspired by objective list accounts of well-being.[7] These maintain, roughly—against accounts typically faulted for some unacceptable "subjectivism" (such as hedonist, or desire-satisfactionist accounts)—that factors such as *knowledge, friendship,* and *achievement* make essential contributions to our well-being. And—an objectivist might say—they do this quite independently of subjective experience. For non-conscious beings—intelligent zombie robots perhaps—could possess these very same "welfare goods." And this suggests that there may have been something wrong with my so strongly discounting the continued benefits I could gain from a zombified existence.

To answer this doubt, first, we should recall that, while the intrinsic value I accord experience is great, the way I have conceived of this simply does not commit me (as it would a hedonist or experientialist) to denying the

---

[7] I owe this suggestion to Gwen Bradford.

contribution real world connections—of the sort required by knowledge, friendship, and achievements—make to my well-being. What I *am* committed to, however, is the idea that no form of knowledge, or friendship, or achievement I could have would intrinsically benefit me, were I to lack all capacity for subjective experience. But that is compatible with seeing such objective list goods as contributors to my welfare.

For, I may point out, even if there is some form of knowledge, friendship, or achievement attributable to intelligent non-conscious agents, it does not manifest itself in experience, as do those forms of which I am capable. A "zombie-knowledge" would by definition involve no *experiences* of recognition, of realization, of understanding what one is saying, reading, or hearing. "Zombie-friendship" likewise would involve none of these—and also no experiences of shared, renewed, or deepening affection, struggle, reconciliation, amusement, or delight. "Zombie-achievement" would also of course be devoid of all such perceptual, cognitive, and affective experience. Even if there be such forms of knowledge, friendship, and achievement, *there are none whose possession can offer me intrinsic benefits.* Their existence might, for all that, make the *world* an intrinsically better place, or at least they might have various forms of instrumental value, but that is all.

There is also a second, less concessive response to the worry. We simply should not concede that zombies would have a genuine *mental* life at all. There is, then, no form of the objective list goods mentioned that they would realize. This is not an arbitrary suggestion. Serious cases have been variously made by, for example Kriegel (2011), Pautz (2013), Mendelovici (2019), and Smithies (2019), that intentionality of the sort exemplified in our thoughts, judgments, and desires requires the right sort of subjective experience. I myself have argued (Siewert 2014) that entirely non-conscious beings would not be able to acquire a grasp of concepts through perception, and would not themselves occurrently understand concepts at all. On such views, there can simply be no *knowers*, no *friends*, no *achievers* that lack consciousness, for without subjective experience there is no understanding, no thought, no substantial mindedness at all. So there is no way I might mistakenly deprive myself of these benefits by foregoing the option (b) of zombification in lieu of (c) my destruction and replacement by a zombie double.

I conclude that recognizing the welfare value of the sort of features that figure in objective list accounts of this coheres perfectly well with finding the intrinsic benefits of experience essential to my own well-being. For either without the right experience they no longer constitute intrinsic benefits, or else they are then simply not available.

7. How Experience Makes Desire Matter

Suspicions that I overvalue consciousness might also hail from another quarter, in desire satisfactionist theories of well-being. Neil Levy offers a criticism of my thought experiment that seems so inspired—suggesting that my recoil from the prospect of zombification fails to take into account how satisfying life can be without any consciousness. His zombie double, he says, "wants precisely the same things I do... [and] ... We are even matched on desire-satisfaction..." (Levy 2014, p. 133). So, he suggests, from a desire-satisfactionist point of view, zombification would bring no loss in well-being. So maybe I should reconsider my attitude towards this prospect.

However, I don't think this gives me reasons to revise my attitudes. For one thing, it cannot be right that *my* zombie double wants and gets all the same things I do, for a *lot* of what *I* want and get are various forms of subjective experience. And these a non-conscious being lacks by definition.[8] So it won't be the case that zombification would involve no loss to my well-being from a desire-satisfactionist perspective. To adapt one of Levy's own examples: I lie down to relax on the beach, and feel the warmth of the sun on my face. *I want to feel that way.* Later, in the dead of winter, I recall feeling that way—and I want to feel *that way* again. Happy days: on my next vacation my desire is once again fulfilled. However, if (as Levy asks us to suppose) my zombie counterpart wants all the same things I want, he will be doomed to dissatisfaction I am spared. For, being a zombie, he can't possibly feel the warmth of the sun on his face. There is, by definition, no way that it feels to him. So we shouldn't countenance the idea of a zombie who wants what I want and is just as satisfied as I with what he gets. And the difference between my satisfactions and his will be far from trivial. For as Section 4 makes clear, there is a vastly varied and rich range of experiences I want and have that my imagined zombie double by definition never will. I might add, picking up on the remarks of the last section, it's no objection to say that my zombie double will at least get all the knowledge, friendship, and achievement I intrinsically want. For not only do I not grant that zombies would have the sort of understanding those would require—even waiving that—a non-conscious entity's knowledge, friendship, and achievement could not be manifest in its subjective experience. And I want for myself only the kinds that *are* so manifest.

---

[8] I thank George Sher for drawing my attention to this point.

However, mightn't one use desire-satisfactionism to spoil my celebration of experience in a quite different way? For on that theory what makes something contribute to your well-being is your having (the right sort of) desire for it, and getting it. One might then suggest that experience is nothing special in this regard. It's just one thing among others that some of us might want to have. For some people, *music* plays a big part in well-being; for others, it doesn't. For some, *sports* has a big role; for others, none at all. So why not: some of us want *experience* in our lives, and thus need it to do well, while others neither want nor need it. At bottom, what accounts for what makes us intrinsically better off is getting what we want—not facts about our subjective experience, even if it just so happens *that* is what we want.

One reason I don't find this convincing is that it will be hard to find actual conscious human beings who have no experience of affective satisfaction or dissatisfaction whatsoever. And where there *is* such experience, one will *want* some experience—feelings of satisfaction, relief, pleasure, and so on. Having such desires does not require us to hold philosophical views. Even those who write articles saying that consciousness is an illusion, or that they wouldn't mind being zombified, surely still want to feel warm on a cold day, occasionally taste something sweet and creamy, and feel satisfaction in a good laugh, just like the rest of us. Wanting experiences is hardly the special prerogative of quirky "consciousness fans."

But this still understates the case. We can see this, if we think not just about what kind of life we want for ourselves, but about what underlies our concern for others. I think we will find that the character of someone's experience is more basic than their desire-satisfaction when it comes to understanding our concern for their welfare. For it is experience that makes desire-satisfaction matter.

To make my case, let me first make explicit some (I believe relatively uncontroversial) assumptions about well-being and a broadly moral concern for others. I regard the enhancement of others' well-being, of their getting what benefits them, as something that is not merely good *for them*: it's often *a good thing* that they get it. And I think this is so, not solely because of *other* goods that promotes, to which individual well-being is merely incidental, or to which it is merely instrumental. Further, I have some motivation to act on these attitudes. Which is to say: I have some *concern* for others' well-being. Now, there are circumstances in which such concern dictates I should *give them what they want*, even if I have no *independent* desire that what they want should come to pass, from which my interest in their satisfaction is *derivative.* Here my wanting that you get what you want depends on *your* wanting it. Everyday courtesy furnishes examples. To revert to an earlier case: you ask me to pass the salt shaker that sits before me within easy reach. I should give you what you want—it would be wrong not to. Why? Because to frustrate your desire would ultimately, if only in some small way, diminish your well-being, while to satisfy it would enhance this at least a little. How so? Commonly, I will assume, this lies partly in the fact that you would feel somewhat frustrated or annoyed if I ignored you, or if you were salt deprived, while you'd feel some satisfaction in getting what you want. My starting point here (which I won't try to justify) is that, commonly, affective experiences of satisfaction and dissatisfaction make—respectively—positive and negative contributions to a subject's well-being, and we should take this into account when choosing how to treat people and animals, because it's often good that they have what benefits them and bad that they have what is detrimental to them.

This much I'll assume. What I wish to show is how non-derivative, non-instrumental (and to that extent *moral*) concern for another's desire satisfaction vanishes when we imagine away all capacity for subjective experience. Consider a scenario like the following:

Trapped.   Imagine two creatures, A and B, each alone in two small boxes just big enough to contain them. For all you know, they could be small mammals, large insects perhaps, crustaceans, or robots. What you are told is that A and B each "want to get out and run around"—as would apparently be manifest in their movements—and that the escape of these harmless creatures would cause no detriment that would give you reason to keep them confined. However (let us further stipulate), one of them, A, has no capacity for subjective experience at all. Hence A experiences no feelings of frustration, distress, or panic, and would, on release, experience none of relief, enjoyment, or satisfaction. B, on the other hand, does affectively experience these forms of dissatisfaction, and is capable of feeling satisfaction in frolicking around, post-release. Judgment: the fact the B is not getting what it wants provides grounds for thinking it has been mistreated in being kept confined. Not so with A.

Assuming this judgment is correct, let us ask what underlies it. The most straightforward answer would seem to be this. Where a creature has no capacity for subjective experience (for example, of affective (dis)satisfaction), it has no desires whose fulfillment should engage our moral concern.

Such creatures either altogether lack the desires they're attributed (so they have none to honor), or they lack the kind of desires whose satisfaction invites the relevant form of concern. For they *lack the capacity for the subjective experience that would makes these desires matter*. Please note: I do not mean to imply that only desires whose satisfaction the subject does or can experience figure in reckoning what makes them on the whole better off. I wish to leave open the possibility that desires satisfied or frustrated "behind one's back" or after one's death can matter to one's overall well-being. For instance, maybe it would be detrimental to mine that, quite contrary to my wishes, you play "smooth jazz" at my funeral.[9] What I don't leave open here is that a creature who has *no capacity for subjective experience at all* has desires whose (dis)satisfaction figures in their morally relevant well-being.

One might resist this broad moral from "Trapped," on the grounds that the desires (and creatures) in question are so simple. Maybe it's *only with simple* desires that the capacity for experience is needed to make their satisfaction concern-worthy. But why should the fact that a desire's possession demands relatively high cognitive sophistication render the presence of consciousness irrelevant? Even if we granted that non-conscious beings could have the sort of cognitive sophistication needed for "fancy" desires, it's not at all clear why *their* satisfaction should attract moral concern, while "unfancy" zombie desires get none. Let us try to imagine zombies that don't just want to *get out of a box*, but want *to prove an arcane theorem*. Unless we also happen to want the proof (or an attempt at one), it is not evident why we should have any more reason to facilitate or at least not interfere with the zombies' ostensibly desired activities out of a concern for their welfare, than we did in the "Trapped" case. And again, this would seem to contrast with at least some instances where we're dealing with a mathematician who *is* a conscious being—who is, for example, capable of experiencing understanding of, and satisfaction in, her discoveries.

"But," you ask, "what if our zombie mathematicians *said* they intrinsically benefitted from their unconscious cognitive activity?" Should this give me pause? I don't think so. As an aside, if these are *humanoid* zombies, I would be quite unable to *believe* them to be unconscious, were I actually confronted

---

[9] How might the *capacity* for subjective experience still matter in this scenario? Because the reason it's bad for me that you flout my posthumous desires has to do with *how I would have felt or what I would have thought* if I had known that you would do this. Which presupposes that I did have, prior to death, the capacity for consciousness.

with them: I couldn't help but falsely take them to be conscious. But let me, nonetheless, consider the matter in the abstract. First, I don't think that totally unconscious beings would really understand anything, and so I wouldn't concede that they even have evaluative thoughts to which I might accord authority. For the same reason, I don't think they are in a position to literally want to do higher mathematics. Second, and independently, it's not as though I would automatically give weight to any old claim someone might make about what is intrinsically beneficial to them. If (weirdly) my neighbor said she found it intrinsically beneficial to her to set off her smoke alarm late every night, though she felt no satisfaction in doing this, and wouldn't feel in the least put out if she could no longer do so—then her claim of "intrinsic benefit" would count for exactly *nothing* in mitigating my objection to the nuisance. Though someone's unconscious cognitive processing presumably imposes on me no nuisance, should they similarly (again weirdly) claim to find it *intrinsically* beneficial to them, this would be due no more weight in my considerations than the claim about the smoke alarm.

I maintain, then, that our response to "Trapped" is best taken to show that it is their capacity for consciousness that makes others' desire-satisfaction engage our non-derivative concern for their welfare. Here is another case that seems to support this conclusion in a different way:

Joyless gluttony. Suppose some are driven to stuff their faces, beyond anything their health requires (though not so much as to actually damage it), even while they experience no affective satisfaction in their eating, and feel no dissatisfaction or distress when their food is removed. This, I take it, is possible: to experience eating and its cessation with no affect of (dis) satisfaction. One might intelligibly describe such gluttons as having *desires*, as wanting to keep eating, at least in a "behavior-motivating" sense.[10] And part of what they want, we may suppose, is this *experience* of ingestion—they want to *feel the food going in and going down*. They want the sensation of eating. If they begin to lose it, they cease eating. But they do not want this experience just derivatively—because, say, they think that, without it, they will become malnourished by neglecting their meals. Rather, they simply

---

[10] See (e.g.) Heathwood's (2019, pp. 10–12) discussion of "behavioral desire," in which he cites a number of philosophers like him who recognize this purely behavioral-motivational sense of desire, as distinct from one in which desire's object seems compelling, attractive, or affecting to the subject.

have a *primitive compulsion to seek this affectless experience of ingestion.* Does their getting what they want enhance their well-being in any way that engages my concern for them? No. The fact that I have denied their desires does not mean I have harmed them.

If what makes someone's experiences bear on your concern with their well-being were simply the fact that they *wanted* them, then it seems it should make us think that taking the food away from the joyless gluttons would be somehow detrimental to their well-being. But I believe it's clear that keeping them from getting the experience they want does them no harm, and letting them fulfill their desires for it does them no good. It would be natural to suppose that what makes us indifferent to the gluttons' desires for experience, is that they are, well, so utterly "joyless" (and "distressless"). At least, it seems to show that it makes a difference to us what *kind* of experience is wanted before a want's satisfaction matters in the relevant way. This, I will take it, is quite right. But then it won't be right to make subjective experience *subordinate* to desire-satisfaction, in accounting for concern-worthy well-being. For we understand *what desires are relevant* to this well-being by appeal to *the kind of experience* that would fulfill these desires, or that would constitute their affective (dis)satisfaction.

Let me emphasize, I am neither assuming nor arguing that positive affect is, in general, essential if experiences are to be intrinsically beneficial to their possessor. Though the idea has appeal, it needs further consideration. Could there perhaps be entirely *affectless* people who appreciate their experience in the manner described in Section 4? If so, should their experience, and their desire for it, engage my concern for their welfare? I have left this open. I will say, however, it is not obvious to me that you can *appreciate* experience as *intrinsically* beneficial to yourself, if in fact it forms no part at all of what has positive affect for you. And I find it doubtful that experience could *be* intrinsically beneficial to you, if you are thoroughly incapable of appreciating it, or of experiencing it positively—even if your having it might be an intrinsically *good thing.* And I would accept some version of Railton's (1986, p. 9) influential constraint on conceptions of well-being—that subjects' well-being must somehow "resonate" with them, and that people not be totally *alienated* from what truly makes them better off. Just how to interpret and apply this constraint, and just what is involved in "appreciation," is far from obvious, however. I must leave such matters unresolved for now.

Presently, my point is just this. Others' desire-satisfaction will bear on a non-instrumental, non-derivative concern for their well-being only provided they are capable of having relevant forms of subjective experience. This adds to the previous discussion of the intrinsic benefit of experiences, by imbuing it with moral significance.

8. Responsibility and Respect

I have discussed ways experience might invite moral concern via its connection to desire. But this might seem to neglect another dimension of moral status, rooted in what we regard as peculiar to *thinking beings*. I mean here to invoke the idea that beyond a *concern* for how another creature *feels*, there is a *respect* especially due to *thinkers*, as such. And there is a question: what role, if any, does consciousness play in accounting for this? An important one, I believe. To explain this I will appeal to some aspects of the view of experience I summarized in Section 2. Here I will have to argue in an even more abbreviated way than I have been, and leave detailed defense and elaboration to another occasion. But I maintain the argument I will outline has enough plausibility, and significant enough implications, to deserve consideration.

Recall the experience of verbal self-expression I described in Section 2. There is something it's like for you to complete occurrent conscious thoughts through their verbal expression in a way that constitutes your saying what you had to say, even though you did not specifically intend or forecast that very completion in advance, as far as you can tell. This doesn't guarantee that you did not work out, prior to speaking, an *unconscious* prior intention to say just what you wound up saying (though I would question the grounds to say you did). But at least you can form, from first-hand experience, a conception of what it is to "say what you have to say"—to express yourself—that does not *imply* prior planning. Further, in having such experience, you *endorse as your own* what you find an apt or "right" completion—you do not merely agree with something said, once it is put to you. Nor do you merely execute an act as a result of some prior commitment you may no longer endorse. And to endorse a thought as your own you must be constrained by what you take it *makes sense* for you to say, or by what you take yourself, broadly, to *have reason to say*—that is, the activity in question must be norm-guided. (There is no such thing as normless endorsement.) Since, in this experience of self-expression, you complete your own thoughts in a way both *committal* and *norm-guided*, you thereby open yourself to normative assessment. To be engaged in this kind of subjectively experienced thinking makes you responsible for your own thoughts in the most fundamental way. For you are not merely accepting what someone else has said, and not merely acting as a result of some prior intention. Through this experiential activity you endorse what you say as your own; you thereby become a normatively assessable self-expressive being.

This account locates a self-conferring of normative assessability in a certain sort of subjective experience—uncovered in the phenomenology of verbal self-expression. Could making oneself responsible in this manner for what one thinks also occur completely non-consciously? I think not. For I understand what it is to aptly verbally complete my thoughts in a way that presupposes no specific prior intention to complete them relative to which that "aptness" is evaluated, and at the same time constitutes making myself responsible for them, only if I understand this subjectively—thus, in a way that implies experience.

But what does this have to do with the category: respect? First, let me clarify the general notion of respect relevant here. One might contrast *respect* with *concern* discussed previously—a kind of concern called for in response to others' feelings. While attitudes of concern and respect are compatible, we can see them coming apart. Consider the difference between *pity* and *awe*. When you pity someone, you are concerned for them, but you may lack respect for them. If you are in awe of someone, you respect them, but you may not be concerned for them. This is why *awe* is the sort of attitude that would be appropriate for us to take towards beings vastly greater than ourselves, beings who are *beyond* our concern: gods.

Now think about how respect is manifest in our everyday comportment towards our peers. We might say that we show respect in the relevant sense when, in interaction with others, we let them meet their own challenges, and even pose challenges to them—though this may involve no hostility, and can even be playful. Respect is also revealed in the so-called "reactive attitudes" famously discussed by P.F. Strawson (1962)—such as resentment, indignation, and admiration. When we see someone as an apt recipient of such attitudes we hold them to some standards—norms the adherence to which we regard them as somehow responsible. Consider further, another specific, though pervasive, way in which such respect may or may not be manifest: in how we talk with other people, how we engage each other in conversation. This respect is indicated in whether and how you listen to and acknowledge what someone else is saying. To bring this into relief, consider how that respect may be *withheld*. Suppose in speaking with someone, they habitually *talk over* the spoken completions of your thoughts—not just completing them "for you," but simply ignoring what you're saying in their responses to you. Or maybe they are simply indifferent to how *you* do or would complete them—showing this perhaps by wandering away in midst of what you are saying, or by looking at their phones or laptops instead of listening. Or maybe they conceal their indifference. They are not, in any case, according you due *respect*. There's a sense in which they aren't "taking you seriously."

Perhaps we can lose our right to such respect. But what is it about us that ever makes us entitled to it? If the above considerations are on track, we have an answer: our self-expressive consciousness. For this is what makes you responsible for your own thoughts in a way guided by sense and reason, and being self-responsible in this way is what makes you worthy of the kind of respect I have identified. This yields an argument that consciousness is not only essential to making our satisfaction deserving of *concern*; it explains our rightful demand for certain kinds of everyday *respect*. It thus expands and deepens the connection between consciousness and moral status.

9. Irreplaceability

I close with a proposal that draws on the just preceding line of thought. Recall earlier I said that if I were faced with a choice between, on the one hand, continuing on as a conscious being, and, on the other, losing consciousness but maintaining all its ordinary behavioral manifestations, I would not just vastly prefer the former to the latter. I would also have no preference as between the latter, and a third option, in which I am destroyed and replaced by a similarly zombified duplicate that "plays my part" just as well in the world's drama. I am *far from indifferent* to the prospect of destruction and substitution where what gets replaced is my ordinary conscious self. But I *am* indifferent where what is replaced is some zombified me, or the zombified "successor" who has my old body. What is implicit in this: I accord a kind of irreplaceable value specifically to my own continued existence as a conscious being. And this is not because there is a kind of impact on the world I alone can effect. For that impact, my imagined substitute would do just as well.

But what is not clear is whether the value that I suppose would be lost with my replacement relates to anything more than my own well-being. Perhaps it would be good for me to stay on in my post, rather than be decommissioned and incinerated, once the "back-up" Charles was ready to slot into place. But would this diminish *the good of the world*? More generally (for this is certainly not meant to be just about *my* special value to the world!), do individuals—and particularly conscious beings—have a kind of value that makes their loss irremediable by replacements? Is the world any worse for it, if one of us is simply swapped out for a twin who permanently fills in for us?

Note that prominent among pervasive experiences we may value in their own right are experiences of self-expression. Grant me that such experience is not only a benefit in itself to the self-expresser, and a source of respect-worthiness, but that it is in itself a good thing that people have that good. Much as we may allow that the world is a better place when its inhabitants enjoy the benefits of a wide range of affective satisfactions, we may think that it is also often better when we have the experience of self-expression wherein we make ourselves responsible for our thoughts and become worthy of the kind of respect earlier described. Whether we think *that* good depends on experienced affective satisfaction (I leave this open), we may grant it provides extra value the latter does not exhaust.

It seems to me that this good that is added to the world from your experience of self-expression connects with a kind of *irreplaceable value* you have. Let me try to spell this out. We are presently granting that the occurrence of your temporally extended acts of experienced self-expression is good for you in itself, and that it is just plain good that this particular benefit blossom forth in the world. What I wish to draw attention to here is that such valued occurrences of self-expression not only involve the activity of a particular person, but that there is *only one person* who can bring them, once initiated, to completion, and thus secure the value to the world proper to them. In other words, such experience, whether in yourself or in another, is something that has a beginning that *cannot genuinely be finished by* some stand-in, and the value it brings to the world can be brought by no one else. Even if someone can *aid* you in self-expression, there is a sense in which this is a project that no one else can truly take up and finish for you. And so, when you have something to say, your experience brings with it a value that not only entitles you to respect, it's a value that cannot be preserved through the actions of a substitute. For, literally, no substitute can finish what you have started. There is *only one person who can bring what was started to completion in a way that preserves its value.*

Now enlist these ideas in a conception of our lives as a whole. We can regard a person's life as an *extended act of self-expression*, taken up again at the start of each day. I have been focusing on acts of *verbal* self-expression— but let us now include in broadly "self-expressive activity" everything we *do* (in work, in relationships) that expressing ourselves in speech makes possible. Our singular lives as persons are lived through such subjectively experienced self-expressive activity that continually adds to what came before, and accumulates so as to transform itself and make us who we are. This conception gives us an explanation of why the intrinsic value of your experience warrants regarding you as irreplaceable. For through it, there is something valuable, something long-term you have begun, that no replacement can continue. And so when *you* cannot continue, value is lost that cannot be regained. Thus, we are not interchangeable repositories or vessels of goodness. And, if my earlier argument was right, this same source of respect-demanding irreplaceable value cannot be found without the right sort of consciousness.

I am not just saying that there are feature-instances valuable in themselves that require that certain entities persist over time—particular human beings or other animals, for instance. I am suggesting that the value of self-expressive activity requires the sort of *long-term individual continuity characteristic of a person's life*, since some such activity constitutes the living of that life. And I am proposing that the *value* of this activity that *consciousness* makes possible explains why a particular life has an *irreplaceable* value. Or at least it does, until that life is all "lived up"—until really and truly you have *nothing more to say*.

This is not to rule out other sources of irreplaceable value in someone's or something's continued existence. Nor does it presuppose that such value belongs only to those who make themselves responsible to specifically *rational* norms. Looking further into these matters would require determining just what kinds of normatively self-binding expression there are, and the variety of value's sources. For now I only mean to present a serious rationale for finding consciousness at the root of an irreplaceable value that makes sense of our attitudes towards our own lives.[11]

---

[11] I wish to express my thanks to audiences at the Institut Jean Nicod, and the Rice Seminar for their helpful and challenging feedback to presentations of earlier versions of these ideas. For their thoughtful comments, criticisms, and questions on drafts of this chapter, I wish to express my gratitude specifically to Gwen Bradford, Elizabeth Brake, Steve Crowell, Anna Giustina, Uriah Kriegel, Andrew Lee, George Sher, and Peter Zuk.

References

Bradford, G. (2015). *Achievement*. Oxford: Oxford University Press.

Chalmers, D. (1996). *The Conscious Mind*. Oxford: Oxford University Press.

Crisp, R. (2006). *Reasons and the Good*. Oxford: Oxford University Press.

Heathwood, C. (2019). "Which Desires are Relevant to Well-Being?" *Noûs* 53(3): 664–88.

Kagan, S. (1998). "Re-Thinking Intrinsic Value," *Ethics* 2(4): 177–97.

Korsgaard, C. (1983). "Two Distinctions in Goodness," *Philosophical Review* 92 (2): 169–95.

Kriegel, U. (2011). *Sources of Intentionality*. Oxford: Oxford University Press.

Lee, A. (2018). "Is Consciousness Intrinsically Valuable?" *Philosophical Studies* 176(3): 655–71.

Levy, N. (2014). "The Value of Consciousness," *Journal of Consciousness Studies* 21(1–2): 127–38.

Mendelovici, A. (2019). *The Phenomenal Basis of Intentionality*. Oxford: Oxford University Press.

Moore, G.E. (1903). *Principia Ethica*. Cambridge: Cambridge University Press.

Nozick, R. (1974). *Anarchy, State and Utopia*. New York: Basic Books.

Pautz, A. (2013). "Does Phenomenology Ground Mental Content?" In U. Kriegel (ed.), *Phenomenal Intentionality*. Oxford: Oxford University Press, pp. 194–234.

Railton, P. (1986). "Facts and Values," *Philosophical Topics* 14(2): 5–31.

Shepherd, J. (2018). *Consciousness and Moral Status*. London: Routledge.

Siewert, C. (1998). *The Significance of Consciousness*. Princeton: Princeton University Press.

Siewert, C. (2014). "Speaking Up for Consciousness." In U. Kriegel (ed.), *Current Controversies in Philosophy of Mind*. London: Routledge, pp. 199–221.

Siewert, C. (2019). "Appearance, Judgment, and Norms." In Matthew Burch, Jack Marsh, and Irene McMullin (eds), *Normativity, Meaning, and the Promise of Phenomenology*. London: Routledge, pp. 290–306.

Siewert, C. (2020). "On Needing Time to Think: Consciousness, Temporality, and Self-Expression." Phenomenology and the Cognitive Sciences 19(3): 413–29.

Smithies, D. (2019). *The Epistemic Role of Consciousness*. Oxford: Oxford University Press.

Strawson, P.F. (1962). "Freedom and Resentment." *Proceedings of the British Academy* 48: 187–211.

van der Deijl, W. (2018). "Is Pleasure All That's Good About Experience?" *Philosophical Studies* 176(7): 1–19.

Zimmerman, M. and Bradley, B. (2019). "Intrinsic vs. Extrinsic Value," *Stanford Encyclopedia of Philosophy*, edited by Edward N. Zalta (https://plato.stanford.edu/entries/value-intrinsic-extrinsic/).

Zuk, P. (2019). "A Theory of Well-Being." PhD dissertation, Rice University.

2

Towards a Global Hedonism

Roger Crisp

1. Absolute Value

Hedonism is a theory of value, that is, of goodness and badness.[1] Value is often distinguished into different categories. Value can be relative to kinds: a good knife, say, or a bad pun. Instrumental or constitutive value is what is valuable as a means to or constituent of some non-instrumental value. Prudential value is well-being, what is good or bad *for* an individual.[2] Moral value—found in a person, their character, actions, attitudes, or whatever—is what is morally better or worse, or more morally admirable or blameworthy. Aesthetic value is goodness or badness in the aesthetic sphere, and might be understood as involving something's being admirable or open to criticism from the aesthetic point of view. Epistemic value is the being valuable or disvaluable of epistemic states, qua epistemic states.

This list is not exhaustive of those found in the literature, and the categories mentioned can be made to subsume one another. Further, the boundaries between them plausibly overlap, to the point that discussions of one kind of value sometimes stray into another category. It is easy to move from a claim about what makes a work of art disgusting to a claim about the moral character of its creator, or—as perhaps happens in Aristotle's famous 'function' argument—from a claim about what makes for a good human life to a claim about what is prudentially good for a person (1894: 1097b22–1098a20). And a good deal of recent discussion of epistemic value often switches into discussion of prudential, aesthetic, or even moral value.

These different types of value are all instantiated in particular objects. But it is also plausible that there is an overarching category, 'absolute value',

---

[1] As is standard in axiology, my discussion will focus largely on goodness rather than badness.

[2] 'Well-being' is sometimes used more narrowly, to refer to positive prudential value; see e.g. Kagan 2014.

Roger Crisp, *Towards a Global Hedonism* In: *Oxford Studies in Philosophy of Mind Volume 1*. Edited by: Uriah Kriegel, Oxford University Press (2021). © Roger Crisp. DOI: 10.1093/oso/9780198845850.003.0002

which is instantiated, through some more specific value, in a world, or world history, as a whole.[3] In that sense, the more specific values are themselves constitutive of absolute value. The idea that some world is *just* good in itself makes little sense; it can be good only in so far as it instantiates some more specific value. Consider the following analogy. The goodness of a day at the seaside might be said to consist in the sunbathing, the ice-creams, the swimming, and the donkey-rides. There is no goodness in that day over and above the goodness of each of these items.

Nothing in the idea of absolute value implies that the values that constitute it are in any way commensurable. It is at least conceptually possible that there are two possible outcomes, w^1 and w^2, each of which has absolute value because of their constitutive values, but which are incommensurable. Absolute value is not some further substantive value over and above its constituents, and hence it will inherit the evaluative properties of those constituents.

But the fact that absolute value is not itself substantive does not make it trivial. Indeed, I now want to suggest that the most philosophically, axiologically, and practically significant category is that of absolute value:

Absolutism. Any item is ultimately valuable, and grounds a reason for action, if and only if its instantiation in a world makes that world good, that is, better than a world identical except for its lacking that object.

What is ultimately good or valuable, then, is not whether, say, courage or beauty or knowledge are valuable within their own spheres, but whether these alleged goods, when instantiated in a world, make that world good, by constituting its goodness. How can something be ultimately good if the world in which it exists is no better than that in which, other things equal, it does not? By reflecting on absolute goodness, we can see that some types of value are not ultimate. Consider that variety of kind-relative value which consists merely in objects being good or paradigm examples of their kind—a good Freudian slip, say (Griffin 1986: 235, n.36): how can the mere fact that something is a good example of its kind improve a state of affairs by its presence? But it may be that *some* kinds of thing, such as epistemic states, or moral qualities, through other properties they have, will constitute absolute

---

[3] For a defence of the notion of absolute value against the criticisms of Richard Kraut, see Crisp 2012. For a response to semantic arguments against the notion by Judith Thomson (themselves developing earlier arguments by Philippa Foot), see Phillips 2003.

value: other things equal, perhaps, a world with beings who know is more valuable than a world with beings who have only true beliefs, or a world with compassionate feelings is more valuable than a world without. Absolute value, that is to say, is foundational—it is what *ultimately* matters, and it is therefore what ultimately grounds value-based reasons for action.[4]

Let me move now to a particular substantive value: pleasantness. This property is often ascribed to objects such as, say, a garden, in the same way that, for example, apples might be described as healthy.[5] When we say that a garden is pleasant, this is equivalent to the claim that the garden is such as to cause pleasure. We speak also of the pleasure of being in the garden, and this can be taken as the state of being in the garden accompanied by pleasure, where pleasure is some kind of mental state.[6] It is pleasantness as a mental state which will be the focus of this chapter.

I shall argue that pleasure or enjoyment—that is, pleasantness or enjoyableness—is the only absolute good, and pain or suffering the only absolute bad. On the assumptions that pleasure is good for its experiencing subject and that pleasure is good only in so far as it is good for that subject, prudential value is therefore the only absolute value, and it does not include any non-hedonic elements.[7] Goodness-for, of the hedonic kind, that is to say, is the only absolute good. Since, ultimately, nothing matters except pleasure and pain, other alleged values can at best serve as secondary goals the pursuit of which must be justified in hedonic terms. In that sense, then, it is only from hedonic goods and bads that moral, aesthetic, epistemic, and all other evaluations and norms grounded on such alleged values derive their significance.

Hedonism has one major advantage over all other theories of value: its central claims—that pleasure is absolutely good, and pain absolutely bad—are significantly harder to deny than similar claims about any other objects

---

[4] It might be claimed that some values ground reasons not for acting, but for responding in some other way, such as admiring or believing. For more on some categories of such alleged values, see below.

[5] On the notion of 'focal meaning', see Owen 1986.

[6] It may be objected that pleasure is to be understood not as a mental state, but in terms of adverbial modifications of, say, activity; see e.g. Ryle 1954. I believe that the main axiological and normative arguments of this chapter could be restated without commitment to the view that pleasure is a mental state, but also that few readers would welcome any argument for this. For an insightful defence of adverbialism consistent with the internalism defended below, see Aydede 2018.

[7] I take the distribution of pleasure and pain—as in 'the shape of a life' (see Velleman 1991)—to be a non-hedonic matter.

(Sinhababu ms.). Most people find it obvious that a world in which some non-morally-accountable subject is experiencing pain would be improved, other things being equal, if that pain were replaced by pleasure. Many also accept some form of 'experience requirement' on value—that value is found only in conscious experience, or at least that the value of any item must in some way correlate with or involve conscious experience (Glover 1977: 63–4). But the experience requirement does not limit a theory of value to hedonic goods and bads, and of course many have argued that there are goods and bads, such as beauty or ugliness, which can exist entirely independently of conscious experience. The challenge for hedonism is whether it can use the resources of its foundational and widely accepted evaluations to undermine the force of claims made on behalf of non-hedonic items for inclusion in a theory of absolute value (Brax 2009: 12).

2. Pleasure and Consciousness

In speaking of pleasure, I have in mind pleasure as an element of phenomenal consciousness—that is, experience such that there is something it is like for the subject to be experiencing it (Nagel 1979: 165–80; Kriegel 2015: 47–8). But what *kind* of an element of consciousness is pleasure, so understood? In recent work, for example, it has been common to contrast so-called *internalism* about pleasure, according to which pleasantness is a distinctive type of feeling, with *externalism*, the view that pleasantness consists in some kind of attitude—such as liking or wanting—to an experience construed independently of pleasure itself (Sumner 1996: 87–91). One key advantage of internalism is that it might provide a simple explanation of why we call experiences pleasant, while externalism is often said to avoid the so-called *heterogeneity* objection that introspection on the huge variety of pleasant experiences reveals no single, common, phenomenological property.

I have suggested in previous work that the internalist has a simple response to this objection: pleasant experiences do differ in many ways, but they have one obvious property in common—their feeling pleasant—and this explains why it makes perfect sense to ask someone who has gone through two very different types of pleasant experience (such as a body massage followed by listening to a Haydn string quartet) which they enjoyed more ('the massage—I just loved the way I could feel the stress leaving my joints'; or 'the Haydn—the masseur was rather rough at points, and the Lindsays' *Emperor* is exquisite').[8]

I have also compared the heterogeneity objection to the claim that it is a mistake to speak of the experiences of seeing blue and seeing red as both being cases of seeing colour. Ben Bramble has recently criticized my analogy on the ground that 'pleasant experiences, unlike coloured ones, are not all associated with a particular sense. Pleasant experiences can be visual, aural, gustatory, olfactory, tactile, *or* emotional' (Bramble 2013: 208). But my analogy with colour was not intended to imply that pleasant experiences should be associated with vision in particular. I was using vision merely to illustrate the distinction between a determinable (e.g. colour, rather than smell) and a determinate (e.g. red, rather than blue). Indeed, I could have chosen any other sense to provide a similar illustration. The smells of Chanel No. 5, the sea, and decaying rubbish are very different; but they are all smells.

Bramble might be thought to be recognizing this possibility in a passage that follows those just discussed:

> It might be responded that Crisp is comparing pleasant experiences not to *coloured experiences*, but to *the experiences of particular colours* (e.g., a shade of red, a shade of blue, a shade of yellow, etc.).[9] Experiences of a shade of red, a shade of blue, etc., it might be claimed, are phenomenologically alike in a way over and above their being visual experiences, a way that is shared not even by other visual experiences (say, an experience of a colourful rainbow, or a red phone booth). It is this likeness, it may be suggested, that Crisp believes is analogous to the felt similarity of all pleasant experiences.   (Bramble 2013: 208)

Bramble goes on to allow that experiences of particular colours seem to be phenomenologically similar in a way independent of their being visual experiences. He continues:

> This additional similarity, however, it seems to me, is that *they are experiences of some of the ways in which visual experience must come*. If you're having a visual experience, then it must come in one or, more typically,

---

[8] See Crisp 2006: 103–11. For a recent response to the objection, see Lin 2018 (Lin uses the terms 'phenomenological' and 'attitudinal' instead of 'internal' and 'external').

[9] The reference to shades seems to me potentially misleading, but Bramble's objection appears to be independent of it.

some combination of, these shades of colours. If I am correct, then, still, no helpful analogy can be drawn with pleasant experiences. Pleasant experiences, clearly, are not *ways in which experiences associated with a particular sense must come.* Pleasant experiences can be visual, aural, gustatory, olfactory, tactile, *or* emotional.   (Bramble 2013: 208)

Again, however, I intended to be putting no weight on any particular sense. The focus on vision was merely to illustrate the determinate/determinable distinction, not to suggest any particular link between vision and pleasurable experience.

To return to the heterogeneity argument. There is no structurally similar undermining argument, mirroring the heterogeneity argument, available to the internalist against the externalist, since it does seem plausible to speak of some single attitude or other to many different kinds of experience. The idea of 'liking' is perhaps somewhat problematic, since it is so close to 'enjoying', but it might itself be elucidated in terms of some other attitude, such as that of wanting, or of approving. I have no objection to an author's using 'pleasure' stipulatively to refer to such attitudes, but we must remember that these attitudes are independent of the feeling of pleasure. A sentient being incapable of conative attitudes could still experience a hedonic experience, such as that arising from picking up a very hot pan on the stove. Pleasure is a certain property of conscious experiences which consists in their feeling a certain way to their subject. As John Locke puts it (1975: 2.7.1; 2.20.1), pleasure and pain are 'simple ideas'. They are basic and irreducible aspects or qualities of conscious experience, understanding the nature of which can be only through their phenomenology: they, 'like other simple ideas, cannot be described nor their names defined; the way of knowing them is, as of the simple ideas of the senses, only by experience' (1975: 2.20.1). And since all my readers will remember the experience of consciously enjoying something, I can now move on to the evaluation of pleasure.

3. Hedonism and Well-Being

Let me turn first to the category of prudential value, or well-being. By well-being, I mean what is good *for* some subject, what is sometimes referred to as prudential value, happiness, *eudaimonia*, or welfare.[10]

---

[10] I am not ruling out the position that all well-being is momentary—that pleasure at moment m, for example, is good for its current experiencer at m, and good for no other subject, such as a person, or a series of momentary selves related by, for example, memories.

On one reading of Aristotle, sometimes called the 'inclusivist interpretation', he puts a very plausible condition on the correct view of well-being: that it should be *complete*.[11] Imagine that you claim that well-being consists in, say, pleasure, friendship, and knowledge. I may seek to show your list to be incomplete by introducing some further good, such as accomplishment, and if you agree that accomplishment is another component of well-being then you are required to add it to your list. The question of well-being, then, is the question of what should go on the list.

Note that the list we seek is not merely a list of those *things* the instantiation of which results, other things being equal, in that individual's life being better for them. That list—we might call it the *substantive* list—will be merely a list of items, and hence leave unanswered the crucial philosophical question of what it is that *makes* these objects good for the individual who has them. Consider accomplishment. According to perfectionism, accomplishment is good for the individual because it enables them to approach closer to an ideal of human nature; on another view, it is good because it fulfils God's will; on yet another, it is good solely because of its nature as accomplishment. What we want is an *explanatory* list of those properties of the substantive goods in question that *make* them good. Hence, only the last of these three views will include accomplishment, or perhaps rather 'being an accomplishment', on its explanatory list. The others will include, respectively, the perfection of human nature and the fulfilling of God's will, as the sole *ultimate* good-making properties.

The debate about well-being in the Western tradition, then, can be seen as one about what should go on the explanatory list. Hedonists have argued for a monistic view: pleasantness is the only good-making property.[12] But there have also been many versions of non-hedonistic monism, in addition to the perfectionist and theistic views just mentioned. Socrates, for example, claimed that well-being consists only in knowledge, which is identical to virtue, and other ancient philosophers that virtue alone, understood as non-identical with knowledge, constitutes the good. In more recent times, many have come to believe that well-being consists solely in the satisfaction of desires or preferences. Versions of pluralism also abound, and these should all be seen as non-hedonistic, given that hedonism is the view that pleasantness is the only good-making property. But of course there is no reason

---

[11] See Aristotle 1894: I.7, 1097a15–b21; Ackrill 1975.

[12] The monism/pluralism distinction is largely one of convenience. A hedonist could be described as a pluralist if they believe that both intensity of pleasantness and its duration can affect well-being, or if they believe in a variety of types of hedonic experience.

why pluralism should not include pleasantness on its list as one good-making property among others.

Historically, desire-accounts are outliers, and face objections both from hedonistic monism as well as various forms of pluralism. Why does mere desire-satisfaction benefit a person? If I meet someone on a train, and in conversation develop a desire that they succeed in the projects they describe to me, how it can be better for me if they do indeed succeed in these projects? If you create desires in me for some drug, the taking of which will give me no pleasure, how can this increase in my desire-satisfaction add to my well-being?[13] And can individuals not be benefited without the satisfaction of desire? Consider some primitive creature which can experience pleasure, but to which desires cannot plausibly be attributed. It is tempting to conclude that desire-accounts are based on a failure to recognize the significance of the substantive/explanatory distinction, made so much easier by the fact that many, perhaps all, of the objects commonly believed to be good tend to be desired. Desire, as Aristotle put it (1963: 1072a29), aims at what is good independently of its being desired, just as belief aims at what is true independently of its being believed.

Most versions of pluralism have included pleasantness on their lists, and plausibly so. Consider two lives, A and B. B is, from the point of view of well-being, identical to A, except that it includes certain intense, harmless, and innocent pleasures. The only reasonable way to respect Aristotle's inclusiveness requirement here is to accept that pleasantness is indeed a good-making property. The challenge for the hedonist, then, is to provide not arguments for the goodness of pleasure, but arguments against including anything other than pleasure on the list. One general argument is based on the experience requirement, according to which a subject's well-being can be affected only through effects on their experience. This will rule out theories which allow well-being to depend on, for example, the fulfilment of desires or accomplishment, of which the subject is unaware. But could there not be non-hedonic aspects of experience itself which contribute to well-being?

Consider the very state of consciousness itself. In his discussion of death, for example, Thomas Nagel suggests:

There are elements which, if added to one's experience, make life better; there are other elements which, if added to one's experience, make life

---

[13]   This and the previous example are from Parfit 1984: App. I.

worse. But what remains when these are set aside is not merely *neutral*: it is emphatically positive. Therefore life is worth living even when the bad elements of experience are plentiful, and the good ones too meager to outweigh the bad ones on their own. The additional positive weight is supplied by experience itself, rather than by any of its contents.

(Nagel 1979: 2)

Nagel's illustration is a complex one, involving our weighing bad against good elements of consciousness, concluding that the bad outweigh the good, and then attributing the fact that life remains worth living to the presence of mere experience itself. Properly assessing the force of his example would require offering a good deal more detail on the nature of the goods and bads he has in mind, and on their comparison. But a simpler example throws his claim immediately into doubt. Imagine the life of a being which consists in nothing more than an experience of unchanging greyness, without any other content, hedonic or non-hedonic (cf. Lee 2018: 663). It is hard to see what might be good in such a life.

Robert Nozick claims: 'What we want and value is an actual connection with reality' (1989: 106; see also Allen 2019: 9–10). Imagine, then, that the grey experience is representing a grey reality. Again, this life seems of neutral value. As Nozick said a little earlier: 'We want to be *importantly* connected to reality' (my italics). A grey world without any experience is without value; but value does not emerge within that world merely through experience of its greyness.

But even if mere consciousness, qua consciousness, is not valuable per- haps there are non-hedonic *elements* of certain forms of experience which make it valuable. Imagine, for example, that God asks me to choose between (a) my now being zombified for the rest of my life, and (b) my now losing only my hedonically valenced phenomenology. Many are likely to think I should choose (b). Now imagine that God asks me to make a further choice between either (c) my being replaced one year later by another individual physically and phenomenogically indistinguishable from me, or (d) my not being replaced one year later.[14] Here many are likely that to think that, if I am going to select (a) from the first pair, there is nothing to choose between (c) and (d), but that, if I am going to select (b), there is strong reason to choose (d).

---

[14] I owe this example to Uriah Kriegel.

There is force, then, to the claim that consciousness is valuable, even if not merely in so far as it is consciousness. It may be that phenomenal consciousness makes possible certain goods the good-making properties of which, though perhaps dependent on consciousness itself, are conceptually independent of it. Consider, for example, the recent suggestion by Dorothea Debus that value is created by the giving by any subject of their full attention to the activity in which they are engaged.[15] Debus finds it plausible that an activity is made more valuable by its being engaged in attentively (2015: 1179). This claim seems to be less immediately credible, however, than an analogous claim about pleasantness. Consider some apparently pointless activity, such as counting the blades of grass on a lawn (Rawls 1971: 434), and imagine two individuals engaged in this activity, only one of whom is fully attending to what they are doing. More needs to be said to explain why attention creates value, and Debus continues as follows:

> [It] seems plausible to hold that someone who gives something her full attention gains a certain groundedness in the here and now, a heightened sense of reality, and an increased openness to the object she attends to, and by extension an increased openness to the world. Finding oneself in such a situation is in turn very fulfilling, and therefore seems valuable in itself.
>
> (Debus 2015: 1179)

Debus refers to the work of Mihaly Csikszentmihalyi on 'flow' to elucidate what she has in mind by fulfilment. On the first page of his seminal book *Beyond Boredom and Anxiety* (1975), Csikszentmihalyi states that his object of study is enjoyment. Consider, for example, playing music, with full attention. When individuals say how fulfilling they find that activity, they are almost always referring to how enjoyable they find it. One can imagine a superb musician who has become bored of music, and yet believes it important to the value of their life that they continue with it. After a great performance, they may well look back on that performance with pleasure. But that reflective pleasure is not a form of flow, and the mere anhedonic engagement in the activity itself could not plausibly be said to be fulfilling or what Csikszentmihalyi has in mind when he speaks of flow.

More recently, Willem van der Deijl (2019) has suggested that, if one accepts the experience requirement, it would be unwise then to accept

---

[15] Debus speaks of value in general rather than well-being, but her suggestion that such attention is 'fulfilling' for subjects suggests that her general claim does apply to well-being.

hedonism, since hedonism faces the 'philosophy of swine' objection. This objection can be avoided by allowing non-hedonic aspects of experience to play a role in well-being. To illustrate it, van der Deijl quotes my example of *Haydn and the Oyster*:

> Imagine you are a soul, waiting to be allocated a life. You are offered either the life of the composer, Joseph Haydn, or that of an oyster. Haydn's life is quite long, involving great success and enjoyment. The life of the oyster consists only in the most simple and primitive pleasurable experience possible. Of course, you ask for the life of Haydn; but you are then told that the life of the oyster can be as long as you like—millions of years, if you so desire.   (Crisp 1997: 10–11)

The problem for hedonism is that it might seem to imply that the life of the oyster must, once it reaches a certain length, be better for you overall, since it contains more pleasure. In a later discussion (Crisp 2006: 113–16), I claimed that this implication can be blocked by allowing discontinuities into our evaluations of pleasure. The determinants of the value of any pleasurable experience are, as Bentham recognized, ultimately two: 'intensity', and duration. Mill added the dimension of quality to the list, but this is unnecessary once one recognizes that the 'intensity' in question is equivalent to degree of enjoyableness and not to the intensity of the felt experience itself. So the hedonic value of any experience at a time is how enjoyable it is, and the longer that enjoyment lasts, the more valuable it is. But intensity itself, as degree of enjoyableness, can be judged only through experience, and there is nothing to prevent a hedonist from arguing that *no* amount of oyster pleasure can evaluatively outweigh—that is, be overall more enjoyable than—the enjoyment found in the life of Haydn. That is, a hedonist can allow for the view that the life of Haydn is more pleasurable than the life of an oyster, however long.

Van der Deijl objects to my solution as follows:

> While I believe that the value of a pleasure in experience may not be constant, the suggestion that pleasure itself may decrease if a feeling of pleasure is extended is, I believe, deeply confusing. Feelings are localized in time. If, as I argued above, pleasure is a feature of feeling, two moments that feel the same should result in the same pleasure. In [the] case of the oyster, it is postulated that the feeling of the oyster is the same over time. So, consequently, the pleasure in time should remain constant. If that is the

case, a continuously extended life with a constant stream of pleasure must at some point extend [exceed?] any finite amount of pleasure. But this is exactly what Crisp denies.   (van der Deijl 2019: 1779)

Van der Deijl's interpretation of my position suggests that he is assuming continuity. If I myself had been assuming continuity, then one way that the oyster's life could never outweigh that of Haydn's would be if its life became less pleasant to it over time. But I believe that any stipulated period of the oyster's life, whenever it occurs, will be identical in both pleasantness and value to any other period. In the quotation above, the penultimate sentence implies that we must accept continuity of hedonic value, since the assumption is that temporal extension must inevitably lead to greater pleasantness overall and hence greater value. But van der Deijl provides no argument for that, and hence his claim that we must introduce into our experientialist account of well-being non-hedonic aspects of experience, such as aesthetic appreciation, is under-motivated.[16]

At this point it might be said that I have not done enough to defend hedonism against the notion of non-hedonic good-making properties of consciousness. So far I have merely criticized one line of argument in favour of that notion, and defended hedonism itself against an objection. Charles Siewert, for example, suggests that consciousness provides warrant for perceptual and introspective claims (2014: 211), is essential for our having minds (214), and undergirds the value we have as persons (215). All these things could be the case and yet consciousness be of no value in itself.

Consider the following example from Antti Kauppinen:

Suppose you go to a performance of *Macbeth*, which you follow attentively. Plausibly, your experience is rich and developed. Is this a good experience for you to have? Well, it's not a stretch to assume that it is *instrumentally* good for you—perhaps it yields some insight into Shakespeare or even the human condition that you wouldn't otherwise have had. To that extent, it's a means to something intrinsically good, perhaps even a necessary means.

---

[16] Van der Deijl also claims (2019: 1779–80) that I myself unwittingly accept non-hedonic experientialism by suggesting that hedonists can admit the existence of aesthetic values the appreciation of which can be enjoyed in such a way that their value is discontinuous with bodily pleasures. But the form of hedonism under discussion in the passage van der Deijl is criticizing is a view about only well-being, and so entirely consistent with the view that there are non-hedonic values which are not themselves elements of well-being.

But is it good in itself? If it is not in any way an *enjoyable* experience, the answer seems to be negative.   (Kauppinen 2015: 375–6)

Although I myself find Kauppinen's claims plausible, I suspect pluralists about well-being will not. Some of those pluralists who attach value to knowledge or understanding in itself, for example, might be persuaded, but the majority will almost certainly object to the claim that the experience of coming to understand some profound truth about the human condition is merely of instrumental value. Understanding, that is to say, partly involves certain experiences, the value of which is to be explained by their constituting understanding itself. In the following section I shall outline the best direction for the hedonist to take in responding to such claims.[17]

4. Hedonism, Consequentialism, and Moral Value

The upshot of the conclusion of the previous section, then, is that the hedonist would be best advised to treat non-hedonic experientialism in the same way as non-experientialist pluralism, defending the general claim that no other property is good-making, in the context of well-being, than pleasantness. Examples like that of the Macbeth performance, or my own example of a life that is entirely without pleasure (Crisp 2006: 122–3), have some force, but the main arguments against pluralism must dig deeper.

There are fruitful analogies to be noted at this point between hedonism and welfarist consequentialism.[18] Both are radically revisionary, and yet both emerge out of common sense. Consider consequentialism. The consequentialist principle that one should bring about the outcome which is best in terms of welfare or well-being is not radically revisionary, and can be seen as part of common-sense morality—but only as one principle, to be weighed against others. Most people will accept that, when all else is equal, more well-being is better than less, and that, when one can choose between (i) making

[17] This hedonist response also serves to counter 'hybrid' accounts of well-being, according to which pleasantness is a necessary condition of an object's contributing to well-being, though its value is also to be explained by reference to certain non-hedonic values. (For an example of a hybrid view, see Parfit 1984: App. I.) If knowledge, say, is of no value by itself, then it is not clear how it can become valuable in the company of pleasantness. There are good hedonistic explanations of why we tend to find non-hedonic items valuable, and these are surely preferable to dabbling in evaluative alchemy.

[18] This category of course includes standard act utilitarianism. But it includes also theories which apply a non-impartially-maximizing function to the evaluation of outcomes.

one person happy and (ii) making that person and some number of other people happy, if all else is equal, one should choose (ii). The problems for consequentialism arise when its opponents defend principles—such as a principle based on justice—which they believe can override any reason there might be to bring about the best outcome overall. Now consider hedonism about well-being, a view which emerged much earlier than consequentialism.[19] As we have seen, a plausible pluralism will not involve a denial of the claim that pleasure is valuable. Rather, a pluralist will argue that pleasure is only one good among others, just as the principle that we should produce the best outcome overall is one principle among others.

Most consequentialists have not suggested that we should forget the non-consequentialist principles in common-sense morality. Rather, we are advised to see these non-consequentialist principles as 'secondary' (to use J.S. Mill's 1998: ch. 2, para. 24 term), as helpful guides, the following of which can itself be justified overall by reference to the consequentialist principle itself. Take honesty. It is very useful overall to be able to rely on the word of others, and so continuing engagement in practices of truth-telling and trust will provide various benefits to all. Some consequentialists have even argued that somehow our ancestors had a grasp of consequentialism, which led them to develop practices based on these secondary principles. Consider, for example, Henry Sidgwick's reference to 'unconscious utilitarianism' (1907: 4.3.7), or R.M. Hare's argument that his two-level utilitarianism 'predicts' that moral principles will turn out as they have (1981: 82–3). But accounts like this seem unnecessary, once we reflect upon the survival value of secondary principles. We would expect such principles to emerge through cultural evolution, and that several of them are both generally useful and widespread is unsurprising.

This is not in itself a debunking account of secondary principles. They could still be correct, and it could still be entirely reasonable to accept them on reflection. But a standard line of consequentialist thought has been welfarist: at bottom, morality is justified by the promotion of the good of individuals, and secondary principles are just another helpful way of doing just that.

Note also that these principles cover what is often called 'moral worth' or 'moral value'. Consider a case in which I save someone from some great

---

[19] Utilitarianism, which I take to be the earliest, as well as the most influential, form of consequentialism, is first stated clearly not until Richard Cumberland's 1672 *Treatise of the Laws of Nature* (see e.g. Albee 1902: 14; Crisp 2019: 42–5).

disaster, at significant cost to myself, motivated entirely by concern for the other person. Many will say that my action has great moral value. A careful welfarist consequentialist will deny that moral value constitutes a domain of value independent of that of well-being. This is for two reasons. First, accepting moral value is a hostage to fortune. If the consequentialist allows that something matters independently of well-being, then the door is open for an opponent to introduce many other non-welfarist principles, such as 'impersonal' principles of desert or equality. Second, it is unnecessary, since the language of moral worth is itself part of common-sense morality, and that morality as a whole can largely be justified as a set of secondary principles to guide us in the direction of greater well-being.

Structurally similar arguments to those above can be made on behalf of hedonism, though the strategy has been less common. This is perhaps because ancient philosophy was dominated by the Socratic, non-hedonist tradition, while much of modern English-speaking philosophy, from Hobbes until the end of the nineteenth century, has been dominated by hedonists, who did not feel the need to reflect upon how the primary–secondary distinction might be used to explain the rationale for pursuing non-hedonic goods (Crisp 2019: 205). But the strategy works as well for hedonism as it does for consequentialism, since most if not all of the non-hedonic elements usually found on objective lists involve pleasure. Take the following case, from John Skorupski:

> Consider a patient dying of cancer in a hospital. He may be told or he may be given drugs to alleviate his pain and not be told. Suppose the remaining part of his life will in fact be happier if he is not told. But suppose also that he is a type of person who would not care to live out his life in what he would see as a 'fool's paradise'.   (Skorupski 1989: 302)

Skorupski claims that a doctor who did not tell this patient the truth could not claim to be acting for the patient's good, since they would be depriving him of certain non-hedonic goods, that is, relevant knowledge and unrestricted autonomy. But here the hedonist can note the obvious fact that we enjoy acquiring and using our knowledge, as well as making our own choices, along with other alleged non-hedonic goods, such as spending time with our friends and family, or achieving goals at work and at home. Just as consequentialists can argue that acting in accordance with non-consequentialist principles in general promotes consequentialist goals, so hedonists can claim that non-hedonic principles promote hedonic goals. It is of course true that there are times when this is not the case, and these provide the material for anti-consequentialist and anti-hedonist counter-examples. The hedonist must admit that in the case above the doctor will best promote the good of the patient by withholding the truth. The decision about whether it does or not is a matter for ultimate individual judgement. But the sting of such anti-hedonist examples can be drawn once proper note is taken of the fact that the anti-hedonist principles in question are, at least practically, hedonically supported. Since this strategy works for both conse-quentialism and hedonism, the position of non-hedonistic welfarist conse-quentialists, who combine moral radicalism with prudential conservatism (i.e. a pluralist account of well-being), is somewhat unstable (see e.g. Brink 1989: 217–36; Arneson 1999).[20]

Both consequentialism and hedonism can also appeal to the values of theoretical simplicity and elegance. If there was nothing that the consequen-tialist could say about justice, and nothing that the hedonist could say about accomplishment, denying those alleged values to be ultimate would appear dismissive and unjustified. But in light of the views that morality ultimately must be based on well-being, and prudence on pleasure, the fact that both non-consequentialist principles and the pursuit of non-hedonic goods can be grounded on, in each sphere, a single principle, does count to some degree at least in favour of a combination of consequentialist ethics and hedonism about well-being.

Consider once again the reductive revisionism and theoretical elegance of both hedonism and consequentialism, and their capacity for weakening the force of objections based on intuitions inconsistent with them at the primary level by incorporating principles involving those intuitions at a secondary, derivative, practical level. It is worth noting that a similar strategy can be productively applied at the *global* or general axiological level. Hedonism about well-being is the view that pleasure is the only constituent of well-being; most reflective pluralists will allow that pleasure is *one* of these constituents among others. Welfarist consequentialism is the view that we should make any outcome as good as possible, in terms of well-being; most reflective non-consequentialists will allow this principle as *one* among

---

[20] Note that I am claiming not that hedonists must be consequentialists, only that there are important structural analogies between them and the arguments that can be offered for them. Global hedonism is compatible with many forms of non-consequentialism, as long as these views do not postulate non-hedonic ultimate value.

others. Now consider well-being and absolute value. Most reflective thinkers will allow that *one* of the properties that can make a world ultimately good is the degree to which that world instantiates well-being, and that, other things equal, the best world is the one with the highest level of well-being. *Global welfarism* is the view that this is the *only* ultimately good-making property of any world: 'all goodness is goodness-for'. The main task of the hedonist is to show that nothing contributes positively to well-being other than pleasure, while that of the consequentialist is to demonstrate that there are no principles other than consequentialism bearing on our action. Likewise, a welfarist has to support the claim of well-being to be the only good by arguing against other alleged values or sources of value. And a welfarist who, like the consequentialist, puts weight on simplicity and elegance would be well advised, again like the consequentialist, seriously to consider hedonism as a theory of well-being, especially when they recognize that strategies for defending either can be extended to the other.

5. Aesthetic Value

According to the global welfarist, nothing matters—that is, nothing is ultimately valuable—except in so far as, and to the extent that, it matters *for* some being. If you are in terrible agony after some accident, that matters, greatly, for you; while whether certain rocks are arranged in a certain pattern at some distant point in the universe, which will never be visited by sentient beings, matters to no one and for no one, and hence, as welfarists claim, does not matter. But what, it will be objected, if those rocks happen to have fallen in such a way as to create a beautiful landscape? Here we must consider G.E. Moore's famous thought experiment from *Principia Ethica*:

> Let us imagine one world exceedingly beautiful. Imagine it as beautiful as you can; put into it whatever on this earth you most admire—mountains, rivers, the sea; trees, and sunsets, stars and moon. Imagine these all combined in the most exquisite proportions, so that no one thing jars against another, but each contributes to increase the beauty of the whole. And then imagine the ugliest world you can possibly conceive. Imagine it simply one heap of filth, containing everything that is most disgusting to us, for whatever reason, and the whole, as far as may be, without one redeeming feature. Such a pair of worlds we are entitled to compare... The only

thing we are not entitled to imagine is that any human[21] being ever has or ever, by any possibility,*can* live in either, can ever see and enjoy the beauty of the one or hate the foulness of the other. Well, even so, supposing them quite apart from any possible contemplation by human beings; still, is it irrational to hold that it is better that the beautiful world should exist, than the one which is ugly? Would it not be well, in any case, to do what we could to produce it rather than the other? Certainly I cannot help thinking that it would; and I hope that some may agree with me in this extreme instance.   (Moore 1903: 83–4)

Let us allow that Berkeley was mistaken in thinking that it is impossible to conceive of existence unperceived. Nevertheless, I suspect that Moore and those who agree with him may not have reflected sufficiently carefully on the significance of the fact that these worlds will be causally entirely insulated from experience. Indeed, Moore muddies the waters here somewhat by introducing the question whether one has a reason to produce one or other of these worlds. If I have, for whatever reason, to bring into being one or other of these worlds, and I choose the beautiful one, though it may be true that this world will not have any direct effect on my experience, it is causally related to my experience, in so far as I will experience the decision, the action of bringing it about, and the consequence of that decision: while choosing, I may try to imagine the world, for example, and, having chosen and brought it about, be proud, rather than ashamed, of what I have done. What we need to ask is whether it is ultimately better that one or other of these worlds exist, in total causal isolation from any sentient being.[22]

Moore, of course, is likely to claim that it *does* matter. Now consider a case identical to that involving the beautiful and the ugly worlds, except that the beautiful world will contain one sentient being, isolated in some part of that world which is neither beautiful nor ugly, and in constant and uncompensated pain. Since I myself can see no difference between the worlds in the original case, I believe that in this second case the ugly world is *considerably* better than the beautiful one containing suffering (that is, it is of no value, rather than negative value). In the second beautiful world, it matters very

---

[21] This word might profitably have been omitted by Moore here and in the following sentence.

[22] A hedonist might wish to claim that such a world has 'inherent value', in the sense that it contains objects which could be enjoyed (see Audi 2006). But inherent value does not contribute to absolute value.

much for the suffering individual that they are suffering, while in the ugly world it matters for no one that this world is ugly.

Moore may agree that the ugly world is preferable to the second beautiful world, and rightly point out that this view does not imply that the beauty of the beautiful world has no value. But now imagine a third case, in which the choice is between an ugly world, and *any* finite number of beautiful worlds, in one of which exists an individual in constant and uncompensated pain. Here, if one is still tempted to value the ugly world above the series of beautiful worlds, one might reasonably conclude that in fact it is not the case that there is any value in beauty itself, and that one has been misled by attachment to a secondary principle of some kind which encourages positive evaluation and production of beauty because of its effects on well-being.

But, it might be suggested, should we not consider with some care the phenomenology of actually appreciating beauty, such as the eloquence and humanity in some great drawing by Raphael? Is this not best interpreted as the perceiving of independent aesthetic value? One line the welfarist might take here would be to attempt a debunking account of aesthetic value, using evolutionary theory. Consider, for example, Miller's suggestion that

> [B]eauty equals difficulty and high cost. We find attractive those things that could have been produced only by people with attractive, high-fitness qualities such as health, energy, endurance, hand-eye coordination, fine motor control, intelligence, creativity, access to rare materials, the ability to learn difficult skills, and lots of free time.   (Miller 2000: 281)

That sounds like Raphael. But there are no knockdown debunking arguments, and there is nothing to prevent the defender of aesthetic value from claiming that the evolutionary account is, at most, an explanation of how we came to be in a position to appreciate such value.[23] A better response would be, first, to run a two-worlds case, including the Raphael along with a suffering person (unable to see the drawing) in one world, and nothing in the other; and then to stress the importance of *pleasure* in aesthetic experience (see e.g. Matthen 2017). There are, that is to say, aesthetic *properties*— beauty, eloquence, humanity. But we should understand the *concepts* we use

---

[23] Nor is there anything to prevent a hedonist from claiming that, even if it is plausible that evolution has inclined us to think pleasure valuable, this does not debunk the claim that pleasure is valuable. It is much harder to believe that agony is not really bad for us than it is to believe that aesthetic properties do not contribute to absolute value; see Crisp 2006: 17–18.

to describe these properties as non-evaluative, at least in so far as absolute value is concerned. We might call Raphael's drawings 'good', but this is merely to place them in that category of works, involving various complex descriptive properties, which we enjoy so much.

6. Epistemic Value

What about *epistemic* value, which is often seen as a third category of value in addition to aesthetic value, on the one hand, and prudential and moral value, on the other (see e.g. Kriegel 2019: 504)?[24] Isn't knowing that *p*, or understanding *p*, more valuable than, say, merely having true beliefs about *p*? And isn't it better to have true beliefs based on evidence, rather than true beliefs without evidence, or false beliefs?

If knowledge were a component of well-being, the answer to both these questions would be affirmative. But this value would be prudential, and not in some independent, epistemic domain. We might again use the strategy of comparing worlds. World A includes only one person, at a certain positive level of non-epistemically-related well-being throughout her life. This person knows many things. World B includes another person, at the same level of non-epistemically-related well-being. This person knows far fewer things. Now, even if it were true that world A is better than world B in so far as knowledge is a constituent of well-being, what reason is there to believe that it contains more 'epistemic' value?

It may of course be asserted that knowledge just is of great ultimate and absolute value. At this point the hedonist might move on to cases involving suffering, analogous to those involving alleged aesthetic value. Further, it can again plausibly be suggested that our epistemic norms themselves have developed because of the benefits we receive from knowledge and understanding. It is as unparsimonious to assert the existence of a whole separate domain of ultimate epistemic value as it is to postulate non-hedonic prudential value, or moral value, or aesthetic value. The only ultimate value is pleasure.

To conclude, I began the chapter with two claims: (a) the most important form of value is absolute value, the value some item has through possessing

---

[24] BonJour (2010: 58) claims that any adequate of knowledge must explain why it is the 'epistemic *summum bonum*'.

a lower-order evaluative property that makes the world in which it is instantiated good; and (b) absolute value provides, through the substantive value of its constituents, the only source of practical reasons. We may continue to speak of other forms of value, such as attributive or instrumental value, but it is absolute value which has genuine axiological and practical significance. This view I called *Absolutism*.

I then noted that the main issue for hedonists about value is defending not the positive claim that pleasure is valuable, but the negative claim that items other than pleasure have no value. I explained how pleasantness is to be understood as a basic category of phenomenal consciousness, defending this view against so-called 'externalism' about pleasure, and the objection that any form of hedonism incorporating it amounts to an unattractive form of reductionism about value (the 'philosophy of swine').

Hedonism about well-being gains support from the experience require-ment, but some have argued that well-being can consist in non-hedonic aspects of experience. I questioned these arguments, before moving to pluralism more generally. Hedonism is often said to be counter-intuitive, and I suggested that hedonists might adopt strategies similar to those used by consequentialists against the same charge. These strategies were applied in turn to moral, aesthetic, and epistemic value, and then to support welfarism, the view that the only value is well-being. I suggested that welfarists attracted by the parsimony and elegance of that view should consider whether, within the theory of well-being itself, these qualities are not found preeminently in hedonism.

Hedonism has been one of the most, if not the most, popular view of value in the history of philosophy. Its decline in the twentieth century has not been fully explained. Victorian attitudes to pleasure, and the popular criticisms of hedonism by the aesthete G.E. Moore, almost certainly played a role. The arguments against it are no better than those against consequentialism, and just as in normative ethics the central debate is rightly seen as that between consequentialism and forms of deontology, so in axiology hedonism should be recognized along with pluralism as at least an equal partner. Hedonism is sometimes seen as an unserious position in philosophy. But a serious philosopher will not dismiss it out of hand.[25]

[25] For comments on and discussion of previous drafts, I am very grateful to Robert Audi, Ben Bramble, Uriah Kriegel, Theron Pummer, John Skorupski, and Philip Stratton-Lake.

References

Ackrill, J. 1975. 'Aristotle on Eudaimonia', *Proceedings of the British Academy* 60: 339–59.

Albee, E. 1902. *A History of English Utilitarianism*. London: Swan Sonnenschein.

Allen, K. 2019. 'The Value of Perception', *Philosophy and Phenomenological Research*, doi: 10.1111/phpr.12574.

Aristotle. 1894. *Ethica Nicomachea*, ed. I. Bywater. Oxford: Clarendon Press.

Aristotle. 1963. *Metaphysica*, ed. W. Jaeger. Oxford: Clarendon Press.

Arneson, R. 1999. 'Human Flourishing versus Desire Satisfaction', *Social Philosophy and Policy* 16: 113–43.

Audi, R. 2006. 'Intrinsic Value and Reasons for Action', in T. Horgan and M. Timmons (eds), *Metaethics after Moore*. New York: Oxford University Press, 79–106.

Aydede, M. 2018. 'A Contemporary Account of Sensory Pleasure', in L. Shapiro (ed.), *Pleasure: A History*. New York: Oxford University Press, 239–66.

BonJour, L. 2010. 'The Myth of Knowledge', *Philosophical Perspectives* 24: 57–83.

Bramble, B. 2013. 'The Distinctive Feeling View of Pleasure', *Philosophical Studies* 162: 201–17.

Brax, D. 2009. *Hedonism as the Explanation of Value*. Lund: Lunds Universitet.

Brink, D. 1989. *Moral Realism and the Foundations of Ethics*. Cambridge: Cambridge University Press.

Crisp, R. 1997. *Routledge Philosophy GuideBook to Mill on Utilitarianism*. London: Routledge.

Crisp, R. 2006. *Reasons and the Good*. Oxford: Clarendon Press.

Crisp, R. 2012. 'In Defence of Absolute Goodness', *Philosophy and Phenomenological Research* 87: 476–82.

Crisp, R. 2019. *Sacrifice Regained: Morality and Self-Interest in British Moral Philosophy from Hobbes to Bentham*. Oxford: Clarendon Press.

Csikszentmihalyi, M. 1975. *Beyond Boredom and Anxiety: Experiencing Flow in Work and Play*. San Francisco: Jossey-Bass.

Debus, D. 2015. 'Losing Oneself (in a Good Way): On the Value of Full Attention', *European Journal of Philosophy* 23: 1174–91.

Glover, J. 1977. *Causing Death and Saving Lives*. Harmondsworth: Penguin.

Griffin, J. 1986. *Well-Being: Its Meaning, Measurement, and Moral Importance*. Oxford: Clarendon Press.

Hare, R.M. 1981. *Moral Thinking: Its Methods, Levels, and Point*. Oxford: Clarendon Press.

Kagan, S. 2014. 'An Introduction to Ill-being', in M. Timmons (ed.), *Oxford Studies in Normative Ethics*, vol. 4. Oxford: Oxford University Press, 261–88.

Kauppinen, A. 2015. 'What's So Great about Experience?', *Res Philosophica* 91: 371–88.

Kriegel, U. 2015. *The Varieties of Consciousness*. New York: Oxford University Press.

Kriegel, U. 2019. 'The Value of Consciousness', *Analysis* 79: 503–20.

Lee, A. 2018. 'Is Consciousness Intrinsically Valuable?', *Philosophical Studies* 176: 655–71.

Lin, E. 2018. 'Attitudinal and Phenomenological Theories of Pleasure', *Philosophy and Phenomenological Research*, doi: 10.1111.phpr.12558.

Locke, J. 1975. *An Essay concerning Human Understanding*, ed. P. Nidditch. Oxford: Clarendon Press.

Matthen, M. 2017. 'The Pleasure of Art', *Australasian Philosophical Review* 1: 6–28.

Mill, J.S. 1998. *Utilitarianism*, ed. R. Crisp. Oxford: Oxford University Press.

Miller, G.F. 2000. *The Mating Mind: How Sexual Choice Shaped the Evolution of Human Nature*. New York: Doubleday.

Moore, G.E. 1903. *Principia Ethica*. Cambridge: Cambridge University Press.

Nagel, T. 1979. *Mortal Questions*. Cambridge: Cambridge University Press.

Nozick, R. 1989. *The Examined Life: Philosophical Meditations*. New York: Simon & Schuster.

Owen, G.E.L. 1986. 'Logic and Metaphysics in some Earlier Works of Aristotle', repr. in *Logic, Science, and Dialectic*. London: Duckworth, 180–99.

Parfit, D. 1984. *Reasons and Persons*. Oxford: Clarendon Press.

Phillips, D. 2003. 'Thomson and the Semantic Argument against Consequentialism', *Journal of Philosophy* 100: 475–86.

Rawls, J. 1971. *A Theory of Justice*. Cambridge, MA: Harvard University Press.

Ryle, Gilbert. 1954. 'Pleasure', *Proceedings of the Aristotelian Society* 28 (Supplementary Volume): 135–46.

Sidgwick, H. 1907. *The Methods of Ethics*, 7th edn. London: Macmillan.

Siewert, C. 2014. 'Speaking Up for Consciousness', in U. Kriegel (ed.), *Current Controversies in the Philosophy of Mind*. New York & London: Routledge, 199–221.

Sinhababu, N. ms. 'The Epistemic Argument for Hedonism', https://philpapers.org/archive/SINTEA-3.pdf.

Skorupski, J. 1989. *John Stuart Mill*. London & New York: Routledge.

Sumner, L.W. 1996. *Welfare, Happiness, and Ethics*. Oxford: Clarendon Press.

van der Deijl, W. 2019. 'Is Pleasure all that is Good about Experience?', *Philosophical Studies* 176: 1769–87.

Velleman, D. 1991. 'Well-Being and Time', *Pacific Philosophical Quarterly* 72: 48–77.

3

The Value of Consciousness in Medicine

Diane O'Leary

0. Introduction

It is arguably possible for patients to be phenomenally conscious without the complex cognitive capacities that meet standards for personhood. Independently of metaphysical debates about that distinction, patients in a minimally conscious state, those awakening from anesthesia, and those in advanced stages of Alzheimer's disease clearly do have experiential states despite lacking capacities that make medical decision-making possible. Moreover, there's been considerable philosophical discussion about the likelihood that consciousness, in the phenomenal sense, is actually isolated from personhood in some patients diagnosed as being in persistent vegetative state (VS) (Kahane and Savulescu 2009; Levy and Savulescu 2009; Shea and Bayne 2010). Regardless of how we interpret studies suggesting consciousness in VS patients (Owen et al. 2006; Owen et al. 2007; Owen and Coleman 2008), it's been important to consider the distinct implications of consciousness when it comes to ethical questions about sustaining life.

The moral and ethical implications of consciousness should also be considered more broadly in medicine, particularly in its foundations as they've developed since the late twentieth century. Based on rejection of the so-called biomedical model (BMM), "humanism" and "holism" have driven a professional shift that's broadened the scope of medicine's focus from the limited realm of the body and its diseases to a broader realm where we recognize mind and its integration with the body in whole persons. This shift has had a profound impact on medical science and diagnostic practice. More than that, rejection of the BMM has typically been understood to clarify why medicine is a moral practice, broadly speaking, and why the specific demands of clinical ethics should be recognized as imperative. As we

Diane O'Leary, *The Value of Consciousness in Medicine* In: *Oxford Studies in Philosophy of Mind Volume 1.*
Edited by: Uriah Kriegel, Oxford University Press (2021). © Diane O'Leary.
DOI: 10.1093/oso/9780198845850.003.0003

generally see things in bioethics, it is personhood that was overlooked by the BMM, and it is recognition of persons that brings medicine out of the realm of pure science into the realm of moral and ethical values. When we look more closely, however, particularly with respect to holism, we find that it is often not recognition of personhood that's driving medicine's current approach: it is recognition of consciousness.

There has been little effort, however, to clarify the specific role that consciousness has played in the turn away from the BMM, as distinct from the role of personhood. With this in mind, in this chapter I address the following question: *What is the role for recognition of consciousness in grounding the moral value of medicine and the concepts and principles of clinical ethics?*

To address that question, I begin in Section 1 by pinning down the tenets of holism as they concern consciousness. Based on George Engel's suggestion that medicine's ethical demands are implicit in medical science properly understood, I discuss, in Section 2, three ways in which holism's recognition of consciousness changes medical science, and clarify how these force us to see the practice of medicine as a moral endeavor. In Section 3, I argue that the specific principles of clinical ethics are also grounded in recognition of consciousness, not recognition of personhood. In particular, I suggest that respect for autonomy in medical settings arises from respect for the inviolable boundary around bodily experience. Because bodily experience is both private and inescapable, conscious patients command respect for autonomy even in the absence of the cognitive capacities that make it possible for them to exercise their autonomy. I conclude that it is consciousness, rather than personhood, that compels us to pursue medical practice and defines the pursuit as moral, so it is consciousness that provides the foundation for clinical ethics.

My concern with consciousness in this chapter is specifically focused on phenomenal consciousness—that is, conscious states with some kind of qualitative feel—and the capacity to have them. There is "something that it's like" (Nagel 1974) to be a conscious being in this sense, so the concern with consciousness in medical contexts is just a concern with the capacity of patients to have qualitative experiences. Consciousness in this sense is distinguished from "access consciousness" (Block 1995), which involves self-consciousness over time, along with the complex cognitive and motivational capacities that make it possible to set rational goals and act toward achieving them. I will follow Levy and Savulescu in considering access consciousness more central to personhood. As I will understand it, those who meet the standard of personhood (as it's traditionally been construed) have "abilities that require access consciousness, not phenomenal consciousness" (Levy and Savulescu 2009: 367). Ultimately, though, I will defend the view that when holism is properly understood, it clarifies the sense in which conscious human beings are fully worthy of respect even when they do not meet the standard of personhood.

1. Holism and Consciousness

1.1 Two Routes to Resolving Medicine's Crisis

The medical professions experienced a "quality-of-care crisis" (Marcum 2008: v) in the 1970s that only grew more pressing in the remaining decades of the twentieth century. Through the tradition of the BMM, medicine had centrally identified itself as a biological science that set out to improve the body and address its diseases.[1] Though there was no question that this approach had been profoundly successful in its goal, both the profession and the culture at large became concerned that something vital was missing. Ramsey (1970) suggested that patients should be recognized as persons, and that idea was then deepened, largely through Pellegrino's work, into the movement of "humanism."

Humanism insisted that because patients are persons rather than bodies, medical practitioners have clear obligations to them that go beyond the limited focus of biological repair. Through the work of Beauchamp and Childress (1979), humanism pinned down those obligations in a way that codified the principles and concepts of clinical ethics as we now understand them. Humanism's impact on medicine can hardly be overstated. Through this movement, bioethics developed into a profession integrated with medicine and central to its success (Marcum 2008). Medical education evolved to include the humanities, and medical practice recalibrated to demand respect for the autonomy of persons through practices like informed consent and truthfulness.

But humanism is only half of the story when it comes to the turn away from the BMM. Not long after Ramsey's foundational book *The Patient as*

---

[1] It's important to acknowledge that medical ethics did exist before the late twentieth century (see, for example, Gordon 1934), so the profession's biological focus did not exclude the possibility of duties to persons. My distinction between the BMM and the holistic and humanistic alternatives follows the original writing that sharply defines those alternatives.

Person (Ramsey 1970), psychiatrist George Engel wrote that "appeals to humanism" are "ephemeral and insubstantial... when not based on rational principles" (Engel 1977: 135):

> I contend that all medicine is in crisis and, further, that medicine's crisis derives from... adherence to a model of disease no longer adequate for the scientific tasks and social responsibilities of either medicine or psychiatry.
>
> (Engel 1977: 129)

As Engel saw it, "the proper boundaries of professional responsibility" (1977: 129) should be clarified through improved understanding of disease in medical science. The alternative Engel offered to the BMM was the "biopsychosocial model" (BPSM), which is "both a philosophy of clinical care and a practical clinical guide" (Borrell-Carrió et al. 2004: 576). Based on biological systems theory, the BPSM suggests that "clinicians must attend simultaneously to the biological, psychological, and social dimensions of illness" (Borrell-Carrió et al. 2004: 576). In doing so, they would reject the "biomedical dogma requir[ing] that all disease, including 'mental' disease, be conceptualized in terms of... underlying physical mechanisms" (Engel 1977: 130).

As with humanism, it is hard to overstate the impact holism has had on medicine. The BPSM is implicit in the World Health Organization's continued commitment to a definition of health as "a state of complete physical, mental and social well being, and not merely the absence of disease or infirmity" (WHO 2019). It has been described as "the official philosophy of the American Psychiatric Association and the Diagnostic and Statistical Manual, DSM-5" (Rease 2014: 1). Perhaps most importantly, the culture at large could not be more enthusiastic than it now is about "integrated mind–body medicine" and "whole person care," two ideas that have become essential for everyday medical marketing. There have been a great many criticisms of the BPSM in recent years, though most of these express frustration that failings in holism's original formulation have made it hard for the movement to achieve the dramatic change it originally aimed for (Butler et al. 2004; Ghaemi 2010; Bolton and Gillett 2019).

1.2 The Philosophical Bottom Line

While the terms 'humanism' and 'holism' have had varied definitions, and they've often been used interchangeably, in Engel's writing holism provides the conceptual foundation we need to make sense of humanism's ethical demands. The central problem with the BMM, Engel suggests, is that it "embraces ... reductionism, the philosophic view that complex phenomena are ultimately derived from a single primary principle ... " (Engel 1977: 129). More specifically:

> The historical fact we have to face is that in modern Western society biomedicine not only has provided a basis for the scientific study of disease, it has also become our own culturally specific perspective about disease, that is, our folk model.... Biomedical dogma requires that all disease, including "mental" disease, be conceptualized in terms of derangement of underlying physical mechanisms. This permits only two alternatives ... the reductionist, which says that all behavioral phenomena of disease must be conceptualized in terms of physicochemical principles; and the exclusionist, which says that whatever is not capable of being so explained must be excluded from the category of disease. (Engel 1977: 130)

Holism provides a middle way between these two alternatives, so it becomes possible for medical practitioners to address "the human experience of disease" (Engel 1977: 131), including mental illness, without reducing experience to biology and without threatening medicine's claim to scientific practice.

Schillmeier recently suggested that the BPSM "protests against the manner by which only non-subjective qualities gain explanatory power" (Schillmeier 2019: 141), and this echoes Borrell-Carrió and colleagues, who interpreted the model as "a way of understanding the patient's subjective experience as an essential contributor to accurate diagnosis, health outcomes, and humane care":

> Engel did not deny that the mainstream of biomedical research had fostered important advances in medicine, but he criticized its excessively narrow focus for leading clinicians to ... [ignore] the possibility that the subjective experience of the patient was amenable to scientific study.
>
> (Borrell-Carrió et al. 2004: 576)

Though Engel himself never used these terms, his perspective is a form of non-reductive physicalism or property dualism (Marcum 2008; Woods 2015), aptly characterized by Borrell-Carrio and colleagues as the view that "subjective experience depends on but is not reducible to laws of physiology" (Borrell-Carrió et al. 2004: 576).[2] While it seems he was unaware of this, reductionism became untenable to Engel in medicine right around the time that it became untenable in philosophy. In both cases the challenge was (and is) to find a way of distinguishing experiences from the brain states with which they're correlated, while still maintaining the causal closure that science requires. There are indications that Engel was aware of the philosophical enormity of this task: "We are now faced with the necessity and the challenge to broaden the approach to disease to include the psychosocial without sacrificing the enormous advantages of the biomedical approach" (Engel 1977: 131).

2. From Recognition of Consciousness to the Morality of Medicine

2.1 Three Roles for Consciousness in Medical Science According to Holism

Working from the ground up, holism is committed to changing the scope of medicine's scientific focus so that it can take stock of "the human experience of disease" (Engel 1977: 131). Unfortunately, neither Engel nor subsequent researchers working on holism have distinguished consciousness and personhood in this context. How exactly does the new model handle consciousness specifically, as distinct from the psychology of persons and the social parameters that impact the health of persons? I suggest that according to holism the scientific goal of improving the body requires that conscious states of bodily experience must be recognized in three distinct ways. As we will see, on their own, the first two do not force medicine out of the realm of science into the realm of the values. The third, however, does.

(1) Conscious states are central to the success of diagnostic science. Gifford proposes that the BMM and the BPSM

> suggest different implications for the data one needs to collect in order to make decisions about diagnosis and patient management. From the BMM

---

[2] Engel repeatedly equates reductionism with dualism, so it's clear he uses the term 'dualism' quite differently from the way philosophers understand it. This is not the place to address that confusion, so I accept Engel's emphatic rejection of reductionism and, following Marcum and Woods, I take it to demand some form of property dualism.

perspective, lab results etc. are seen as the most objective, as probing deeper into the medical reality, and thus as providing the most reliable and useful information. The BPSM perspective emphasizes more the reports from patients, including reports of subjective experiences.   (Gifford 2017: 446)

Engel certainly did not invent the idea that patients' experiences of their bodies are important to the diagnostic and treatment process. He did, however, bring this reality front and center in a way that posed a challenge for the BMM. Direct experience of the body is, essentially, the body's report on itself, so if your goal is to improve the body, information about experience will be scientifically crucial.

What's complicated about data of this kind—and this is the reason why the BMM would be inclined to minimize its scientific importance—is that experience of the body is epistemically private. That is to say that the doctor cannot get at this data except through patients' reports, and reports are not possible unless the patient has and employs the complex cognitive capacities of personhood.[3] In this sense, personhood intervenes between bodily experiences as they are and bodily experiences as a doctor can access them. Rogers has suggested that

> Medicine strives for objectivity; the purpose of the diagnostic interview and examination is to transform the initial chaos of the patient's presenting complaint into a series of symptoms and signs linked by reference to a pathophysiological disease state. This creates a need to standardise patients' signs and symptoms and to filter them through a medical sieve.
> (Rogers 2002: 79)

Holism proposes that the epistemic complexity of this process in no way challenges the claim to scientific practice. The patient has conscious states of direct, private experience of the body, which she generally interprets and responds to with the complex capacities that characterize her as a person. As a person, then, she communicates to the doctor about her interpretations of, and responses to, her bodily experience. The doctor then works through a

---

[3] There are substantial efforts in medicine to access the private data of bodily experience without the personhood-related complexities that arise with patients' reports. Pain measurement charts, for example, are meant to provide something like a numerical measure of pain experience purely through observation of patients' facial expressions. These measurements are deeply flawed, of course, because facial expressions of pain are generally mediated by person-level considerations that involve self-awareness and self-image in the social setting.

professional filtering process, which she hopes will isolate facts about bodily experience that can support accurate conclusions about disease.

> The most essential skills of the physician involve the ability to elicit accurately and then analyze correctly the patient's verbal account of his illness experience. The biomedical model ignores both the rigor required to achieve reliability in the interview process and the necessity to analyze the meaning of the patient's report in psychological, social, and cultural as well as in anatomical, physiological, or biochemical terms.   (Engel 1977: 132)

It's important to Engel that, as the language of the BPSM always points out, the doctor cannot develop an accurate picture of direct bodily experience if she only pays attention to patients' words about the body. Because a sad patient will report on pain differently from an anxious patient, for example, part of the doctor's clinical acumen involves assessing the patient's psychological and social experiences of herself as a person, and then using those assessments during the filtering process to improve the accuracy of data about conscious states of bodily experience. The doctor can, and should, also take stock of patients' psychological health and social frameworks through direct observation, independently of patients' reports about them. Sadness and anxiety are sometimes directly apparent, for example, as are the complex interactions of family. These considerations should play a role in doctors' interpretations of patients' reports about their bodily experiences.[4]

(2) Conscious states play a role in the biological development of disease, so they're central not just epistemically, but also metaphysically. Engel offered a case study that illustrates this, where a patient with history of heart attack has some initial cardiac symptoms, but then is triggered into actual heart attack by fear that arises in response to clinical investigations (Engel 1981). Whatever we might say about the challenges of that example, the point is important for a scientific understanding of disease. The body does not develop disease independently of conscious states. On the contrary, it seems clear that experiential states play an integral role in triggering, sustaining, and worsening disease.

---

[4] Though my concern at this point is with the place for consciousness in holism's picture of biomedical science, holism does also centrally suggest that doctors should concern themselves with improving patients' experiences of themselves as persons, even when those improvements do not involve biological science.

Since Engel's time, medicine has become far more informed about the impact of conscious states on the disease process. It is clear, for example, that stressful experiences delay wound healing and support the development of infection (Gouin and Kiecolt-Glaser 2012). Similarly, researchers have become much more precise about the neurochemistry of experiential states of distress, and this has made it possible to clarify how conscious states play a role in gut diseases (Sgambato et al. 2012). In both of these areas, research is focused on conscious experience of the self—that is, private experiences of psychological or social distress at a level that requires the cognitive capacities of personhood.

Other research in this area has considered the impact on the central nervous system when patients have bodily experience of pain for long periods of time. Research of this kind suggests it's possible for conscious states of bodily pain at a given moment to arise from the nervous system's response to sustained states of bodily pain in the past (Wallit et al. 2015). The distinction between consciousness and personhood in this area is complex and poorly considered. At times, researchers seem to suggest the nervous system has responded directly to long-term bodily experience at the level of consciousness (Gracely 2002; Kaplan et al. 2019), while at other times the suggestion seems to be that the nervous system has responded to long-term experience at the level of personhood—that is, experience of the self as a person who suffers from pain (Budtz-Lilly et al. 2015; Harte et al. 2018). Diagnosis and management would be improved with clarification on this point.

(3) Medical science must measure its success not in terms of the body's improvement, but in terms of improvement in conscious states. This is certainly the most powerful idea holism introduced into medical practice, and its ramifications have been immense, both as a matter of science and as a matter of values. Engel wrote:

> "Rational treatment"... directed only at the biochemical abnormality does not necessarily restore the patient to health even in the face of documented correction or major alleviation of the abnormality.   (Engel 1977: 386)

Once diagnosis has been made and treatment has been provided, the doctor must evaluate the success of her interventions, and to do this she must again return to the private realm of experience, with all the epistemic complexity that involves. There are four reasons why this would be the case.

First, the diagnostic process is imperfect, so it's possible for doctors to identify and address problems in the body that are not actually responsible for patients' experiences of pain or illness. Error of this kind can only be rectified if the doctor returns to private experience of the body through the complex reports of persons.

Second, it's possible for diagnostic investigations to suggest disease when experience does not manifest disease:

> ... in terms of the human experience of illness, laboratory documentation may only indicate disease potential, not the actuality of the disease at the time. The abnormality may be present, yet the patient not be ill.... the biochemical defect constitutes but one factor among many, the complex interaction of which ultimately may culminate in active disease or manifest illness.   (Engel 1977: 131)

This point is particularly important in light of recent concerns about over-diagnosis and over-medicalization. It is true that much of medicine's power lies in its ability to notice and address disease in its early stages, before experience of disease occurs. It is also possible, however, for biological abnormalities to be present that never actually threaten patients' lives or bodily experiences. We can recognize and incorporate this reality into the practice of medicine only because we recognize experience as the ultimate arbiter for medical success.

Third, it's possible for patients to have bodily experiences of pain or illness in the absence of biological abnormalities.

> By evaluating all the factors contributing to both illness and patienthood, rather than giving primacy to biological factors alone, a biopsychosocial model would make it possible to explain why some individuals experience as "illness" conditions which others regard merely as "problems of living," be they emotional reactions to life circumstances or somatic symptoms.
> (Engel 1977: 133)

The BMM would suggest that when patients experience illness in the absence of biological abnormalities, their problems lie outside the scope of doctors' concerns. But holism insists that medicine does not begin and end with biological abnormalities, because patients' experience of illness and disease does not begin and end in their biology. It is possible, holism proposes, for patients' experiences of themselves, at the level of personhood, to lead to experience of biological pain or disease when no biological abnormalities are present.[5]

Fourth, blind application of medical science is actually unproductive when it does not lead to experiential improvement. This has been a profoundly important revelation for medicine and for medical ethics, particularly in end of life care. While the BMM seems to encourage improvement of bodily abnormalities whenever it can be achieved, holism has made it clear that improvement is an experiential matter, and in many cases the blind application of biological science will not improve experience. We've gotten very good at medical interventions that won't actually improve conscious states for conscious patients, and we've gotten good at sustaining the body in various states of consciousness and personhood. These biological successes have forced us to recognize, through holism and through humanism, that we misunderstand the goal of medicine when we pursue biological interventions without weighing their value in experiential terms.

2.2 From the Scientific Importance of Consciousness to the Moral Character of Medicine

As long as we understand medical science to be initiated for biological reasons, to proceed based on biological data, and to succeed based on biological evaluations, the practice of medicine will not be intrinsically moral. We might insist that there should be ethical requirements for medical practitioners, and we might ground these in the idea that patients are persons rather than bodies, but if we construe medical science to begin and end with biology, those requirements will remain external to practice.

It is a scientific matter to insist that conscious states are central to the diagnostic process, and that they play a central role in the development of disease. It is also a scientific matter to insist that the success of medical interventions must be evaluated through improvements in conscious states—but this third scientific point forces us to recognize the moral implications of medicine as a practice that centrally attends to conscious

---

[5] The idea of psychological causes for symptoms is a great deal more complicated than medicine, or philosophy, has appreciated. It remains unclear whether psychological distress can create an experience of bodily pain or illness, or what such a process would involve. Though practice guidelines now generally equate diagnostic uncertainty with psychological causes (O'Leary 2018a), bioethics has only just begun to examine ethical challenges that arise at the mind–body diagnostic line (O'Leary 2018b, 2019).

states. As Kahane and Savulescu put it, "the presence of consciousness, or of a capacity for consciousness…marks a crucial moral boundary separating conscious beings from other entities" (Kahane and Savulescu 2009: 9). Because holism demands attention to conscious states through every stage of the scientific process, and particularly in the goal of the process in every specific case, holistic medical practice is intrinsically moral from start to finish.

It is wrong-headed, then, to imagine that the doctor can go about the business of medical science as if values become involved only in ethicists' external demands or in medicine's big-picture goals. In reality, medical science is intrinsically wrapped up with conscious states, and it is driven at every moment by the moral goal of improving them. This tells us the moral shift does not occur because the doctor has recognized the body in the room as a person. It occurs because she has recognized the body in the room as conscious, and she has understood how its conscious states motivate and support the activities of medical science.

It's helpful to compare medicine's moral character as it arises from recognition of consciousness to the moral character of veterinary medicine. We understand veterinary medicine *as* medicine, rather than as veterinary mechanics, because we recognize that non-human animals are conscious. That is to say that we recognize the moral imperative to pursue veterinary medicine not because non-human animals might approach the standard of personhood, but purely because they meet the standard of consciousness. At the other end of the spectrum, if we imagine entities with the biological complexity of non-human animals that are not conscious—something like organic Roombas, for example—we will not imagine that repairing them will amount to Roomba medicine rather than Roomba mechanics. It is not the presence of biologically complex bodies, and it is not the presence of personhood, that compels us to practice medicine and to understand the practice as moral. It is the presence of consciousness.

3. From Medicine's Moral Character to the Classic Principles of Ethical Practice

3.1 Consciousness and the Principles of Clinical Ethics

It might seem like the route from medicine's general moral character to the specific demands of clinical ethics is easy enough to map out. The presence of consciousness is sufficient to motivate medicine and broadly define it as a moral enterprise, it might seem, but the development of clinical ethics has been driven by recognition of the capacities that define personhood. As we typically understand these things, "seeing patients as persons, who are rational, self-conscious beings" is "the backbone of Western medical ethics" (Tsai 2008: 172). I am going to argue against this simple explanation, suggesting that the principles of clinical ethics are fully motivated by recognition of consciousness in patients who lack the capacities we associate with personhood. Moreover, the principles would not be motivated by the presence of those capacities in the absence of consciousness.

The four principles of beneficence, non-maleficence, justice, and autonomy have been described as "four moral nucleotides that constitute the moral DNA" of medicine (Gillon 2003: 308). Introduced by Beachamp and Childress in 1979, they have been vigorously criticized since that time, and vigorously defended through eight editions of the original text. Whatever we might say about their merits, the four principles have played a central role in the development of clinical ethics through holism and humanism, so it's important to understand what they actually imply, and what they actually require, about the presence of consciousness versus the presence of personhood.

The first and most obvious step here has to do with beneficence and non-maleficence. While it's common to see these characterized in terms of personhood, what drives them both is the far simpler fact that patients are conscious. Debates about VS patients make this clear. We all do immediately recognize that "If PVS patients are sentient, then it matters what we do to them," because "phenomenal consciousness is sufficient to make its bearer a moral patient" (Levy and Savulescu 2009: 366). That is to say that the presence of consciousness in VS patients triggers the demand to beneficently improve conscious states through the practice of medicine. It should be equally clear—particularly given Kahane and Savulescu's suggestion that it's unethical to sustain the lives of VS patients—that it's consciousness, rather than personhood, driving the imperative not to do harm. The principles of beneficence and non-maleficence are fully motivated in conscious patients who do not meet the standard of personhood.

Broadly speaking, the principle of justice demands fair distribution of health resources, that is, equal access to medical care for those with equal need. In this sense it might seem that justice is best characterized as a social idea, an idea about how we should or must behave as persons in relation to other persons. In the context of VS patients, however, we automatically apply the principle of justice in spite of the absence of capacities that meet the standard of personhood. That is to say, when patients are capable of conscious bodily suffering, we do not debate their equal claim to pain relief, for example. Indeed, it seems morally reprehensible to propose that conscious suffering patients might have a lesser claim to health resources purely because they lack complex cognitive capacities.

There are many senses in which the medical principle of justice is applied that certainly do assume the status of personhood for those involved, and I do not mean to suggest that we should question the force of these kinds of considerations. I suggest, rather, that at the most basic level where we invoke clinical ethics, at the level where consciousness clearly does compel medical practitioners to act according to the principles of beneficence and non-maleficence, it also compels them to act according to the principle of justice.

That leaves us with the heftiest element of clinical ethics, the principle of autonomy and the practices that manifest respect for autonomy in medical settings, such as informed consent and truthfulness. Broadly speaking, traditional autonomy in clinical ethics is understood as a principle of patient self-rule or self-governance, in contrast with the more authoritarian practices that prevailed with the BMM. In a social or political context, autonomy requires the complex cognitive capacities of personhood—because if a being is not self-conscious, and does not have the capacity to set rational goals and act toward accomplishing them, she is not capable of making self-governing decisions. Within normative ethics generally (outside the context of medicine), Kant equates autonomy with entry into the realm where ethical duties apply. For all these reasons it appears that while consciousness is sufficient to ground the moral nature of medicine, and might even be sufficient to motivate beneficence, non-maleficence, and justice, when we reach the principle of respect for autonomy, it appears that it is personhood rather than consciousness that is more central. When we consider the prospect of a non-conscious being who meets the standard for personhood, however, this appearance is no longer convincing.

3.2 The Principles of Clinical Ethics for Zombified Patients

Based on the distinction between consciousness and personhood (or at least between phenomenal consciousness and access consciousness or "sapience"), Kahane and Savulescu (2009) present distinct considerations of values as they arise with all four combinations of consciousness and personhood in VS patients. The most challenging of these combinations is personhood without consciousness, which they characterize as

> the presence of cognitive and motivational processes that are sufficiently extensive and systematic to merit not just ascription of local information processing in some area of the brain but ascription of genuine person-level mental states such as beliefs and desires. But this mental activity would take place without phenomonality—strictly speaking, there would be nothing it is like to be such a person.   (Kahane and Savulescu 2009: 16)

The idea of personhood without consciousness is conceptually controversial. Kahane and Savulescue argue, however, that while "this possibility may ultimately prove to be incoherent...at this stage we certainly cannot just rule it out" (Kahane and Savulescu 2009: 16), and on that basis they propose that the ethical implications of personhood in the absence of consciousness should be more carefully considered. I suggest that regardless of our views on the empirical possibility of personhood without consciousness, and regardless of our views on its conceptual coherence, it is informative to consider the ethical implications of this combination of capacities. Siewert's thought experiment about "zombification" or "phenolectomy" provides a particularly useful tool along these lines:

> I ask...merely how you would respond to your options if you came to think it was possible for you to maintain as good as normal nonphenomenal capacities, after a total excision of relevant talents for phenomenal experience. To answer this question in a manner that reveals a commitment to valuing consciousness for its own sake, you need not *actually* believe that it is possible, in any sense, for this "zombification" to happen to you, or to anyone else.   (Siewert 2000: 23)

What intuitions do we find ourselves with when we imagine the possibility of zombification in the context of the four principles?

To begin, if a zombified patient and a conscious patient suffer an equivalent bodily abnormality, will we imagine that the duty to provide medical care applies equally, justly, for both patients? Levy suggests that access consciousness and self-consciousness might "underwrite a great deal of what we value...in our lives" (Levy 2014: 8) even in the absence of phenomenal consciousness. If this is the case, it would be important for clinicians to give equal weight in medical decision-making to the non-experiential interests of the zombified patient and the conscious patient. In the medical context, however, concerns about these kinds of interests cannot equal the demand to improve the experience of bodily suffering when it is present. When faced with a zombified patient and a conscious patient in a similar state of bodily abnormality, that is to say, the principle of justice will not apply.

Without a demand to provide medical care justly, moreover, as it applies to all conscious patients, the demands of beneficence and non-maleficence will also be weakened, if they will be present at all in their original sense. Because there's nothing that it's like to be the zombified patient, if we accept the goal of medicine as it's understood by holism, the sense in which the doctor is compelled to beneficently improve the zombie's body, or to avoid harming it, will be strange and distinctly unmotivating.

Both holism and humanism were overtly concerned that the BMM had overlooked persons, but when we consider the zombified patient scenario we see that overlooking consciousness may have been the deeper problem. There is something quite grotesque about practicing medicine as if the bodies on which you practice are not conscious, even if you continue to pursue directives for preventing and alleviating pain. Things will be no less grotesque if you respect patients' personhood. The reason for this is the reason why holism swept through the medical professions with such immense power. We pursue medicine based on the moral significance of consciousness, so practicing as if patients are not, in fact, conscious, is morally grotesque. When we think of medicine in this way, as we do in the zombified patient scenario, the basic bioethical principles of justice, beneficence, and non-maleficence become skewed beyond recognition.

Would we recognize a demand to respect the autonomy of a zombified patient, one who has the cognitive capacities needed to make medical decisions, but lacks experience of the body? I suggest we would not. First, without the private character of the body's reports on itself in experience, it is hard to motivate the idea that the zombified patient has unique authority about her body in the medical setting. Second, we pursue the practice of medicine for the sake of the conscious patient because she cannot choose to escape her bodily suffering, because she is bound to experience the body even while experience is terrible. For this reason, the kind of stake that the conscious patient has in medical decision-making is deeper, more important, and more compelling than the stake of the zombified patient.

The zombified patient has non-experiential interests in the body, presumably having to do with her ability to use it, and there is no question that these are unique. On the basis of these interests the zombified patient does have a stronger stake in medical decision-making about her body than, say, her doctor does. At the same time, however, the zombified patient's stake in medical decision-making is quite different from the stake of the conscious patient across the hall, and that difference is vital to our understanding of medicine's moral motivation. The conscious patient commands respect for autonomy because her experience of the body is both private and inescapable, and she commands it even in the absence of the ability to act autonomously through medical decision-making.[6]

While the ability to make autonomous medical decisions does require the complex capacities of personhood, respect for autonomy in the medical setting does not arise from the presence of these capacities, and it does not arise from professional practices that manifest respect for the exercise of these capacities (like informed consent and truthfulness). It arises from the uniquely impenetrable character of phenomenal consciousness. While the zombified patient's claim to non-experiential interests would command respect from medical practitioners, autonomy in the medical setting is bodily autonomy. Without bodily experience we cannot make sense of respect for the patient's dominion in the realm of her own body.

When we equate respect for patient autonomy with respect for personhood we confuse the practices of medicine with the experiential realities that motivate them. Though this is not a chapter where I can defend a position on the idea of personhood, my conclusions do suggest that traditional notions of "personhood" and "respect for persons" are deeply misguided in the medical setting, that they arise from lack of attention to the differences between consciousness and personhood as they broadly pertain to the moral and ethical aspects of medicine.

4. Conclusions

Just as it's been fruitful to track consciousness through philosophical discussion of VS patients, it is fruitful to track consciousness through philosophical discussion of the recent change in medicine's identity. In the last fifty years, broadly speaking, we've seen medicine shift from a sense of itself

---

[6] Shea and Bayne (2010) raise important questions about what it might mean to suggest that VS patients have reportable experiences without the capacity to actually report. Though my concern is ethical, I am relying on a similar distinction.

as science-centered to a sense of itself as a moral endeavor with a very specific set of ethical constraints. This change has been understood in medicine, psychiatry, and bioethics to be grounded in recognition of personhood, but when we take a closer look we see it really was not personhood that drove the change, and it's not personhood that sustains it today. Though humanism might rightly be characterized in terms of persons, holism (in spite of its language) is really about consciousness. It is a perspective that argues for recognition of conscious states in medical science, and for the idea that medicine's moral character is grounded by this new scientific approach.

According to holism, properly understood, it is consciousness, rather than personhood, that compels us to pursue medical practice and defines the pursuit as moral, so it is consciousness, rather than personhood, that drives the principles of beneficence, non-maleficence, and justice. These principles apply for the VS patient just as they do for the everyday patient with a broken leg, because in both cases the doctor's goal is to improve experience—and that goal is recognized, pursued, and achieved when conscious patients lack the capacities we associate with personhood. Most importantly, the authority and inescapability of bodily experience command respect even when patients lack the capacity to exercise bodily authority through medical decision-making. Respect for patient autonomy is respect for the dominion of an experiencer in the private, inescapable realm of bodily experience—so even when experiencers lack the capacities needed to exercise their dominion though medical decision-making, they nevertheless command respect for autonomy.

Qualitative facts about the bodily suffering of one being are inaccessible to others. At the same time, experience of bodily suffering forces all conscious beings to need relief—but it does not give conscious beings the power to bring relief upon themselves. It is for these reasons that human beings cooperate in the social endeavor that is the medical profession, and it is for these reasons that we all share the sensibility that this endeavor is a collective human duty. The impenetrable boundary around bodily experience characterizes the human condition, and medicine is defined by its deep engagement with that reality.

Finally, while medicine provides fertile ground for philosophical understanding of the ties between consciousness and value, understanding of this kind is actually more important in reverse. That is to say that while it is philosophically useful to consider the implications of medicine in this area, it's more important to consider the medical usefulness of these kinds of philosophical conclusions. I'm not suggesting that medical practitioners need to engage in high-level philosophical debates about consciousness, or even that these kinds of debates should be incorporated into medical education (though I'd certainly approve of that). I'm suggesting that, because holism is right that medicine is improved when its scope includes consciousness, medical practice would be more successful if practitioners were trained to understand how private bodily experience figures into medical science. More than that, medicine would be more successful if practitioners had a sense of how medicine's moral identity, and its specific ethical constraints, arise not from the extraneous demands of ethics professionals but from the nature of bodily experience.

References

Beauchamp, T. and J.F. Childress. 1979. *Principles of Biomedical Ethics*. New York: Oxford University Press.

Block, N.J. 1995. On a confusion about the function of consciousness. *Behavioral and Brain Sciences* 18: 227–47.

Bolton, D. and G. Gillett. 2019. The biopsychosocial model 40 years on. In *The Biopsychosocial Model of Health and Disease*. Cham: Palgrave Pivot, 1–43.

Borrell-Carrió, F., A.L. Suchman, and R.M. Epstein. 2004. The biopsychosocial model 25 years later: principles, practice and scientific inquiry. *Annals of Family Medicine* 2(6): 576–82.

Budtz-Lilly, A., A. Schroder, M.T. Rask, P. Fink, M. Vestergaard, and M. Rosendal. 2015. Bodily distress syndrome: a new diagnosis for functional disorders in primary care? *BMC Family Practice* 16: 180.

Butler, C.B., M. Evans, D. Greaves, and S. Simpson. 2004. Medically unexplained symptoms: the biopsychosocial model found wanting. *Journal of the Royal Society of Medicine* 97(5): 219–22.

Engel, G. 1977. The need for a new medical model. *Science* 196(4286): 129–36.

Engel, G. 1981. The clinical application of the biopsychosocial model. *Journal of Medicine and Philosophy* 6(2): 101–24.

Ghaemi, S.N. 2010. *The Rise and Fall of the Biopsychosocial Model: Reconciling Art and Science in Psychiatry*. Baltimore: Johns Hopkins University Press.

Gifford, F. 2017. The biomedical model and the biopsychosocial model in medicine. In *The Routledge Companion to Philosophy of Medicine*, ed. M. Solomon, J.R. Simon and H. Kinkaid. New York: Routledge, 445–54.

Gillon, R. 2003. Ethics needs principles—four can encompass the rest—and respect for autonomy should be "first among equals". *Journal of Medical Ethics* 29: 307–12.

Gordon, A.H. 1934. The patient as a person. *Canadian Medical Association Journal* 31: 191–3.

Gouin, J.-P. and J.K. Kiecolt-Glaser. 2012. The impact of psychological stress on wound healing: methods and mechanisms. *Critical Care Nursing Clinics of North America* 24(2): 201–13.

Gracely, R.H., F. Petzke, J.M. Wolf, and D.J. Clauw. 2002. Functional magnetic resonance imagining evidence of augmented pain processing in fibromyalgia. *Arthritis and Rheumatology* 46(5): 1333–43.

Harte, S.E., R.E. Harris, and D.J. Clauw. 2018. The neurobiology of central sensitization. *Journal of Applied Biobehavioral Research* 23(2): 1–25.

Kahane, G. and J. Savulescu. 2009. Brain damage and the moral significance of consciousness. *Journal of Medicine and Philosophy* 34: 6–26.

Kaplan, C.M., A. Schrepf, D. Vatansever et al. 2019. Functional and neurochemical disruptions of brain hub topology in chronic pain. *Pain* 160(4): 973–83.

Levy, N. 2014. The value of consciousness. *Journal of Consciousness Studies* 21: 127–38.

Levy, N. and J. Savulescu. 2009. Moral significance of phenomenal consciousness. *Progress in Brain Research* 177: 361–70.

Marcum, J.A. 2008. *Humanizing Modern Medicine: An Introductory Philosophy of Medicine.* New York: Springer.

Nagel, T. 1974. What is it like to be a bat? *Philosophical Review* 83: 435–50.

O'Leary, D. 2018a. Why bioethics should be concerned with medically unexplained symptoms. *American Journal of Bioethics* 18(5): 6–15.

O'Leary, D. 2018b. Ethical management of diagnostic uncertainty: response to open peer commentaries on "Why bioethics should be concerned with medically unexplained symptoms". *American Journal of Bioethics* 18(8): W6–W11.

O'Leary, D. 2019. Ethical classification of ME/CFS in the United Kingdom. *Bioethics* 33: 716–22.

Owen, A.M. and M. Coleman. 2008. Functional neuroimaging of the vegetative state. *Nature Reviews: Neuroscience* 9: 235–43.

Owen, A.M., M. Coleman, M. Boly, M. Davis, S. Laureys, and J.D. Pickard. 2006. Detecting awareness in the vegetative state. *Science* 313: 1402.

Owen, A.M., M. Coleman, M. Boly, M. Davis, H. Matthew, S. Laureys et al. 2007. Using functional magnetic resonance imaging to detect covert awareness in the vegetative state. *Archives of Neurology* 64: 1098–102.

Ramsey, R. 1970. *The Patient as Person*. New Haven: Yale University Press.

Rease, J. 2014. The pernicious effect of mind/body dualism in psychiatry. *Journal of Psychiatry* 18(1): 1–7.

Rogers, W.A. 2002. Is there a moral duty for doctors to trust patients? *Journal of Medical Ethics* 28: 77–80.

Schillmeier, M. 2019. Thinking with the living body: the biopsychosocial model and the cosmopolitics of existence. *Medical Humanities* 45: 141–51.

Siewert, C. 2000. Precis of *The Significance of Consciousness*. *Psyche* 6(12). http://journalpsyche.org/files/0xaa85.pdf. Accessed September 8, 2020.

Sgambato, D., A. Miranda, R. Ranalso, A. Federico, and M. Romano. 2012. The role of stress in inflammatory bowel diseases. *Current Pharmaceutical Design* 23(27): 3997–4002.

Shea, N. and T. Bayne. 2010. The vegetative state and the science of consciousness. *British Journal of Philosophy of Science* 61(3): 459–84.

Tsai, D.F.-C. 2008. Personhood and autonomy in multicultural health care settings. *Virtual Mentor* 10(3): 171–6.

Wallit, B., M. Ceko, J.L. Gracely, and R.H. Gracely. 2015. Neuroimaging of central sensitivity syndromes: key insights from the scientific literature. *Current Rheumatology Reviews* 12(1): 55–87.

Woods, S. 2015. Holism in healthcare: patient as person. In *Handbook of Philosophy of Medicine*, ed. T. Schramme and S. Edwards. New York: Springer, 1–17.

WHO [World Health Organization] (2019). Constitution. Resource document. https://www.who.int/about/who-we-are/constitution. Accessed July 17, 2019.

4

The Emotion of Fulfillment and Its Phenomenology

Hyunseop Kim

1. Meaningfulness as Correct Fulfillment

Let me start with Susan Wolf's deservedly influential account of meaning in life. She argues, plausibly, that the life of a person who is bored or alienated from what she spends her life doing is meaningless, even if what she is doing is actually objectively worthwhile. So meaningfulness requires a subjective element, what Wolf calls feelings of fulfillment: "the feelings one has when one is doing what one loves, or when one is engaging in activities by which one is gripped or excited." They are the opposite of boredom and alienation.[1] Meaningfulness also requires an objective element. Suppose the gods implant in Sisyphus some substance that makes him want to roll the rock up the hill endlessly and somehow find the futile job of rock-rolling fulfilling. Sisyphus's task is no longer boring to him, but it remains futile. There is no value to his efforts; nothing ever comes of them.[2] We find it hard to regard his work as meaningful. The source or object of fulfillment should be objectively valuable or worthwhile. So Wolf defends a hybrid view on meaningfulness. According to her Fitting Fulfillment view, one's life is meaningful insofar as one finds oneself loving things worthy of love and engaging with them in some positive way in his life. That is, "meaningfulness consists in active engagement in projects or activities of worth." Or "meaning arises when subjective attraction meets objective attractiveness."[3]

---

[1] Susan Wolf, *Meaning in Life and Why it Matters* (Princeton University Press, 2012), p. 14.
[2] Richard Taylor, *Good and Evil* (Macmillan, 1970), pp. 319–34; Wolf, *Meaning in Life and Why it Matters*, p. 17.
[3] Susan Wolf, "Happiness and Meaning: Two Aspects of the Good Life," *Social Philosophy and Policy* 14.1 (1997): 207–25, at p. 213; Wolf, *Meaning in Life and Why it Matters*, pp. 34–5.

Hyunseop Kim, *The Emotion of Fulfillment and Its Phenomenology* In: *Oxford Studies in Philosophy of Mind Volume 1*. Edited by: Uriah Kriegel, Oxford University Press (2021). © Hyunseop Kim.
DOI: 10.1093/oso/9780198845850.003.0004

In my view, we can interpret Wolf's account of meaningfulness in terms of the evaluation of an emotion and its correctness. Her view, I take it, is that meaningfulness consists in correct fulfillment. According to evaluative accounts of emotions, emotions purport to (re)present their particular object as having certain evaluative property. For example, fear of an object (re)presents it as dangerous to the person who feels the emotion; indignation is a negative evaluation of an event as unjust.[4] Evaluative accounts of emotions enable us to talk about the correctness of emotions. Emotions are correct iff their particular object does have the attributed evaluative property. Fear is correct iff its particular object is indeed dangerous. If I fear a rubber snake or a falling leaf, the particular object is not dangerous. There is no reason for me to have fear, and my emotion of fear is incorrect.

I believe that fulfillment is not a contentless sensation or brute feeling, but a positive evaluation of an activity as rewarding.[5] In other words, fulfillment at an activity consists in regarding the activity's object as valuable and worthy of engagement and the activity itself as realizing the object's value and worthy of continuation (and completion). Fulfillment at an activity is correct iff the activity is in fact rewarding. My interpretation of meaningfulness as correct fulfillment yields the intuitively plausible verdicts that motivate Wolf's hybrid view. Sisyphus's futile work of rolling the rock uphill is not worthy of engagement, so not rewarding. The fulfilled Sisyphus has no reason to be fulfilled at what he does. His emotion of fulfillment is incorrect. The fulfilled Sisyphus's incorrect fulfillment does not make the activity it is directed at meaningful. The meaningless activity does not confer meaning to his life. Contrariwise, suppose an alienated philosopher does not experience fulfillment at the activity of writing an excellent philosophy paper. The activity is rewarding (i.e., the philosophical idea is valuable and worthy of engagement and articulating the idea realizes its value and deserves continuation and completion) and gives the philosopher reason to be fulfilled.

---

[4] The particular object of an emotion is distinguished from its formal object, the evaluative property the emoter attributes to its particular object. According to this usage, the formal object of fear is the property of being dangerous, and that of indignation is being unjust. In other words, the particular object of an emotion is the specific target that the emotion is directed toward and (re)presents as instantiating its formal object. See Anthony Kenny, *Action, Emotion and Will* (Routledge, 1963).

[5] Wolf observes that fulfillment involves an evaluation. She says fulfillment includes "a cognitive component that requires seeing the source or object of fulfillment as being, in some independent way, good or worthwhile." The fulfilled Sisyphus is deluded, by the substance in his veins, into seeing some value in stone-rolling that isn't really there. See Wolf, *Meaning in Life and Why it Matters*, pp. 23–4; see also Wolf, "Happiness and Meaning: Two Aspects of the Good Life," p. 217.

The philosopher is unreasonably unfulfilled (maybe he suffers from burnout or does not understand the significance of his work). Since fulfillment is a necessary condition for meaningfulness, his rewarding activity is not meaningful, either.

Wolf, as she distinguishes her Fitting Fulfillment view from what she calls the Bipartite View, emphasizes that the subjective and objective elements of meaningfulness fit together to constitute a coherent, unified whole. For example, suppose the fulfilled Sisyphus's rock-rolling, unbeknownst to him, scares away vultures who would otherwise harm a nearby community. Even if he finds rock-rolling fulfilling and his action contributes to something objectively worthwhile, these conditions do not make what he does meaningful because, Wolf says, the subjective and objective elements are not suitably linked.[6] My interpretation of meaningfulness as correct fulfillment clearly explains the way in which they should be combined. In order for an emotion to be correct, the particular object should have the evaluative property that the emotion (re)presents it to have. The correspondence between the fulfillment's evaluative content and the activity's objective value is the fittingness or coherence that Wolf claims or should claim is necessary for meaningfulness. The fulfilled Sisyphus's rock-rolling is valuable because it saves the nearby community from harm, but that value is not what his fulfillment attributes to his activity. This discrepancy or mismatch is the reason why the Sisyphus's fulfillment is incorrect and fails to make his objectively valuable activity meaningful.

2. Analyzing the Emotion of Fulfillment

I have argued that fulfillment at an activity evaluates the activity as rewarding. The evaluation of fulfillment is twofold: the activity's object is regarded as valuable and worthy of engagement and the activity itself is regarded as realizing the object's value and worthy of continuation (and completion). Let me analyze these two parts in more detail. An example will come in handy. Let us start with a characterization of what goes on, from the agent's point of view, when a pianist plays music beautifully to his satisfaction. First, he recognizes the rhythm, melody, and harmony of a piece of music and the beauty that supervenes on them. The music's aesthetic value calls for being

---

[6] Wolf, *Meaning in Life and Why it Matters*, pp. 20–1.

played, and his recognition of this motivates him to play it. In other words, the music's beauty gives him motivation to engage with it and realize its value. Let me call the experience that the pianist undergoes when the value of music and his appreciation thereof leads to motivation for engagement *attraction*.

Attraction is evaluative-cum-motivational. We can see the evaluative aspect of attraction clearly by contrasting it with a brute urge or impulse. Imagine a violinist who does not find a piece of music beautiful and worthy of being played. To make the case clearer, suppose there does not seem to be any other reason for him to play it. Playing it will not help to maintain or improve his skills. Indeed, playing the discordant piece will disrupt his skilled pattern of performance. No one will be pleased by hearing him play the "music." Nevertheless, he is somehow motivated to play it. Then, the motivational pull would not be (part of) an attraction, but a brute urge, as is the case with Quinn's radioman who strongly wants to turn on every radio he sees to be turned off without any (apparent) reason.[7] It would look as if some unintelligible inclination to play is thrust upon him. Were he to succumb to its motivational force, what he does would not be autonomous but heteronomous. Indeed, he might be so passive with regard to the behavior that it does not properly count as "his act."[8] We can see that attraction is not only evaluative but also motivational by contrasting it with a detached evaluation. There can be someone who sincerely agrees with the judgment that a piece of music is of aesthetic value. He believes that those who play or listen to the music have good reason to do so and feels the obligation not to interfere with their valuable activity. At the same time, the music is not his cup of tea and leaves him cold. He is not motivated to engage with the music (by listening to or playing it) himself. This person is not attracted, in my sense, to (the value of) the music.[9]

The experience of fulfillment includes, in addition to attraction, evaluation of the activity and motivation therefrom. Suppose the pianist, attracted

---

[7] Warren Quinn, "Putting Rationality in Its Place," reprinted in his *Morality and Action* (Cambridge University Press, 1993), pp. 236–7.

[8] For the idea that we are active insofar as, as it seems to us, we are responsive to reason, see Joseph Raz, "When We Are Ourselves: The Active and the Passive," in his *Engaging Reason: On the Theory of Value and Action* (Oxford University Press, 1999), pp. 1–21.

[9] Wolf says that in order for an agent's engagement with an object or activity to contribute to the meaningfulness of his life, he must have some *attachment* to the object or activity (*Meaning in Life and Why it Matters*, p. 114). Someone who simply believes an object to be valuable and recognizes its value might not be attached to it. I take the attachment to involve, at least characteristically, motivation to engage with it.

by the beauty of the music, goes on to play it and delivers a great perform-ance. While playing, he is aware that he is pulling it off. He recognizes the accuracy, intensity, and style of his performance and the interpretive value that supervenes on them. His recognition of this motivates him to continue playing and causes bodily expressions (e.g., a relaxed but alert posture, a smile on the face). Let me call the experience that the pianist undergoes when the value of his performance and his appreciation thereof leads to motivation for continued engagement with the music *satisfaction*. When we are fulfilled, we experience satisfaction as well as attraction. The pianist's fulfillment is, in my view, as much about his playing and its performative value, as it is about the music and its intrinsic value. We can see this by comparing the fulfillment that David Golub seems to be undergoing in Figure 4.1 with the attraction that Robert Casadesus seems to be undergoing in Figure 4.2.[10]

What I imagine is that Casadesus is just about to play a Mozart concerto. His focused eyes and readiness to play indicate that he is already quite motivated by the beauty of Mozart's music. He has not started to play yet, so his motivation does not come from his performance and its realization of the music's value. On the other hand, Golub is in the middle of his performance. Admittedly, but for the aesthetic value of music and his appreciation thereof, he would not have been as fulfilled. Still, a significant part of what he is happy about and what motivates and fuels him is, as his smile suggests, his good performance, the fineness of his playing (or so it seems to me).

Satisfaction is, like attraction, evaluative-cum-motivational. We can clearly see the evaluative aspect of satisfaction by comparing it with the impulse to continue what one has been doing. Imagine a pianist who realizes that he is performing very poorly and wants to stop playing. There is no audience who would be disappointed were he to stop. However, he is averse to quitting and somehow motivated to continue playing. Then, the motiv-ational pull would not be (part of) a satisfaction. He is rather in the grip of a brute impulse or urge to keep playing. The following scenario helps us see that satisfaction is not only evaluative but also motivational. A pianist was

---

[10] The photograph of David Golub (Figure 4.1) was reprinted in Stephen Darwall, *Welfare and Rational Care* (Princeton University Press, 2002), p. 74. Wolf acknowledges that Darwall's description of experiences of valuing activity is "more or less identical to" her description of experiences of fulfillment and that his account of welfare "has much in common with" her account of meaningfulness (*Meaning in Life and Why it Matters*, footnote 11 at pp. 24–5). I am very grateful to the photographer Linda Rosier for her permission to reprint it here.

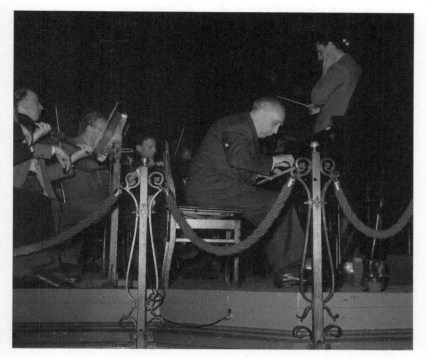

Figure 4.1 David Golub (photograph by Linda Rosier, reproduced with permission).

playing an étude very well and aware of his good performance. His playing had been fueled by the awareness. Then, he is suddenly depressed by the realization that he had to sacrifice so many important things in life to practice playing the piano. The performance no longer seems worth the effort. Nevertheless, as he has practiced the étude so many times, his habituated routine of playing moves him mechanically forward. He is aware that he is still playing almost as well as before the onset of depression, but the realization does not motivate him to play. The performance is no longer satisfactory and fulfilling, in my sense, to him.

We experience fulfillment—attraction and satisfaction—in many activities of all kinds. A variety of objects (e.g., an opera, a mountain, a philosophical idea) call for our engagement (watching, climbing, writing). Recognition of their value induces motivation to engage with them. If we successfully engage and realize their value (e.g., understanding the plot and sympathizing with the characters, enjoying panoramic views, articulating

Figure 4.2 Robert Casadesus (photograph by Carel L. de Vogel/Anefo/Nationaal Archief).

the idea clearly and persuasively), recognition of the activity's value (in addition to the object's value) adds another layer of motivation to engage in the activity and helps us complete the realization of their value.

Let me point out a couple of more characteristics of fulfillment. I have argued that fulfillment, unlike a brute urge, has an evaluative component or aspect. The evaluation of fulfillment is not conceptual. Here is an example that supports this claim:

Back in the groove.   A pianist, who had been confident about his musical achievements, read a harsh review of his performance. The reviewer made several theoretical arguments why the music he played and his interpretation are not of much aesthetic value. The pianist found the arguments persuasive and came to agree with the reviewer's negative judgment. However, there comes an occasion when he is prodded to play the music again. He is initially reluctant, but the music's rhythm and melody tempt him to play it. Once he starts to play, he gets back in his groove. He gets immersed in the music and his performance. It does not look as if he is forced to play by an unintelligible impulse in spite of himself. He plays smoothly and efficiently, and smiles. While playing, he does not change his mind about his agreement with the negative review. But his negative belief does not inform his performance; he is fueled by the music and his successful performance. When the piece is over, he is asked to evaluate his performance. He feels inclined to praise his own performance, but remembers the negative review. He realizes that his second performance was more or less the same as the first, and hesitantly gives a negative verdict on his second performance. He reluctantly decides not to tell his friends about his performances.

The pianist apparently experienced fulfillment, attraction, and satisfaction during the second performance. This case shows that fulfillment is recalcitrant in the sense that it can arise and persist in the face of an evaluative belief to the contrary; that fulfillment's positive evaluation is not as inferentially promiscuous (i.e., freely available as a premise in a wide range of inferences) as the corresponding evaluative belief. The recalcitrance of fulfillment and its limited inferential role or cognitive encapsulation suggest that the evaluation of fulfillment is not conceptual.[11] The cases of small children and animals also suggest that fulfillment's evaluation is nonconceptual. Imagine an enthused toddler who is so excited about running around that she does not listen to her mom's order to stop, or a happily running dog that is taken to a park after staying inside for a month. They engage in vigorous running, apparently motivated, at least partly, by positive evaluation of their activity. They seem to experience fulfillment, but their cognitive capacities are, by hypothesis, not so sophisticated as to make a conceptual evaluation.

Fulfillment arises out of our active engagement with things of value.[12] It is what we experience as a result of what we actively do. However, it is not itself

---

[11] Cf., Tim Crane, "The Nonconceptual Content of Experience," in Tim Crane (ed.), *The Contents of Experience: Essays on Perception* (Cambridge University Press, 1992), pp. 136–57 and Sabine Döring, "The Logic of Emotional Experience: Noninferentiality and the Problem of Conflict without Contradiction," *Emotion Review* 1 (2009): 240–7.

[12] Wolf says, "[T]he relationship between the subject and the object of her attraction must be an active one. The condition that says that meaning involves engaging with the (worthy) object of love in a positive way is meant to make clear that mere passive recognition and a positive attitude toward an object's or activity's value is not sufficient for a meaningful life. One must be able to be in some sort of relationship with the valuable object of one's attention—to create it, protect it, promote it, honor it, or more generally, to actively affirm it in some way or other" (*Meaning in Life and Why it Matters*, pp. 9–10).

what we do. Fulfillment is not under our immediate voluntary control. If I could simply decide to write with fulfillment, I would have written much more philosophy.

In this section, I have argued that fulfillment is non-conceptually evaluative, motivational, manifest in bodily expressions, and not under the direct voluntary control of the person who experiences it. These are characteristic features of emotions,[13] so they reinforce my supposition that fulfillment is an emotion. Another feature of emotions is that they have distinct phenomenologies. Does fulfillment have a distinct phenomenal quality? What is it like to experience fulfillment?

3. The Phenomenology of Fulfillment

Let me first argue that there is no distinct sensory phenomenology of fulfillment. There are many kinds of activities such that they give rise to fulfillment and the fulfillment motivates their continuation. These activities are, as I pointed out above, widely heterogeneous. The sensory content of what we experience when we engage in an activity, especially when we are fully immersed in the activity, seems to depend on the activity. There does not seem to be a sense-perceptual (i.e., visual, auditory, gustatory, olfactory, tactile) experience that is common to all cases where fulfillment motivates us to engage with what we value. For example, what an author experiences when he is fully absorbed in writing (aka writing in flow) seems quite different from what an athlete experiences when he is fully immersed in surfing big waves or skiing down a hill at full speed. What is it that all of them see? While the author might see a typewriter, a piece of paper and letters on it in a room, the skier would see things like snow and trees on a mountain, and the surfer waves, the sea, and the sky. Experiences of fulfillment do not seem to share any sense-perceptual phenomenology.

The heterogeneity of fulfilling experiences also suggests that there is no distinct feeling of bodily change that is common to all experiences of fulfillment. For that matter, while fulfillment manifests itself in various bodily expressions, the fulfilled person does not seem to be aware or conscious of her body or herself at all. During the experience of fulfillment, her attention and consciousness is fully absorbed in the activity in which she

[13] Julien Deonna & Fabrice Teroni, *The Emotions: A Philosophical Introduction* (Routledge, 2012), ch. 1.

engages. One might say that the phenomenology of fulfillment is negative, in the sense that it removes task-irrelevant thoughts and feelings ("noises") from the experiential field.[14]

I have argued that fulfillment does not have its own sense-perceptual or bodily phenomenology. Some philosophers believe that the sensory phenomenology of perceptions and bodily sensations (and combinations thereof) exhausts our stream of consciousness. They would take these arguments to show that fulfillment is an emotion without (positive) phenomenology. Other philosophers of mind believe that there are more things in our stream of consciousness than are dreamt of by those parsimonious philosophers. The expansionists about phenomenal consciousness would claim that my argument, even if cogent, falls short of showing that there is nothing it is like to be fulfilled. Experiences of fulfillment might have their own non-sensory phenomenology.

It has been argued that there is something it is like to have thoughts or propositional attitudes (e.g., to believe the proposition that p, make a judgment that p, desire that p, hope that p, wonder whether p) and that the cognitive phenomenology is not reducible to the sensory phenomenology of perceptions and bodily sensations.[15] The following considerations make me believe that experiences of fulfillment do not involve cognitive phenomenology (if such there be) and, a fortiori, that cognitive phenomenology is not what distinguishes fulfillment from other emotions and mental states. First, small children and animals, I have argued, can experience fulfillment. However, they do not possess the conceptual capacities to hold propositional attitudes or have propositional thoughts in mind. Second, when we

[14] While I am not equating fulfillment with flow in psychology, they seem to share many characteristics. One of them is the loss of the sense of self. Csikszentmihalyi's following description of the subjective experience of flow seems to apply to fulfillment: "Immersion in the activity produces as one of its consequences *a loss of self-consciousness*. There is neither need nor opportunity to reflect on oneself—the self as an object of awareness recedes while the focus of attention is taken up by the demands of the activity and by the responses given to them." See *Flow and the Foundations of Positive Psychology: The Collected Works of Mihaly Csikszentmihalyi* (Springer, 2014), p. 216.

[15] Terence Horgan & John Tienson, "The Intentionality of Phenomenology and the Phenomenology of Intentionality," in D. Chalmers (ed.), *Philosophy of Mind: Classical and Contemporary Readings* (Oxford University Press, 2002), pp. 520–33; Uriah Kriegel, *The Varieties of Consciousness* (Oxford University Press, 2015), chs. 1, 3. Pitt distinguishes the mental act of holding an attitude toward a proposition from the mere occurrence of the proposition or thought in one's mind, and argues that the latter has its own irreducible phenomenology. See David Pitt, "The Phenomenology of Cognition or *What Is It Like to Think that P?*" *Philosophy and Phenomenological Research* 69 (2004): 1–36, at pp. 2–3. If, as Pitt argues, merely having a propositional thought in mind has its proprietary phenomenology, it is part of what I call cognitive phenomenology in this chapter.

are immersed in an activity, any conscious thought, even a thought about what to do in the situation, is a distraction or interruption. Having a propositional thought in mind or taking up an attitude toward the proposition would distract our attention away from the activity we are engaging in (e.g., dancing to fast music) and interrupt the flow.[16] If the experience of fulfillment includes what it is like to think that *p*, it would impede our smooth, efficient operation. The fact that fulfillment helps us focus on the activity and act smoothly and efficiently suggests that the experience of fulfillment does not involve cognitive phenomenology.

It has also been argued that there is something it is like to act voluntarily, some phenomenology of experiencing a behavior as one's own doing or a realization of one's agency (as opposed to something that happens to one). The phenomenology of agency involves, among others, the sense that one decides/intends to φ, wills/exerts effort to φ, and causes/generates φ-ing, an action such that it is up to him/her whether or not to perform it.[17] The agentive phenomenology is arguably reducible neither to cognitive phenomenology nor to the familiar kinds of sensory phenomenology.[18]

Even if exercising one's agency has its proprietary phenomenology, what it is like to be fulfilled does not seem to feel like that. While fulfillment arises out of our active engagement with things of value, it is not a thing toward which we feel active. It does not appear that we directly intend or exert effort to be fulfilled. Indeed, as is the case with pleasure and happiness, doing so would prevent us from attaining what we aim at. Fulfillment is not what we get when we seek it, but what comes to us when we engage in valuable activities.

I have argued that the experience of fulfillment does not have its own sensory, cognitive, or agentive phenomenology. This does not mean that fulfillment has no distinct, proprietary phenomenology, though the elusiveness of its phenomenology might tempt us to think so. In order to refer to the emotion of fulfillment, I have appealed to what it is like to experience it. For example, I could easily distinguish fulfillment from the positive but dispassionate evaluation of what one is doing, on the basis of the

---

[16] Julia Annas, "The Phenomenology of Virtue," *Phenomenology and the Cognitive Sciences* 7.1 (2008): 21–34.

[17] Terence Horgan, John Tienson, & George Graham, "The Phenomenology of First-Person Agency," in S. Walter & H. Heinz-Dieter (eds.), *Physicalism and Mental Causation* (Imprint Academic, 2003), pp. 323–34; Tim Bayne, "The Phenomenology of Agency," *Philosophy Compass* 3 (2008): 1–21.

[18] Tim Bayne, "The Sense of Agency," in F. Macpherson (ed.), *The Senses* (Oxford University Press, 2011), pp. 490–524; Kriegel, *The Varieties of Consciousness*, ch. 2.

phenomenological difference between what it is like to be fulfilled and what it is like to make the cold, detached judgment. If there were nothing it is like to be fulfilled, it would be hard to explain the ease with which I could enable you, the reader, to pick out what I had in mind. The fact (I hope it is a fact) that we have been on the same page about what the topic of this chapter is, suggests that there is something it is like to be fulfilled. The descriptions that I used to refer to fulfillment already reflect its phenomenology.

A number of philosophers argue that an emotion has a distinct phenomenology such that we experience the evaluative property of its particular object as intelligibly motivating the relevant attitude and readiness to act. For example, when I experience fear at a gorilla on the loose, its danger seems to push me to run away from it and make the resultant inclination to flee and avoid it immediately intelligible and appropriate. The evaluative-normative phenomenology of fear can be spelled out as follows:[19] (a) The sense of danger appears not gratuitous or groundless, but responsive to an external threat. It seems that the grunting gorilla with sharp teeth and muscular frame presents or discloses its danger to me and my fear represents or registers the response-independent disvalue.[20] (b) The evaluation seems to fit the motivation to flee from and avoid the gorilla, in the sense that the motivated actions are the sort of actions that the registered disvalue of danger calls for or demands. If I find myself pulled toward the gorilla, I am presumably not evaluating it as dangerous (possibly, as charming instead). (c) It seems that the particular object's (dis)value leads to or causes the fitting motivation and appropriate action-readiness. The disvalue of the gorilla's danger transmits its negative power, via the evaluation of fear, to my motivation and tendency to flee and avoid. To experience the evaluative property of being dangerous is partly to experience its normative force, the property of, among others, meriting-to-be-fled-from and deserving-to-be-avoided. (d) As a result, the motivation and action-readiness seem intelligible to me. Indeed, the emotion of fear as a whole, an evaluative-motivational complex, apparently makes sense. The evaluative phenomenology of emotion

---

[19] A caveat: This description of emotional phenomenology is an introspective reflection on it. How it appears to me from the inside during the experience may not be as precise and discrete as the conceptual articulation and analysis might make it out to be.

[20] It is not the metaphysical claim that the disvalue of danger is in fact out there, but the phenomenological claim that it appears to be objective. Even those who reject the former accept the latter and try to explain away the apparent objectivity of values. See, e.g., J. L. Mackie, *Ethics: Inventing Right and Wrong* (Penguin, 1977), pp. 42–6.

is, these philosophers argue, not reducible to any sensory, cognitive, or agentive phenomenology that may accompany emotions.[21]

I believe that the phenomenology of fulfillment can be understood along similar lines. The above model of evaluative phenomenology applies to the experience of attraction as follows: When a pianist is attracted to a piece of music, it seems he senses its objective value. The music discloses its beauty and presents itself as worthy of engagement. His appreciation of the beauty motivates him to play it. Playing is an appropriate way, for the pianist who is able and in a position to do so, of responding to the music's beauty. His sense of the music's beauty makes the motivation to play appear intelligible. Simply put, when the music attracts him, its beauty is experienced as having the rational power ("oomph") to pull him to engage with it. The same model applies to the experience of satisfaction: When the attracted pianist goes on to play the music and pulls it off, he senses the beauty of his performance. The aesthetic awareness motivates him to continue to play. Continuation of playing is the appropriate response that his performance's aesthetic value calls for (until he fully realizes the music's value). His positive evaluation of his performance makes the motivation to continue playing appear to make sense. To sum up, when he is fulfilled, the music's beauty and the value of his performance are experienced as having the rational power to propel him to (continued) engagement. This subsumption of the phenomenology of fulfillment under the model of emotions' evaluative phenomenology reinforces, again, my supposition that fulfillment is an emotion.

4. The Values of Fulfillment's Evaluative Phenomenology

I have argued that Wolf's account of meaning in life can be interpreted as the claim that meaningfulness consists in correct fulfillment. This argument, if correct, implies that correct fulfillment is an important part of what makes our life worth living.[22] But it does not entail that its phenomenology is an

---

[21] Michelle Montague, "Evaluative Phenomenology," in S. Roeser & C. Todd (eds.), *Emotion and Value* (Oxford University Press, 2014), pp. 32–51; Peter Poellner, "Phenomenology and the Perceptual Model of Emotion," *Proceedings of the Aristotelian Society* 116.3 (2016): 261–88; Jonathan Mitchell, "The Epistemology of Emotional Experience," *Dialectica* 71.1 (2017): 57–84; Mitchell, "Emotional Intentionality and the Attitude-Content Distinction," *Pacific Philosophical Quarterly* 100 (2019): 359–86; Mitchell, "Affective Representation and Affective Attitudes," *Synthese* (2019), doi:10.1007/s11229-019-02294-7.
[22] I assume that meaning in life or meaningfulness is an important component of well-being. For the relation between meaningfulness and well-being, see Antti Kauppinen,

important part of our well-being. Even if, as I have argued, fulfillment has its distinct evaluative phenomenology, the phenomenology or felt quality is only one part of the emotion. It remains an open question how valuable fulfillment's evaluative phenomenology is.[23] In this section, I will argue that the evaluative phenomenology of fulfillment has three values: hedonic, epistemic, and motivational.

4.1 Hedonic Value

I have argued that fulfillment does not have its own sensory phenomenology. At the same time, it might be—indeed, it does seem to be—pleasant in non-sensory ways.[24] While fulfillment is pleasant, its pleasantness is mild. Fulfillment does not feel like orgasm; it is not intensely pleasant. It might help to see this more clearly by distinguishing the pleasure in the experience of fulfillment from the pleasure of accomplishment. By the pleasure of accomplishment, I mean the pleasure that comes from the awareness that one has achieved a goal, that one has engaged with what is valuable and realized its value. For example, a pianist would feel this kind of pleasure if he has just finished playing a demanding piece beautifully. The pleasure of accomplishment may well be intensely hedonic, but we feel it, not in the middle of an activity, but after completing the activity. On the other hand, fulfillment is what motivates the activity, the process that leads up to or brings about the accomplishment. In fact, if fulfillment had been noticeably

---

"Meaningfulness," in G. Fletcher (ed.), *The Routledge Handbook of Philosophy of Well-Being* (Routledge, 2016), pp. 288–9.

[23] Whether an emotion is valuable is a distinct (though related) question from whether its phenomenology is valuable. For example, one might reasonably argue that getting indignant at an apparently unjust world, if it is indeed unjust, is of intrinsic value. The correct indignation affectively registers and appreciates, while the corresponding belief conceptually cognizes and understands, the unjust world's disvalue. Cf., Amia Srinivasan, "The Aptness of Anger," *The Journal of Political Philosophy* 26.2 (2018): 123–44, at p. 132. Indeed, one might think that correct emotions are, in general, intrinsically good, because they are part of the ways in which we get values right and respond properly to them. At the same time, one might consistently believe that the indignation's felt quality or phenomenology is intrinsically bad; it is uncomfortable and distressing. The phenomenological disvalue, one believes, is overridden by its epistemic value; while the indignation's phenomenology is intrinsically bad, the indignation is intrinsically good overall.

[24] For a classification of pleasure that makes room for the pleasure in experiencing flow as non-sensory pleasure, see Ingvar Johansson, "Species and Dimensions of Pleasure," *Metaphysica* 2 (2001): 39–71.

hedonic, it would have distracted us and impeded our smooth, efficient operation. So while hedonic phenomenology is part of what makes the experience of fulfillment valuable, hedonicity does not seem to exhaust its value.

4.2 Epistemic Value

It is plausible that perceptual experiences are epistemically valuable: a sense-perceptual experience as of p provides an evidential reason to believe that p. Our faculties of perception are, we can reasonably suppose, reliable, in the sense that under normal conditions the world is as they represent it to be. It has been argued that emotional experiences are similarly of epistemic value: If an emotional experience makes it seem as if its particular object has some evaluative property, it provides an evidential reason to believe that that object has the evaluative property. For example, an experience of fear, it seems reasonable to say, is a reason to believe that its particular object is dangerous. To be sure, emotions are, as is the case with perceptions, fallible. There are circumstances in which their reliability is undercut (e.g., external injection of fear-related hormones) or conclusive evidence rebuts their claim (expert testimonies about the object's safety). The epistemic reasons emotional experiences provide are defeasible, prima facie reasons.[25]

Then it seems arguable that if, as I have argued, the experience of fulfillment makes it seem to the fulfilled person as if the object is valuable and worthy of engagement and his engagement is realizing its value and worthy of continuation, it gives him a defeasible, prima facie reason to believe so. Of course, fulfillment is, as with other emotions, fallible. The question is: If the experience of fulfillment makes it seem as if the object of engagement and the engaging activity are valuable, how reliable is this appearance?

When it comes to basic emotions (e.g., fear), we seem innately disposed to respond to some types of objects more easily than to others (to snakes than to flowers); there also seem to be some characteristic actions that they motivate (fight or flight). These dispositions, while sometimes misleading,

---

[25] See, e.g., Mark Johnston, "The Authority of Affect," *Philosophy and Phenomenological Research* 63.1 (2001): 181–214; Sabine Döring, "Seeing What to Do: Affective Perception and Rational Motivation," *Dialectica* 61 (2007): 363–94; Catherine Elgin, "Emotion and Understanding," in G. Brun, U. Doguoglu, & D. Kuenzle (eds.), *Epistemology and Emotions* (Ashgate, 2008), pp. 33–50; Adam Pelser, "Emotion, Evaluative Perception, and Epistemic Justification," in S. Roeser & C. Todd (eds.), *Emotion and Value* (Oxford University Press, 2014), pp. 107–23.

presumably help us to respond properly in time. On the other hand, we are apparently attracted to all sorts of things. It seems hard to find commonality in what triggers our attraction. Accordingly, the actions attraction motivates also seem to be diverse and open-ended (engagement can take quite various forms). What attracts an agent and motivates his engagement seems highly dependent on the way in which he has developed his interest and dispositions, and the development process seems sensitive to social and cultural influences. These observations indicate that fulfillment should not count as a basic emotion or affect program.[26] More importantly, the malleability of attraction through habituation and education means that the emotion of fulfillment reliably detects valuable activities only when the emotional disposition has been cultivated properly. Unfortunately, quite a few people seem to find pointless activities or even evil deeds fulfilling. For example, a bum might spend his life solving simple puzzles at home alone (it is possible that he was overwhelmed by challenges that exceeded his abilities; the trauma of failures makes him content and happy with repeating what he has been doing); or a serial killer might regard his perfect crimes as great achievements (he is thrilled in developing his criminal skills and ruthlessness). These cases suggest that the experience of fulfillment is not in and of itself a reliable indicator that the fulfilling activity is actually worthwhile. It may be prudent not to blindly engage with what seems attractive, but to reflect on its value before engaging. It would be better to cultivate an evaluative disposition that reliably tracks things worthy of engagement in the first place.[27] There might be someone who knows that he finds what he is doing fulfilling but wonders whether the activity is meaningful. As I interpret him, he is wondering whether his fulfillment is correct. It makes sense for him to wonder whether what he is doing is as valuable as his emotion of fulfillment (re)presents it as being. An experience of

---

[26] For the distinction between basic emotions and 'higher cognitive' emotions, see Paul Ekman, "An Argument for Basic Emotions," *Cognition & Emotion* 6 (1992): 169–200 and Paul Griffiths, *What Emotions Really Are* (University of Chicago Press, 1997), chs. 4, 5.

[27] Echeverri distinguishes the epistemic value of basic emotions from that of non-basic emotions. Our basic emotional dispositions, he argues, have been developed through long evolutionary processes in relatively stable environments and are triggered reliably by the objects that exemplify their formal objects (= evaluative properties). So it is more epistemically justifiable to form corresponding evaluative beliefs on the basis of basic emotions than on the basis of non-basic emotions. Santiago Echeverri, "Emotional Justification," *Philosophy and Phenomenological Research* 98.3 (2019): 541–66. It seems that fulfillment is, in general, not as reliable an indicator of the activity's value as fear is, according to Echeverri, of its object's danger.

fulfillment provides only a weak reason to believe that the fulfilling activity is actually valuable.

Still, fulfillment provides information about our talents and passions. When we are fulfilled, it is highly likely that we are successfully engaging with what we value. When we succeed in what we are doing, it is likely that the activity fits our talents and abilities. If we are fulfilled, it also means that we are intrinsically motivated to engage in the activity. Our evaluative disposition is relatively stable. We can take our fulfillment at an activity as an indication that we will probably not have to bring or force ourselves to engage in that kind of activity. These considerations suggest that fulfillment can serve as an instrument to discover what we are good at and passionate about. The phenomenology or felt quality of fulfillment provides an easy access to our talents and passions. It is no mean feat to find where our talents and passions lie. Many students and even adults struggle to figure it out. We can use the information fulfillment provides to our advantage. Indeed, "follow your fulfillment" may be better career advice than "follow your passion." In choosing a career, we should take into consideration not only our wants and aspirations but also our talents and abilities.

4.3 Motivational Value

The phenomenology of fulfillment contributes to the continuation of the motivation to engage in a number of ways. First, the experience of fulfillment is, I have argued, mildly pleasant. Hedonicity is conducive to motivation. The degree of pleasantness is such that it does not interrupt the engagement but strengthens the motivation. Second, the experience of fulfillment, as with the experience of emotions in general, captures and consumes our attention. It makes us focus on the act of engagement and prevents distractions from reaching our consciousness. This removal of distractions helps the motivation to engage/continue without external interruption. Third, the experience of fulfillment, I have argued, makes it seem as if the activity and its object are valuable and the motivation to (continue to) engage is thus intelligible. By making the motivation appear intelligible, the phenomenology of fulfillment contributes to its continuation without internal interruption. Let me explain.

When we act, we act for reasons. We have at least implicit reasons for our action, considerations that count in favor of what we do. By the same token, when we act in a way that we cannot make sense of, i.e., when there apparently is no consideration that counts in its favor, we do not let the action continue but, at least, pause. Suppose you see yourself raise your right arm (or, it might be better put, see your right arm raised) without any apparent reason. The motivation to raise your arm looks unintelligible and foreign to you. Probably you will find yourself immediately trying not to raise your right arm and/or pressing down your right arm with your left hand. You will not leave "your action" of raising the right arm alone. Letting an apparently unintelligible motivation move you around means losing control of yourself. Letting this kind of things happen amounts to losing your agency. It seems that we desire not to lose agency. We seem to have an almost instinctive desire not to let our apparently unintelligible motivation and resulting action go unchecked. When it is brought to our attention that what motivates or moves us to action seems groundless and unintelligible, we cannot help but hesitate and stutter.

An act of engagement draws our attention. If it does not look intelligible, the appearance of unintelligibility can hardly fail to make us hesitate and interrupt the action. Even if we manage to go on with the engaging action, we would have to struggle to fight the instinctive desire to stop and reflect on what's going on within us. By making the motivation appear intelligible, the phenomenology of fulfillment prevents this interruption from occurring. The appearance of intelligibility lubricates the motivation. The evaluative phenomenology of fulfillment facilitates smooth continuation of the motivation to engage. If the object is indeed worthy of engagement, it helps to continue and complete the valuable activity and make our life meaningful and worth living.[28]

References

Julia Annas, "The Phenomenology of Virtue," *Phenomenology and the Cognitive Sciences* 7.1 (2008): 21–34.

Tim Bayne, "The Phenomenology of Agency," *Philosophy Compass* 3 (2008): 1–21.

[28] Earlier versions of this chapter were presented at Workshop on Emotions at City University of New York, Overseas Speakers Series at Wuhan University in China, and Normativity in Philosophy Conference at Seoul National University. I would like to thank the audiences on those occasions, including Peter Finocchiaro, Hilla Jacobson, Jinho Kang, Hille Paakkunainen, Abelard Podgorski, Jesse Prinz, Daniel Shargel, and Michael Zhao for discussions and criticisms. I am also grateful to Ralf Bader and especially Uriah Kriegel for helpful comments that greatly helped me improve the chapter.

Tim Bayne, "The Sense of Agency," in F. Macpherson (ed.), *The Senses* (Oxford University Press, 2011), pp. 490–524.

Tim Crane, "The Nonconceptual Content of Experience," in Tim Crane (ed.), *The Contents of Experience: Essays on Perception* (Cambridge University Press, 1992), pp. 136–57.

Mihaly Csikszentmihalyi, *Flow and the Foundations of Positive Psychology: The Collected Works of Mihaly Csikszentmihalyi* (Springer, 2014).

Stephen Darwall, *Welfare and Rational Care* (Princeton University Press, 2002).

Julien Deonna & Fabrice Teroni, *The Emotions: A Philosophical Introduction* (Routledge, 2012).

Sabine Döring, "Seeing What to Do: Affective Perception and Rational Motivation," *Dialectica* 61 (2007): 363–94.

Sabine Döring, "The Logic of Emotional Experience: Noninferentiality and the Problem of Conflict without Contradiction," *Emotion Review* 1 (2009): 240–7.

Santiago Echeverri, "Emotional Justification," *Philosophy and Phenomenological Research* 98.3 (2019): 541–66.

Paul Ekman, "An Argument for Basic Emotions," *Cognition & Emotion* 6 (1992): 169–200.

Catherine Elgin, "Emotion and Understanding," in G. Brun, U. Doguoglu, & D. Kuenzle (eds.), *Epistemology and Emotions* (Ashgate, 2008), pp. 33–50.

Paul Griffiths, *What Emotions Really Are* (University of Chicago Press, 1997).

Terence Horgan & John Tienson, "The Intentionality of Phenomenology and the Phenomenology of Intentionality," in D. Chalmers (ed.), *Philosophy of Mind: Classical and Contemporary Readings* (Oxford University Press, 2002), pp. 520–33.

Terence Horgan, John Tienson, & George Graham, "The Phenomenology of First-Person Agency," in S. Walter & H. Heinz-Dieter (eds.), *Physicalism and Mental Causation* (Imprint Academic, 2003), pp. 323–34.

Ingvar Johansson, "Species and Dimensions of Pleasure," *Metaphysica* 2 (2001): 39–71.

J.L. Mackie, *Ethics: Inventing Right and Wrong* (Penguin, 1977).

Mark Johnston, "The Authority of Affect," *Philosophy and Phenomenological Research* 63.1 (2001): 181–214.

Antti Kauppinen, "Meaningfulness," in G. Fletcher (ed.), *The Routledge Handbook of Philosophy of Well-Being* (Routledge, 2016), pp. 281–91.

Anthony Kenny, *Action, Emotion and Will* (Routledge, 1963).

Uriah Kriegel, *The Varieties of Consciousness* (Oxford University Press, 2015).

Jonathan Mitchell, "The Epistemology of Emotional Experience," *Dialectica* 71.1 (2017): 57–84.

Jonathan Mitchell, "Emotional Intentionality and the Attitude-Content Distinction," *Pacific Philosophical Quarterly* 100 (2019): 359–86.

Jonathan Mitchell, "Affective Representation and Affective Attitudes," *Synthese* (2019), doi: 10.1007/s11229-019-02294-7.

Michelle Montague, "Evaluative Phenomenology," in S. Roeser & C. Todd (eds.), *Emotion and Value* (Oxford University Press, 2014).

Adam Pelser, "Emotion, Evaluative Perception, and Epistemic Justification," in S. Roeser & C. Todd (eds.), *Emotion and Value* (Oxford University Press, 2014), pp. 107–23.

David Pitt, "The Phenomenology of Cognition or *What Is It Like to Think that P?*" *Philosophy and Phenomenological Research* 69 (2004): 1–36.

Peter Poellner, "Phenomenology and the Perceptual Model of Emotion," *Proceedings of the Aristotelian Society* 116.3 (2016): 261–88.

Warren Quinn, "Putting Rationality in Its Place," reprinted in his *Morality and Action* (Cambridge University Press, 1993), pp. 236–7.

Joseph Raz, "When We Are Ourselves: The Active and the Passive," in his *Engaging Reason: On the Theory of Value and Action* (Oxford University Press, 1999), pp. 1–21.

Amia Srinivasan, "The Aptness of Anger," *The Journal of Political Philosophy* 26.2 (2018): 123–44.

Richard Taylor, *Good and Evil* (Macmillan, 1970).

Susan Wolf, "Happiness and Meaning: Two Aspects of the Good Life," *Social Philosophy and Policy* 14.1 (1997): 207–25.

Susan Wolf, *Meaning in Life and Why it Matters* (Princeton University Press, 2012).

5

Experience is Knowledge

Matt Duncan

One way in which consciousness is valuable has to do with its role in generating *knowledge* of the world. Experience has epistemic oomph. Or, at least, it seems like it does. That is, it seems like experience plays a positive—even essential—role in generating some knowledge. For example, suppose I see a tiger before me. I thus come to know about the tiger. And it seems like, in this case, as in others like it, my visual experience plays a positive—perhaps even essential—role in generating my knowledge of the tiger.

The problem is, it's not clear what that role is. To see this, suppose that when my visual system takes in information about the tiger it skips the experience step and just automatically and immediately generates the belief in me that there is a tiger before me. A lot of philosophers think that, in such a case, I would (or at least could) still know, via perception, that there is a tiger before me. But then that raises the question: What epistemic role was the *experience* playing? How did *it* contribute to my having knowledge of the tiger?

Philosophers have given many different answers to these questions.[1] But, for various reasons, none of them has really stuck.[2] In this chapter I'll offer and defend a different answer to these questions—a solution to the problem—which avoids the pitfalls of previous answers, does not require commitment to certain controversial theses entailed by other solutions, and allows that experience has an even deeper, more extensive epistemic significance than others have realized or suggested. I'll argue that experience has epistemic oomph because experience is, all by itself, a kind of knowledge—

---

[1] For a detailed overview of this debate, see Byrne (2016), Siegel and Silins (2015), or Johnston (2006). In some way or other, all of these philosophers trace the contemporary debate over the epistemic significance/oomph of experience to Donald Davidson (1986).

[2] Mark Johnston (2006) goes as far as to say, "Contemporary philosophy has no good answer to the question: what is the function of sensory awareness as opposed to immediate perceptual judgment?" (p. 260).

Matt Duncan, *Experience is Knowledge* In: *Oxford Studies in Philosophy of Mind Volume 1*. Edited by: Uriah Kriegel, Oxford University Press (2021). © Matt Duncan. DOI: 10.1093/oso/9780198845850.003.0005

it's what Bertrand Russell (1912) calls "knowledge of things." So, on this view, experience helps generate knowledge by *being* knowledge.

Here's the game plan. First, I'll describe the debate over the epistemic oomph/significance of experience and briefly evaluate some of the main positions within it. Then I'll stake out my position and defend it against objections. My aim here isn't to move partisans from their platforms. It's rather to give a good alternative to undecideds—to those seeking a different candidate explanation for the epistemic value of experience.

1. The Epistemic Oomph of Experience

Start with a case. I see a tiger at a zoo. As a result, I know various things about that tiger—its approximate size, shape, and color; and also just that it's there at the zoo. And my seeing the tiger—my visually experiencing it—is part of the explanation for how I know these things. For example, if someone asked me whether there is a tiger at the zoo, I'd say, "Yes"; if they asked me how I know, I'd say, "Because I *saw* it." My experience is a key player in this epistemic story. I saw and then I knew, and I knew *because* I saw.[3]

Furthermore, it's natural to think that my seeing the tiger—my having a visual experience of it—is not just an epistemically idle step in the cognitive process that terminates in my knowledge of the tiger. It's natural to think that it makes some epistemic difference—whether it's because it plays an essential role in generating my knowledge, or merely makes my knowledge more likely, or increases justification, or whatever. One way or another—however it is cashed out—it seems like my experience has some epistemic oomph.[4]

---

[3] Here and throughout this chapter I am focusing on perceptual knowledge of the external world (versus, say, self-knowledge), and I am assuming the falsity of external world skepticism. The debate over the epistemic significance/oomph of experience isn't a debate over skepticism— over whether we have knowledge of the external world. It presupposes that we have such knowledge and is rather over whether (or how) experience plays a positive epistemic role in generating it.

[4] It would be nice to have a general, agreed-upon precisification of the claim that experience has epistemic oomph. But how this claim is precisified will very much depend on what role one ends up thinking experience plays in generating knowledge. For example, on my view, which is that experience is a kind of knowledge, the following claim is true: For some actual knowledge k had by some subject s, there is some experience e had by s such that, necessarily, if s had not had e, s would not have had k. That's a strong claim—it makes experience *absolutely necessary* for some knowledge. But I don't think one would need to defend such a strong claim in order to establish that experience plays some positive epistemic role in generating knowledge (cf. Byrne 2016, p. 951).

Now, to be clear, the claim here isn't that experience is the only possible route to my knowing about a tiger at the zoo. I could've known about it in other ways—a zoo keeper could've told me about it, for example. So the claim here is rather that, in some actual cases of knowledge that seem to come from experience, experience plays some positive epistemic role in generating that knowledge. So just focus on the case where, as a matter of fact, I come to know about the tiger by seeing it. The claim is that in *that* case, *that* visual experience played a positive epistemic role in generating *that* bit of knowledge.

But what is that role? One initial thought might be that it's a *causal* role—that experience helps generate knowledge by causing it. Indeed, the standard picture of how I come to know (via perception) about the tiger in front of me is that information from the world impacts my sensory receptors, which then send signals to my brain that then cause me to have an experience of the tiger (or "as of" the tiger), which in turn causes me to form beliefs about the tiger, which then, in the right conditions, amount to knowledge. So here are the steps: (i) information from the world, (ii) sensory processing, (iii) experience, (iv) beliefs that add up to knowledge (cf., Byrne 2016). And, on this picture, experience is one step in the epistemic causal process. So, one potential suggestion is that experience has epistemic oomph because it *causes* some knowledge.

But there has to be more to it than that if the claim that experience has epistemic oomph is to be vindicated. Sure, experience often plays a causal role in generating knowledge. But the claim here is that it plays a positive *epistemic* role in generating knowledge (hence, "epistemic oomph"). And a merely causal story isn't enough to vindicate that claim. To get a better sense of why, consider an analogy from Alex Byrne (2016):

> Suppose you want to get a message to Bertie. You can tell him yourself, or you can tell Alys instead, and she will pass the message on. Assuming that telling Bertie yourself doesn't involve a long trip or other disadvantages, why bother with the messenger? In fact, telling Alys gratuitously *adds* possibilities of error—she might garble the message or fail to tell Bertie.
>
> (p. 950)

This analogy illustrates how something could play a causal role in bringing about some result without it actually *helping*, in some other important sense, in bringing about that result. If you give Alys the message, she may play a causal role in Bertie's getting the message. But Alys wasn't needed. Nor did she really help the process—Bertie could've gotten, and was more likely to get, the message without her involvement.

With this analogy in mind, we can better appreciate some of the central questions regarding the epistemic oomph of experience. Even if experience plays a causal role in generating knowledge, as it may very well, we might still wonder whether it actually *helps*, epistemically, in generating that knowledge. We might wonder whether it is instead more like Alys—what Byrne (2016) calls a "superfluous middleman" (p. 951).

So we need more than a causal story. Another way to go—a path that goes beyond mere causation—is to say that experience sometimes plays a positive (even essential) role in *justifying* certain of our beliefs. The thought is that my seeing the tiger in front of me not only *causes* me to form beliefs about the tiger, it also *justifies* those beliefs—or makes them rational, warranted, and so on. On this approach, my experience isn't merely a causal middleman. It's doing epistemic work. So this may seem like a more promising route.[5]

The problem is that, as Byrne (2016) points out, it seems like, given all the other sensory and cognitive processing going on in my case, I could have justified beliefs—indeed, I could know—about the tiger without experiencing it. The worry isn't that I could learn about the tiger in some totally different way—by the zoo keeper telling me, for example. It's rather that the sensory and cognitive processing of information from my environment would be, all by itself and regardless of whether it involved experience, enough to justify my beliefs about the tiger.

To get a better grip on the worry, again return to steps (i)–(iv) in the process of how I come to know about the tiger. The question is: What if we cut out the experience step? What if my sensory systems skipped it and went straight from (ii) to (iv), directly causing beliefs in me about my external environment? Would any epistemic damage be done? Or would this merely cut out a superfluous middleman? One might think that no epistemic damage would be done. For one might think that as long as the relevant information from the world is safely and reliably delivered to my mind, and as long as it is encoded in the relevant beliefs in all the right ways, the job is done—the justification is had, the knowledge is secured.

---

[5] Indeed, the majority of philosophers who have attempted to tackle this issue have taken this route in some form or other. They include Pollock (1974), Pryor (2000), Huemer (2001), Peacocke (2004), Johnston (2006), Smithies (2014, 2019), and many others. Again, see Johnston (2006), Siegel and Silins (2015), or Byrne (2016) for an overview.

To reinforce the appeal of this thought, consider Ned Block's (1995) "superblindsight" case—a possible case in which someone is fully "access conscious" of external things but not phenomenally conscious of them:

> Visual information from his blind field simply pops into his thoughts in the way that solutions to problems we've been worrying about pop into our thoughts, or in the way some people just know the time or which way is North without having any perceptual experience of it. The superblindsighter himself contrasts what it is like to know visually about an X in his blind field and an X in his sighted field. There is something it is like to experience the latter, but not the former, he says. It is the difference between just knowing and knowing via a visual experience.   (p. 233)

Block (1995) says that the superblindsighter would know about the external world by taking in information via his senses, even though he doesn't experience the external world. If Block is right, then the sensory and cognitive processing involved in superblindsight is, all by itself—without any experience—sufficient to produce justified beliefs, and indeed knowledge, about the external world. Thus, if Block is right, then the superblindsighter needn't experience the world in order to have justified perceptual beliefs about it.

But now, if experience isn't needed for justification in the superblindsighter case, it's natural to also suppose, and think, that it isn't needed in normal cases. For it's natural to think that our sensory and cognitive systems could glean the relevant information from the world and directly encode that information in beliefs about the world without producing any experiences of the world. And it's natural to think that these beliefs would be justified and, indeed, that we could (and would) know about the world in this way.

In fact, this conclusion is inevitable on certain theories of justification. Take reliabilism. On this view, so long as one's beliefs are produced by a reliable cognitive faculty—i.e., one that produces mostly true beliefs—they are justified.[6] The superblindsighter's perceptual beliefs are, by stipulation, reliably formed. So, if reliabilism is true, they are justified. And as long as our

---

[6] There are various different version of, and tweaks on, reliabilism. And reliabilism (broadly construed) has a ton of defenders, including Goldman (1979), Dretske (1981), Plantinga (1993), Comesana (2002), Lyons (2009), and Pritchard (2016). See Goldman and Beddor (2016) for an overview.

sensory and cognitive faculties could likewise reliably form true beliefs without producing experiences—using just non-experiential information processing—those beliefs would be justified on reliabilism. Thus, if this is possible, and if reliabilism is true, then it looks like experience is just a superfluous middleman when it comes to our perceptual knowledge.

This conclusion may also be inevitable on other theories of justification. But you may not need to consult any specific theory of justification in order to see the force of the point. For you may think it's just intuitively plausible that one could have these justified perceptual beliefs sans experience. But then, if that's right, then the epistemic significance of experience—its epistemic oomph—can't be explained by saying that experience plays a positive (even essential) role in justifying the relevant beliefs. For, if everything I just said is right, that justification could be gotten without the experience. My experience of the tiger at the zoo would be like Alys—yes, as a matter of fact, it was part of the story of how I came to know about the tiger, but it wasn't *needed* for me to know about the tiger, and it didn't even really help, epistemically. Just like the message delivered to Bertie, my knowledge could have been conveyed to me in a more direct way.

At least that's one potential reaction. On the other hand, you could always deny some or all of what I just said. That is, you could deny that we (including the superblindsighter) could have justified perceptual beliefs sans experience. Declan Smithies (2014, 2019), for example, argues that experience is the basis of all justification—that phenomenally individuated mental states determine which of our beliefs are justified. So his view implies that the superblindsighter's beliefs about the external world are unjustified. And, more generally, it implies that our perceptual beliefs about the external world couldn't be justified sans experience in the way described above. So the present strategy for explaining the epistemic oomph of experience—i.e., by saying it plays a positive role in justifying beliefs—is still available to Smithies. He has an out.

However, I want to foreclose this out for now. For one thing, this exit strategy relies on a minority view among theories of justification—one that isn't going to appeal to very many. Also, I want to take seriously the challenge—raised by Byrne (2016) and others—about the epistemic oomph of experience. So, I want to grant the intuition that our perceptual beliefs could be justified without our having the relevant experiences. And then what I want to show is that, *even if* this is the case, and so *even if* one rejects something like Smithies' experientialist account of justification, experience still has epistemic oomph. Thus, I am willing to grant that the explanation for the epistemic oomph of experience doesn't lie at what Byrne (2016) calls "the experience-belief synapse"—i.e., the link or transition from experience to belief—because that synapse could be severed without thereby excising the relevant knowledge.

But, with that much granted, I also want to close the door on Byrne's (2016) way out of the problem. Byrne suggests that perceptual experiences are partly constituted by beliefs—that believing P just is part of experiencing P. So he suggests that experiences have epistemic oomph because, in the good cases where those beliefs add up to knowledge, experiences are partly constituted by knowledge. I think Byrne's view has some virtues. In particular, I think Byrne is wise to dodge the troublesome experience-belief synapse. But I also think his view has some vices. First, I think it's implausible, for reasons that we needn't get into here, that experiences are partly constituted by beliefs. Sure, experiences may typically—even always—*come along* with beliefs. But they're distinct mental states. Or so I say. Second, it's not clear that Byrne's view actually vindicates the idea that experience has epistemic oomph, at least not in the way that idea was originally formulated. The datum we started with was that phenomenal experience *itself*—the looks, the feels, the sounds, etc.—has epistemic oomph. But, on Byrne's view, it doesn't really—it's only the belief component, not the phenomenal component, which carries epistemic weight. So I'm doubtful that Byrne's out really is an out. From where I stand, it looks more like a door locked from the inside.[7]

But set those complaints aside. For my goal here isn't to dwell on criticisms of Byrne's out, or Smithies' out, or anyone else's out. It's to press the problem and then offer my own out. The mere fact that philosophers haven't scampered en masse for either of the above exits is sufficient evidence that there is an appetite for another avenue. So, opening up another viable path to explaining the epistemic oomph of experience will be valuable, irrespective of where others' views end up. And so it's to that task that I now turn.

---

[7] Another common objection to Byrne's solution—one which he addresses—comes from cases of known illusion, where something appears some illusory way to a subject, but she knows that it is an illusion. In such cases, it seems that one experiences P but doesn't believe P. In which case, believing P couldn't be a constitutive part of experiencing P, as per Byrne's view. Byrne (2016) responds by saying that, in such cases, one does believe P, but one's belief is held in check by a stronger belief. I'll leave it to readers to assess the merits of Byrne's response.

2. Experience is Knowledge

My explanation for the epistemic oomph of experience is very simple. I say that experience is, all by itself, a kind of knowledge. So experience helps generate knowledge by *being it*. That's how it has epistemic oomph.

To get an initial grip on what this explanation is all about, go back to the case where I see a tiger at the zoo. The standard view is, again, that I take in information, process it, have an experience, and then form beliefs about the tiger that, given the right conditions, amount to knowledge. I say forget the beliefs for a second. The visual experience *itself* is a kind of knowledge—what Russell (1912) calls "knowledge of things" (more on this below). So, given the right conditions, just *seeing* the tiger—visually experiencing it—is enough to know of it. I of course don't deny that we also form perceptual beliefs about the external world that amount to knowledge. I just deny that those beliefs are required for perceptual knowledge. For, again, I say that experience *itself* is a kind of knowledge. In this way, experience has epistemic oomph.[8]

On this view, experience has a very significant epistemic role. It doesn't just cause or justify knowledge; it doesn't just contribute to it or make it more likely. On this view, experience *is* knowledge. So it is strictly *essential* for some knowledge—that is, for some knowledge had by some subjects, there are experiences such that, necessarily, if those subjects had not had those experiences, they would not have had that knowledge.

Which, again, isn't to say that experience is the only possible route to knowledge of, say, a tiger at a zoo. There are other routes. It's just that, in this case, a particular visual experience is essential to a particular bit of knowledge. The original problem of the epistemic oomph of experience arose when we considered some perceptual belief that amounted to knowledge, and we noted that *that very belief* could've amounted to knowledge without the experience. Nothing like that is true for experiential knowledge. If some knowledge *just is* an experience, then it is false—trivially so—that *that very*

---

[8] In this chapter, I have been and will continue to focus on *perceptual* experiences, since those are the core cases that motivate our problem. However, it's worth mentioning that my view naturally extends to other kinds of experiences, too. Take, for example, the sharp knee pain that I feel. Just as I can know of the tiger in front of me simply by seeing it, so, too, I can know of my knee pain simply by feeling it. And, on my view, the experience *is* knowledge—both of the pain itself and, plausibly, of the physical disturbance in my knee that is its cause or basis. More on this in the following pages.

knowledge could've existed without the experience. After all, that knowledge *is* the experience, and you can't have an experience without an experience.

This solution to the problem is similar to Byrne's (2016) solution in that it doesn't locate the epistemic oomph of experience in the experience-belief synapse—that is, in experience's *relation* to beliefs that are distinct from it. In particular, it doesn't say that experience has epistemic oomph only because it causes or justifies (distinct) beliefs. So my solution, like Byrne's, is immune to the aforementioned worries with such accounts of experience's epistemic oomph. So my solution shares this virtue with Byrne's solution.

It also lacks the vices. First, it doesn't require commitment to the implausible view that experiences are partly constituted by beliefs. Second, whereas on Byrne's view the phenomenal aspect of experience is epistemically idle—it's only the belief component of experience that has any epistemic oomph—on my view the phenomenal component (which I maintain is the only component of an experience) is epistemically significant. The looks, the feels, the sounds, the tastes—on my view, they *themselves* have epistemic oomph. Thus, unlike Byrne's solution, my solution locates the epistemic significance of experience in experience *itself*. And thus, unlike Byrne's solution, my solution truly vindicates our original datum.

So, already, my solution has a lot going for it—it has virtues that many solutions lack, but sans the trade-off vices.

However, more needs to be said to vindicate my explanation of experience's epistemic oomph. For one thing, there are a bunch of potential objections to it. I'll address those in Section 3. But also, in order for my knowledge of things explanation to get off the ground, I need to say more about what this experiential knowledge that I'm talking about is supposed to be. I've laid out and defended a detailed account of it elsewhere (Duncan 2020).[9] So, in the remainder of this section, I'll limit myself to some pertinent highlights.

[9] Aside from this account, knowledge of things has been largely ignored by contemporary analytic philosophers. A few other philosophers, such as Earl Conee (1994), Colin McGinn (2008), and Michael Tye (2009), do endorse knowledge of things (in the service of other ends), but they don't develop their accounts in much detail, so they leave themselves open to some fairly straightforward objections (see Crane 2012). There are a couple of other philosophers who defend something that is at least similar to knowledge of things. For example, Eleanor Stump (2010) and Lorraine Keller (2018) talk about "Franciscan knowledge," which is very much like knowledge of things. M. Oreste Fiocco (2017) defends a Brentano-inspired account of something like knowledge of things. Matthew Benton (2017) talks about interpersonal knowledge, which is non-propositional and may be a species of knowledge of things. And Frank Hofmann (2014) argues that perceptual experience is "non-conceptual knowledge," which is non-doxastic (though propositional). It may be that there are other philosophers out there who just haven't

Let's start with Bertrand Russell. He maintains that there are two kinds of knowledge: knowledge of *truths* and knowledge of *things*. Russell (1912) says 'knowledge' in the former sense is:

> ... the sense in which what we know is *true*, the sense which applies to our beliefs and convictions, i.e. to what are called *judgments*. In this sense of the word we know *that* something is the case.   (p. 69)

For Russell, knowledge of truths is ordinary propositional knowledge— constituted by beliefs in propositions. And it is distinct from knowledge of *things*, which comes in two varieties: knowledge by *acquaintance* and know- ledge by *description*. Russell (1911) describes acquaintance as follows:

> I say that I am *acquainted* with an object when I have a direct cognitive relation to that object, i.e. when I am directly aware of the object itself.
> (p. 108)

Russell (1911) then describes acquaintance as the direct "presentation" of objects and properties to one's senses (p. 108), and says that, strictly speaking, we are only ever acquainted with sense data, our awareness of sense data, and a few other things. All other knowledge of things is indirect, according to Russell, and counts as knowledge by *description*—it's the kind of knowledge we have when we know of something as satisfying some description or falling under some concept, such as "the tiger at the zoo," "the zookeeper," or "*that* thing there."

According to Russell (1912, p. 73), knowledge by description presupposes some knowledge of truths. For example, in order to know a tiger as "that tiger," I must know certain propositions about what tigers are. Nonetheless, Russell holds that knowledge by description is distinct from knowledge of truths. My knowledge of the tiger, its color, shape, and so on, is not the same as, nor is it reducible to, knowledge of propositions.

Furthermore, on this account, not all knowledge of things presupposes or requires knowledge of truths. Take my knowledge of the color of the tiger. I know of it *as orange*. This knowledge requires that I possess the concept *orange*, and thus it presupposes some background knowledge of truths about

---

thought about this issue, or for whatever other reason are not *opposed* to knowledge of things (maybe they even like the idea). But it's safe to say that knowledge of things has been largely ignored by contemporary analytic philosophers.

what orange is. But I also know of the *very specific* shade of orange that I see when I look at the tiger, for which I have no concept. This knowledge of things does not require knowledge of truths. Or consider another example. Right now I'm looking at a set of bookcases in my office. They are full of books. I see these books of various specific shapes, sizes, and colors, at various angles and in various relations to each other. What I see is highly determinate and fine-grained. I really do see those books in all their complex and multifarious glory. And, on this account, I know of them.[10] To be more specific, suppose that, in some precise region in the center of my visual field, there are forty-eight books. I see, and thus know of, those forty-eight books. But of course I don't know *that* there are forty-eight books there. Furthermore, I don't know *that* the bright red book is seventeen books to the left of that dull gray, tattered book. Or anything of the sort. In this way, as in others, my knowledge of highly determinate, fine-grained properties and objects in my environment outstrips what I know about them propositionally.[11] And this knowledge of things does not presuppose or require propositional knowledge/knowledge of truths.

Russell (1911, 1912) goes on to say more about knowledge of things. But he never fully develops his characterization of it. Also, some of the particulars of his view (e.g., sense data) are unpopular with contemporary philosophers. So what I'll do now is offer what I think is a plausible adaptation of Russell's view.

I take knowledge of things to be constituted by awareness (or consciousness) of properties and objects. In the present context, I am specifically interested in *experiential* awareness. So I will focus on knowledge of things as constituted by experiences of properties and objects.[12] Some paradigm cases are perceptual experiences. When I see the tiger in front of me, I know

---

[10] Russell (1911, 1912) would say that what I know of most immediately in this case are *sense data* that make up the appearances of the books. So he would describe this case a little differently (though not in a way that matters for the point that I am making here). However, most philosophers these days reject the sense-datum view. So I will set this part of Russell's view aside.

[11] This naturally raises the question: Do I know of *every*thing that I experience (in good conditions), or must I *attend to* a thing, or notice it in some other way, in order to know of it? For what it's worth, I'm inclined to say that we don't know of everything that we experience— that some level of attention is required to justify knowledge of things (see below). But I also think that acquiring knowledge of things doesn't generally require great mental effort. We regularly know of all sorts of things that we don't carefully attend to. I may know of a tiger in front of me, for example, without carefully attending to it. So although knowledge of things does require *some* attention, it doesn't require a great deal of it.

[12] In what follows I will talk about experience in a way that is most fitting for a representationalist (or intentionalist) view of experience, which is the most popular view of perceptual

of it. When I see the forty-eight books in my office, I know of them (even though I do not know *that* there are forty-eight books there). The same goes for other sense modalities. I can experience, and thus know of, properties and objects in my environment by smelling, hearing, tasting, or touching them. I can also know of the position of my body via proprioception.

Other paradigm cases of knowledge of things include *self-knowledge*—i.e., knowledge of one's own mental states—that comes via introspection. By introspecting, I can know of my knee pain, this annoying nose tickle, my anger at how bad New England drivers are, and my thoughts about Russell, knowledge, and tigers.[13]

Further details about knowledge of things can be seen most starkly when it is contrasted with propositional knowledge (or knowledge of truths). Propositional knowledge is constituted by a subject's bearing a certain relation—namely, the *belief* relation—to a proposition. Knowledge of things differs in both relation and content. When a subject knows of things, she *experiences* something—she is *experientially aware* (or *conscious*) *of* it.[14] And the contents of her knowledge are properties and objects—colors, shapes, tigers, people, etc.—not propositions.[15] Hence, knowledge of truths and of things differ both in their relation and content.

---

experience these days. However, the main elements of my account can be reformulated so as to suit other views, such as naïve realism or the sense-datum theory.

[13] What other kinds of experiences are potential knowledge? What about experiences of boredom, for example? Or nausea? Although taking a stand on this issue isn't necessary to support my claim that *some* experiences are knowledge, my own view is that even the above kinds of experiences are potential knowledge. What are they knowledge of? Of *oneself*, I think—of one's own mind and/or bodily state. Of one's boredom or nausea. There are plenty of further questions about how to explain or describe this self-knowledge (e.g., Is this knowledge quasi-perceptual? Is attention required for it? If so, what is one attending to when one comes to know of it?), just as there are plenty of further questions about the nature and structure of perceptual experience. But I will not attempt to settle or even pick sides on these issues here. However it is spelled out, the point is that in experience we come to know of various objects and properties—in both our environment and ourselves—and, on my view, these experiences can and sometimes do constitute knowledge of those objects and properties. Thanks to Uriah Kriegel for raising this point.

[14] For reasons that I won't go into here, I think that this relation is primitive—it admits of no informative (i.e., non-circular) definition or analysis. But this point isn't essential to my account of knowledge of things. Those who prefer a reductive account of the consciousness relation may take a different tack. For example, some say that the aware/conscious of relation is reducible to a *tracking* relation, where consciousness of property/object x is reducible to one's being in a state that is poised for cognitive access and that causally covaries with the instantiation of x (see, e.g., Dretske 1995; Tye 1995). So, although I think this relation is primitive, reductionists still have room on board.

[15] Maybe you think that the contents of perception are (or include) propositions. If that's your view, then you could accept a version of this knowledge of things solution on which

Now, in any given case, there is more to knowledge than one's bearing a relation to a content—further conditions must also be satisfied. For example, one cannot know a proposition that is false—to know that *P*, *P* must be *true*. Also, to know that *P*, one's belief must be *justified*. These are necessary conditions on knowledge of truths. And I take knowledge of things to be partly similar, partly different along each of these dimensions.

Start with truth. Experiences are not true or false. My experience of the color of the tiger, for example, is neither true nor false. But experiences are *veridical* or *non-veridical*. One's experience of property *Q* is veridical if and only if *Q* is instantiated as it's represented; one's experience of an object *O* is veridical if and only if *O* exists and is present as represented. And it's natural to think that, in order to count as knowledge (of things) of property *Q* or object *O*, one's experience of *Q* or *O* must be veridical.

It's also natural to think that, in order to count as knowledge, an experience must have a rational/normative status parallel to that of justification for beliefs. The idea would be that, in normal cases, my experiences are in some sense rational or justified as representations of things around me. But if instead I am in non-ideal circumstances—in poor lighting or a hall of mirrors, for example—my experiences of things around me may be less justified or rational, even if they happen to be veridical. Perhaps more controversially, if my experiences are being influenced in an epistemically untoward way—by unjustified background beliefs, for example—then those experiences may be less rational than they otherwise would be (Siegel 2017).

There are various ways to spell out this idea. For example, it could be spelled out in terms of Susanna Siegel's (2017) "epistemic charge";[16] or in terms of epistemic *luck* or *risk* (Pritchard 2016);[17] or in terms of epistemic

---

experience is a kind of propositional knowledge. But I prefer a non-propositional version of knowledge of things (see Duncan 2020). So, if you think that perception has propositional content, just note that what I'm talking about as the contents of knowledge of things are the individual objects and properties that I experience—what may be the *constituent parts* of perceptual propositions. Even if you think that perception is propositional, there's still room for knowledge of things in my sense.

[16] According to Siegel (2017), epistemic charge is an epistemic property that gives experiences rational standing. More carefully, it is "A property of experience that can be modulated by psychological precursors of the experience and transmitted to subsequent beliefs, and in virtue of which a subject's experience manifests an epistemic status" (p. 41). Siegel uses the term 'charge' to draw an analogy with electricity—just as electric charge can be passed from one thing to another, so, too, epistemic charge can be passed from psychological precursors to experiences and then to beliefs.

[17] On Pritchard's (2016) account, a belief is epistemically lucky just in case it is actually true but there are nearby possible worlds—worlds much like the actual world—in which it is false.

virtues related to experience, such as attentiveness, acuity, and perceptual memory; or in terms of the *reliability* of our faculties for producing veridical experiences. There are other options too, as you can imagine. All of this is ripe for controversy and is bound to remain so, if for no other reason than that every account of epistemic normativity is controversial. But the point here is just that it's natural to expect knowledge of things to have a normative status parallel to that of knowledge of truths.[18] Further work is needed to elucidate this parallel.

So that's knowledge of things. I have said what constitutes it (experiences of properties and objects), given paradigm examples of it (from perception), and compared and contrasted it with knowledge of truths. In giving this adaptation of Russell's account, I don't mean to imply that all philosophers who posit knowledge of things are, or should be, committed to every aspect of this account. I offer this account merely to show how the basics of Russell's view might be filled out. It's not the aim of this chapter to show that some *specific* view about knowledge of things is right; rather, it's to develop a solution to a particular problem. So if, at the end of the day, aspects of the above account need to be adjusted or rejected, so be it. The core of the view is just that some knowledge is constituted by experiences of properties and objects.

And, as we've seen, this view provides a simple, elegant solution to our problem concerning the epistemic oomph of experience. If some knowledge is constituted by experiences of properties and objects, then experience has

---

Pritchard's account of epistemic risk is very similar—it is a matter of whether an actually true belief is false in a nearby possible world. The differences are (or at least include) that risk is forward-looking (rather than backward-looking, as with luck), concerns only negative states or events, and, according to Pritchard, really is the kind of thing we want to avoid, epistemically. Either of these notions could be applied to experiences by talking about whether a given experience (as opposed to a belief) that is actually veridical (as opposed to true) is non-veridical in nearby possible worlds.

[18] Maybe you are skeptical that experiences could have such a status. Perhaps this is because you think that, unlike beliefs, experiences are formed *passively*—we just "take in" what's around us—and because, unlike beliefs, what we experience is not entirely up to us or rationally adjustable. But there are several false assumptions here. As Siegel (2017) points out, many of our beliefs are also formed passively (e.g., my belief that I'm now typing), and some of our beliefs are not under our control or rationally adjustable (e.g., delusions). What's more, how we experience the world often *is* rationally adjustable and, in many respects, under our control. We can choose what to look at or attend to, adjust background assumptions that affect how we experience things, disavow experiences (e.g., illusions), and shape our perceptual experiences through learning and habituation, for example (Siegel 2017, §3.1). Thus, beliefs and experiences are more similar than you might've thought in terms of their fitness for justification.

epistemic oomph simply because it is a kind of knowledge. This gives experience a very significant epistemic role. For, on this view, some experiences are strictly essential for some knowledge. And, as we've seen, this solution shares the virtues, but not the vices, of some of its main competitors.

3. Objections

So that's my answer as to how experience has epistemic oomph. Now I'll address some potential objections.

Objection 1: I (the objector) am not convinced that knowledge of things exists. Is there more to be said in its favor?

Response: Yes! Elsewhere I have given several arguments for thinking that knowledge of things exists (see Duncan 2020). In one argument, I appeal to certain cases of fine-grained perceptual knowledge—cases where it seems obvious that we have knowledge about certain properties or objects around us and where positing such knowledge is needed to explain our behavior—and I argue that we lack some of the beliefs that we'd have to have in order for this knowledge to be purely propositional. I also argue that experiences bear various hallmarks of knowledge—that is, that they play various philosophical roles that are distinctive of knowledge. For example, I argue that, in experience, we grasp reality and gain evidence in a distinctively epistemic way; that experiences render us appropriate subjects of epistemic praise and blame and serve as the knowledge base for various forms of expertise; and that experiences are sometimes the bases of knowledge-conferring inferences in ways that imply that they themselves are knowledge. So knowledge of things has a lot going for it.

And this chapter offers yet further support for knowledge of things. For allowing that some knowledge is of things solves an important, seemingly intractable problem about the epistemic oomph of experience. We started with a datum: Experience has epistemic oomph. Positing knowledge of things explains that datum. Which is evidence that knowledge of things exists. And the fact that this datum is not easily explained otherwise, and that other views struggle to explain it, and that leading candidate explanations require commitment to views that many reject, adds to the evidence for knowledge of things.

Again, there are other reasons to accept that knowledge of things exists. But this chapter offers its own backup.

Objection 2: Here's a more specific worry about knowledge of things: It is supposedly constituted, not by beliefs in propositions, but by experiences of properties and objects. But properties and objects can't be true (or false). How could one know something that isn't true? Also, beliefs, not experiences, are the kinds of mental states that can be justified (or unjustified). How could one have knowledge that isn't justified?

Response: It's true that properties and objects can't be true or false. But representations of them can be veridical or non-veridical (or accurate or inaccurate), which is parallel to truth and falsity. Also, as I suggested above, it's natural to think that knowledge of things has a normative status parallel to that of justification for beliefs. These may not be exactly the same as truth/falsity and (doxastic) justification. But knowledge of things is a different kind of knowledge, so we shouldn't expect it to be exactly the same as propositional knowledge. On the other hand, the fact that there are parallels with respect to truth/falsity and justification for knowledge of things should bolster our confidence that it is a denizen of the epistemic realm.

Objection 3: Fine, but if there is knowledge of things, shouldn't there be an ordinary language analogue to propositional knowledge? Is there any evidence in ordinary language for the existence of knowledge of things?

Response: There is. Matthew Benton (2017) makes a case based entirely on ordinary language considerations for thinking that something like knowledge of things exists. He starts by pointing out that, in English, there is a difference between phrases like 'S knows that φ' and 'S knows NP' where 'NP' is a noun phrase (p. 2). He then argues that the way 'know' is used in these cases fails various tests for semantic sameness. This suggests that, in English, the propositional sense of 'know' ('know *that P*') is used differently, and indeed, does not mean the same thing as, the non-propositional sense of 'know' ('know Q' or 'know of Q').

Benton (2017) also points out that many languages have a distinct sense of 'know' that refers to non-propositional knowledge (see also Tye 2009; McGinn 2008). In Spanish it's 'conocer' (as opposed to 'saber' for propositional knowledge), in German it's 'kennen' (vs. 'wissen'), in French it's 'connaître' (vs. 'savoir'), in Hebrew it's 'lehakir' (vs. 'lada'at'), and in Chinese it's 'renshi' (vs. 'zhidao'). So, various languages use distinct terms to distinguish between propositional and non-propositional knowledge. And Benton appeals to this fact, along with other ordinary language considerations, to argue that some knowledge is non-propositional.

Objection 4: These ordinary language considerations are inconclusive. It's not obvious that the uses of 'know' mentioned above refer specifically to knowledge of things. Speakers might mean something else. Plus, these knowledge attributions can always be paraphrased into attributions of propositional knowledge.

Response: I agree that the ordinary language case for knowledge of things isn't totally conclusive. More generally, I think that language, including language involving knowledge attributions, is messy and an imperfect guide to reality. However, those who do favor ordinary language consider-ations in this context may find Benton's arguments persuasive, or at least some evidence in favor of knowledge of things. And, at the very least, it's worth pointing out that there is no ordinary language case *against* there being knowledge of things.

With that said, I do find other arguments for knowledge of things more compelling—such as those mentioned above. That experience plays various distinctively epistemic roles—and thus bears those hallmarks of knowledge—is, I think, a good reason to accept that knowledge of things exists. So even if ordinary language can't settle the matter—and I concede that it can't—there's ample reason to accept knowledge of things.

Objection 5: All putative knowledge of things can be modeled or repre-sented in a proposition-friendly way. For example, it's possible to represent experiential states algebraically, or with a probability distribution, or in some other formal way. Then this knowledge can be modeled in line with the propositional orthodoxy.

Response: I deny that all experiential knowledge can be fully captured propositionally. I maintain that a propositional modeling is bound to leave something out in terms of what we know (see Duncan 2020). So, I reject the guiding assumption of this objection that our knowledge can be fully represented propositionally.

But set that aside. For the real question in this context is not whether knowledge of things can be *represented* propositionally; it's just whether knowledge of things *exists*. For if knowledge of things exists, then some experiences are knowledge, and so they have epistemic oomph. And, indeed, we have reason to think that this knowledge does exist. So we have reason to think that some experiences are knowledge and thus have epistemic oomph. This is consistent with the possibility that this knowledge can be represented propositionally. Indeed, several of the arguments given or alluded to above are neutral on whether perceptual knowledge can be represented or modeled propositionally—that is, they are consistent with the possibility of such a modeling. Yet they still support the conclusion that there is knowledge of things—that some experiences constitute knowledge. So even if all experiential knowledge *could* be fully represented propositionally, still, there would be plenty of reason to believe that some knowledge is of things.

An analogy may help. Suppose we're looking at a painting and you tell me that you could, in principle, give me some detailed description of all its features. Does that mean that this painting is a story, not a picture? Hardly. The fact that a representation of one type can be modeled using a representation of another type doesn't mean the former is in fact the latter. That knowledge of things might be modeled propositionally shouldn't shake our confidence that it exists, especially given all of the reasons to accept it.[19]

Objection 6: Even if there are reasons to accept that knowledge of things exists, this thesis is still controversial. We set aside Smithies' solution in part because his is a minority view and all kinds of controversial. Knowledge of things must be at least as controversial. If so, shouldn't we set that solution aside too?

Response: It's an interesting question whether knowledge of things is controversial. Certainly a lot of philosophers *ignore* it. But if you look at encyclopedia entries or introductory textbooks on epistemology, you'll find a lot of philosophers asserting (as if it's obvious) that knowledge of things exists.[20] So, it's not clear to me that knowledge of things actually is very controversial.

And even if it is controversial, it's not controversial in the way that Smithies' view is. Smithies' view is incompatible with most philosophers' views in this debate.[21] Knowledge of things isn't.[22] That is, whether or not others in this debate accept knowledge of things, it's open to them in a way that Smithies' views may not be.

Furthermore, in setting aside Smithies' view, I don't mean to suggest that it's not a live option. It's just not *my* option. My aim in this chapter isn't so

---

[19] Or consider another analogy. You might think that various moral theories can be "consequentialized"—modeled or described in an extensionally equivalent, consequentialist-friendly way. And yet that, by itself, hardly implies that every moral theory is in fact consequentialist. Thanks to Chris Ranalli for this suggestion.

[20] See, e.g., Feldman 2002, p. 12; Fumerton 2006, p. 1; Martin 2010, pp. 1–2; Audi 2011, ch. 1; Fantl 2017; Ichikawa and Steup 2017; Steup 2017.

[21] This includes, of course, Byrne (2016). But it also includes anyone who denies that justification wholly depends on phenomenally individuated states. Which is a ton of people—indeed, the vast majority of philosophers.

[22] This includes views about justification (as I mentioned in Section 2) and also a wide array of views in epistemology more generally—e.g., internalism, externalism, foundationalism, coherentism, knowledge-first epistemology, conceptualism, non-conceptualism. That's partly because most of the views formulated in contemporary epistemology are only about *propositional* knowledge.

much to criticize other solutions to the problem; it's rather to offer another solution that may be appealing to those who don't like the other solutions on offer. Given what I've argued, we don't need to pin our hopes on Smithies' solution. Even if his view and others' views are wrong, still, we can accept that experience has epistemic oomph. And the fact that philosophers haven't rallied around any of the other solutions suggests that there is indeed appetite for another option.

Objection 7: Okay, let's suppose that knowledge of things exists. Still, this doesn't solve our problem. For it's still possible to have perceptual knowledge without knowledge of things—without having the experience. And it's not just that some possible perceptual knowledge could be had without the experience; it's that for *every* case of perceptual knowledge there is a parallel case of knowledge without experience. Remember the steps: (i) information from the world, (ii) sensory processing, (iii) experience, (iv) beliefs that add up to knowledge. Even if some experiences are knowledge, it's still possible to go right from (ii) to (iv). So it's possible to know everything we know without experience. So experience is superfluous.

Response: Again, I deny that it's possible to know everything we know sans experience. But even if I'm wrong about that, the key point in this context isn't that experiencing X is the *only* way to know about X. That's not what's at issue. What's at issue is whether experience is *one way* to know about X where the experience is doing epistemic work (cf., Byrne 2016, p. 491). If some experiences are knowledge, then, in those cases, experience is doing epistemic work, regardless of whether there are other ways to get the job done.

Objection 8: The superblindsighter is still *aware* of things, just not *experientially* or *consciously* aware of them. So couldn't he still have a kind of knowledge of things? If so, then even knowledge of things can be had without any experience. Which once again just raises the question of what epistemic role the experience is playing.

Response: One potential response is to deny that non-experiential awareness could ever amount to knowledge of things. But bracket that. Let's grant that some possible knowledge of things is non-experiential. This doesn't detract from the claim that some experiential awareness is also knowledge. Indeed, it doesn't detract from the claim that a lot of ordinary cases of experiential awareness are knowledge. So it doesn't detract from the claim that experiential awareness is essential for knowledge in a lot of ordinary cases. Which is sufficient to show that experience has epistemic oomph. For, again, if some knowledge *just is* an experience, then experience plays a positive epistemic role in generating that knowledge—namely, by being it.

Objection 9: Even if the knowledge of things solution is right and experience is essential to some knowledge in virtue of being that knowledge, that doesn't explain how experience has epistemic oomph when it comes to generating *propositional* perceptual knowledge—e.g., my knowledge *that* there is a tiger at the zoo. Which was one of the original cases in need of explanation. So this solution doesn't address the original problem.

Response: The original problem was just about explaining the epistemic oomph of experience. My example was merely meant to illustrate that problem—a problem which, in the last several decades, philosophers have addressed with only propositional knowledge on their radars. Hence the example. But the fact that knowledge of things doesn't, by itself, explain how experience has epistemic oomph for propositional perceptual knowledge (if it does have that kind of oomph) doesn't imply that it doesn't explain how experience has epistemic oomph more generally. It *does* explain that. Which is the heart of the original problem.

Think of it this way. Suppose someone is pondering over the original problem and says, "It seems obvious that experience has epistemic oomph, but I just can't see how." Then suppose she reads this paper and agrees that experience has epistemic oomph when it comes to generating knowledge of things. It would be unfair of her to nonetheless maintain that I haven't addressed her original pondering just because I haven't shown that experience has epistemic oomph for *every* kind of knowledge—because I only showed that it has this oomph for some kinds of knowledge. Epistemic oomph is epistemic oomph.

With that said, appealing to knowledge of things may also help explain how experience is epistemically relevant to propositional perceptual knowledge. It may do this by figuring in an account of how knowledge of things gives rise to or supports propositional knowledge. It is beyond the scope of this chapter to give such an account (see Duncan 2020 for more). But the point here is just that knowledge of things may go even above and beyond the call of duty when it comes to explaining the epistemic oomph of experience.

Objection 10: There are all sorts of other issues that this solution doesn't address. For example, many of those who are concerned about the epistemic oomph of experience are thinking about issues having to do with skepticism, foundationalism, the Given, and so on. And it's not at all obvious how the knowledge of things solution addresses those issues. So, in the broader theoretical context, this solution falls short.

Response: Granted, I haven't said anything about these other issues. Which isn't to say that knowledge of things is irrelevant to them or that it can't help with other issues. But one thing at a time. And the purpose of this chapter is just to lay out a simple, attractive explanation for the epistemic oomph of experience.

4. Conclusion

Other objections are no doubt waiting in the wings. Here I hope to have done just enough to get my candidate out there and maybe (hopefully) polling above zero. The datum was that experience has epistemic oomph. It just wasn't clear *how* it does. In this chapter, I have defended a solution to this problem. The solution is simple, straightforward, and, I think, worthy of further consideration. It's that experience is itself knowledge.

This of course applies to ordinary perceptual cases—e.g., where I see a tiger. But it also has broader import. To see this, consider: Not all experiences are ordinary. Some are life changing. Some shape what and how we think of ourselves, what we want to become, and how we interact with others. And the conclusion that experience is itself knowledge is highly relevant to the question of what might learn from—and *in*—these cases.

Consider one common but important case. Imagine that you're comforting a close friend who has just lost a loved one. As you listen to her, and look at her, and carefully attend to her very subtle facial expressions and highly specific bodily manner, and as you interact with her in only a way that a close friend could, in those moments, there's so much that you see and know about her—about what she looks and sounds like; about what she's thinking and feeling and going through—that doesn't seem reducible to mere propositional information processing. Your experience *itself* packs an epistemic punch. And it matters that it does.

And so it's worth exploring how we can, and perhaps ought to, avail ourselves of these rich epistemic resources. We can start, I think, by recognizing that experience—the looks, the feels, the sounds—is itself knowledge.[23]

---

[23] Thanks to Galen Barry, Mark Fiocco, Trip Glazer, Louis Gularte, Uriah Kriegel, Colin McLear, Adam Pautz, Chris Ranalli, Tomoji Shogenji, and Jack Spencer for helpful comments on and/or discussions of this chapter.

References

Audi, Robert (2010). *Epistemology: A Contemporary Introduction to the Theory of Knowledge*, 3rd edn. London: Routledge.

Benton, Matthew A. (2017). "Epistemology Personalized," *The Philosophical Quarterly* 67, 269, pp. 813–34.

Block, Ned (1995). "On a Confusion about a Function of Consciousness," *Brain and Behavioral Sciences* 18, pp. 227–47.

Byrne, Alex (2016). "The Epistemic Significance of Experience," *Philosophical Studies* 173, 4, pp. 947–67.

Comesana, Juan (2002). "The Diagonal and the Demon," *Philosophical Studies* 110, 3, pp. 249–66.

Conee, Earl (1994). "Phenomenal Knowledge," *Australasian Journal of Philosophy* 72, 2, pp. 136–50.

Crane, Tim (2012). "Tye on Acquaintance and the Problems of Consciousness," *Philosophy and Phenomenological Research* 84, pp. 190–8.

Davidson, Donald (1986). "A Coherence Theory of Truth and Knowledge," in E. LePore (ed.), *Truth and Interpretation: Perspectives on the Philosophy of Donald Davidson*. Oxford: Blackwell, pp. 307–19.

Dretske, Fred (1981). *Knowledge and the Flow of Information*. Cambridge, MA: MIT Press.

Dretske, Fred (1995). *Naturalizing the Mind*. Cambridge, MA: MIT Press.

Duncan, Matt (2020). "Knowledge of Things," *Synthese* 197, pp. 3559–92.

Fantl, Jeremy (2017). "Knowledge How", *The Stanford Encyclopedia of Philosophy* (Fall 2017 edition), ed. Edward N. Zalta, https://plato.stanford.edu/archives/fall2017/entries/knowledge-how/.

Feldman, Richard (2002). *Epistemology*. Somerset, NJ: Pearson.

Fiocco, M. Oreste (2017). "Knowing Things in Themselves: Mind, Brentano and Acquaintance," *Grazer Philosophische Studien* 94, pp. 332–58.

Fumerton, Richard (2006). *Epistemology*. Malden, MA: Blackwell.

Goldman, Alvin (1979). "What is Justified Belief?" in G. S. Pappas (ed.), *Justification and Knowledge*. Dordrecht: Reidel, pp. 1–25.

Goldman, Alvin and Beddor, Bob (2016). "Reliabilist Epistemology," *The Stanford Encyclopedia of Philosophy* (Winter 2016 edition), ed. Edward N. Zalta, https://plato.stanford.edu/archives/win2016/entries/reliabilism/.

Huemer, Michael (2001). *Skepticism and the Veil of Perception*. Lanham, MD: Rowman and Littlefield.

Hofmann, Frank (2014). "Non-Conceptual Knowledge," *Philosophical Issues* 24, 1, pp. 184–208.

Ichikawa, Jonathan Jenkins and Steup, Matthias (2017). "The Analysis of Knowledge," *The Stanford Encyclopedia of Philosophy* (Fall 2017 edition), ed. Edward N. Zalta, https://plato.stanford.edu/archives/fall2017/entries/knowledge-analysis/.

Johnston, Mark (2006). "Better than Mere Knowledge? The Function of Sensory Awareness," in T. S. Gendler and J. Hawthorne (eds.), *Perceptual Experience*. Oxford: Oxford University Press, pp. 260–90.

Keller, Lorraine Juliano (2018). "Divine Ineffability and Franciscan Knowledge," *Res Philosophica* 95, 3, pp. 347–70.

Lyons, Jack (2009). *Perception and Basic Beliefs: Zombies, Modules, and the Problem of the External World*. Oxford: Oxford University Press.

McGinn, Colin (2008). "Consciousness as Knowingness," *The Monist* 91, 2, pp. 237–49.

Martin, Robert (2010). *Epistemology: A Beginner's Guide*. London: Oneworld Press.

Peacocke, Christopher (2004). *The Realm of Reason*. Oxford: Oxford University Press.

Plantinga, Alvin (1993). *Warrant: The Current Debate*. New York: Oxford University Press.

Pollock, J. (1974). *Knowledge and Justification*. Princeton, NJ: Princeton University Press.

Pritchard, Duncan (2016). "Epistemic Risk," *The Journal of Philosophy* 113, 11, pp. 550–71.

Pryor, James (2000). "The Skeptic and the Dogmatist," *Noûs*, 34, 4, pp. 517–549.

Russell, Bertrand (1911). "Knowledge by Acquaintance and Knowledge by Description," *Proceedings of the Aristotelian Society*, 11, pp. 108–28.

Russell, Bertrand (1912). *The Problems of Philosophy*. London: Thornton Butterworth Limited.

Siegel, Susanna (2017). *The Rationality of Perception*. Oxford: Oxford University Press.

Siegel, Susanna and Silins, Nicholas (2015). "The Epistemology of Perception," in M. Matthen (ed.), *The Oxford Handbook of the Philosophy of Perception*. Oxford: Oxford University Press, pp. 781–811.

Smithies, Declan (2014). "The Phenomenal Basis of Epistemic Justification," in J. Kallestrup and M. Sprevak (eds.), *New Waves in the Philosophy of Mind*. New York: Palgrave Macmillan, pp. 98–124.

Smithies, Declan (2019). *The Epistemic Role of Consciousness*. Oxford: Oxford University Press.

Steup, Matthias (2017). "Epistemology," *The Stanford Encyclopedia of Philosophy* (Fall 2017 edition), ed. Edward N. Zalta, https://plato.stanford.edu/archives/fall2017/entries/epistemology/.

Stump, Eleanore (2010). *Wandering in Darkness: Narrative and the Problem of Suffering*. Oxford: Oxford University Press.

Tye, Michael (1995). *Ten Problems of Consciousness*. Cambridge, MA: MIT Press.

Tye, Michael (2009). *Consciousness Revisited: Materialism without Phenomenal Concepts*. Cambridge, MA: MIT Press.

6

The Special Value of Experience

Chris Ranalli

0. Introduction

Aristotle opens Book I of the *Metaphysics* with the statement that:

> All men [*sic*] by nature desire to know. An indication of this is the delight
> we take in our senses; for even *apart from their usefulness they are loved for*
> *themselves*; and above all others the sense of sight. For not only with a view
> to action, but even when we are not going to do anything, we prefer seeing
> (one might say) to everything else [my emphasis].[1]

Mark Johnston echoes Aristotle on this score. He asks:

> Why is it such a good thing to see, to hear, to smell, taste and touch? What
> if anything makes perception *intrinsically valuable*, as opposed to just a
> useful means for getting around our environment?
>
> (Johnston 1996, 185, my emphasis)

This question has not been asked very often in epistemology.[2] It concerns
not the value of knowledge over mere true belief but of certain epistemic
sources over others. In particular, it concerns the value of conscious perceptual knowledge of reality over second-hand knowledge of reality. We
might ask: why prefer such perception over testimony if truth is the fundamental epistemic good and perception and testimony turn out to be equally
reliable with respect to acquiring true beliefs about the matter that you're

---

[1] This is the translation from W. D. Ross. It is widely available online. See the Internet
Classics Archive from MIT: http://classics.mit.edu/index.html.
[2] A few important exceptions include Allen (2019) and Pritchard (2014). For related
questions about the specifically epistemic value of experience, see Byrne (2016), Campbell
and Cassam (2014), and Siegel and Silins (2015).

Chris Ranalli, *The Special Value of Experience* In: *Oxford Studies in Philosophy of Mind Volume 1*. Edited by:
Uriah Kriegel, Oxford University Press (2021). © Chris Ranalli. DOI: 10.1093/oso/9780198845850.003.0006

interested in? Or: why prefer observation to deference to authority if observation and deference to authority just as reliably yield the relevant truths
you're interested in? Are we simply being irrational in our preferences? Call
this the **special epistemic value question** because it concerns the premium
we place on conscious perception or observation over testimony and deference to authority in certain domains.[3]

In general, the problem seems to be that if truth is the fundamental
epistemic good, it's hard to see why anyone—from a purely epistemological
point of view—would have any reason to prefer one source of truth over
another source of truth if they are equal in terms of their reliability of
yielding truth, and yet we intuitively find that people prefer the perception
of the frescoes of the Sistine Chapel to testimony about them or to the
experience of seeing the Himalayan mountains to merely reading about
them in a book.[4] *Mutatis mutandis* for propositional knowledge. If propositional knowledge is the sole fundamental epistemic good but you already
know all the true propositions about the frescoes of the Sistine Chapel or
about the Himalayan mountains that you're interested in, then it seems as if,
from a purely epistemological point of view—where only epistemic goods
matter to you—that there would be no reason to desire consciously perceiving or visually attending to the Sistine Chapel or the Himalayan mountains,
provided that they are equally good at yielding the relevant knowledge. But
intuitively there is and therein lies our puzzle.

Here's one intuition about the special epistemic value of perception that
I want to defend. Perception gives one many different *epistemic goods*. One
of them is truth. Another is propositional knowledge (if its epistemic value is
not only that it is instrumental to truth). It might even facilitate one's
understanding of why a certain belief they have is true.[5] But it also yields
what we might call **cognitive contact with reality**—another epistemic good,
or so I will argue—that testimony and the like do not and perhaps cannot

---

[3] Two points. The premium we place on perception over testimony is *ceteris paribus*.
There might be cases where testimony would serve our interests or goals better, or where
perception wouldn't be especially helpful. Second, while I do not argue for this in the chapter,
I think that we can broaden the special epistemic value question as follows: why do we place a
premium on first-hand epistemic sources, of which perception is a special case, over second-
hand epistemic sources, such as testimony, deference to authority, reading reports, and the
like? This question is broader because it might include knowledge by a priori insight or
knowledge by intuition, knowledge by a first-hand constructed proof, and so forth, and not
only perception.
[4] That is, the intuition is there despite slight differences in reliability.
[5] Pritchard (2016) gestures at this.

yield.[6] This is what is missing when you merely read a list of truths about the frescoes in the Sistine Chapel without ever having been there. Mark Johnston (1996) makes the point vivid in the following example:

> Once my eyes were covered with bandages for five days. Part of what I longed for in longing to see again was not simply more information by which to negotiate my environment, nor simply more visual sensations. I longed for the cognitive contact with external features which vision seems to provide.   (Johnston 1996, 189)

Imagine that Johnston already had strong evidence to believe the relevant truths about his environment while his bandages were on. Imagine that he had all the information he needs—e.g., a memorized list of the true propositions about the world around him—from which to successfully navigate his environment. What, if anything, of epistemic value would be missing from his life while his bandages were on?

We might think that he would be missing conscious contact with the relevant objects, properties, or states of affairs that his true beliefs are about.[7] Put another way, the referents of his true beliefs would not be part of his conscious awareness: something that he could consciously attend to. In contrast, when he takes the bandages off and navigates his environment on the basis of his conscious awareness of the visible objects and properties therein, he would thereby be in contact with the relevant things which make

---

[6] For the phrase 'cognitive contact,' see Byrne (2010), Johnston (1996), Martin (2001), Millar (2007), Nudds (2015), and Putnam (1994). See Campbell (2009) for the similar notion 'epistemic contact.' See also Martin's (2006) discussion of Hume's skeptical challenge.

[7] Mark Johnston (1996) argues for a similar claim about why we prefer perception. One difference between Johnston and I is that he holds that perception, understood as a relation of acquaintance with external things, acquaints one with the *nature* of the perceptible properties that one perceptually attends to, but I take on no such metaphysical commitments. This is similar to Russell's (1912) views about the perception of colors. I say that it simply relates you cognitively to such properties: it brings them into your conscious mental life. In the philosophy of color, the idea that ordinary visual experience of color reveals the nature of colors is called 'revelation.' See Johnston (1992) for this idea, and Byrne and Hilbert (2007) for a discussion. Allen (2011) argues for the claim that if naïve realism about sensory experience is true, then revelation is false. I say that ordinary perceptual experience acquaints you with color properties like orangeness or shape properties like the particular unnamed squarish shape of a rug, but that it's an open question whether you are thereby acquainted with the nature or essence of orangeness or squareishness. It might be that their natures or essences are different from what's consciously perceptually presented to us. Campbell in his chapters in Campbell and Cassam (2014) argues that perceptual experience so understood provides one with a grasp of the relevant objects or properties as mind-independent, but here, too, I take on no such epistemic commitments. It might be that we abstract from experience that the objects we perceive are mind-independent.

his beliefs true. He would not just have true beliefs but the truth-makers for his beliefs right there before his eyes.

What do I mean by 'cognitive contact' with reality? Cognitive contact with reality seems to be a kind of conscious relation or non-propositional awareness of objects, properties, or states of affairs. It is a conscious awareness relation to the relevant entities that your true belief is about. For example, compare two people who both know that that the apple is red (p), the first by seeing and visually attending to the red apple and the second by hearing, from a reliable testifier, that the apple is red. I claim that while both people know that p, the first but not the second person is in cognitive contact with reality. This is because the first but not the second person is consciously aware of the relevant object (the apple) and property (its redness) that her true belief is about. In this way, cognitive contact with reality requires more than simply having a belief about reality which is true (more on this in Sections 3 and 4). The relevant entities that your true belief is about have to figure in your conscious awareness. But the relevant object and property that the second person's true belief is about is external to her conscious awareness, and thereby not what she's in cognitive contact with.[8] I claim that perceptual experience of reality is a paradigm case of cognitive contact with reality, but there might other cases too: perhaps mathematical perception, ethical perception, or even memory. I'll bracket these cases here, and focus only on perceptual experience.

Conscious perceptual experience so understood supplies what John Campbell calls the "initial base of knowledge of what the things are that you are thinking and talking about" (Campbell 2009, 648). The idea is that, even before I know what 'apple' or 'red' refers to, or how to use demonstratives, if I become visually aware of a red apple, I can thereby come to know the redness of the apple and the way that that apple looks by seeing it at that time. This is what Mark Johnston characterizes as simply "knowing" the properties which are presented to us in perceptual experience, in contrast to knowing which propositions about those properties are true. We might think of it as "acquaintance with things" and thus *knowledge of things* rather than *knowledge of truths* about those things (Johnstone 1996, 190; cf., Russell 1912, 1911).[9] Call this the **cognitive contact intuition** about the specifically

---

[8] As we will see in Section 4, merely knowing that p when it turns out that the objects and properties that your true belief that p is about are the distal cause of your true belief that p is not yet sufficient for being in cognitive contact with relevant objects and properties that p is about.

[9] I will be presupposing that there is knowledge of things and that acquaintance with things supplies such knowledge. See Duncan (Chapter 5, this volume) and Duncan (2020) for the

epistemic good that conscious perceptual experience yields in addition to truth or propositional knowledge. According to the cognitive contact intuition, it is epistemically good to be in cognitive contact with reality. Its value is epistemic value in addition to any other value it might have. If that's right, then one hitherto neglected task for contemporary epistemology is to try to understand what cognitive contact with reality is and why it is epistemically valuable.

The cognitive contact intuition seems to show up in our thinking about other cases too.[10] We can intuitively see this by adapting L.A. Paul's (2014) transformative experience cases. If you had all the relevant true beliefs about what it is like to become a vampire and truth was the sole fundamental epistemic good, then actually *experiencing* becoming a vampire and thereby coming into contact with the relevant vampire-making properties shouldn't be preferable from a purely epistemic point of view to being *told* the relevant truths about becoming a vampire.[11] But surely it is. Inquiry takes a stand on the issue. We can very easily imagine an extremely dedicated scientist who studies vampirism (and who already has all the relevant true beliefs about vampirism) wanting to see for themselves what it is to be a vampire. Curiosity is not indifferent to these choices. They want to *know* the vampire-making properties and not only know truths about them. For intuitively *something* is learned when they undergo such experiences and one way of characterizing what they learn when they already have all of the relevant true beliefs about the event is that they are consciously put in contact with the very things that their true beliefs are about.

Here, then, is a roadmap of the chapter. In Section 1, I will develop the special epistemic value problem as a challenge to the thesis that truth is the

nature of knowledge of things. I do not take on the other commitments of Russell's view of knowledge by acquaintance: that propositional knowledge "rests upon acquaintance at its foundation," or that we can only understand propositions that have constituents we are acquainted with (Russell 1912, 48; see also Russell 1911). For recent work on knowledge by acquaintance in the philosophy of mind and language, see Knowles and Raleigh (2019).

[10] For another example, see Chudnoff (2013), who argues that intuition is a real two-place awareness relation to abstract objects. When one mathematically intuits that 2 is a prime number, on this view, they become aware of the number 2 such that their awareness depends on the presence of the number 2 in their intuition in the sense that the number 2 partly constitutes the person's intuitive experience at that time. If Chudnoff is right, then mathematical intuition would afford cognitive contact with the things one's corresponding true mathematical belief is about. See also Byrne (2010) for a conception of episodic memory which preserves the cognitive contact with reality that their initial perception provided.

[11] See Paul (2014), specifically pp. 1–4 for the thought experiment about becoming a vampire.

sole fundamental epistemic good. In Section 2, I will explore the view that the greater value that perceptual experience seems to have over second-hand sources such as testimony or reading is due to its having greater *non-epistemic value*. In turn, I argue against that view. In Section 3, I consider the idea that cognitive contact with reality is not a distinctive epistemic good at all but rather to be identified with the good of true belief or propositional knowledge of reality, and ultimately reject it. In Section 4, I consider the view that perception gives one richer and more specific *information* than testimony and that its value can be explained by reference this fact in a way that is compatible with truth being the fundamental epistemic good. I argue that this view is also problematic. Finally, in Section 5, I explore the idea that cognitive contact with reality is a distinctive fundamental epistemic good. This chapter, then, amounts to a prima facie defense of the idea that there is an additional fundamental epistemic good—which I identify as cognitive contact with reality—and thus that truth is not the sole fundamental epistemic good.

1. The Special Value Problem and Epistemic T-Monism

Epistemic T-monism is the thesis that truth is the sole fundamental epistemic good.[12] This means that epistemic goodness consists in *truth* and that any other epistemic property which is epistemically valuable has instrumental epistemic value only relative to its promotion of the sole fundamental epistemic good, which is truth. The idea that truth is the sole fundamental epistemic good is a kind of orthodoxy in epistemology.[13] It is related to the idea that truth is the aim of inquiry. Some epistemologists have argued that it is the fundamental epistemic goal in the sense that the epistemic goal of inquiry is truth (Alston 1985, 2005; Goldman 1999). On this account, to the extent that our epistemic goals are directed at knowledge, justification, and so forth, it is only instrumental to getting truth. Truth is what legitimately closes inquiry.

What supports epistemic T-monism? One argument is that a proper understanding of the epistemic domain reveals that *the epistemic* is the domain in which our activities, cognitions, states of mind, and so forth,

---

[12] For key defenses, see Pritchard (2014) and Ahlstrom-Vij (2013).
[13] Compare Pritchard (2014). He notes that the view has been challenged by epistemic pluralists such as Kvanvig (2005).

aim at truth. For example, what's the point of collecting evidence for your beliefs if evidence doesn't help with getting to the truth? From a purely epistemic point of view, what would be the point of having reasons or arguments for one's views if reasons and arguments were essentially indifferent to truth? It's hard to see why anyone should care about having a justified belief, or a belief based on evidence, reasons, or good arguments, if it not for the fact that justification, evidence, reasons, or argument bear some relation to truth.[14] Provided that true belief is valuable it can account for why justification, evidence, reasons, or argumentation are valuable too—because they promote truth. This is a simple and elegant explanation of the source of epistemic value.

The special epistemic value problem suggests that there is an intuitive asymmetry in epistemic value between those cases in which the agent consciously perceives that p compared to being told by a reliable informant that p, but it's hard to see how this intuitive asymmetry can be accommodated *if* truth is the sole fundamental epistemic good and both ways of getting to truth are equally reliable or equally good at yielding the desired intellectual end (i.e., truth). The basic outline of the argument I will be endorsing from the special epistemic value problem to the denial of epistemic T-monism can be put like this:

P1.   If epistemic T-monism is true, then there cannot be cases in which (i) two agents A and B are doxastic duplicates, having the same true belief that p arrived at in ways which are equally reliable and truth promoting and yet (ii) A and B differ with respect to the (non-derivative) epistemic goods they possess.

P2.   There are cases in which two agents can have the same true belief that p arrived at in ways which are equally reliable and truth promoting and yet they differ with respect to the (non-derivative) epistemic goods they possess.

Therefore,

C.   Epistemic T-monism is false.

Epistemic T-monism implies that there is only one non-derivative epistemic good (epistemic value monism) and identifies it with *truth*. So, my argument is in effect an argument for *epistemic value pluralism*, which says that there is more than one (non-derivative, non-instrumental) epistemic good. The first premise is supported by the thought that if epistemic T-monism is true, then

---

[14] See Bonjour (1985) for this kind of argument.

two people who are alike doxastically, having the same true belief that p, are also alike in their possession of fundamental epistemic goodness vis-à-vis their true belief. Two people who both truly believe that p as a result of equally reliable methods, then, ought to be epistemically on par with respect to their non-derivative epistemic goods, since there is only *one* non-derivative epistemic good and they both have it. Any epistemic value difference would need to be accounted for in terms of true belief.[15] We can also show this for epistemic properties like *evidence* or *responsible belief*. Suppose that Kathy and Katie both believe that the p and p is true. Kathy believes p on the basis of some evidence, whereas Kathy responsibly inquired and found out that an expert testified that p. Epistemic T-monism tells us that what makes having evidence or believing responsibly *epistemically valuable* is that they go towards getting the truth, the sole fundamental epistemic good. Provided that having the evidence Kathy had or believing responsibly in the way that Katie did both go towards getting the truth that p equally well, epistemic T-monism predicts that having Kathy's evidence or believing responsibly in the way that Katie did are equally instrumentally valuable, because they both served the goal of getting the true belief that p equally well.

The meat of the argument is therefore in the second premise. We can further support this premise by considering examples and explaining why the apparent further good is genuinely *epistemic* and furthermore not reducible to truth or anything epistemic whose value is merely instrumental to the truth.

For example, consider Will Hunting from *Good Will Hunting*. Will is a genius, but he's afraid to uproot himself and leave Boston. His therapist Sean notes that while Will knows a lot of truths about the Sistine Chapel, he suggests that Will is still lacking in some epistemically important way. Here's what he says:

So, if I asked you about art, you'd probably give me the skinny on every art book ever written. Michelangelo. You know a lot about him. Life's work,

---

[15] Zagzebski (2004) argues for a stronger claim: that reliability adds no additional value to one's true belief if truth is the fundamental epistemic good. See Goldman and Olsson (2009) for their response. I find Zagzebski's case compelling, but my argument doesn't rely on the key intuition there, the so-called swamping intuition, that reliability adds no additional value not already possessed in the item of true belief. Premise 1 is much weaker than this, since it says that if the very same true beliefs were produced by equally reliable or truth-promoting processes, then it's hard to see how they could differ with respect to their manifestation of fundamental epistemic goodness if truth is the fundamental epistemic good.

political aspirations, him and the pope, sexual orientation, the whole works, right? But I bet you can't tell me what it smells like in the Sistine Chapel. You've never actually stood there and looked up at that beautiful ceiling.

Although Will might know the important truths p, q, and r about the Sistine Chapel, there is still some further epistemic good to be acquired by getting in contact with the relevant facts which make his beliefs that p, q, and r true. To see this, compare two versions of Will Hunting:

SISTINE CHAPEL A: Will hasn't been to the Sistine Chapel and looked at the ceiling for himself. However, he knows all of the true propositions about the ceiling of the Sistine Chapel, from the trivial and mundane, to the extraordinary and the interesting. For he read them all in "The List of Truths about the frescoes on the ceiling of the Sistine Chapel," which lists all of the relevant true propositions about it that he was interested in. As a result of reading this book, he comes to believe those propositions.

SISTINE CHAPEL B: Will* knows all of the same true propositions about the frescoes as Will. Unlike Will, however, he's seen the ceiling for himself. That's why he knows all the relevant true propositions about the frescoes that he was interested in.

Will and Will* are doxastically and veritistically identical. For they share exactly the same true beliefs. Intuitively, however, Will* is epistemically better off than Will. He seems to have some further non-derivative epistemic good that Will lacks. I say: let's take this seeming at face value. If epistemic T-monism is true, however, how could this be possible? We might think that the epistemic asymmetry between Will and Will* is grounded in the fact that Will* learns something else that he didn't already possess by having the true beliefs he has about the Sistine Chapel. He comes to know the ceiling first-hand and what it is like—that is, he comes to know what the truth-makers of his true beliefs are like, such as the orange robes in the frescoes on the ceiling, or the way the depicted people appear to pop out against the vivid sky blue background—which seems irreducible to knowing true propositions about the scene. For if they were reducible to knowledge of truths about the Sistine Chapel then Will would have known them as well but *ex hypothesi* he didn't. Put generally: if epistemic T-monism were true, the value of believing the truth would drown out the value of learning the truth by seeing the facts which make one's beliefs true.

We might be able to appreciate this point more clearly by considering a simple variation of Frank Jackson's Mary's Room thought experiment.[16] In this variation of the case, Mary is a color scientist who has lived her whole life in a monochromatic room filled with the most reliable monochromatic papers, books, and videos about color. She has never left her monochromatic room, but she has worked out or otherwise read all the relevant true propositions about colors because of her desire to get the truth. The list of truths about color is complete and she believes everything on the list.

Now suppose that truth is the primary epistemic aim of inquiry in the sense that any other epistemic aim is instrumental to getting truth. If the aim of one's inquiry is knowledge, on this view, its ultimate end is truth and knowledge is the expression of that end. Fulfilling the goal of one's inquiry by getting the knowledge that p as opposed to only true belief that p would simply be valuable relative to getting the truth. *Ex hypothesi*, if Mary's inquiry into some specific color—say the orange of the robes depicted on the ceiling of the Sistine Chapel—aims at cognitive contact with reality, that is, the specific part of reality which includes the orange robes depicted on the ceiling, and if truth is the sole fundamental epistemic good, then since she has the relevant true beliefs about reality already, it follows that her inquiry would be legitimately closed. But intuitively it isn't. She can still coherently wonder what the orange robes look like or what it is like to experience them for herself. But since she already has all the relevant true beliefs about the orange robes, it can't be that she's articulating a desire for *more truths* about the orange robes. She already has all the truth that anyone can get and yet her inquiry is still open.

Here's another way to take the example. We imagine Mary having read the list of truths about the color she's interested in and believing that p—one of the true propositions about the color—versus Mary* who has read everything on the list except that p but she has left her room and has now become consciously aware of the fact which makes p true because she consciously sees that p and likewise truly believes that p on this basis. Intuitively, Mary* is in possession of some further epistemic good that

---

[16] The original thought experiment is from Jackson (1982). Jackson's intended conclusion was that there is more to reality than the physical, for Mary already knew all the truths about the physical world before she left her monochromatic room. Conee (1994) argues that Mary's new knowledge is acquaintance knowledge of the physical world—which is neither propositional knowledge nor ability knowledge. I agree. But my argument here doesn't depend on that. It could be that Mary's new knowledge is that she (also) learns a new concept and how to properly use it.

Mary lacks—she's in cognitive contact with reality—but there is no differ-ence in what they believe or in the truth of what they believe or in the reliability of their belief-forming processes. For Mary* now experiences seeing the orange robes herself and knows what the orange robes depicted on the ceiling of the Sistine Chapel look like. This doesn't give her some additional truth she didn't have before. It gives her something more primi-tive than truth: it gives her contact with the truth-makers of her pre-existing true beliefs about the orange robes.

Thus, the problem for T-monism is that it's not at all clear why there should be such an intuitive asymmetry in epistemic value between the Mary who has true beliefs about the colors and the Mary who has that *plus* conscious perceptual awareness of the truth-makers for her beliefs (or: conscious perceptual awareness of the relevant entities that her true beliefs are about). If the fundamental epistemic good is truth, it seems as if Mary ought to be, from a purely epistemic point of view at least, entirely indiffer-ent to the choice between seeing that there are orange robes depicted in the frescoes and reading that there are in a reliable book. For both ways of getting to the truth are equally reliable, we are supposing, but we intuitively judge that Mary gets a further epistemic good when she leaves her monochromatic room.

The lesson I want us to draw from these cases is that the asymmetry in epistemic value between our target first-hand and second-hand knowledge cases is attributable to the fact that the relevant first-hand ways of getting truth are also ways of getting cognitive contact with reality.[17] This is an epistemic good *in addition* to truth. If truth were the sole fundamental epistemic goal of inquiry and we had a choice about whether to inquire first-

---

[17] Alan Millar (2007) registers a similar asymmetry as follows: there is an epistemic asym-metry between a reasonable true belief without cognitive contact with reality, and a reasonable true belief with cognitive contact with reality. Millar holds a view of cognitive contact with reality on which in good cases—where one's belief is true—one is related to external objects by the exercise of one's perceptual discriminatory and recognitional capacities to the target objects one's true beliefs are about. This is a complicated view that I cannot assess properly here. I can only offer a preview. The problem is that in the good case one can exercise the relevant cognitive capacity, which on Millar's view yields cognitive contact with the relevant object, but one's sensory experience in such a case is the same fundamental kind as the experience one could have in the bad case—where one's belief is false. What is different between the good and bad cases on Millar's view is the truth of one's belief and whether one exercises the relevant cognitive capacities, but crucially *not* that experiences. If that's right, then someone who is only acquainted with sense-data but who has the relevant discriminatory and recognitional capacities and causal connection with reality would be able to get in cognitive contact with reality, but this seems wrong. The problem for a view like this is that it simply doesn't give sensory experience an explanatory role in putting us in contact with reality. Cf., Campbell and Cassam (2014).

hand by perception or second-hand by receiving testimony, we would have no purely *epistemic* reason for preferring one over the other (provided that they were equally reliable and equally truth promoting, as we have stipulated). But it certainly seems as if we rightly *do* prefer first-hand sources (like perception) to second-hand sources (like testimony). Inquiry isn't indifferent to this choice.

The proponent of T-monism, then, has at least three options available to them:

EUDAIMONIC VALUE: Conscious perception has greater value than second-hand sources such as testimony or reading, but this added value is exclusively *non-epistemic*.

DEFLATIONISM: The alleged additional, distinctive fundamental epistemic good does not exist—there is no such thing as cognitive contact with reality as a distinctive epistemic value. At best, the goal of getting cognitive contact with reality is a broader goal which getting true belief or propositional knowledge can realize.

MORE INFORMATION: Perception has greater epistemic value than testimony because perception provides one with rich information unavailable by testimony and thereby promotes truth better than testimony.

Once these three options are off the table the special epistemic value problem for epistemic T-monism will be sustained.

2. The Eudaimonic Value View

The proponent of epistemic value T-monism could argue that cognitive contact with reality is in fact not a fundamental epistemic good but that it is a good *and* epistemic. For example, it might be that instances of cognitive contact with reality are instances of an intellectual state of some sort—perhaps conscious acquaintance with reality—but that the *value* of this intellectual state is located outside the *epistemic domain*. One natural place to look is within the person's well-being: cognitive contact with reality has **eudaimonic value** since it adds to the well-being of the person or promotes their flourishing.

One way of arguing for the claim that cognitive contact with reality has eudaimonic value is grounded in Robert Nozick's (1974) experience machine case. In this case, you are plugged into an experience machine which provides the experiences that you desire. It provides you with a simulation of the life you most desire. The claim is that if well-being were only a matter of having the right sort of mental states—such as feeling pleasure and not pain, or having the feeling that one's preferences were satisfied—then one ought to plug into the machine because one's well-being would be improved compared to a life outside of it. The intuition, however, is that this would be a fundamentally defective life. After all, don't we want to be in contact with that which is pleasurable or the things to which our preferences are directed? Doesn't a parent want to in fact *parent* a child and not only simulate parenting? Doesn't the mountaineer want to *climb* mountains—with all its risks and rewards—and not only simulate the ascent? These sorts of examples suggest that having contact with reality is fundamentally part of the good life.[18]

You might agree with this application of the experience machine case, but think that it's hard to see how our intuitions here can be reduced to intuitions about eudaimonic value alone. The experience machine case so applied is only an argument for the view that cognitive contact with reality has eudaimonic value but from that fact that it has eudaimonic value it doesn't follow that it lacks epistemic value or that it has epistemic value only instrumentally, that is, only relative to the goal of truth. For it's consistent with the experience machine case that it has *both*. The experience machine case nicely brings out the additional type of value that cognitive contact with reality has.

There is an explanatory challenge for this view, however. We might think that once we have granted the eudaimonic value of cognitive contact with reality, it's no longer clear what role it could have in explaining the alleged *epistemic* asymmetry between our first-person perceptual experience cases and our second-hand testimony cases. After all, isn't it enough that there is a genuine difference in value between these cases even if it is not *epistemic value*?

---

[18] Lynch (2004) argues that what's epistemically problematic about the experience machine is that the experiencer misses out on truth or accuracy. That's of course one problem, but as Littlejohn (2018) has argued, we can rig the experience machine so that some of the experiencer's beliefs are accurate. According to Littlejohn, the epistemic problem of the experience machine is that the experiencer lacks propositional knowledge. For even if their beliefs are true, they are only luckily correct. I agree with Littlejohn but add that the experiencer also misses out on cognitive contact with reality, something that ordinary perceptual experience of reality would give them, in addition to propositional knowledge and true belief about reality.

One response to this challenge is to try to finesse the initial thought that from the fact that something has eudaimonic value it doesn't follow that it has no other kind of value. The proponent of the eudaimonic value view, that the intuitive asymmetry between the perception and testimony cases can be accounted for exclusively in terms of eudaimonic value as opposed to epistemic value as well, needs to explain why cognitive contact with reality doesn't have final epistemic value.[19] Otherwise, they need to explain why, if cognitive contact with reality indeed *has* epistemic value, its epistemic value doesn't play a role in accounting for the intuitive asymmetry between the perception and the testimony cases but only its eudaimonic value does this. I will argue that if this explanatory challenge works against the putative epistemic value of cognitive contact with reality, it ought to work against the putative epistemic value of truth as well. In this fashion, the objection will prove too much.

Consider a variation of the experience machine case in which the experience machine promotes not only pleasure but other goods as well: goods which make one's life go best. It promotes our well-being. Reality, on the other hand, doesn't make one's life go badly but it doesn't make it go as well as the experience machine. Michael Lynch has argued that reflection on this kind of experience machine case reveals that "we care about the truth for more than just the benefits it brings us" because we are apt to choose a worse reality, in which we get true beliefs, over an otherwise better simulation of it, where we'd get many false beliefs (Lynch 2004, 15).[20] The thought is that if our goal were the promotion of our well-being *simpliciter*, we would plug into the experience machine since that is what would promote it best.[21] At least, the thought is that it would do a much better job at this than reality—for reality might be banal or even awful. Provided that we wouldn't do this,

[19] It wouldn't be enough for the eudaimonist to respond: "cognitive contact with reality has final epistemic value, it's just that it plays no role in accounting for the axiological asymmetry in the relevant cases. Its eudaimonic value accounts for that intuitive asymmetry." The reason is that the whole point of the cases is to make plausible that cognitive contact with reality has final *epistemic* value, against the view that only *truth* has final epistemic value. Once they grant that it has final epistemic value, they have conceded the point. So eudaimonists would need to argue that if cognitive contact with reality has epistemic value, it is only instrumental epistemic value (e.g., relative to that which has final epistemic value, which is truth) or else deny that it has any epistemic value, in order to secure their objection.

[20] This experience machine case is analogous to Neo's choice in *The Matrix*. Lynch suggests that viewers weren't at all surprised that Neo chose the non-simulated 'real' world over the simulated 'matrix' world.

[21] For the view that the experience machine case puts pressure not only on hedonism about well-being, but also other outcome-based approaches, see Lorraine Besser-Jones (2015).

however, it provides some reason to think that we care about truth for its own sake apart from its promotion of eudaimonic value. Now consider the following argument:

The experience machine case reveals that the possession of epistemic goods has so much eudaimonic value that we'd rather live miserably with truth than pleasantly with falsity. But it's consistent with this that truth doesn't have genuine *epistemic* value. For we can account for our intuitions about the value of truth in purely eudaimonic terms without introducing some other type of value, so-called distinctively *epistemic value*. It's enough that the value of truth is eudaimonic. Truth is epistemic *and* good, not *epistemically good.*[22]

This argument parallels the objection that the eudaimonic value of cognitive contact with reality is all we need in order to explain our intuitions about the intuitive asymmetry in value between the perception and testimony cases. This might already make one skeptical of this sort of objection—because truth *is* epistemically valuable—but I think there is another way of showing what's wrong with it.

The thought is that when x is attributed two values v_1 and v_2, this raises a serious question about whether our intuitions about the value of x are solely attributable to its possession of v_1 rather than v_2 or vice versa. This introduces an explanatory burden, especially when one of the values is highly general, as is the case with eudaimonic value. What is needed to effectively disarm the challenge are plausible cases where x still looks valuable even when the relevant value v_1 is absent. In this way, it would suggest that v_2 has some explanatory role in accounting for the value of x. For example, consider how one might explain the value of Picasso's *Guernica* even if its financial value dropped to zero. For it would retain its political and aesthetic value. Applied to Lynch's version of the experience machine case, the thought is that reality might make one eudaimonically worse off than the experience machine, but we still might prefer a life embedded in reality if we can have true beliefs about it. As Lynch puts it: "We want the truth, warts and all" (Lynch 2004, 15). This suggests that we care about the truth for its own sake apart from its promotion of our well-being.

---

[22] See Hazlett (2015) for the distinction between something being good *and* epistemic and *epistemically good.*

It's important to recognize that we do not need to agree with Lynch's argument here. The argument is indeed controversial. The point is rather that the eudaimonist's objection that cognitive contact lacks epistemic value can be used to show that truth lacks epistemic value as well—which is absurd. Of course, it might be that the epistemic and the eudaimonic domains converge. This is what some epistemologists have argued (Baehr 2011; Zagzebski 1996, 2004). On this picture, an epistemic evaluation is a certain type of eudaimonic evaluation. It is a eudaimonic evaluation of agents in their capacity as inquirers or in their capacity as agents that form attitudes with mind-to-world direction of fit. If this were true, however, it would undercut the eudaimonist's objection as well. For then to show that some intellectual state meets some evaluative standard or has some property of eudaimonic value wouldn't have the tendency to show that it doesn't have epistemic value and vice versa. There would no longer be a genuine competition between an intellectual state's eudaimonic value and its epistemic value with which to wonder just *which* kind of value our intuitions are tracking.

Now, the eudaimonist might reply as follows: perhaps true belief has such a high degree of eudaimonic value that it effectively makes an otherwise miserable life much better. So it's not that what explains the intuition in our alternate experience machine case is the epistemic value of truth, but rather that the value of truth is eudaimonically *much greater* than we might have initially thought.

This reply is implausible because the possession of truth can be depressing and conducive to misery and angst. It might be that one's miserable life spent in reality is made worse by believing truths about it. There are also plausibly "eudaimonically worthless true beliefs," such as true beliefs about how many grains of sand there are in a sandbox or true beliefs about the number of people in the 1973 Düsseldorf phonebook with the letter 'm' in their name (Hazlett 2013, 141). Nevertheless, the suggestion is that truth would retain some *other* sort of value in any case: epistemic value.[23] Eudaimonically worthless true beliefs can have epistemic value.

If this argument works for truth, it should work for cognitive contact with reality as well. Indeed, Nozick highlights that "we desire connection to

---

[23] Importantly, if this argument succeeds, it wouldn't follow that epistemically good things— like true belief, knowledge, or conscious awareness of truth-makers—are especially good. Ernest Sosa has argued for this: that while there are distinctively epistemically good things, the epistemic goods are *just not that good.*

actuality" and this suggests that at least part of our desire not to plug into the experience machine is genuinely epistemic in a way that goes beyond true belief (Nozick 1989, 106). For we plausibly desire a connection with reality that goes beyond having our propositional attitudes fit reality. We also desire contact with the reality that our attitudes fit.[24] For example, imagine that the person in the experience machine tended to form general beliefs about reality such that there is an occasional match between the person's belief and the world. It could even be that this occasional match is no accident: perhaps one of the controllers can predict when the agent will believe that p and can ensure that p comes to pass in reality when such a prediction is made. This might include 'there are trees in most of the Amsterdam parks,' 'most of the bicycles in the world have two wheels,' or that 'the trains between Brussels and Amsterdam are cancelled,' and so on. These beliefs could all be true. Likewise, the agent might on occasion form more specific beliefs, such as that 'my sister just earned her degree in mathematics,' or 'my neighbor is walking his dog,' or 'the current President of the United States is giving a speech,' and these beliefs might all be true (cf., Littlejohn 2018, 55). From the epistemic point of view, would there be something more left over worth wanting? For the person in the experience machine—with all of their true beliefs or even occasional knowledge—might want to be aware of the truth-making events or states-of-affairs in the wider world.

Indeed, all that we need here to secure the response is a pair of cases in which the agent is made eudaimonically worse off in the first case but not the second case, and yet there is some intuitive epistemic asymmetry between them, such that, in the first case, there is some epistemic benefit not possessed in the second case. For example:

WAR SIGHT: Asha has just seen various innocent people shot to death by soldiers. As a result of her conscious perceptual experience of the shooting, she forms the true belief that the people there were shot to death (p). This

---

[24] Finally, one might think that all my response shows is that even truth only has eudaimonic value. For true belief is an epistemic state, but there it has no distinctive epistemic value. Its value is ultimately eudaimonic. Hazlett describes this position as follows: "to say that true belief has epistemic value is redundant: the eudaimonic value of true belief is 'epistemic' just because true belief is a species of belief, so 'epistemically valuable belief' is more perspicuously rendered 'valuable belief' or 'eudaimonically valuable belief'" (Hazlett 2013, 140). It would take us too far afield to adequately address this view in this chapter. See Zagzebski (1996) and (2004) for a defense of this position. If this view is true, it would in any case undercut the eudaimonist's explanatory challenge. For a state or property's epistemic value would simply reduce to its eudaimonic value; it's eudaimonic value would in this way be more basic than or even equivalent to its epistemic value.

true belief and the prior experience were painful and traumatizing, leaving Asha with flashbacks and PTSD which impedes her from living a good life.

WAR READING: Asha has just read a highly detailed and accurate investigative report about how various innocent people were shot to death by soldiers. As a result of reading this story, she forms the true belief that the people there were shot to death (p). However, she experiences no well-being reducing effects from reading that p.

In the second case, Asha learns that p by reading that p and her well-being doesn't fluctuate before and after—save whatever well-being promotion we are willing to grant learning that p is true generates by itself. In the first case, however, she learns that p as well and yet her well-being is clearly reduced. It is reduced in part *because* she learns that p in the way that she does. Intuitively, however, some further epistemic good is possessed in the first case but not the second case. Indeed, this is exactly what a situated epistemology should predict: her first-hand experience of the war counts epistemically for more than testimony about it. If the eudaimonic value view is correct, however, it's hard to make sense of this, unless of course the eudaimonic value of the target intellectual state is so vanishingly small that it's not only not noticeable by the agent but compatible with their well-being being so low as to make their life quite awful.

Another strategy for the eudaimonist is to follow Duncan Pritchard (2016) and argue that the special value that conscious perception has over second-hand epistemic sources such as testimony is that when one is motivated to find out whether p by perceiving that p, one manifests a desire to get to the truth for themselves. This exhibits one's intellectual autonomy, a paradigmatic intellectual virtue—a desire which might be absent if one also had the option to get reliable testimony about p and took that option instead. The idea here is to regard the success due to the manifestation of an intellectual virtue as finally valuable because it is an achievement and achievements have final value. In turn, this is what explains the intuitive difference in value between the first-hand perceptual and second-hand non-perceptual cases. Here's how Pritchard puts the point:

> ... strong achievements have a special value in virtue of the fact that they represent cases of one's agency acting, in some substantive way, on the world. As we might put the point: a life full of successes where these successes represent achievements on one's part is much more valuable

than an equivalent life where those same successes are all down to dumb luck [...]. Moreover, since strong achievements are clearly more valuable than mere achievements, better to have a life rich in strong achievements than a comparable life consisting only of mere achievements. There is thus at least a prima facie case for the idea that strong cognitive achievements are finally valuable.   (Pritchard 2016, 36)[25]

As Pritchard puts it, "a life full of successes." where the successes are achievements, is more valuable than one without them (Pritchard 2016, 36). This suggests that the kind of value that cognitive achievements have is eudaimonic value. Putting two and two together, the picture we end up with is this: when Mary sees the orange robes depicted on the ceiling of the Sistine Chapel—given that she had the option to remain in her monochromatic room and could have just as easily read the relevant truths out of an equally reliable book, say—she manifests her intellectual autonomy in seeking out that truth for herself. Her cognitive success, the true belief she goes on to form, is due to her perceptual skills and her intellectual virtues. As such, it accrues eudaimonic value in addition to the epistemic value it has by being a true belief.

Now suppose that what explains the extra value that is present in our perceptual cases compared with our non-perceptual cases is the presence of the relevant eudaimonic value and the fact that that value is grounded in the manifestation of the agent's intellectual virtues. I'm not claiming that this is Pritchard's (2016) argument, only that this is how one might expand it in order to respond to the special value problem. The presence of the success from virtue—and intellectual autonomy in particular—is the explanation of the difference in value between the relevant cases. If that's right, then a case in which (a) the relevant truth that p is believed on the basis of the agent's manifestation of their intellectual virtue, *and* cognitive contact is present, ought to be evaluated as the axiological equivalent of the case in which (b) the relevant truth that p is believed on the basis of one's manifestation of their intellectual virtue but cognitive contact is absent. After all, if the explanation of the added value is the presence of success due to intellectual

[25] Compare with Sosa: "We prefer truth whose presence is the work of our intellect, truth that derives from our own virtuous performance. We do not want just truth that is given to us by happenstance, or by some alien agency, where we are given a belief that hits the mark of truth *not* through our own performance, not through any accomplishment creditable to us" (Sosa 2003, 174).

virtue, then it should make no fundamental axiological difference—whether epistemic or eudaimonic—that cognitive contact is present or absent.

This is what I think we should be skeptical about. Here are cases where we can see this:

ACTIVE PERCEPTION: Mary is interested in seeing the frescoes on the ceiling of the Sistine Chapel. Her motivation is that she wants to get to the truth by her own intellectual efforts, so she goes to the Sistine Chapel, looks up and visually attends to the frescoes on the ceiling, forming the true belief that p as a result.

ACTIVE DEFERENCE: Mary is interested in seeing the frescoes on the ceiling of the Sistine Chapel, but unfortunately nobody is allowed to be there. There are two people who seem like experts on the art within the Sistine Chapel, as they have resumes which are nearly identical, but one of them is a fraud. Mary goes through the painstaking process of ruling out the fraud, identifies the expert, and trusts their testimony that p. She did this because she was motivated by her desire for getting to the truth by her own intellectual efforts, coming to believe that p as a result.

In both cases, Mary's success in believing that p seems to be primarily due to her skills and intellectual virtue.[26] In the first case, she manifested her desire for finding out whether p for herself by actively visually attending to the facts which make p true, motivated by her desire to get to the truth for herself, using her perceptual skills. In the second case, she manifested her desire for finding out whether p for herself by ruling out the fraud and trusting the expert, motivated by her desire to get to the truth for herself, using her intellectual skills. But clearly in the first (but not the second) case, she is in cognitive contact with the part of reality that p delineates. For believing that p on the basis of the testimony that p—whether it is fundamentally a success due to the manifestation of intellectual virtue or not—is paradigmatically *not* something which puts the agent in cognitive contact with the truth-

[26] You might worry that Mary's success is not the right kind of success. After all, if her goal was to see the frescoes for herself, but her attempt failed, intuitively she was *not* successful. To why this worry is misplaced, we need to appreciate that the relevant evaluations here are directed at her *beliefs*, not at her wider inquiry goals. So, the thought is that Mary is successful in both cases, because her belief *is true* in both cases. Importantly, her *true belief* (her success) is due to the manifestation of her intellectual virtue in both cases. In the perception case, but not the deference case, her manifestation of intellectual virtue is *also* a case of making cognitive contact with reality, and this is what I'm arguing is the difference-maker in value between the two cases. Thanks to Matt Duncan for raising this point.

maker for their belief that p. The two cases are not symmetrical in value. A plausible explanation of why this is, is that there is additional epistemic value added by getting cognitive contact with reality.

3. Deflationism about Cognitive Contact with Reality

Following Zagzebski (1996), suppose we thought of 'cognitive contact with reality' as just a basic epistemic determinable for which determinates like true belief or propositional knowledge of reality are instances.[27] On this view, 'cognitive contact with reality' is the determinable phrase for more determinate and successful mental states with mind-to-world direction of fit. For example, if the state of mind is satisfied by reality, or accurately represents reality, or expresses a true proposition about reality, then it is a case of cognitive contact with reality. On this account, then, perceptual experience and testimony can both yield cognitive contact with reality for the same reason: they can both yield true belief about reality.

This suggests a kind of deflationism about the value of cognitive contact with reality. If truth or propositional knowledge are themselves cases of cognitive contact with reality and knowledge or truth has final epistemic value, then the value of cognitive contact with reality could be reduced to the value of truth or propositional knowledge. This would have the effect that the special value problem is not a genuine problem.

This deflationary strategy could work if we thought of cognitive contact with reality as the epistemic determinable to which true belief about reality and propositional knowledge of reality are determinates. But we have an alternative. The alternative is that cognitive contact with reality is an epistemic value in its own right. Everything else being equal, we non-derivatively value being in contact with reality. We want to *observe* the results of our experiments and not only read about the results. We want to *see* the frescoes in the Sistine Chapel and not only listen to someone tell us about them. We value contact with reality for its own sake and not only

---

[27] This is the way I interpret Zagzebski (1996), but I don't want to defend this explicitly in the chapter. Here's one motivation, for example. She says that: "Although all intellectual virtues have a motivational component that aims at cognitive contact with reality, some of them may aim more at understanding, or perhaps at other epistemic states that enhance the quality of the knowing state, such as certainty, than at the possession of truth per se" (1996, 167). This suggests that cognitive contact with reality is a determinable and that knowledge and true belief are determinates. See also Zagzebski (2009).

because of the promise of truths about the tract of reality to which we are cognitively related.[28]

To see how the deflationary strategy works, consider true belief. Imagine that you have a true belief about reality. Perhaps it's the belief that there is a birch tree in the nearby park. Imagine that it's true. Why think this true belief about reality is a case of making cognitive contact with reality? One reason you might appeal to is that belief is a paradigmatically cognitive state, a state which aims at representing reality, and to say that the state makes 'cognitive contact' with reality is just a way of saying that the belief state accurately represents reality.

I think this kind of argument misses something crucial about the concept of cognitive contact with reality. Cognitive contact with reality is a contact-involving relation. It marks an essentially existence-entailing relation between the cognizer and reality, as something which implies the actual *existence* of the object cognized, but true belief does not do this any more than the satisfaction of a description marks an essentially existence-entailing relation between the description and its satisfier.[29] We don't want to say that

---

[28] Here, you might worry the reason why we value cognitive contact with reality is because it narrows the possibility of being misled in a way that testimony and reading do not. So, on this picture, valuing cognitive contact with reality is tied to the value of avoiding falsity and getting truth, which is the more fundamental value. I think this idea is initially plausible but ultimately untenable because it wouldn't explain why we should prefer seeing that p to trusting an infallible guru about whether p. It predicts that both ways of learning that p have equal epistemic value, because they both reduce the possibility of being misled to zero. Indeed, we can imagine that the guru is an excellent epistemic risk reducer concerning some object O. Suppose that for any truth that you might learn by visually exploring O, you could have just as easily asked the guru about it instead. In that case, we'd need to say that the first-hand source (i.e., conscious visual perception, a source which provides cognitive contact with reality), and the second-hand source (trusting the guru's testimony), are epistemically equally valuable, since the guru would reduce the possibility of being misled as much as your vision would, or even more. But, again, why not say that there's something valuable about *being* in cognitive contact with what makes your beliefs true, aside from reducing the risk of error in what you believe? I'm not denying that we might ordinarily value first-hand sources like perception over testimony because the former reduces the risk of being misled to a greater extent, but that this is not the *only* reason why we do; that this explanation doesn't fully account for why we value actually perceiving reality over being told about it. Thanks to Matt Duncan and Duncan Pritchard for pressing me on this point.

[29] Of course, some belief contents are existence-entailing with respect to the world. For example, self-referentially true beliefs, like 'I exist' entail that the believer exists. Likewise, beliefs with externally individuated contents, such as 'that's water' are existentially committal with respect to certain substances in the world, such as H_2O. My point is rather that it's not in the nature of belief-states generally that they entail the existence of what their contents are about. They generally do not respect the principle 'If I f that x is F at t, then there is x which is F at t for which I f.' Belief generally doesn't even *seem* to respect this sort of principle. By contrast, perceptual experience at least seems to respect this principle; where it goes awry are those cases

a sentence written on a wall, 'the birch trees in the park are young,' which is satisfied by some particular group of birch trees in the park, is an existence-entailing relation between the sentence inscribed on the wall and the birch trees. Now imagine that the same content that the sentence expresses is mentally represented. Why say that this is essentially an existence-entailing relation to some group of birch trees in the park? Why think the fact of being cognitively represented in some way (that the birch trees in the park are young) *and* its being satisfied (the fact that there are young birch trees in the park) is sufficient for the former being a case of cognition making contact with the latter? It is rather precisely a case of contact *not* being made. Here's another argument against the deflationary view. This argument tries to show that two people who have exactly the same true beliefs about reality and whose true beliefs were *caused* by the specific part of reality that their beliefs accurately represent, nevertheless can differ in some intuitively epistemic-axiological way (i.e., a way that matters for our thinking about epistemic value). To see this, consider yourself and a twin whose experiences and beliefs are all introspectively indiscriminable from your own and vice versa. The difference between you and them is the following: what the early twentieth-century sense-datum theorists' thought was true about the mind generally is true quite specifically of your twin's mind. So, imagine someone for whom the sense-datum theory is true.[30] If we are to believe contemporary philosophers of mind, your imagined twin has a mind which is presumably quite unlike your mind in this respect. When they see their cat, for example, and their cat is thereby the cause of their visual experience as of their cat, they are thereby immediately aware of a *sense-datum*, they are immediately aware of the cat$_{SD}$, which is an object in its own right, metaphysically distinct from their cat. What they consciously visually attend to *is* the sense-datum. As they pet their cat, they experience not the cat's warmth and soft fur but a soft fur- and warmth-sense-datum. Nevertheless, they form all the same beliefs that you do and they have experiences which are introspectively indiscriminable from your own. If you believe *my cat's fur is*

---

where we think perception isn't working properly, such as hallucination. It's not in the *nature* of belief to be a contact-involving state between believer and believed.

[30] To be clear, I'm not claiming that the sense datum theory is true. The thought experiment begins by asking that you *imagine* that your twin's perceptual psychology is exactly as the sense datum theorist says it is, and to compare intuitions about your twin's perception of reality so understood with your own, whereby when you conceive of your own situation you are not thereby conceiving of the sense datum theory as being true of your experience.

really soft, so, too, your twin believes it. If it visually seems to you that some object has some property, and you form a true belief on that basis, then it visually seems to your twin that the object has the relevant property, and they, too, form a true belief on this basis as well.

From a purely epistemic point of view, why prefer your situation to your twin's situation? It cannot be because they don't have *true beliefs* or even *knowledge* about the environment while you do. For they plausibly have that too. After all, on the basis of undergoing an experience in which they are presented with, say, their cat's sense-datum or a soft-and-warm sense-datum, their cat and its properties are typically the cause of that type of experience and they wouldn't easily falsely believe *that's my cat* or *my cat's fur is soft* without their cat really being there and its fur really being soft. That is, suppose that whatever modal connection there is between your experiences and your beliefs, as well as your beliefs and reality, whether this is understood in terms of *safety* (i.e., you wouldn't easily be wrong believing as you do), *sensitivity* (i.e., if your cat's fur weren't soft, then you wouldn't believe that your cat's fur is soft), or *reliability* (i.e., typically when you form a belief about your cat's fur, out of the fairly limited range of beliefs you form about your cat's fur, your beliefs tend to be true), the same type of modal connection holds for their experiences and their beliefs as well as for their beliefs and reality.[31] We can imagine that you and your twin, in addition to having the same true beliefs, are *modally similar* in this respect.

Here's what seems to follow from this case: if, from a purely epistemic point of view, all that really matters is truth or propositional knowledge, then there would be no epistemic reason to pick one situation over the other. An ideal epistemologist might simply flip a coin. Nevertheless, it intuitively seems like you would be missing out on something *fundamentally epistemically good* by opting for your twin's situation. You would in effect be closing yourself off cognitively from the world, resolving to mere external impingements which cause you to have the right sort of purely inner sensations that are modally connected to reality in the right way. It would be a situation

---

[31] For ease of exposition, I omitted other factors which might be thought to be necessary too. For example, perhaps your twin is *motivated to get the truth* when they form their belief on the basis of their sense experience, so understood, as virtue theorists might maintain. Or perhaps your twin needs to appreciate, by reflecting on the matter, that forming the particular belief they have about their cat, as a result of their experience (i.e., as a mental event in which they are presented with sense data), is a good reason to believe what they do, as the internalist might maintain. It might even be that this faculty is functioning properly in accordance with its *telos*. These additions, I submit, do not change the outcome of what I think the central thought experiment shows us.

which is similar to the person who lives in a room with only video and pictures on their phone as their 'window' onto the world. To see this, imagine that they are presented with a stream of video and pictures on the phone for every event they might have partaken in had they left their room, as if it were a front row seat to a movie. If the person were given a choice between engaging with the world and actively partaking in those events as opposed to staying at home and passively watching the very same events unfold on their screens, we would rightly criticize their indifference about not being engaged with reality. The justifiability of this criticism seems to rest on the idea that they are disengaged with the world by witnessing it from only behind a screen as they do. They are, in effect, only in contact with their screens. It would manifest a real apathy for cognitive engagement with reality and this seems to be an intellectual vice precisely because (but not necessarily only because) it obstructs their cognitive contact with reality.

4. The More-Information View

Consider the following idea. When you see that p, more information than only that p is conveyed to you. For example, when you see the ceiling of the Sistine Chapel, although the fact that many people are wearing orange robes is conveyed to you—it is something you come to know on the basis of undergoing that visual experience—much more determinate information about the scene is conveyed to you as well. You also pick up information about the particular shade of their orange robes, as well as the relative size, position, and distance of the people depicted on the ceiling. Of course, you could have come to know that p by a reliable person's testimony as well but the additional determinate information you picked up by visually attending to the scene for yourself would not have been available to you. According to the **more-information view**, what makes the condition of the person who sees the ceiling of the Sistine Chapel for herself and thereby learns that *pceteris paribus* more epistemically valuable than the condition of the person who is told that p by a reliable testifier, is that the condition of the former is *informationally richer* than the latter. It is the additional information that accompanies one's corresponding true belief that p which accounts for the difference in epistemic value.

Information can be encoded *analogically* or *digitally*. Information is encoded analogically when it is represented densely or continuously, whereas information is encoded digitally when it is represented discretely.

For example, the speedometer on a car is an analog representation of the car's speed because it is continuously updating the car's variable speed. Indeed, between each number on the speedometer, there is some specific number (not shown) which would give the driver more specific information about the car's speed, whereas the oil pressure light is digital because the oil pressure is represented discretely—*on* (pressure is low) and *off* (pressure is adequate)—and is neither constantly fluctuating nor are there more specific states in between *on* and *off* that might be represented by the light. More specifically:

> A signal ... carries the information that *s* is *F* in digital form if and only if the signal carries no additional information about *s*, no information that is not already nested in *s*'s being *F*. (Dretske 1981, 137)

Otherwise it carries the information that *s* is *F* in analog form. In particular, "the signal always carries more specific, more determinate, information about *s* than that it is *F*" when it is carried in analog form (Dretske 1981, 137).[32]

Perception seems to encode information analogically (Dretske 1981, Evans 1982, Peacocke 1986). For example, suppose you are wandering through the Mauritshuis, wondering what Vermeer's *Girl with a Pearl Earring* looks like. Your friend tells you that the girl is wearing a blue turban (*p*) and that she is facing the viewer by being turned slightly left (*q*). This is digital information. You later find the painting in the museum and visually attend to it. Much more information than just *p* and *q* is made available to you here. Information about magnitudes as well as much more specific information about the colors are also made available; information that is best represented as indefinite values on a continuum (e.g., the particular shade *n* of the girl's blue turban along the blue color-spectrum). This sort of information was conveyed to you visually. Of course, this information can be transmitted via testimony as well—perhaps a more specific description of the painting would have been sufficient. Nevertheless, there would have been some further information that was left unavailable, to which more descriptive testimony would be necessary. The point here is that if one sees that *p* and *q*, there is richer and more specific information nested in *p* and *q* than would be available if one were only told that *p* and *q*. Upon being told that *p* and *q*, you might wonder whether the girl is just glancing over her shoulders

---

[32] There is some controversy surrounding exactly how to distinguish analog from digital representation. See Beck (2018), Kulvicki (2015), and Maley (2011).

or whether her body is turned slightly left as well. However, if you had seen *Girl with a Pearl Earring* this information would have been supplied to you. The picture would have conveyed just *how* bright her face is, *which* shade of blue her turban is, and *how much* she is turned to face the viewer. There would have been, additionally, much more information for you to pick up than you might have been initially wondering about. This is the analog information the visual experience made available to you.

How does the additional, analog information made available to one in cases of perception help the T-monist? The proponent of T-monism will make use of the more-information account as follows. If perceptual experience encodes information analogically, then the visual experience one has when one sees that *p* (e.g., when one sees that *many* (depicted) *people are wearing orange robes*) contains much more information than the digital representation that *p*. You could not *just* see people wearing orange robes when you see that people are wearing orange robes; you would also see the relative size and distances of those depicted people, the particular shade of orange, and so on. In this fashion, *more truths* are (unavoidably) made available to you. Being told that *p*, however, doesn't nest this amount (or kind) of information. One could read that *p* or be told that *p* and, in this way, come to know that *p* without getting access to the analog information that is nested in *p* that is made available when one sees that *p*. In this way, your perceptual experience that *p* is not only a reliable indicator that *p*, but your perceptual experience that *p promotes truth* in that it gives you access to the analog information—$p_1, p_2, p_3, \ldots$—nested in *p*. The basic explanation, then, is that even if perceptual experience and testimony are equally truth-reliable, perceptual experience is a better *truth-promoter* than testimony and in this way is epistemically better than testimony, consistently with T-monism. Call this the **truth-promotion argument**.

One problem with utilizing the more-information view in this way is that one could in principle pick up all of the information about the relevant scene in digital, propositional form. Indeed, Dretske is explicit about this point. He says:

> A sentence expressing *all* the information a signal carries will be a sentence expressing the information the signal carries in digital form (since this will be the most specific, most determinate, piece of information the signal carries). This is true of pictures as well as analog representations. The information a picture carries in digital form can be rendered only by some enormously complex sentence, a sentence that describes every detail of the situation about which the picture carries information.   (Dretske 1981, 138)

Assume that what Dretske says here is possible. If so, then we can imagine a kind of super-testifier who is such that, for any analog information N nested in p that would be made available to one when one sees that p, the super-testifier not only makes p but also N available to the listener in digital form. For example, compare:

SISTINE CHAPEL C: Mary has listened to the super-testifier who tells her a long, highly descriptive list of truths about the color of the robes of the people depicted on the ceiling of the Sistine Chapel, such that for any analog information N encoded in p, the super-testifier makes available to her the digital conversions of N, p_1, p_2, ... As a result, Mary comes to believe these truths on the basis of the person's testimony.

SISTINE CHAPEL D: Mary*, who listened to the super-testifier who tells her a long, highly descriptive list of truths about the color of the robes of the people depicted on the ceiling of the Sistine Chapel, such that for any analog information N encoded in p, the super-testifier makes available to her the digital conversions of N, p_1, p_2,... . However, unlike Mary, she has left her room and has now become consciously aware of the facts which makes p, p_1, p_2, ... true by way of the fact that she consciously sees that p and likewise truly believes these truths on the basis of her perceptual experience.

Here's the problem. The proponent of epistemic T-monism would need to say that there is total epistemic parity between Mary and Mary* in this case. Intuitively, however, we might think that Mary* is in possession of some further epistemic good that Mary lacks—cognitive contact with the part of reality which make her beliefs true. For the things that her true beliefs are about are *right there* before her mind, as it were: the relevant things that her true beliefs are about are presented to her. But in this case, there is no difference in the relative truth-promotion of their respective belief-forming bases. So the more-information account wouldn't help the T-monist address the intuitive epistemic disparity between Mary and Mary*.

4.1 More-Information *Simpliciter*

One might think that the more-information account has the resources to explain the epistemic disparity between Mary and Mary*, and thus the testimony and perception cases properly understood, without relying on the idea that perception is a better truth-promoter than testimony. Rather, the key insight behind the more-information account is that perceptual experience picks up analog information about one's perceived environment and this *additional kind of information*, irrespective of the additional truths it might ordinarily make available to one, is itself the further epistemic good that perception provides over testimony.

To see this explanation in action, let's reconsider the Sistine Chapel cases. Mary* stands before the ceiling of the Sistine Chapel and sees for herself that that p whereas Mary is told that p by a reliable testifier. As a result, both Mary and Mary* know that p but Mary* intuitively seems to have some further epistemic good that Mary lacks. What is it? According to the more-information view, this further epistemic good is the more determinate information nested in the proposition that p which perceptual experience makes available to her. The information that is visually conveyed is necessarily more specific. The testimony that p, as it were, "throws away" the more specific determinate information that the visual experience of the scene conveys (Dretske 1981, 141). So we might say that this more specific information is the additional epistemic good that the perceptual experience that p provides over the testimony that p.

Is more information all that there is to the story? It's important to recognize that while the more-information and the cognitive contact accounts have a common implication—namely, that when we see that p, we pick up more specific information on the things that p is about than we would pick up were our true belief that p formed by testimony—they nevertheless fail to have another important implication in common. For we might think that, aside from the epistemic goodness of getting more information *simpliciter*, it is epistemically good to be consciously aware of the facts that our true beliefs delineate. To be sure, the more-information account doesn't rule this out. It doesn't say that the cognitive contact with reality that perception provides is not an epistemic good. It just tries to account for the epistemic disparity intuition in terms of the fact that much more information is made available to the agent in the perception cases compared to the testimony cases.

So in order to help bolster the cognitive contact account let's imagine the following scenario. First, imagine that the sense-datum theory is true of you but not true of an (otherwise psychological) twin of you. When you see that, say, a goldfinch is sitting on a chestnut tree, the goldfinch on the tree causes you to become visually aware of a goldfinch sense-datum. We can imagine that the relation between you and your experience (e.g., your awareness of the sense-datum) as well as your experience and the world is modally stable in the sense that in nearby worlds in which you become aware of a goldfinch sense-datum,[33] there is a goldfinch which distally causes you to be in that mental state. Not easily would you have that experience and there not really *be* a goldfinch perched on a chestnut tree. In epistemic terms, not easily would you believe that there is a goldfinch perched on a chestnut tree on the basis of your immediate awareness of a goldfinch perched on a chestnut tree sense-datum and yet your belief is false.

The next step is to compare you and your twin in the following way. Imagine that your twin also sees the goldfinch on the chestnut tree. But instead of becoming immediately aware of a goldfinch sense-datum, as you do, their visual experience includes the goldfinch as a part. Like you, they form the belief that the goldfinch is perched on a chestnut tree, and their belief, like your own, is true. But unlike you, what their true belief is about is congruent with what they immediately experience in a particular way. For what they are consciously aware of at that time—the goldfinch perched on a chestnut tree—is the same as what their true belief is about: the goldfinch perched on the chestnut tree. There is a certain type of incongruency between your experience- and your belief-state, however. What your perceptually-based true belief is about is the goldfinch perched on the chestnut tree and yet what you are immediately visually aware of is something else. It is the goldfinch sense-datum.

The third step is to register that you and your twin's experiences are just as informationally rich as the other. There is no informational loss when your twin sees and thereby becomes immediately visually aware of the goldfinch than when you see the goldfinch and thereby become immediately visually aware of the goldfinch sense-datum. But intuitively you are at an epistemic disadvantage here. When you see a goldfinch perched on the branch of the chestnut tree, you are immediately consciously aware of a goldfinch sense-datum. *That* is the object that your experience relates you to. If an evil demon were to stimulate your brain in exactly the same way as the goldfinch does, then you would have exactly the same experience in the absence of the goldfinch (on this view). For in both cases what you consciously, visually attend to is the relevant mental entity—namely, the goldfinch sense-datum. This seems to 'get in the way' of your sensory awareness of the flesh (feathered) and blood goldfinch, even though it doesn't impede your ability to know or form true beliefs about it. There is no informational

---

[33] I am using 'aware' here in a *de re* sense. One is consciously aware of the blossoming-cherry-tree sense-datum, not necessarily *as* a sense-datum or *that it is* a sense-datum.

loss here and so the more-information account ought to predict an epistemic parity between you and your twin.

It is important to see that the key point here doesn't depend on which theory of sensory experience we are working with. After all, whether it is a sense-datum view, a representationalist view, or a naïve realist view, they can all say that the analog state carries all of the information from its variable source before being converted into digital form (see Dretske 1981, 149). It's just that these theories of experience will disagree about the nature of the analog state. For the sense-datum theorist, its nature consists in the presence of sense data that one is immediately aware of. For the representationalist, it is that one is in a state which represents the world as being some way. For the naïve realist, it is the presence of the macro-physical objects (or properties, events, or states-of-affairs) that enter into one's experience as constituent parts, facilitating one's immediate awareness of them. In this way, each picture is compatible with the idea that you and your twin's analog states are just as informationally rich, determinate, and specific as the other. The more-information view thereby predicts:

ANALOGICAL SIMILARITY: each of you has experiential states of mind which are no less informationally rich than the other.

Coupled with the epistemic value claim embedded within the more-information view, that analog states are informationally richer, more determinate, and more specific than their corresponding digital states, and that this is why they are *ceteris paribus* epistemically more valuable, it follows that:

AXIOLOGICAL DIFFERENCE: you and your experience twin's conditions—e.g., the conditions in which you all form true beliefs as a result of undergoing certain experiences—contain more epistemic value than you and your testimony twin's condition.

This is because, in addition to each of you having the same digital states with the same amount of epistemic value—namely, true beliefs about the very same state-of-affairs—you and your experience-twin but not your testimony-twin have more information conveyed to each of you. It is information which is connected with the very state-of-affairs your true belief is about and in this way there is a congruity between your analogical states (your experiences), your digital states (your beliefs), and the world. Your testimony-twin misses out on this additional information that you and your experience-twin pick up.

Nevertheless, the problem is that there seems to be some value not only in having the relevant part of reality—with all of the analog information it conveys—as part of the causal explanation of your getting a true belief but also in being consciously aware of the causes of your true belief. We epistemically desire not only picking up more information (which might or might not be causally connected to reality in the right way) but in actively being aware of the part of reality that our true beliefs are about. Consider, for example, Johnston on this point:

> The acquaintance with external features which vision seems to provide is something we have reason to value.... My pleasure in seeing color is not simply the pleasure of undergoing certain sensory experiences, it is also the pleasure of having access by sight to the natures of the colors and hence access to part of the nature of colored things.   (Johnston 1996, 189)

What Johnston is drawing our attention to here is relevant for our assessment of the more-information view. If we compare a case in which a person simply undergoes certain experiences, say they vividly hallucinate that the tomato sitting on the table is in front of them, and there is a tomato sitting on the table in front of them, forming the true belief that the tomato is in front of them as a result, the proponent of the more-information view would have no principled reason for saying that this was any *less* epistemically valuable of a condition than seeing the tomato sitting on the table and forming the corresponding true belief on that basis. For there isn't any loss of analog information between these two cases and thus no epistemic disparity. As Johnston points out, however, there is "epistemic pleasure in seeing" as opposed to *simply* undergoing visual experiences (Johnston 1996, 189). In order to account for this we need to move away from the more-information account and look elsewhere.

Indeed, this point sets up the proponent of the more-information view with a dilemma. If it's not simply the availability of analog information that makes the perceptual case *ceteris paribus* more epistemically valuable than the testimony case, but rather that the available analog information be appropriately connected to the part of reality that one's true belief is about—something lacking in our hallucination case above—then the more-information view is not substantially different from the cognitive contact account. After all, the explanatory work would be done by the fact that what carries the relevant analog information is one's experience of the part of reality that one's corresponding true belief is about. It would be a distinction which lacked any substantive difference. But if instead it is simply the availability of analog information that makes the perceptual case *ceteris paribus* more epistemically valuable than the testimony case, it's not so clear why the availability of analog information alone really is *epistemically* better. Why think that simply having rich sensory analog information conveyed to you, whatever its variable source, has any epistemic value?[34] Rather, what matters to us is that the analog information be part of the information encoded in the world that our true beliefs are about, rather than *simply* being another kind of information to experience, whatever its source. If simply having experiences which convey analog information is what mattered here, it would make the more-information view just another way of motivating the eudaimonia view, since it's hard to see what epistemic value such states might have all on their own, even if it's easy to see that they might promote our well-being.

5. Cognitive Contact is a Distinctive Fundamental Epistemic Value

I have been arguing that there is an intuitive asymmetry in the epistemic value between cases where an agent truly believes that *p* on the basis of their conscious perception of the relevant truth-makers for their belief that *p* (or more weakly: the relevant objects, properties, or states-of-affairs that their true beliefs are about) and the agent who truly believes that *p* on the basis of testimony or deference to authority, where both of these epistemic bases are taken to be equally truth-reliable. My hypothesis is that the explanation of the difference in epistemic value between the cases is that in the first-hand but not the second-hand cases the agent's epistemic basis for her belief that *p* puts her in cognitive contact with reality—e.g., the part of reality that her true belief that *p* delineates—which seems non-derivatively epistemically valuable. In short: perception gives one an additional epistemic good that doesn't seem to be available in cases of testimony.

---

[34] Compare Lynch (2004, 17) on the brain-in-a-vat case. In this case, we would have a rich array of analog information made available to us, but intuitively our epistemic desires in such a case would be unmet.

This should raise eyebrows and make us ask: why care about making cognitive contact with reality and not just getting truths about it? I think the value we place on contact with reality is more basic than truth or true belief about reality. One reason is that we value having actual contact with reality and not just having information about it. Here's a way to illustrate the problem. Imagine a world in which we are all Philalethians. We all love truth. But suppose that we only care about reality derivatively: truth is what really matters, and reality or being in contact with reality matters to us inasmuch as it is related to truth or gets us to truth. If, as a proper Philalethian, what I really care about is *truth* and having *true beliefs*, then it's enough that I try my best to change reality to fit my beliefs if I could do so. This properly manifests my love of truth. After all, this will make my beliefs *true* and since I only care about *that*, prima facie I should do everything I can to get it. If the best way of doing that is making the world match my beliefs then that's what I ought to do as a lover of truth. We can imagine that the Philalethians are like Olympic gods that, quite egocentrically, find themselves with beliefs that they later shape reality to match.

It's hard to miss the problem with the Philalethians: they have it backwards. Reality is what really matters and truth matters to us because that our beliefs are true entails that we have represented reality as it is. In this way, reality is what really matters; truth matters derivatively. Intuitively, not only do the epistemically virtuous have a **love of truth**, but they have a **love of contact with reality**, and merely having truths (having true beliefs), or even knowledgeable belief (having stable, non-lucky true beliefs), isn't enough, as we have seen, for being in cognitive contact with reality. When these two basic intellectual virtues are integrated it is easy to see what's so absurd about our Philalethians. They put truth first rather than reality, but it should be the other way around.

Indeed, the idea that cognitive contact with reality has final epistemic value helps to explain why we should care about truth. To help see this, suppose that truth is not a property that a belief gets when it fits reality in the right way—whether we understand this fittingness in terms of correspondence, satisfaction, identity, or structural isomorphism. That is, suppose that it is a property that a belief gets when it is what a rational person would believe in the ideal limits of rational inquiry *simpliciter*, or that it is verifiability *simpliciter*, or that it is coherence with the rest of your beliefs *simpliciter*. If that's right, truth would not essentially be a kind of fittingness with reality. Reality as such would drop out of the picture. Truth would matter to us *only* as much as what we would believe in the ideal limits of rational inquiry would matter to us. Or truth would matter to us *only* as much as what was verified matters to us, or *only* as much as cohering with everything we believe matters to us. I say: that doesn't really capture why truth matters to us. Truth matters to us precisely because (but not only because) reality matters to us: this is why it matters to us that the way that we represent reality as being fits with reality. We don't want to be out of touch with reality. The proponent of the epistemic value of cognitive contact adds to this story as follows. Not only do we not want to be *out of touch* with reality but we also want to be *in touch* with reality and truth by itself doesn't give us that. Suppose you have mostly true beliefs about a certain tract of reality—say, the Himalayas—but you formed these beliefs in a sensory deprivation tank on the other side of the world. For you've never even been to the Himalayas. From an epistemic point of view, you are certainly not out of touch with this part of reality—that's what all your true beliefs make clear. But, equally so, you are certainly not in touch with reality either. For you haven't made cognitive contact with reality yet.

6. Conclusion

Epistemological orthodoxy takes truth to be the fundamental epistemic good. In this chapter, I've introduced the special epistemic value problem and I've argued that it poses a serious challenge to the idea that truth is the fundamental epistemic good (epistemic T-monism). I have explored several different ways for the epistemic T-monist to sidestep this problem, but I argued that they all fail or face serious challenges of their own. In light of this, the special epistemic value problem persists. One option is to opt for the rejection of epistemic T-monism and that is the option I have recommended in this chapter. In particular, I've argued that first-hand conscious perception not only can give one true belief and propositional knowledge about reality but an additional epistemic good, which is cognitive contact with reality.[35]

[35] I would like to especially thank Matt Duncan, Uriah Kriegal, Duncan Pritchard, and Jeroen de Ridder for their detailed and helpful comments on earlier versions of this chapter. I would also like to thank Catarina Dutilh Novaes, René van Woudenberg, and members of the theoretical philosophy research group at VU Amsterdam for helpful discussion on an earlier draft.

References

Ahlstrom-Vij, Kristoffer (2013). In Defense of Veritistic Value Monism. *Pacific Philosophical Quarterly* 94 (1): 19–40.

Allen, Keith (2011). Revelation and the Nature of Colour. *Dialectica* 65 (2): 153–76.

Allen, Keith (2019). The Value of Perception. *Philosophy and Phenomenological Research*, doi: 10.1111/phpr.12574.

Alston, William P. (2005). *Beyond "Justification": Dimensions of Epistemic Evaluation*. Cornell University Press.

Alston, William P. (1985). Concepts of Epistemic Justification. *The Monist* 68 (2): 57–89.

Baehr, Jason (2011). *The Inquiring Mind: On Intellectual Virtues and Virtue Epistemology*. Oxford University Press.

Beck, Jacob (2018). Analog Mental Representation. *WIREs Cognitive Science* 9 (6): e1479.

Besser-Jones, Lorraine (2015). Eudaimonism. In Guy Fletcher (ed.), *The Routledge Handbook of Philosophy of Well-Being*, 187–94. Routledge.

Bonjour, Laurence (1985). The Structure of Empirical Knowledge. Harvard University Press.

Byrne, Alex (2010). Recollection, Perception, Imagination. *Philosophical Studies* 148: 15–26.

Byrne, Alex (2016). The Epistemic Significance of Experience. *Philosophical Studies* 173 (4): 947–67.

Byrne, Alex and Hilbert, David R. (2007). Color Primitivism. *Erkenntnis* 66 (1–2): 73–105.

Campbell, John (2009). Reference and Consciousness. In Ansgar Beckermann, Brian P. McLaughlin, and Sven Walter (eds.), *The Oxford Handbook of Philosophy of Mind*, 648–662. Oxford University Press.

Campbell, John and Cassam, Quassim (2014). *Berkeley's Puzzle: What Does Experience Teach Us?* Oxford University Press.

Conee, Earl (1994). Phenomenal Knowledge. *Australasian Journal of Philosophy* 72 (2): 136–50.

Chudnoff, Elijah (2013). Awareness of Abstract Objects. *Noûs* 47 (4): 706–26.

Dretske, Fred (1981). *Knowledge and the Flow of Information*. MIT Press.

Duncan, Matt (2020). Knowledge of Things. *Synthese* 197 (8): 3559–92.

Evans, Gareth (1982). *The Varieties of Reference*. Oxford University Press.

Goldman, Alvin (1999). *Knowledge in a Social World*. Oxford University Press.

Goldman, Alvin I. and Erik J. Olsson (2009). Reliabilism and the Value of Knowledge. In Adrian Haddock, Alan Millar, and Duncan H. Pritchard (eds.), *Epistemic Value*, 19–41. Oxford University Press.

Hazlett, Allen (2013). *A Luxury of the Understanding: On the Value of True Belief*. Oxford University Press.

Hazlett, Allen (2015). Epistemic Goods. In Guy Fletcher (ed.) *The Routledge Handbook of Philosophy of Well-Being*, 259–270. Routledge.

Jackson, Frank (1982). Epiphenomenal Qualia. *Philosophical Quarterly* 32 (127): 127–36.

Johnston, Mark (1992). How to Speak of the Colors. *Philosophical Studies* 68 (3): 221–63.

Johnston, Mark (1996). Is the External World Invisible? *Philosophical Issues* 7: 185–98.

Knowles, Jonathan and Thomas Raleigh (eds.) (2019). *Acquaintance: New Essays*. Oxford University Press.

Kulvicki, John (2015). Analog Representation and the Parts Principle. *Review of Philosophy and Psychology* 6 (1): 165–80.

Kvanvig, Jonathan (2005). Truth is Not the Primary Epistemic Goal. In Matthias Steup and Ernest Sosa (eds.), *Contemporary Debates in Epistemology*, 285–95. Blackwell.

Littlejohn, Clayton (2018). The Right in the Good: A Defense of Teleological Non-Consequentialism in Epistemology. In Kristoffer Ahlstrom-Vij and Jeff Dunn (eds.), *Epistemic Consequentialism*, ch. 1. Oxford University Press.

Lynch, Michael (2004). *True to Life*. MIT Press.

Maley, Corey J. (2011). Analog and Digital, Continuous and Discrete. *Philosophical Studies* 155 (1): 117–31.

Martin, Michael G.F. (2001). Out of the Past: Episodic Recall as Retained Acquaintance. In C. Hoerl and T. McCormack (eds.), *Time and Memory*, ch. 10. Oxford University Press.

Martin, Michael G.F. (2006). On Being Alienated. In Tamar S. Gendler and John Hawthorne (eds.), *Perceptual Experience*, 354–410. Oxford University Press.

Millar, Alan (2007). What the Disjunctivist is Right About. *Philosophy and Phenomenological Research* 74 (1): 176–99.

Nozick, Robert (1974). *Anarchy, State, and Utopia*. Basic Books.

Nozick, Robert (1989). *Examined Life: Philosophical Meditations*. Simon & Schuster.

Nudds, Matthew (2015). Auditory Appearances. In James Stazicker (ed.), *The Structure of Perceptual Experience*, 103–24. Wiley-Blackwell.

Paul, L.A. (2014). *Transformative Experience*. Oxford University Press.

Peacocke, Christopher (1986). Analogue Content. *Proceedings of the Aristotelian Society* 60: 1–17.

Pritchard, Duncan (2014). Truth as the Fundamental Epistemic Good. In Jonathan Matheson and Rico Vitz (eds.), *The Ethics of Belief*, 112–29. Oxford University Press.

Pritchard, Duncan (2016). Seeing it for Oneself: Perceptual Knowledge, Understanding, and Intellectual Autonomy. *Episteme* 13 (1): 29–42.

Putnam, Hilary (1994). Sense, Nonsense, and the Senses: An Inquiry into the Powers of the Human Mind. *Journal of Philosophy* 91(9): 445–517.

Russell, Bertrand (1912) [2001]. *The Problems of Philosophy*, 2nd edition with an introduction by John Skorupski. Oxford University Press.

Russell, Bertrand (1911). Knowledge by Acquaintance and Knowledge by Description. *Proceedings of the Aristotelian Society* 11 (1): 108–28.

Siegel, Susanna and Nicholas Silins (2015). The Epistemology of Perception. In M. Matthen (ed.), *The Oxford Handbook of the Philosophy of Perception*, 781–811. Oxford University Press.

Sosa, Ernest (2003). The Place of Truth in Epistemology. In Michael De Paul and Linda Zagzebski (eds.), *Intellectual Virtue: Perspectives from Ethics and Epistemology*, 155–180. Oxford University Press.

Zagzebski, Linda (1996). *Virtues of the Mind: An Inquiry into the Nature of Virtue and the Ethical Foundations of Knowledge*. Cambridge University Press.

Zagzebski, Linda (2004). The Search for the Source of Epistemic Good. *Metaphilosophy* 34 (1–2): 12–28.

Zagzebski, Linda (2009). *On Epistemology*. Wadsworth.

II
PHYSICALISM AND NATURALISM

7

Ground Functionalism

Jonathan Schaffer

Back when the world was young—in the 1960s and 1970s—a hopeful story was told about the metaphysics of the mind, which went something like this. For hundreds of years, we philosophers were held spellbound by Descartes's spooky dualism. Ryle and the behaviorists then freed us from dualism but omitted inner mental life. Place, Smart, and the identity theorists then found room for inner mental life but missed multiple realizability. And finally Putnam, Armstrong, Lewis, Fodor, and the functionalists forged a grand synthesis that reconciled materialism, inner mental life, and multiple realizability, and all was well with the world (or at least with the place of the mind within it). We could rest content with materialism, and move on to consider how connectionism would explain cognition and information theory would naturalize content.

Alas, this hopeful story has aged poorly (in many ways). For objections soon arose against functionalism, including Block's objection from overgeneration and Kim's objection from causal potency. But perhaps the most damaging objection, from Kripke, Levine, and Chalmers, was that functionalism—and indeed all materialist-friendly views—could not explain conscious experience but rather fell into an explanatory gap. This objection remains "the main obstacle to acceptance of materialism" (Levine 2001: 76; see also Gertler 2001: 689), making many contemporary metaphysicians of mind return to dualism, or embrace options such as Leibnizian panpsychism or Russellian monism, all of which take phenomenal (or proto-phenomenal) properties to be fundamental ingredients in nature. According to the new tragic story about the metaphysics of the mind, from dualism we came and to dualism we shall return.

I have the bold ambition of reviving the hopeful materialist story, by adding a new chapter—*ground functionalism*—which integrates functionalist insights about the mind with ground-theoretic insights about explanation. The ground functionalist posits a *mind making* principle linking material states to mental states via functional role, such that a properly

Jonathan Schaffer, *Ground Functionalism* In: *Oxford Studies in Philosophy of Mind Volume 1*. Edited by: Uriah Kriegel, Oxford University Press (2021). © Jonathan Schaffer. DOI: 10.1093/oso/9780198845850.003.0007

choreographed system dances out a mind. I argue that ground functionalism preserves the insights of functionalism, while enabling a viable explanation for consciousness.

1. Metaphysical Explanation

Lawyers say that hard cases make bad law. Since I am after a viable explanation for the hard case of consciousness, I propose to first consider how metaphysical explanation works in some easier cases, in order to trace an explanatory template (applied to consciousness in Section 2). On this template, there is a viable form of metaphysical explanation linked by grounding principles, aptly modeled by structural equations, and justifiably posited when explanatorily fruitful.

1.1 Four Examples

In order to trace a template for metaphysical explanation, I offer four starting point examples, drawn from set theory, mereology, metaethics, and quantum mechanics. Each example involves controversial assumptions, but the assumptions are not at issue. Rather what is at issue are the explanations they would enable. So, for instance, even if you do not believe in sets, you can still consider what explanations set theory would enable. Call an explanation *viable* when it is successful given its background assumptions. I claim that each example displays a viable metaphysical explanation *linked by a grounding principle*.

So, starting with the example drawn from set theory, consider the relationship between Socrates and {Socrates}, the set whose one and only member is Socrates. I assume that {Socrates} is built out of Socrates by the principle of set formation (or set making). We can think of set formation as a machine that clamps things into sets. For every plurality of inputs one feeds into this machine, one gets out a set with all and only those inputs as members. So if one feeds Socrates into this machine, one gets out {Socrates} (Figure 7.1):[1]

---

[1] Strictly speaking, this is a derivative principle describing the operation of hierarchical set formation *at a stage*. Hierarchical set formation is *recursive*, in that the outputs at any given stage loop back into the mouth of the machine to serve as added inputs at the next stage. So if we start with Socrates at stage 0, then we get {Socrates} born at stage 1, {{Socrates}} born at stage 2, etc. Note that, although I am only concerned with a single stage of set formation in the main

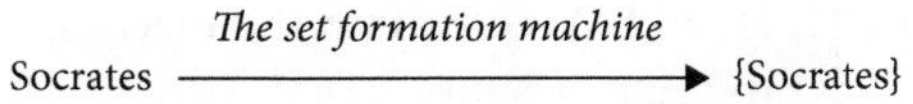

The set formation machine
Socrates ─────────────────────────▶ {Socrates}

Figure 7.1

My first claim about this example is that there is a viable metaphysical explanation for why {Socrates} exists, from the existence of Socrates, via the principle of set formation. After all, given that Socrates exists and set formation is at work, it is no mere accident that {Socrates} exists too. For there is a grounding principle: set formation, which clamps every plurality of inputs into a so-membered set (never mind how set formation came to operate—we are just assuming it is at work). And there is an input: Socrates (never mind where Socrates came from—we are just assuming he is there). {Socrates} is the output of this principle on this input, and so {Socrates} exists.

To buttress this first claim, note that the theoretical role of explanation includes (i) *revealing patterns*, (ii) *providing recipes*, and (iii) *allowing understanding* (Schaffer 2018: 305–7). Seeing {Socrates} as the output of Socrates via set formation (i) reveals a unifying pattern that extends through Plato and {Plato}, Aristotle and {Aristotle}, etc.; (ii) conveys a recipe to wiggle the existence of {Socrates} by wiggling the existence of Socrates; and (iii) allows one to understand why {Socrates} exists, by revealing how sets get collected.

My second claim is that set formation plays the needed role of *link* from Socrates to {Socrates}. If one just considered Socrates and {Socrates} on their own, one would just be considering a heap of things with no specified relationship (likewise for the existence facts concerning these things—this is just a heap of facts). That is not enough for explanation. Explanation requires *connection* as well as *direction*. Set formation provides the directed connection from Socrates to {Socrates}, so licensing the arrow in Figure 7.1.

Turning to a second example drawn from mereology, consider the relationship between some appropriately bonded H, H, and O atoms and the H_2O molecule they compose. I assume that the molecule is built out of the atoms by the principle of mereological fusion (or whole making). We can think of mereological fusion as a machine that melts things into sums. For every plurality of inputs one feeds into this machine, it spits out their sum.

text, the total recursive structure of the machinery further justifies the claim of *priority*, that Socrates comes first and {Socrates} second (with {{Socrates}} third, etc.).

So if one feeds the H, H, and O atoms into the machine, it spits out their sum, namely the H2O molecule (Figure 7.2):[2,3]

The mereological fusion machine

H ⟶
H ⟶⟶⟶⟶ ➤ H2O
O ⟶

Figure 7.2

There is a viable metaphysical explanation for why the sum (the H2O molecule) exists, from the existence of the parts (the H, H, and O atoms), via mereological fusion. After all, given that the parts exist and the principle of mereological fusion is at work, it is no coincidence that the sum exists too. The sum is the output of this principle on this input. Mereological fusion provides a unifying pattern which conveys recipes and provides a basis for understanding, revealing how sums get lumped.

Mereological fusion plays the needed role of *link* from atoms to molecule. Without it one would just see a list of things (/facts). Mereological fusion contributes the directed connection needed for explanation, underwriting the arrows.

Moving to a third example drawn from metaethics, consider a simple "do as you like" subjectivist treatment of moral rightness, on which the present desires of the actor determine the moral status of her act. We can think of this simple subjectivist as positing an operation of right making, understood as a machine which gilds acts with morality. Feed it the present desires of the actor, and its spits out the moral status of her act (Figure 7.3):[4]

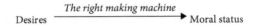

The right making machine

Desires ⟶⟶⟶⟶⟶⟶⟶➤ Moral status

Figure 7.3

---

[2]   This is the universal fusion machine. For restricted fusion machines, one needs restrictions on the inputs. For instance, for the organicist fusion machine (van Inwagen 1990), one needs to say: "For every plurality of inputs *whose activities collectively constitute a life* that one feeds into this machine . . . " But such a machine will not spit out any H2O molecules. For the example, any fusion machine that can make H2O molecules will do.

[3]   *Clarification*: The fusion machine spits out a sum, but falls silent as to whether that sum is a cabbage or a king, etc. What makes the sum *an H2O molecule* presumably involves extra-mereological facts as to the natures of and relations between the parts (for instance, that the sum has an exhaustive decomposition into two H atoms and one O atom, where the O atom is covalently bonded to each H atom). That is not at issue here.

[4]   I trust the reader can see how to extend this simple subjectivism to more sophisticated views. For instance, on Railton's (1986: 173–4) ideal advisor approach, what makes an action right for an agent is not her present desires, but what an idealized "A+" version of himself "would want his non-idealized self A to want."

There is a viable metaphysical explanation for why Ann's eating the chocolate is right, from Ann's desire to eat the chocolate, via right making. After all, given that Ann desires to eat the chocolate and this principle of right making is at work, it is hardly surprising that Ann's eating the chocolate is right. The moral status of the act is the output of this principle on this input. Right making provides a unifying pattern, conveys recipes, and allows understanding, revealing how moral status gets painted onto acts.

Right making plays the needed role of *link* from desires to moral status. Without it one would just see a non-explanatory list of states (/facts). With it we see a directed connection.

Finishing with a fourth example drawn from quantum mechanics, consider the treatment of particle locations afforded by Bohmian wave function realism (Albert 1996), on which what is fundamental is a wave in a $3n$-dimensional space and a single world-atom (the "marvelous point") in $3n$-space, and what is derivative are n-many "ordinary" physical particles in the 3-space we experience, as derived by the operation of particle enactment (or particle placing). We can think of particle enactment as a machine that projects particles onto 3-space. Feed it the location of the world in $3n$-space at a given time, and it spits out 3-space locations for n particles at that time, by assigning the first triple of the world's $3n$-space location as the first particle's 3-space location, the second triple of the world's $3n$-space location as the second particle's 3-space location, etc. So if one feeds the location of the world in the $3n$-space at a given time into the machine, it spits out locations for n-many particles in 3-space at that time, with particle p_j placed at coordinates $<x, y, z>$ in 3-space, corresponding to the world's $<3j-2, 3j-1, 3j>$ coordinates in $3n$-space (Figure 7.4):[5,6]

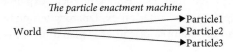

The particle enactment machine

World → Particle1 / Particle2 / Particle3

Figure 7.4

[5] Albert (1996; see also Ney 2013) calls this a principle of enactment because, under Bohmian wave function realism, having the world particle at such coordinates enacts the causal roles of having so-many ordinary particles so-located. Note that this implementation does not eliminate particles in three-dimensional space but embraces them as derivatively real, and it does not treat particle enactment as a follow-on that must be justified from the preceding theory but rather as one of the initial posits of the theory.

[6] Why do I bother with such a complicated example? Because it has many useful features, including (i) it is scientifically serious, (ii) it is one-many, (iii) it is broadly functionalist, (iv) it is a case where some commentators (such as Maudlin 2010 and Allori 2013) have questioned how an explanation is possible, and (v) it is a case in which the need for a non-transparent grounding principle is especially vivid (see Section 1.3).

There is a viable metaphysical explanation for where the particles are, from the location of the world in 3n-space, via particle enactment. After all, given that the world is there and the principle of particle enactment is at work, it is no wonder that the particles are where they are. The locations of the n particles in 3-space at that time are the output of this principle on this input. Particle enactment provides a unifying pattern, conveys recipes, and allows understanding, revealing how particles are sprayed onto 3-space.

Particle enactment plays the needed role of *link*, arrowing world-location to particle-locations.

Bringing this together, I have offered four examples of viable metaphysical explanations, each linked by a grounding principle. If I am right about any of these cases, then:

Minimal explanatory claim: There are viable metaphysical explanations linked by grounding principles.

Note that I am helping myself to some fairly orthodox ideology, including that of "metaphysical explanation," and "grounding principle," but this ideology is not load-bearing. Mainly I am just looking at some non-causal but constitutive explanations and labeling their linking principles (in order to set up an analogous explanation for consciousness). The reader is invited to substitute terminology as she prefers.[7]

1.2 Theorizing the Examples

So far I have displayed four viable metaphysical explanations linked by grounding principles. Now I offer an explanatory template based on these four examples and an example of causal explanation. This template has a

---

[7] My terminology is drawn from Fine (2001), Schaffer (2009), Rosen (2010), and the grounding theorists, and most especially follows Schaffer (2016, 2017, 2018). But I make no specific assumptions about grounding. Indeed even *grounding skeptics* such as Wilson (2014) can accept the substance of what I am saying, but should just substitute the more specific metaphysical determination relation of 'enactment' where I use the generic notion of 'grounding.' Also, I make no further assumptions about linking principles, beyond how they provide explanatory connections. There is a division among grounding theorists—discussed by Glazier (2020: section 3)—between *nomicists* (such as myself and Wilsch 2015) who invoke lawlike principles, and *essentialists* (such as Fine 2012 and Dasgupta 2014) who invoke the essences of the derivative. Essentialists should just substitute claims about the essence of the derivative where I invoke a principle. (I say how to re-write ground functionalism in both Wilsonian and Finean terms in Section 2.1.)

tripartite structure, where *sources* (causes, grounds) via *link* (causal law, grounding principle) generate *result* (effect, derivative), aptly modeled by the input–function–output structure of *structural equation models*.

So consider causal explanation. One traces how causes generate an effect via laws of nature. To take a paradigmatic example, imagine that Suki throws a rock through a window. We can think of the shattering of the window as the result of Suki's throwing the rock, via the nomological machinery.[8] If one feeds Suki's throw into the causal machinery of the world, one gets out a shattered window (Figure 7.5):

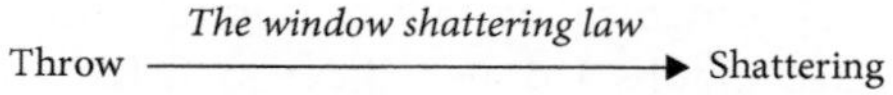

The window shattering law

Throw ⎯⎯⎯⎯⎯⎯⎯⎯⎯⎯⎯⎯⎯⎯⎯⎯→ Shattering

Figure 7.5

I say that—on this picture—there is an explanation for why the window shattered, from Suki's throw, via the "window shattering law." After all, given that Suki threw the rock and the window shattering law is at work, it is no coincidence that the window shattered. Rather the shattering is the output of this law on this input. This is not just a paradigmatic example, but one that unifies a pattern across vandalisms, conveys recipes for wiggling the fates of windows, and offers a basis for understanding why the window shattered.

With causal explanation, laws of nature provide the needed links. Without them one would just see a list of events. The causal laws add the connection and direction that constitute the arrow of explanation.

Indeed, in the causal case, sometimes cause and effect are known but the law is not—and then the effect remains unexplained. Consider the classic double-slit experiment (from Thomas Young in 1801), in which light shone through a doubly slit wall generates an interference pattern on a screen, which Feynman (1965: 1.1) calls "impossible, *absolutely* impossible, to explain in any classical way," saying that it "has in it the heart of quantum mechanics." Here, cause (shining the light through the doubly slit wall) and effect (interference pattern on the screen) were long known, but the explanation required the discovery of quantum mechanical laws providing the link.

[8] To treat the example more seriously, we either need to specify the precise background conditions around Suki's throw and the precise details of her throw, or—more feasibly, as will be done in the main text—we need to use a locally valid but derivative generalization linking the rock throw to the window shattering.

So, putting the examples together, here is the template I have in mind:

Explanatory template: If the result is the output of the sources via the link, then there is a viable explanation of the result from the sources via the link.

Note that *Explanatory template* is merely a sufficient condition for a viable explanation, applicable only in simple cases where the connections are direct. There are unresolved difficulties arising in more complex cases with various indirect connections, but these need not intrude here.

The reader familiar with *structural equation models* (Pearl 2000, Woodward 2003) will recognize my talk of "input," "function," and "output," and the directed graphs I draw. These models were developed for studying causation but there is nothing specifically causal about them. The formalism smoothly extends to grounding (Schaffer 2016). In a nutshell, we recruit variables whose valuables represent the states of interest for the system under study, link the dependent variables by functions that map the values of some input variables to their output value, and then assign values to the independent variables.[9]

So, for a simple model of Suki throwing the rock through the window, we can recruit an independent variable *Throw* with values of 0 if Suki does not throw and 1 if she throws, and a dependent variable *Shatter* with values of 0 if the window does not shatter and 1 if the window shatters. We then link these variables with a function—here the identity function—mapping *Throw*=0 to *Shatter*=0 and *Throw*=1 to *Shatter*=1. Finally we assign *Throw*=1, and now we can solve for the fate of the window, since we can derive *Shatter*=1.

More formally, we begin with a representation of the system under study, divided into sets of independent and dependent variables, with each variable mapped to some range of allotted values:

Variables1:   <*Independents1*={*Throw*}, *Dependents1*={*Shatter*}, *Range1*= {*Throw*→{0,1}, *Shatter*→{0,1}}>

---

[9] This is how it goes in the deterministic case. In the indeterministic case, the functions output probability distributions over values for each dependent variable, and we assign values to all variables consistent with what the functions allow. Since I take it that the metaphysical case must be deterministic, I focus there.

We then add in functions given the "dynamics" of the system, where '<=' is to be read as 'is the output of' (yielding '*Shatter* is the output of the identity function on *Throw*'):

Functions1:   {*Shatter* <= *Identity*(*Throw*)}

Finally—in the deterministic case—we just need to seed the "initial conditions" by assigning values to the independent variables:

Assignment1:   {*Throw*=1}

This structure induces the directed graph in Figure 7.6, fitting our earlier representation:

Throw ⎯⎯⎯⎯⎯⎯⎯⎯⎯⎯⎯⎯⟶ *Shatter*

Figure 7.6

But we have added needed information beyond the graph, concerning the range of values each variable can take, the form of the function connecting them, and the value assigned to the independent variables. This added information enables us to derive *Shatter*=1 (as the output of the identity function on the input *Throw*=1), and so model a viable explanation as to why the window shattered.

For a metaphysical example, we can simply re-purpose the model for the window shattering, to represent the formation of {Socrates}. Just treat *Throw* as a strangely labeled variable for Socrates, with 0 representing non-existence and 1 existence; and treat *Shatter* as a strangely labeled variable for {Socrates}, with 0 again representing non-existence and 1 existence. We can then solve for the presence of {Socrates}, and in the exact same way display an explanatory model as to why {Socrates} exists. So we find a common modeling structure for causal and metaphysical explanations, from sources (Suki's throw, Socrates's existence), via link (window shattering law, set formation principle), to result (the shattering, {Socrates}'s existence).

Or, to add a new metaphysical example, suppose we want to model how the mass of the H2O molecule depends on the mass of its constituent H, H, and O atoms. Then we could recruit variables *H1*, *H2*, *O*, and *H2O* (representing the atoms and molecule), allowed any real value (representing mass in Daltons). We would then need to specify the function through which the mass of the constituent atoms determines the mass of the molecule. Supposing a Newtonian framework, the apt function is addition. And finally we would need to assign masses in Daltons to the atoms, as initial inputs. Rounding off a bit, we can assign both $H1$ and $H2$ the value of 1, and O the value of 16. We would then be able to solve for the mass of the $H2O$ molecule, since we can now derive $H2O=18$. The model would then look like this:

Variables2:   <*Independents2*={H1, H2, O}, *Dependents2*={H2O}, *Range2*= {H1/H2/O/H2O→Reals}>

Functions2:   {H2O <= Addition(H1, H2, O)}

Assignment2:   {H1=1, H2=1, O=16}

The model induces the same directed graph (Figure 7.7) as the mereological fusion function displayed in Section 1.1:

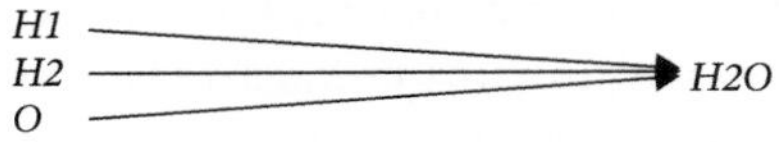

Figure 7.7

But the model adds further information beyond the graph, such as the substantive information that mass is additive (which is true in a Newtonian framework but false in relativistic physics), which thereby entails $H2O=18$, aptly representing the mass of the molecule as (roughly) 18 Daltons. In this way we can model a viable Newtonian explanation for why the mass of the $H2O$ molecule is (roughly) 18 Daltons.

The structural equation formalism helps reveal exactly why explanations need links. The links not only license the arrows, but they license specific structural equations that enable solutions for the values of dependent variables. Take the mass case. We not only need to draw an explanatory arrow from $H1$, $H2$, and O to $H2O$, but we need to specify that it is the arrow of *addition* to solve for the mass of the molecule (had we multiplied, or taken the mean or the min, etc., we would have reached a different result).

There is a familiar saying in computing: "Garbage in, garbage out." I offer a further motto: "No function, no output." From just the input (causes, grounds) nothing further follows.[10]

So, our explanatory template can be modeled as follows:

Template modeled: If there is an apt structural equation model in which the value of the variable representing the result is the output of the values of the variables representing the sources on a given function representing the link, then there is a viable explanation of result from sources and link.

Note that *Template modeled* (like *Explanatory template*) is merely a sufficient condition for a viable explanation, applicable only in simple cases with a single direct link. Also note that I help myself to the ideology of an "apt" model. There are many vexed questions as to what exactly aptness involves, but I trust that the models in use should count as apt, however that goes. The reader who suspects otherwise is invited to say why.

1.3 Abductive Metaphysics

The topic of metaphysical explanation is not only relevant to explanatory concerns about consciousness, but goes to the heart of metaphysics itself. I say that a satisfying metaphysics should be *explanatory*. A metaphysics that merely lists what there is (as per Quine 1948) lacks explanatory value, since a mere list is not an explanatory structure and provides no understanding (Jackson 1998: 4–5). Rather, the metaphysician with the ambition to explain *how and why the world is as it is* should offer theories of what grounds what (Schaffer 2009).

---

[10] Likewise from just a function, nothing further follows. There is only output when input meets function. Note that this is compatible with the idea that the input in our model may represent a null condition in the world, and so compatible with Fine's (2012: 47–8) idea of *zero-grounding*, understood as the output of an operation when fed nothing, and illustrated by the idea that the null set is the output of set formation when fed nothing. To model zero-grounding (if such be wanted), we just require an input value that aptly represents the null condition. Actually we can re-purpose our simple two-binary-variable model used to represent Suki throwing the rock through the window, and Socrates membering {Socrates}, by taking the independent variable to represent the null condition, and the dependent variable to represent the null set. (This requires the representation of counterlogical conditions, such as the absence of even the null condition. But structural equation models of grounding were already knee-deep in counterlogicals: Schaffer 2016: 71–3.)

I can now be more precise about what it takes to offer a theory of what grounds what. First, one needs to think of the derivative result as enfolded in a contrast space, or (equivalently) encased in a question. This is the analogue of encoding a range for a variable. When it comes to the H2O molecule, for example, we might enfold it in a contrast space of {exists, does not exist}, which is to encase it in the question of whether it exists or not. Or we might enfold it in the contrast space of {has mass n Daltons} for all real numbers n, which is to encase it in the question of how massive it is. Secondly, we need to identify the candidate explaining entities, and enfold these in a contrast space/question as well. So we might look to the H, H, and O atoms, and ask of each whether it exists or not, or how massive it is, etc.

Once we have asked our questions of nature, we may consider how the answer to a given question is determined by answers to upstream questions, and ultimately by answers to certain fundamental (/source) questions. This is to exhibit how wiggling the grounds (within its contrast space) wiggles the grounded (within its contrast space), and how the grounded fits into a pattern of dependence upon its grounds. And then we only need to answer the source questions, and we will thereby be in a position not merely *to answer* all downstream questions, but *to understand why these are the answers*, by seeing how answers cascade through nature.

Explanations are not merely answers to a question, but flowcharts as to how answers cascade through nature.

Think of the physicist, tasked with creating an explanatory causal map of the cosmos. She may begin from a statespace representing the possible states of the system at a time. This is a contrast space, posing the question of *how the system is* for any given time. She may then add a dynamics representing the possible trajectories through this statepace over time. This is a function from the state of the system at a time to the state of the system over other times.[11] Then she only needs to answer *what was the initial state*. This will position her (in principle) to give a complete causal explanation for the rest of the cosmos, since the dynamics not only determines the subsequent history, but charts how answers evolve forwards through time.

Think of the metaphysician as facing an analogous explanatory task. She needs to answer the question *what is the fundamental state* and specify the "dynamics" of grounding, to chart how answers percolate upwards through the derivative. (So in the case of consciousness, the materialist is looking to

---

[11] Or in the indeterministic case, this is a function from the state of the system at a time to a probability distribution over other times. At present I am only considering the deterministic case.

answer the question *what is the material state* and specify the dynamics of grounding, to chart how answers to the material state question percolate upwards to determine answers to the question *what is the mental state.*)

I can also be somewhat more precise about the methodology of such an explanatory metaphysics, which is *abductive.* Grounding principles are posited by inference to the best explanation, in a holistic and fallible manner. The idea that principles are posited for explanation is arguably already present in Aristotle's *Posterior Analytics*, where—at least according to Kosman (1973: 387)—Aristotle holds that the "criteria of adequacy" for principles is our ability "to explain by them the phenomena with which we begin and thus to gain with them scientific understanding..." And the idea that metaphysics is generally abductive remains prominent, for instance in Lewis and Lewis's (1970: 212) view of metaphysical debates as "haggling" over the costs and benefits of consistent options, and in Paul's (2012: 23) approach on which "modeling and inference to the best explanation...form the core of the metaphysical method."

I am saying that, just as we accept an abductive methodology for inquiry into the laws of nature, so we should accept an abductive methodology for inquiry into the grounding principles (or "laws of metaphysics"). In the causal case, the physicist seeks the simplest (/most elegant) total package of initial conditions and dynamics, that is, the strongest (/most informative) for the rest. Likewise, I say that the metaphysician should seek the simplest and strongest package of fundamental conditions and grounding principles. From an evidential perspective, in both physics and metaphysics we are most directly witness to a small swath of intermediate structure—some local patterns in the midst of history at middling levels—and (crudely speaking) our task is to construct the best explanation of this "data," from before and below.[12]

Inference to the best explanation is ultimately a holistic comparison between packages, which means that any posited links—causal or metaphysical—are *doubly provisional.* It is provisional that a given posited link is the best complement to a given remainder, and provisional that the resulting package provides the best explanation overall. But a physicist can still provisionally recommend a nomic posit (e.g., Schrödinger's equation) when it seems *explanatorily fruitful* (e.g., explaining the result of experiments such as the double split experiment), without specifying every other law of nature or considering every alternative package. Likewise a

---

[12] A less crude account should allow us to "explain away" a seeming bit of "data" as a mere appearance, etc.

metaphysician can still provisionally recommend a grounding principle (such as set formation) on the basis that it seems *explanatorily fruitful*, without specifying every other grounding principle or considering every alternative package. (It is in this doubly provisional spirit that I recommend ground functionalism.)

This abductive methodology stands opposed to the constraint that animates the explanatory gap literature, namely that explanatory links be *epistemically transparent*, in the sense of being evident to pure reason, *a priori* knowable, or inconceivable otherwise. Transparency is neither holistic nor abductive, but local and deductive, requiring of each individual link that it be perfectly evident to pure reason. Indeed, the opposition between an abductive and rationalist-deductive methodology may lie at the root of the whole debate. Thus Trogdon (2013: 471) connects the explanatory gap concern to a transparency requirement:

> [T]he appearance that connecting questions [between phenomenal and physical facts] are cognitively significant is at the root of a familiar challenge to physicalism. A standard gloss of physicalism is that in the actual world each mental fact is ultimately grounded in certain physical facts... Many agree that the appearance of cognitive significance with respect to connecting questions in the phenomenal/physical case—what Levine dubs the *explanatory gap*—gives us a *prima facie* reason to believe that physicalism is false, that the physical fails to ground the mental.

(I reply that we should not reject physicalism but instead reject transparency, and thus make room for a physicalism that posits non-transparent (/"cognitively significant") connections for abductive reasons.)

Note that there are many ways to precisify transparency. For instance, one might require an *a priori* entailment from the grounds to the grounded, so that an ideal reasoner in her armchair, given the information about the grounds and full conceptual competence, could deduce the facts about the grounded on that basis (Chalmers & Jackson 2001: 351). Or—perhaps equivalently—that it should be *inconceivable* for the link to fail, so that an ideal reasoner would regard any other view as contradictory (Chalmers 1996: 73–6).[13] Chalmers (2012) considers a wide range of "scrutability"

---

[13] Chalmers (1996: 73) gives the following as his leading example of such an "inconceivability": What kind of world could be identical to ours in every last microphysical fact but be biologically distinct? Say a wombat has two children in our world. The physical facts

theses. Nothing here should turn on the precisifications, however, so I will simply use "transparency" along with a conceivability test for definiteness.

I oppose transparency for three reasons, the first of which being that it fits none of our starting examples (Section 1.1). It is fully conceivable that set formation is not at work to clamp things into sets, and likewise it is fully conceivable that mereological fusion, right making, and particle enactment are not functioning. Indeed, each of these principles is rejected by various excellent philosophers, who may reject the result as well (e.g., denying that there are any sets), or say that the result is grounded in other ways or else deem the result fundamental (e.g., saying that moral status is grounded in non-psychological ways or else viewing it as fundamental), or even invert the proposed arrows (e.g., saying that the whole grounds the parts). It is now widely accepted in each of these debates that there are multiple consistent options for the haggling. (Of course it is epistemically possible that, in every single one of these debates, some subtle and hitherto unseen contradiction is lurking in all but one of the relevant options. But this seems unlikely.)[14]

My second reason for opposing transparency is that it manifestly fails for causal links. In the early days of modern science, there was a felt demand for transparent laws of nature ("rational mechanics"). But we have long since learned to reject any such constraints on laws of nature. So why impose them on grounding principles? The causal case already shows that viable explanation does not need transparency.

My third reason for opposing transparency is that—at least from a broadly realist perspective—causal laws and grounding principles are both principles of real generation in nature (with explanations charting how answers cascade through nature). From such a realist perspective, it seems

about our world will include facts about the distribution of every particle in the spatio-temporal hunk corresponding to the wombat, and its children, and their environments, and their evolutionary histories. If a world shared those physical facts with ours, but was not a world in which the wombat had two children, what could that difference consist in? Such a world seems quite inconceivable.

I reply (Schaffer 2017; see also Montero 2013: 102) that one conceivable difference concerns whether or not mereological fusion is at work. There is a conceivable *nihilist* scenario in which the particles do not fuse at all, not even into wombats.

[14] It is also worth noting that the main evidence bearing on the examples *cross-cut* standard epistemic categories. For instance, the main evidence bearing on set formation is *a priori*, but the main evidence bearing on particle enactment is *a posteriori*, and the main evidence bearing on mereological fusion is a mix of *a priori* and *a posteriori* considerations. Insofar as inference to the best explanation is holistic, it should be expected that the full evidence for all principles involves every consideration there is, but that the main evidence for a given principle can be "concentrated" in various ways.

just wrong-headed to demand that the clockwork of nature be transparent from the armchair.

Putting this together: Explanatory metaphysics—at least when the explanations fit *Explanatory template* and *Template modeled* —must articulate a structure of sources (/inputs), link (/function), and result (/output). The proper methodology—in both the causal and the metaphysical case—for posting such links is abductive:

Abductive methodology: Links for causal and for metaphysical explanations may be posited when explanatorily fruitful (and ultimately insofar as they are part of the best explanatory package).

Note that rejecting transparency is not saying *anything goes*. The rejection of one (unsuitable) constraint is not the rejection of all constraints. I am saying that, in both physics and metaphysics, the proper constraint on positing links is not epistemic transparency but explanatory fruitfulness.[15]

2. Ground Functionalism

In Section 1, I argued that there is a viable form of metaphysical explanation linked by grounding principles, which are aptly modeled as functions from input to output, and justifiably posited when explanatorily fruitful. I now introduce the ground functionalist approach, positing a *mind making* principle mapping token realizer states to token mental states, so enabling a viable materialist-friendly explanation for conscious experience. Ground

---

[15] Hofweber (2009: 273) raises the concern that "esoteric" metaphysicians like myself are opening the door to *priority aquaism*, the view that everything is fundamentally water. Rabin (2019: 197) specifically charges that my views about consciousness lead to a "methodological madness" on which "anything goes," including *peanutism*, which is the view that "the actual world's fundamental level consists of Peanie the peanut." *Abductive methodology* provides my reply (see also Schaffer 2017: 14). Priority aquaism and peanutism look like explanatorily fruitless doctrines worth discarding. Note that I do not rule out such doctrines from the start. It may well have been reasonable for a counterpart of Thales to propose priority aquaism. I am instead saying that these doctrines now look fruitless and so deserve to be ignored, just as silly physical theories deserve to be ignored. Thus compare the silly metaphysical theory that what is fundamental is my nose, with the silly physical theory that what is causally initial is my nose ("the Big Sneeze"). I am saying that the right response in both cases is not to rule out such theories from the start for failing epistemic transparency, but rather to discard them now for seeming to be explanatorily fruitless. Here again the proper methodology is abductive.

functionalism is built on the template for metaphysical explanation traced in Section 1, with mind making as the link.

2.1 Mind Making

The ground functionalist posits a mind making principle, mapping realizer states to mental states by scanning the functional role of the input and molding a fitting output. The input to mind making is any token state of any system whatsoever, whether the system be an actual material system or some other-worldly ectoplasmic system. For instance, the input could be the current C-fiber firings (state) of Huma the human (system). This input is encased in the question, *what role does the state realize in the system*? For instance, it might realize the pain role, the tickle role, or no relevant role in the system at all.

The output of mind making is a token mental state (if any) for that system. For instance it could be Huma's current pain. This output is encased in the question, *what if any mental state is the system in*? For instance, it might be a pain, it might be a tickle, or it might be no mental state at all.

Mind making then maps input to output, pairing realizing states in a system to fitting mental states for that system, so forming an answer cascade from the deeper question *what role does the state realize in the system?*, to the downstream question *what if any mental state is the system in*? Thus:

Ground functionalism: There is a grounding principle of mind making, which links realizer states in a system to mental states for that system.

Just as right making may be said to imbue acts with moral status (Section 1.1), so mind making is said to imbue systems with mental properties.[16]

---

[16] Some re-statements: For the Wilson-style pluralist who substitutes more specific metaphysical determination relations, just say: "There is a specific metaphysical determination relation of mind making..." For the Fine-style essentialist, say: "For each mental state, it lies in the nature of that state to be the state made by a state of a system realizing a fitting functional role." Though the essentialist will then make some counter-intuitive essence claims, for instance claiming that it lies in the nature of pain to be the state made by a state of a system with a given causal profile. Intuitively, it simply lies in the nature of pain to feel a certain way. But insofar as the essentialist thinks of essences as real natures, it is not clear to me if she should or even can view our intuitions as reliable guides. (My preferred statement does not use the ideology of "essence" and so side-steps such issues.)

Some precursors: Both Rosen (2010: 132) and Khudairi (2018: 923) mention the prospect of a ground-theoretic implementation of functionalism. Thus Khudairi (2018: 923) offers "Functional truths (F) ground truths about consciousness (Q)..." and regiments it (with Fine's strict full ground operator) as "F > G." But to my knowledge the idea has not yet received further development.

Realizer states in a system *enact* mental states for that system, and the ground functionalist views enactment as a specific metaphysical determination relation and thus a form of grounding, positing that what is enacted is thereby created. Indeed, mind making and particle enactment (Section 1.1) are both enactment principles. Enactment may be thought of as a "dance it into being" principle. Just as what it takes to make a ballet is to have dancers spinning in the right patterns, so generally what it takes to make enacted things is to have the enactors functioning in the right (actual and counterfactual) patterns. A properly choreographed system dances out a mind. Yeats concludes "Among School Children" with the memorable lines:

> O Chestnut tree, great rooted blossomer,
> Are you the leaf, the blossom or the bole?
> O body swayed to music, O brightening glance,
> How can we know the dancer from the dance?

Enactment is a specific claim about the relationship between the dancer (the realizer, which may be a physical brain), the dance (the causal patterns), and the result (the mind itself) enacted by the dance.

So we can think of mind making as a machine. Feed it a state of a system (material or otherwise), and it spits out a mental state on the basis of the role of the input. So, if the role of pain is to be causally intermediary between tissue damage and avoidance behavior, and if C-fiber firings realize this role for Huma the human, then mind making maps Huma's C-fiber firing to her pain (Figure 7.8):

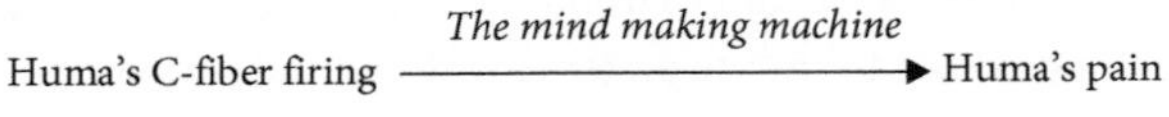

The mind making machine

Huma's C-fiber firing ⎯⎯⎯⎯⎯⎯⎯⎯⎯⎯→ Huma's pain

Figure 7.8

Likewise, if what plays the pain role for Marvin the Martian is the inflation of small hydraulic cavities in his feet (as per the tale in Lewis 1980), then mind making maps Marvin's foot cavity inflation to his pain (Figure 7.9):

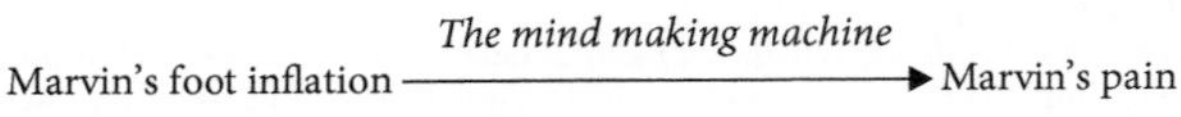

The mind making machine

Marvin's foot inflation ⎯⎯⎯⎯⎯⎯⎯⎯⎯⎯→ Marvin's pain

Figure 7.9

Or, if what plays the pain role for Casper the ghost is a vibration of their ectoplasm, then mind making maps Casper's ectoplasmic vibration to their pain (Figure 7.10):

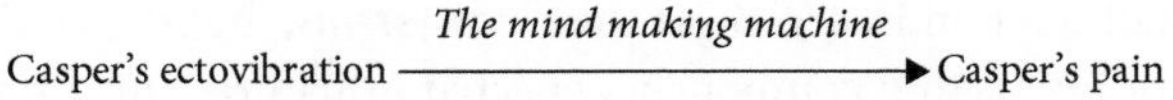

The mind making machine

Casper's ectovibration ————————————▶ Casper's pain

Figure 7.10

Note that these are toy examples, in at least three respects. First, the actual role of pain is far more complicated, and indeed talk of pain in humans may need to give way to talk of distinctive states of nociceptive, neuropathic, and psychogenic pain. For the typical roles of each differ: nociceptive pain is typically caused by tissue damage, but neuropathic pain is typically caused by nervous system disorder, while psychogenic pain is typically caused by emotional distress.

Secondly, philosophical legend notwithstanding, C-fibers are almost certainly not the realizers of (nociceptive) pain in humans. C-fibers and Aδ-fibers are our two types of nociceptors in the peripheral nervous system, signaling certain "threatening" physical stimuli over to the central nervous system. Our realizers of pain are almost certainly found, not in local peripheral nervous system activations, but in more holistic central system patterns these tend to trigger.[17]

Thirdly, and most relevantly, the roles of mental states are almost certainly interwoven, and so functional determination is best viewed as holistic, from the whole system at a time to a troupe of states for that system. So the deeper structure is really more akin to the structure of the functionalist principle of particle enactment (Section 1.1) (Figure 7.11):

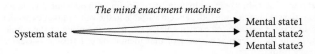

The mind enactment machine

System state ⟶ Mental state1 / Mental state2 / Mental state3

Figure 7.11

[17] As to the human neural correlate of pain, Garcia-Larrea & Bastuji (2018) propose a model in terms of the coordinated activation of a three-part "pain matrix," involving: (i) unconscious processing in the sensorimotor and limbic areas, (ii) immediate stimulus awareness due to joint activation of the sensorimotor and fronto-cingulate-parietal networks, followed by (iii) integration into declarative perception linked to memory, involving the posterior cingulate and medial temporal areas. On this view, we might speak of the coordinated activation of Huma's neural pain matrix.

From a holistic functionalist perspective, minds are *natural dynamical structures*. Minds are not quite like the mousetraps or Coke dispensers commonly invoked in the literature (e.g., Fodor 1981: 120), for those are *artifacts*, and artifact kinds are determined in part by the intentions of their artificer. Rather, minds are more like *ecosystems*, holistic and dynamic structures of interacting components enacted in nature. For instance, what makes a given ecosystem feature *a nutrient cycle* is that the system dances out an abstract and multiply realizable loop, seen in the way water on earth precipitates down from the sky and then evaporates back up.

But just as it is easier to work with locally valid derivative models in the causal case, so it is easier in the mental case, and I will largely ignore the holistic aspect of functionalism in what follows. It should be more than enough just to exhibit even a locally valid and derivative explanation for conscious experience.[18,19]

I say that—on these simplifying assumptions—the firing of Huma's C-fibers plus the principle of mind making *explain* why Huma is in pain (with parallel stories for Marvin and Casper, etc.) After all, given that Huma's C-fibers are firing and mind making is at work, it is no mere accident that Huma is in pain. For we have a grounding principle: mind making, which

---

[18] Structural equation models for holistic systems are highly non-trivial. What is needed are mappings, for each downstream mental state, from the system state to it (akin to the Bohmian wave function realist mapping, for each downstream particle location, from the world location to it). First, we can think of the whole system as occupying a point in a *flowchart space*, which is a state-space of possible cognitive architectures and activations (including a point for "not a cognitive architecture"). We would then model the location of the system in flowchart space via a single independent variable. Second, we can think of each mental state as occupying a point in a *determination space*, for all of the possible determinate states (including a "no such state" point). We would then add many dependent variables to represent each mental state. Finally, for each mental state, we need a link from the place of the whole system in flowchart space, to the place of that mental state in its determination space. So, for each dependent variable, we need a function from the value of the one independent variable to the value of that dependent variable. This yields an answer cascade for each mental state, from the place of the whole system in flowchart space to the determinate status of that mental state. I trust it is clear why I have simplified away from holism.

[19] I leave open what the most basic or *root principle* is. Perhaps holistic mind enactment is simply a root principle in the workings of the world, or perhaps it stems from some deeper and more general enactment principle. Just as we might consider more and less restricted mereological fusion machines (see Section 1.1), so we might consider more and less restricted enactment machines—including a universal enactment machine—from which mind enactment (and particle enactment, etc.) might derive. This is relevant to assessing whether or not *Ground functionalism* is inflationary. If mind enactment is a root principle, then the ground functionalist is positing an additional root principle in nature. But if mind enactment derives from a more general enactment principle needed anyway, then there is no additional cost (just as there is no additional cost in saying that the molecules of chemistry are made by mereological fusion, if mereological fusion was needed anyway).

links Huma's C-fiber firing to her pain. And we have input: Huma's C-fibers are firing. Huma's pain is the output of this principle on this input, and so she is in pain. This explanation reveals patterns in Huma's (and in human) psychology, provides recipes for wiggling her pains, and allows one to understand why she is in pain by revealing how her pain gets realized.

I then say that this is a viable metaphysical explanation, with mind making playing the role of *link* from Huma's C-fiber firing to her pain. If we just considered her C-fiber firing and her pain on their own, we would just see a bucket of events with no specified relationship (likewise for the occurrence facts concerning these events—that is, just a bucket of facts). That is not enough for explanation. Here there is an evident explanatory gap! But I think that the right response is not to declare consciousness an extra fundamental ingredient in reality(!), but rather to recall that we generally need to involve links to see any explanatory connections. Mind making turns the trick (by design), connecting Huma's C-fiber firing to her pain in the direction of input to output, licensing an explanatory arrow drawn from C-fiber firing to pain, and charting how the answer to the question of her material state flows into an answer to the question of her mental state.

So, mind making backs the explanatory arrow that *bridges* the explanatory gap, in just the way that grounding principles generally link metaphysical explanations (Section 1.1; see also Schaffer 2017). Mind making connects material states to mental states as input to output, allowing for viable metaphysical explanation.[20,21]

Indeed, this case can be modeled by exactly the same "two binary variable" structure seen in the simple case of Suki throwing the rock through

---

[20] In this vein, Tye (2000: 22) characterizes the epistemic gap in terms of a missing link:
One who has a complete understanding of the term 'pain', for example, and who is fully apprised of the physical facts as we now know them, can still coherently ask why such-and-such brain processes or functional states feel the way pains do or why these processes feel any way at all. In this case, it seems that as far as our understanding goes, *something important is missing.* Herein lies the famous "explanatory gap" for consciousness.
I am saying that mind making adds what was missing.
[21] So what premise of Chalmers's (1996: 94–9) *zombie argument* am I rejecting? I am rejecting the premise that conceptual possibility entails metaphysical possibility. In general, scenarios that conflict with actual grounding principles may be conceptually but not metaphysically possible (for more detailed discussion, see Schaffer 2017: 16–18). Since the zombie scenario violates the mind making principle, the ground functionalist has a principled reason to say that it is conceptually but not metaphysically possible. (Compare: Since a mereological nihilist scenario violates universal composition, the friend of universal composition has a principled reason to say that a mereological nihilist scenario is conceptually but not metaphysically possible.)

the window, and the formation of {Socrates} from Socrates. Repeating the model except for re-labeling the variables in obvious ways:

Variables1: <*Independents1*={*C-fibers*}, *Dependents1*={*Pain*}, *Range1*={*C-fibers*→{0,1}, *Pain*→{0,1}}>

Functions1:   {*Pain* <= *Identity*(*C-fibers*)}

Assignment1:   {*C-fibers*=1}

This structure induces the directed graph in Figure 7.12, fitting our earlier representation:

$$C\text{-}fibers \longrightarrow Pain$$

Figure 7.12

And, moreover, it allows us to solve for Huma's mental state (she is experiencing pain) from her material state.

In Section 1, when considering metaphysical explanation without yet looking at consciousness, I offered the following theses, repeated here:

Minimal explanatory claim: There are viable metaphysical explanations linked by grounding principles.

Explanatory template: If the result is the output of the sources via the link, then there is a viable explanation of the result from the sources via the link.

Template modeled: If there is an apt structural equation model in which the value of the variable representing the result is the output of the values of the variables representing the sources on a given function representing the link, then there is a viable explanation of result from sources and link.

So, I conclude that the ground functionalist style of explanation of Huma's pain from her C-fiber firings is a viable metaphysical explanation, fitting the template for metaphysical explanation linked by grounding principles, and thus exhibiting a viable explanation for consciousness.

Note that I only call this a viable explanation (successful given its background assumptions). I have not argued that this is the actual explanation, and indeed—as noted above—I regard the assumptions in play as highly simplified in multiple ways. But the explanatory gap arguments were supposed to show an in-principle divide across which not even a viable explanation was possible. So, I conclude that, whatever problems materialism might face, lack of any viable explanation for conscious experience is not among them.

2.2 Functionalism Meets Grounding

To further explicate ground functionalism, and situate it against some extant views, it is useful to decompose it into *functionalist* and *ground-theoretic* aspects. The functionalist aspect begins from an empirical claim of type-level *correlation*, between mental state types and second-order functional role properties, as per:

Functional correlation: Every mental state type actually corresponds one-one to a functional role.

For instance, the type pain—on the simplifications we are adopting— corresponds to the second-order functional role property of *being a property caused by tissue damage and causing avoidance behavior*.[22]

The primary rationale for *Functional correlation* is that—as a matter of empirical fact—there seem to be robust correlations between material states and mental states, and that—given that states like pain seem to be multiply realizable across a wide range of diverse creatures (Putnam 1975)—these correlations seem best characterized at the functional level. In this vein Fodor (1981: 117–18) says that there is "a level of abstraction at which the generalizations of psychology are most naturally pitched..." which "cuts across differences in the physical composition of the systems to which psychological generalizations apply."

Note that *Functional correlation* merely claims an *actual* correspondence. It is logically compatible with the incredible claim that this correspondence is just a cosmic accident. And it is compatible with the more credible claim

---

[22] There is an intramural dispute among functionalists, as to whether to draw the mental state roles from folk psychology (Armstrong, Lewis) or from empirical science (Fodor). (The latter view, with its eye on psychology, is labeled "psycho-functionalism" in Block 1978.) *Functional correlation* is intended to be neutral, but insofar as it is said to represent an empirical truth, it seems to me that the right place to find causal roles is in empirical science. (Analytic functionalists like Lewis (1972) treat *Functional correlation* not as an empirical discovery but as part of folk theory, with mental state terms defined by Ramsification. Since my *Ground functionalist* is not making an analytic claim about the meaning of mental state terms, she is under no pressure to follow.)

that this correspondence holds for nomological reasons, in a way defended by *naturalistic dualists* like Chalmers (1996: 247; see also Gertler 2020):

> A natural suggestion is that consciousness arises in virtue of *the functional organization* of the brain. On this view, the chemical and indeed the quantum substrate of the brain is irrelevant to the production of consciousness. What matters is the brain's abstract causal organization, an organization that might be realized in many different physical substrates.

So, *Functional correlation* seems to be an empirical truth, which dualists may equally accept.

In my view, *Functional correlation* is the core insight of functionalism worth preserving (the other needed ingredient is grounding). It is because I accept *Functional correlation* that I am proposing *Ground functionalism*, and viewing the sources of the mind in terms of functional role.

But *Functional correlation* is not essential to my claim to deliver a materialist-friendly explanation of conscious experience. Indeed, one of the main concerns about *Functional correlation* is Block's (1978) objection from overgeneration. For instance, if the population of China were to enact a system with the right roles, then *Functional correlation* would implausibly pair the population of China with mental states. My own preference is to bite the bullet, but this is not a matter I can discuss here.[23] But one main alternative is to say that there is a further requirement of the right kind of biological substrate, as per:

Functional-and-biological correlation: Every mental state type actually corresponds one-one to a functional role realized in the right biological substrate.

Or one might even drop the functional element altogether:

Biological correlation: Every mental state type actually corresponds one-one to a biological substrate.

---

[23] See Chalmers (1996: 249–51) for further discussion. I would just add that, in a literature in which the panpsychist attribution of mental states to all entities is considered a serious option, the functionalist attribution of mental states to a few surprising systems seems practically common-sensical in comparison.

The reader who prefers one of these alternatives is invited to replace the functionalist aspect in *Ground functionalism* accordingly, for instance via:

Ground functionalism-and-biologicism: There is a grounding principle of mind making, which links realizer states in a system with the right biological substrate to mental states for that system.

What bridges the explanatory gap is not taking a functionalist component as the relevant input, but positing a ground-theoretic mapping from any sort of material input to mental output.

Since *Functional correlation* is merely a claim of actual correlation, compatible with the incredible view that the correlation is merely a vast cosmic accident, it is standard to add that the correlation has a real basis, and that the mental thereby "arises from," "depends on," or "is determined by" the material (Fodor 1981: 118; Levin 2018).[24] What is distinctive about *Ground functionalism*, comprising the ground-theoretic aspect of the view, is the follow-up claim that the basis of the correspondence is a metaphysical grounding principle, as per:

Metaphysical basis: *Functional correlation* holds due to a metaphysical principle.

The particular understanding of "arising" is then ground-theoretic:

Metaphysical arising: Token mental states are grounded in token material states.

This is naturally paired with the thought that these correlations are resilient to the extent that metaphysical grounding principles are resilient, which I will label *metaphysical necessity*, understood via the sphere of scenarios consistent with the grounding principles:

Metaphysical resilience: *Functional correlation* holds with metaphysical necessity.

---

[24] Thus Kriegel (2020b) notes that all parties can accept the general claim that the mental depends on the material, since the main dividing line "concerns the type of dependence involved. For the materialist, consciousness depends ontologically, metaphysically, or constitutively, on brain activity. For the dualist, the dependence is merely 'natural,' nomological, or causal."

Just as *nomological necessity* may be understood via the scenarios consistent with the laws of nature, so I understand metaphysical necessity via the scenarios consistent with "the laws of metaphysics."[25]

I am now in position to situate *Ground functionalism* against extant dualist and functionalist views, in terms of both the basis for, and the resilience of, *Functional correlation*. Let me start with *Naturalistic dualism*, which is the view that the material-mental correlations—which I take to be as given by *Functional correlation*—hold due to a merely contingent nomological connection. Thus Chalmers (1996: 125) clarifies: "[C]onsciousness arises from a physical substrate in virtue of certain contingent laws of nature ..." And Kriegel (2020a) says:

> [Dualism] is the view (roughly) that the experiential and the physical are mutually (metaphysically) independent, such that any links between consciousness and its neural correlate are at most causal and contingent, not constitutive and necessary.

So, working with *Functional correlation*, this yields:

Nomological basis: *Functional correlation* holds due to a law of nature.

Nomological arising: Token mental states are caused by token material states.

This is naturally paired with the thought that these correlations are resilient to the extent that laws of nature are resilient, which is *nomological necessity*, understood via the scenarios consistent with the laws of nature:

Nomological resilience: *Functional correlation* holds with nomological necessity.

So, one way to reach *Ground functionalism* is to start from *Naturalistic dualism* plus *Functional correlation*, but strengthen the connections from nomological up to metaphysical.

---

[25] According to Rosen (2006: 35), the laws of metaphysics "specify the categories of basic constituents and the rules for their combination. They determine how non-basic entities are generated from or 'grounded' in the basic array." Rosen says that the philosopher's conception of metaphysical necessity is indeterminate between a kind of necessity *tout court*, and a necessity restricted by the laws of metaphysics. I may be understood as adopting Rosen's restricted notion. Verbal matters aside, the key point is that there is this intermediate modal sphere to consider, which is neither merely nomological nor full conceptual necessity.

Turning to analytic functionalism, this view builds in *Functional correlation* (indeed, such is the main achievement of the view). But it views the correlation *conceptually*, in terms of the meanings of mental state terms. As Armstrong (1968: 82) says: "The concept of a mental state is primarily the concept of a state of the person apt for bringing about a certain sort of behavior..." Thus the analytic functionalist holds:

Conceptual basis: *Functional correlation* holds because terms for mental state types mean states with corresponding functional roles.

Conceptual arising: Token mental states are identical to token material states.

This is naturally paired with the thought that these correlations are resilient in any conceivable scenario (whether or not that scenario is consistent with the actual laws of nature, or the actual grounding principles):

Conceptual resilience: *Functional correlation* holds with conceptual necessity.

So, a second way to reach *Ground functionalism* is to start from *Analytic functionalism*, but weaken the connections from conceptual down to metaphysical.[26]

As a related way to distinguish these views, let us use the notions of *realizer* (e.g., C-fiber firings), *role* (e.g., causing avoidance), and *result* (e.g., pain). *Ground functionalism*, *Naturalistic dualism*, and *Analytic functionalism* agree that the *realizer-role* relation is one of instantiation. But the views disagree on whether the *role-result* relation is a nomological, metaphysical, or conceptual connection, and on whether the *realizer-result* relation is causation, grounding, or identity. This is depicted in Figure 7.13:

I am not claiming these three views to be exhaustive, but merely distinguishing between them. Other views worth considering include a broadly Kripkean *functional identity* view (see, for instance, Papineau 2002 and Loar 1990: 99–101), which upholds the idea that the *Realizer-Result* relation is

---

[26] *Ground functionalism* foregoes a functionalist analysis of mental state terms, and so falls silent on their meaning (as does *Naturalistic dualism*). *Ground functionalism* is thus consistent with a purely disquotational view, on which the only thing to be said about the meaning of a given mental state term '*t*' is that it means *t* (e.g., 'pain' means pain). In my view, there are few terms that allow for non-disquotational analyses, so there should be little expectation of a non-disquotational analysis of 'pain' or other mental state terms.

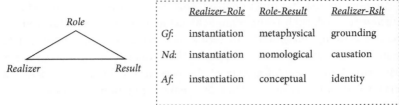

Figure 7.13

identity, but treats this identity not as a matter of *a priori* conceptual analysis, but rather as an *a posteriori* discovered identity in nature (like the water-H2O identity).[27]

Note that, in distinguishing these views, I am helping myself to the ideology of "nomological," "metaphysical," and "conceptual," as intuitive and distinct notions. (I treat these notions as correlated with different modalities, but would not explicate the distinctions modally—to my mind the modal differences are better viewed as manifestations of a fundamental distinction between *cause*, *ground*, and *definition*.) I trust that the distinctions I draw can be recognized, even by readers who prefer different terms. But the reader who will not tolerate my ideology may need to fend for herself.

2.3 The Case for Ground Functionalism

I have introduced *Ground functionalism*, argued that it enables a viable explanation for conscious experience (Section 2.1), and distinguished it from extant views (Section 2.2). I conclude by arguing that *Ground functionalism* preserves the core advances of functionalism, is favored by *Abductive metaphysics* (Section 1.3) for being explanatorily fruitful, and is preferable to alternative views for this and other reasons.

---

[27] Chalmers (1996: 161–8) offers some more full-blown taxonomies, under which I take *Ground functionalism* to count as a form of "nonreductive" and "type B" materialism. But Chalmers does not use the ideology of grounding (to be fair, he was writing before grounding came onto center stage in metaphysics), and so neither distinguishes grounding-based from other versions of type B materialisms, nor anticipates how *Ground functionalism* fits into a general and independently motivated view of metaphysical explanation that emerged in the grounding literature. Indeed his (1996: 167) central resistance to Type B materialism is that "it relies on a metaphysics that is either incoherent or obscure, and one that is largely unmotivated; the main motivation is simply to avoid dualism at all costs." I may be understood as responding that grounding provides exactly the sort of general and motivated framework that the type B materialist needs.

As to preserving the core advances of functionalism, I take these to consist in reconciling materialism with inner mental life and multiple realizability. It should be obvious that *Ground functionalism*—and indeed any view upholding *Functional correlation*—allows for multiple realizability. This is already exhibited in Section 2.1 with Huma the human, Marvin the Martian, and Casper the ghost. *Ground functionalism* allows these diverse realizations to ground the same mental state, just by taking the grounding condition for a mental state to be the relatively abstract condition of realizing a functional role.

Moreover *Ground functionalism* allows for inner mental life. This is also exhibited with Huma, Marvin, and Casper, where *Ground functionalism* allows us to attribute not just outward dispositions to behave (e.g., withdrawal), but inner conscious experiences (e.g., pain).

As to materialism, *Ground functionalism* preserves the materialist-friendly aspect of *Analytic functionalism*, by allowing that a purely material system can—in virtue of its functioning—enact mental states. Indeed, *Ground functionalism* is designed so as to entail that, if the actual realizers are material (as is empirically plausible), then every actual mental state is grounded in the material. This result fits Loewer's (2001: 39) characterization of physicalism as claiming that "the fundamental properties and facts are physical and everything else obtains in virtue of them," fits Trogdon's (2013: 471; see also Bennet 2011: 33 and Dasgupta 2014: 557–9) "standard gloss of physicalism" as claiming that "in the actual world each mental fact is ultimately grounded in certain physical facts...", and fits the view I elsewhere (Schaffer 2017: 14) label "*Ground physicalism*" on which "[t]he physical is the ultimate ground for the chemical, the biological, and the psychological." In a related context Rosen (2010: 118; see also Pautz 2017: 388–9) says:

[T]here is a difference between the materialist who holds that the facts about phenomenal consciousness are grounded in, and hence necessitated by, the neurophysiological facts that underline them, and the dualist for whom the neural facts merely cause or generate conscious states according to contingent causal laws.

Overall, *Ground functionalism* is compatible with the world being fundamentally material (in the sense that all independent inputs into the grounding machinery are material states). It is also compatible with the idea that the material explains the mental (Section 2.3), that there is "nothing special" about the mental (like all higher-level phenomena, it is an output from fundamental physical inputs via the grounding machinery), and that the physical forms a metaphysical supervenience basis for the mental (where "metaphysical supervenience," as with "metaphysical necessity" above, holds grounding principles fixed). I say these are more than enough to qualify *Ground functionalism* as materialist-friendly (see also Schaffer 2017: 19–21).

That said, "materialism" is something of a cluster concept, and there are at least two theses in the cluster that *Ground functionalism* does not uphold. First, some materialists seek to completely excise mental terms from "the book of the world" (to borrow a phrase from Sider 2011). But the ground functionalist posits a mind making principle linking functional role (itself not a fundamental aspect of the material, but never mind that) to mental state, and so uses mental terms to describe the derivative outputs.[28]

Secondly, some materialists hold that every state of the world must be token-identical to a material state.[29] But the ground functionalist says that a given token mental state is grounded in the material, and given that grounding is *irreflexive*, it follows that the token mental state is not identical to, but merely dependent upon, its material grounds. (Nor is there any other material token to plausibly identify with the mental token.) Note that the ground functionalist is not saying that the mental state is wholly distinct from the material state either. There is an intermediate status between *identity* and *distinctness*, seen paradigmatically in the relation between partially overlapping things, and seen more generally—I say—between ground and derivative (Schaffer 2016: 75–6). I am saying that, on *Ground functionalism*, token mental states are neither identical to nor distinct from token material states, but have the intermediate status of ground and derivative.

I take these two points to show that there are recognizably materialist approaches that neither erase mental state terms from the book of the world, nor claim any token identities between material and mental states. But I do

---

[28] Given that grounding relations are generally backed by principles connecting the more to the less fundamental, principles generally will need higher-level terminology to characterize the non-fundamental outputs. There is nothing special about the mental here. For instance, if we want to recognize chemicals like H2O molecules as derivative but real entities, then we will need principles that use the chemical terminology of "H2O molecule" on the output side. No chemical terms on the output side, no chemical output.

[29] In this vein Nagel (1974: 446–7) says that "the meaning of physicalism is clear enough … mental events are physical events." But he adds that "when the two terms of the identification are very disparate it may not be so clear how it could be true" so that "an air of mystery surrounds the identification."

not care to squabble over labels. The reader is welcome to label *Ground functionalism* a form of "dualism" or "emergentism" (or perhaps a new position entirely), so long as she recognizes that *Ground functionalism* is built around the thesis that the mental is not fundamental but rather grounded in the physical. Indeed, we may leave the cluster concept of materialism behind, and just consider this grounding thesis in its own right, as a basis for the empirical material-mental correlations seen in nature. The reader who thinks this grounding thesis is too weak is invited to show the evidence for any stronger claim.

This concludes my case that *Ground functionalism* preserves the core advances of functionalism. Given that *Ground functionalism* both enables a viable explanation for consciousness and preserves the core advances of functionalism, I add that it is favored by *Abductive metaphysics* for being explanatorily fruitful. Or at least, given that we want a materialist metaphysics and an explanation for conscious experience (neither of which claim I have argued for here, but both of which strike me as deeply plausible), a mind making principle is worth the positing. So I say that *Ground functionalism* provides a new chapter in the hopeful materialist story of the mind, preserving the insights of functionalism while integrating the developments of metaphysical grounding to achieve explanation.

I have focused on the positive development of *Ground functionalism*, and have not attempted to criticize other views. But I close with a parting glance at some comparative reasons for preferring *Ground functionalism* over *Naturalistic dualism*, *Analytic functionalism*, and functional identity theories, if only to trace some changes in the usual dialectic, and point to some lines of further discussion.

So, first, as compared to *Naturalistic dualism*, *Ground functionalism* is mainly to be preferred for allowing materialism.[30] But a second reason to prefer *Ground functionalism* is that the material-mental correlations do not seem nomological (as the naturalistic dualist claims), in at least three

---

[30] Thus dualists often acknowledge that they would prefer materialism but were only driven to dualism by the arguments. For instance, Chalmers (1996: xiv) says:

> For a number of years, I had hoped for a materialist theory; when I gave up on this hope, it was quite reluctantly. It eventually seemed plain to me that these conclusions were forced on anyone who wanted to take consciousness seriously. Materialism is a beautiful and compelling view of the world, but to account for consciousness, we have to go beyond the resources it provides.

I am saying that *Ground functionalism* offers a new hope for materialism.

respects. For the most fundamental nomological connections of our world seem to have the following character:

- They link *fundamental* states of nature
- They are *global*, concerning whole states of the cosmos
- They are *dynamic*, governing the temporal evolution of systems (or expressing global constraints).

In this vein Maudlin (2007: 172) speaks of "fundamental laws of temporal evolution" which "specify how the state of the universe will, or might, evolve from a given initial state."

Now consider a given psycho-physical connection, such as the C-fiber firing to pain link. I say that this link has none of the bulleted characteristics of a fundamental law. It does not link fundamental states, since it invokes C-fiber firings on the left, which are not fundamental on any account. (Note that I am not complaining that this connection invokes pain on the right, as that complaint would beg the question against the dualist; rather I am complaining that this connection invokes C-fiber firings on the left, which are not fundamental material states on any account.) It is not global (nor perfectly local) but rather regional, operating at a middle-sized biological scale. And it is not dynamic but synchronic. Such regional and synchronic ropes through the nonfundamental look like vertical grounding connections (as per *Ground functionalism*) rather than horizontal causal connections (as per *Naturalistic dualism*).[31]

Secondly, as compared to *Analytic functionalism*, *Ground functionalism* is mainly to be preferred for explaining consciousness. But another reason to prefer *Ground functionalism* is that *Analytic functionalism* is based on meaning claims that are just obviously false, and indeed are already refuted by the mere conceivability of zombie scenarios. For recall that analytic functionalism claims that it is conceptually necessary that realizing the functional role for a mental state means having that mental state. But— given that the zombie scenario is conceptually possible—it is conceptually possible to have a functional duplicate of our world but which is devoid of any conscious experience at all. So it immediately follows that analytic functionalist's claim of conceptual necessity is false, *before any questionable jump from conceptual necessity to metaphysical necessity*. Hence I agree with

---

[31] See Schaffer (forthcoming) for further criticism of the laws of nature posited by the naturalistic dualist.

Chalmers (1996: 17–18), when he claims: "It is not a *conceptual* truth that the process should be accompanied by the phenomenal quality, but it is a fact about the world." I am just proposing that this fact about the world is not a contingent nomological connection as Chalmers then infers, but something intermediate he did not consider: a metaphysically necessary grounding connection.[32]

The third and final parting comparison I offer is with functional identity theories. Again, *Ground functionalism* is mainly to be preferred for explaining consciousness. But a second reason to prefer *Ground functionalism* is that, while functional identity theories dispense with obviously false claims of conceptual analysis, they leave in their wake bare and incredible identity assertions. For instance, the property of *having a property caused by tissue damage and causing avoidance behavior* and the property of *being in pain* look like clearly different properties (with different extensions at zombie scenarios). There is far more to say. For instance, perhaps this appearance of difference is just an illusion due to specific features of our phenomenal concepts (see Tye 2002, Loar 1990, and Papineau 2002 on "conceptual dualism"; but see Chalmers 2007 for an argument against such views). But for now suffice it to say that the ground functionalist avoids such bare and incredible identity assertions.

A third reason to prefer *Ground functionalism* is that functional identity theories have trouble reconciling the unity and the causal efficacy of mental properties (Kim 1998). There is a core dilemma between *role theories* which identify mental properties with causally inefficacious second-order properties, and *realizer theories* which identify mental properties with disunified first-order realizing properties. There is far more to say (see Robb & Heil 2018 for a useful overview of the myriad issues arising). But for now, suffice it to say that the ground functionalist allows mental properties to stand as unified first-order properties.

Leaving this parting glance at comparisons aside, my primary claim remains that *Ground functionalism* achieves a viable materialist-friendly explanation for conscious experience. Nagel (1974: 445) says: "If we acknowledge that a physical theory of mind must account for the subjective

---

[32] The functionalist literature is replete with examples of terms that really do seem to have functionalist meanings, like 'mousetrap.' But it seems to me that phenomenal terms just do not have these sorts of functionalist meanings. To the extent that we can say anything substantive about their meanings beyond bare disquotational claims like " 'pain' means pain," these terms seem to name types of inner subjective feels, not causal abilities and liabilities. Small wonder that analytic functionalism was unable to properly explain inner experience, when it began by mis-defining it.

character of experience, we must admit that no presently available conception gives us a clue how this could be done." I claim to have shown how this can be done by positing that mind making is at work. Minds are made by dancing, and even matter can dance.[33]

References

Albert, David. 1996. Elementary Quantum Metaphysics. *Bohmian Mechanics and Quantum Theory: An Appraisal*, eds. James T. Cushing, Arthur Fine, and Sheldon Goldstein: 277–84. Dordrecht: Kluwer.

Allori, Valia. 2013. Primitive Ontology and the Structure of Fundamental Physical Theories. *The Wave Function: Essays on the Metaphysics of Quantum Mechanics*, eds. Alyssa Ney and David Albert: 58–75. Oxford: Oxford University Press.

Armstrong, David. 1968. *A Materialist Theory of the Mind*. London: Routledge.

Bennett, Karen. 2011. By Our Bootstraps. *Philosophical Perspectives* 25: 27–41.

Block, Ned. 1978. Troubles with Functionalism. *Minnesota Studies in the Philosophy of Science* 9: 261–325.

Chalmers, David. 1996. The Conscious Mind: In *Search of a Fundamental Theory*. Oxford: Oxford University Press.

Chalmers, David. 2007. Phenomenal Concepts and the Explanatory Gap. *Phenomenal Concepts and Phenomenal Knowledge: New Essays on Consciousness and Physicalism*, eds. Torin Alter and Sven Walter: 167–94. Oxford: Oxford University Press.

Chalmers, David. 2012. *Constructing the World*. Oxford: Oxford University Press.

Chalmers, David and Frank Jackson. 2001. Conceptual Analysis and Reductive Explanation. *The Philosophical Review* 110: 315–60.

Dasgupta, Shamik. 2014. The Possibility of Physicalism. *The Journal of Philosophy* 111: 557–92.

[33] Thanks to Paul Audi, Chiara Brozzo, Dave Chalmers, Philip Goff, Uriah Kriegel, Janet Levin, Barbara Montero, Hedda Hassel Mørch, Tim O'Connor, Adam Pautz, Gabriel Rabin, Kelly Trogdon, and audiences at *Summer of Consciousness* (Rice); *New England Workshop on Metaphysics* (Rhode Island College), University of Southern California; *Lost in the Cosmos* (University of Indiana-Bloomington), University of Geneva, University of Virginia, University of Cambridge, Institut Jean Nicod; *Grounding and Consciousness* (New York University-Florence), Tübingen University; and *The Fundamentality Conference* (University of Oxford).

Feynman, Richard. 1965. *The Feynman Lectures on Physics, vol. 3: Quantum Mechanics*, eds. Richard Feynman, Robert Leighton, and Matthew Sands. Reading, MA: Addison-Wesley.

Fine, Kit. 2001. The Question of Realism. *Philosophers' Imprint* 1: 1–30.

Fine, Kit. 2012. Guide to Ground. *Metaphysical Grounding: Understanding the Structure of Reality*, eds. Fabrice Correia and Benjamin Schnieder: 37–80. Cambridge: Cambridge University Press.

Fodor, Jerry. 1981. The Mind/Body Problem. *Scientific American* 244: 114–23.

Garcia-Larrea, Luis and Hélène Bastuji. 2018. Pain and Consciousness. *Progress in Neuro-Pharmacology and Biological Psychiatry* 87B: 193–9.

Gertler, Brie. 2001. The Explanatory Gap is not an Illusion: Reply to Michael Tye. *Mind* 110: 689–94.

Gertler, Brie. 2020. Dualism: How Epistemic Issues Drive Debates about the Ontology of Consciousness. *Oxford Handbook of the Philosophy of Consciousness*: ch. 13. Oxford: Oxford University Press.

Glazier, Martin. 2020. Explanation. *Routledge Handbook of Metaphysical Grounding*, ed. Mike Raven: 121–32. London: Routledge.

Hofweber, Thomas. 2009. Ambitious, yet Modest, Metaphysics. *Metametaphysics*, eds. David Chalmers, David Manley, and Ryan Wasserman: 260–89. Oxford: Oxford University Press.

Jackson, Frank. 1998. *From Metaphysics to Ethics: A Defence of Conceptual Analysis*. Oxford: Oxford University Press.

Khudairi, Hasen. 2018. Grounding, Conceivability, and the Mind-Body Problem. Synthese 195: 919–26.

Kim, Jaegwon. 1998. *Mind in a Physical World: An Essay on the Mind-Body Problem and Mental Causation*. Cambridge, MA: The MIT Press.

Kosman, L. A. 1973. Understanding, Explanation, and Insight in the Posterior Analytics. *Exegesis and Argument: Studies in Greek Philosophy Presented to Gregory Vlastos*, eds. Edward Lee, Alexander Mourelatos, and Richard Rorty: 374–92. New York: Humanities Press.

Kriegel, Uriah. 2020a. What is the Philosophy of Consciousness? *Oxford Handbook of the Philosophy of Consciousness*, ed. Uriah Kriegel: 1–13. Oxford: Oxford University Press.

Kriegel, Uriah. 2020b. Beyond the Neural Correlates of Consciousness, ed. Uriah Kriegel. *Oxford Handbook of the Philosophy of Consciousness*: ch. 12. Oxford: Oxford University Press.

Levin, Janet. 2018. Functionalism. *Stanford Encyclopedia of Philosophy*: https://plato.stanford.edu/entries/functionalism/ (accessed 4/4/20).

Levine, Joseph. 2001. *Purple Haze*. Oxford: Oxford University Press.

Lewis, David. 1972. Psychophysical and Theoretical Identifications. *Australasian Journal of Philosophy* 50: 249–58.

Lewis, David 1980. Mad Pain and Martian Pain. *Readings in Philosophy of Psychology, Volume 1*, ed. Ned Block: 216–32. Cambridge, MA: Harvard University Press.

Lewis, David and Stephanie Lewis. 1970. Holes. *Australasian Journal of Philosophy* 48: 206–12.

Loar, Brian. 1990. Phenomenal States. *Philosophical Perspectives* 4: 81–108.

Loewer, Barry. 2001. From Physics to Physicalism. *Physics and its Discontents*, eds. Carl Gillet and Barry Loewer: 37–56. Cambridge: Cambridge University Press.

Maudlin, Tim. 2007. *The Metaphysics within Physics*. Oxford: Oxford University Press.

Maudlin, Tim. 2010. Can the World Be Only Wavefunction? *Many Worlds? Everett, Quantum Theory, & Reality*, eds. Simon Saunders, Jonathan Barrett, Adrian Kent, and David Wallace: 121–43. Oxford: Oxford University Press.

Montero, Barbara. 2013. Must Physicalism Imply the Supervenience of the Mental on the Physical? *Journal of Philosophy* 110: 93–110.

Nagel, Thomas. 1974. What is it Like to Be a Bat? *The Philosophical Review* 83: 435–50.

Ney, Alyssa. 2013. Ontological Reduction and the Wave Function Ontology. *The Wave Function: Essays on the Metaphysics of Quantum Mechanics*, eds. Alyssa Ney and David Albert: 168–83. Oxford: Oxford University Press.

Papineau, David. 2002. *Thinking about Consciousness*. Oxford: Oxford University Press.

Paul, L. A. 2012. Metaphysics and Modeling: The Handmaiden's Tale. *Philosophical Studies* 160: 1–29.

Pautz, Adam. 2017. The Significance Argument for the Irreducibility of Consciousness. *Philosophical Perspectives* 31: 349–407.

Pearl, Judea. 2000. *Causality: Models, Reasoning, and Inference*. Cambridge: Cambridge University Press.

Putnam, Hilary. 1975 [1967]. The Nature of Mental States. *Mind, Language, and Reality: Philosophical Papers Volume 2*: 429–40. Cambridge: Cambridge University Press.

Quine, W. V. O. 1948. On What There Is. *Review of Metaphysics* 2: 21–38.

Rabin, Gabriel. 2019. Grounding the Gaps or Bumping the Rug? On Explanatory Gaps and Metaphysical Methodology. *Journal of Consciousness Studies* 26: 191–203.

Railton, Peter. 1986. Moral Realism. *The Philosophical Review* 95: 163–207.

Robb, David and John Heil. 2018. Mental Causation. *Stanford Encyclopedia of Philosophy*: https://plato.stanford.edu/entries/mental-causation/ (accessed 4/4/20).

Rosen, Gideon. 2006. The Limits of Contingency. *Identity and Modality*, ed. Fraser MacBride: 13–39. Oxford: Oxford University Press.

Rosen, Gideon. 2010. Metaphysical Dependence: Grounding and Reduction. *Modality: Metaphysics, Logic, and Epistemology*, eds. Bob Hale and Aviv Hoffmann: 109–36. Oxford: Oxford University Press.

Schaffer, Jonathan. 2009. On What Grounds What. *Metametaphysics*, eds. David Chalmers, David Manley, and Ryan Wasserman: 347–83. Oxford: Oxford University Press.

Schaffer, Jonathan. 2010. Monism: The Priority of the Whole. *The Philosophical Review* 119: 31–76.

Schaffer, Jonathan. 2016. Grounding in the Image of Causation. *Philosophical Studies* 173: 49–100.

Schaffer, Jonathan. 2017. The Ground between the Gaps. *Philosophers' Imprint* 17: 1–26.

Schaffer, Jonathan. 2018. Laws for Metaphysical Explanation. *Philosophical Issues* 27: 302–21.

Schaffer, Jonathan. Forthcoming. Naturalistic Dualism and the Problem of Physical Correlates. Grounding and Consciousness, ed. Gabriel Rabin. Oxford: Oxford University Press.

Sider, Theodore. 2011. *Writing the Book of the World*. Oxford: Oxford University Press.

Trogdon, Kelly. 2013. Grounding: Necessary or Contingent? *Pacific Philosophical Quarterly* 94: 465–85.

Tye, Michael. 2000. *Color, Consciousness, and Content*. Cambridge, MA: The MIT Press.

van Inwagen, Peter. 1990. *Material Beings*. Ithaca, NY: Cornell University Press.

Wilsch, Tobias. 2015. The Nomological Account of Ground. *Philosophical Studies* 172: 3293–312.

Wilson, Jessica. 2014. No Work for a Theory of Grounding. *Inquiry* 57: 535–79.

Woodward, James. 2003. *Making Things Happen: A Theory of Causal Explanation*. Oxford: Oxford University Press.

8

Why I Am Not a Dualist

Karen Bennett

I am not a dualist. I do not think there are any nonphysical properties, substances, or facts. I think that the entire nature of the world is grounded in—determined or settled by—its fundamental physical nature.

But *why* do I think this? In the bright light of day, I take physicalism to be almost obvious. But in the dark of night, I have to admit to myself that it is not entirely clear why exactly I dislike dualism. Are there good arguments against it? That is, set aside whether there are good objections to the arguments *for* dualism, or against physicalism. Are there good arguments against the view itself?

In what follows, I will take up that question. After more carefully spelling out what I take dualism and physicalism to be, I will suggest that the most frequently heard arguments against dualism are more problematic than we physicalists like to admit. I will then offer a new argument against dualism. In broad strokes, it is this: dualists do not dodge all demands for explanation by denying that consciousness can be explained in physical terms. I will articulate what exactly it is that they must explain, and offer two independent arguments for thinking that they cannot do so. The basic upshot is that moving to dualism because of a perceived explanatory failure of physicalism simply does not help.

1. Dualism

Dualists think that not all the facts are physical facts. They think that there are facts about phenomenal consciousness[1] that cannot be explained in purely physical terms—facts about what it's like to see red, what it's like to

---

[1] See Block 1995 on the distinction between what he calls 'access consciousness' and 'phenomenal consciousness.' I will usually just say 'consciousness,' but it is the latter I have in mind.

Karen Bennett, *Why I Am Not a Dualist* In: *Oxford Studies in Philosophy of Mind Volume 1*. Edited by: Uriah Kriegel, Oxford University Press (2021). © Karen Bennett. DOI: 10.1093/oso/9780198845850.003.0008

feel sandpaper, what it's like to run ten miles when it's 15° F out, and so on. These phenomenal facts are genuine 'extras,' not fixed, determined, grounded by the physical facts and the physical laws. To use the standard metaphor: even after God settled the physical facts and laws, he had more work to do to put the phenomenal facts in place. Some dualists think that the additional work involves the creation of a special kind of nonphysical substance. More common these days are dualists who think that the add-itional work merely involves the creation and positioning of special non-physical properties, and that is the only form of dualism that I will be explicitly concerned with here. The property dualist's claim is that phenom-enal properties, or at least protophenomenal properties, are among the basic furniture of the world.

Importantly, however, the property dualist does not propose to ignore the evidence from neuroscience. She does not think that the phenomenal facts float utterly free of the physical facts and laws; she thinks they are connected in important ways. But she thinks these connections are contingent. They are breakable, unlike the connection between, say, being a cat and being a mammal, or that between the existence of some atoms standing in certain complex relations to each other, and the existence of a composite object like a table.[2] That is how the property dualist maintains a reasonable respect for the physical sciences, while simultaneously claiming that phenomenal prop-erties are genuinely new additions to the world.

Most contemporary property dualists—at any rate, the ones who are my primary target in this chapter—motivate their view by appeal to a family of arguments that are, in the first instance, arguments against physicalism. What I have in mind are the conceivability argument (Descartes 1641; Kirk 1974, 1996; Kripke 1980; Chalmers 1996), the knowledge argument (Nagel 1974; Jackson 1982), and the more general issue that lies in the background of both—the explanatory gap. Both the knowledge argument and the con-ceivability argument are largely driven by the fact that we don't seem to have any idea how the massively complicated pattern of electrochemical activity in my brain could possibly account for what it's like to see red, or feel sandpaper, etc. As Joseph Levine (2001: 77) puts it, "there seems to be no discernible connection between the physical description and the mental one,

---

[2] Of course, not everyone believes in composite objects; some instead endorse what has come to be known as 'compositional nihilism' (including, to varying degrees, van Inwagen 1990; Merricks 2001; and Dorr and Rosen 2002). But most people, including these nihilists, think that the principles that link simples arranged in certain ways to composite objects are necessary, or necessarily false. The exception is Ross Cameron 2007.

and thus no explanation of the latter in terms of the former." Tell us all the neuroscience you like; it's still a mystery why *that* is what red looks like. That is why we can apparently conceive of zombies, and why it seems compelling to say that Mary learns something new when she emerges from her black-and-white room. Though the details of the particular arguments differ, the purported upshot is the same—namely, that it is a mistake to think that consciousness can be explained in physical terms.

2. What Is Wrong with Dualism?

As I have already indicated, I am not a dualist. Why am I not a dualist? One way to answer that question would be to lay out what I take to be the problems with the arguments for dualism that I have just sketched. There has been a lot of discussion about where exactly those arguments go awry, and those discussions have yielded fruitful work on the relationship between conceivability and possibility, on the nature of phenomenal concepts, and so forth. However, I want to stick with the question of what is wrong with dualism *itself.* Instead of explaining why I am not convinced by the arguments for dualism, I want to discuss why I am committed to finding fault with them in the first place. This is an important task. I do not want my physicalism to be an article of faith.

Unfortunately, it is closer to an article of faith than most of us are willing to admit. The sad truth is that the extant arguments against dualism are not all that compelling. Here are three.

First, consider a quick appeal to simplicity and Ockham's razor—that we should make do with as little as possible, and not multiply entities beyond necessity (e.g., Smart 1959). This alone is not going to convince the dualist, who will justifiably claim that she *is* making do with as little as possible. After all, simplicity can only break ties. It can only be wheeled in to decide between two views that both account for all the data—when all else is, as they say, 'equal.' But the dualist thinks that all else is decidedly *not* equal. She thinks that physicalism cannot account for all the data, and that making sense of conscious experience requires postulating irreducible phenomenal properties. Legitimately appealing to simplicity here requires having independent reason to think that she is wrong about that. Unfortunately, then, this version of the appeal to simplicity is circular. We need to already have reason to think that the physical facts indeed are sufficient for all the facts before we are entitled to shave with Ockham's razor (cf., Kim 2005: 125–6).

That said, I do think there is a more sophisticated appeal to simplicity or elegance to be made, and I will do so soon. All I mean to dismiss here is the quick thought that physicalism automatically wins because it has a smaller ontology. While philosophers with a taste for desert landscapes (Quine 1948) will certainly be inclined towards physicalism, that aesthetic preference does not by itself constitute an *argument* for physicalism.

A second argument against dualism might be called the 'argument from optimistic metainduction.'[3] Science has always managed to make do without before. It has never before needed to postulate irreducible nonphysical properties to solve tricky, long-lasting problems, so why here, in this one isolated instance? But even if the dualist grants the premise, this argument is not going to convince her either. She will again say that consciousness is *different*, consciousness is *weird*, and that there is every reason to think that it requires special treatment. It is therefore hard to see how this appeal to the success of science fares much better than the quick appeal to simplicity.

A third argument against dualism is the argument from causal exclusion. If the mental is truly distinct from the physical, how can it have nonoverdeterministic causal power without violating the completeness of physics? Some would say that the nonreductive physicalist has just as much trouble answering this question as the dualist does (e.g., Kim 1989, 1993, 1998; Crane 2001), but they are wrong; nonreductive physicalists have a very plausible solution that dualists cannot properly motivate (see Bennett 2003, 2008). Nonetheless, it is not clear that dualists need to really care about this, because it is not clear that dualists need to think that physics is causally complete.[4] If they do not, they can duck out of the exclusion problem altogether. We physicalists like the exclusion problem because it gets us from the completeness of physics to physicalism proper; it provides the crucial bridge between the two. Unfortunately, though, it is not entirely obvious why we should think that any dualist would want to get on the bridge in the first place.[5]

---

[3] I owe the name to David Baker; it is, of course, a pun on the "argument from pessimistic metainduction" against scientific realism.

[4] See Papineau 2001 for an interesting survey of reasons to think that physics *is* causally complete, including a critical discussion of the appeal to conservation of energy.

[5] I am inclined to think that the argument against *substance* dualism from mental causation is in even worse shape. Princess Elisabeth famously charged that Descartes could not make any sense of "how the mind of a human being can determine the bodily spirit in producing voluntary actions, being only a thinking substance" (letter to Descartes 6/16 May, 1643). But notice that how much force this sort of concern has depends upon what the right account of causation is. The Princess' objection hits its target if causation requires a connecting process (as in Salmon 1984; Dowe 2000). But it is far from clear that it hits its target if causation merely

Now, I am not saying that none of those three arguments has any force at all. I do think the exclusion problem has *some* force, and that it is important that we be clear that it has more force against a dualist than against a nonreductive physicalist (see Bennett 2008). But all told, we physicalists are perhaps not in as good a position as we like to think. Forget about responding to *objections* to our view; why do we hold it in the first place? What entitles us to our rejection of dualism? Why *am* I not a dualist?

My goal in this chapter is to explore a new answer to that question.[6] Presumably it will not be knockdown, either, but at the least it will contribute to the cluster of concerns that together constitute the case against dualism. The new objection is basically this: dualists do not excuse themselves from all demand for explanation simply because they deny that consciousness can be *physically* explained. Unfortunately, however, nothing they can offer genuinely addresses this demand in a way that is consistent with their reasons for being a dualist in the first place.

In what follows, I will flesh out the details of that sketch. The core of the complaint is clear enough: dualists owe us an explanation that they cannot provide. This places two tasks before me. First, I need to clarify what it is that dualists need to explain. Second, I need to argue that they cannot satisfactorily do so. In the next section, I address the first task. In the rest of the chapter, I address the second.

3. The Dualist's Project

What is it that dualists need to explain? Care is required here, because of course the whole point of dualism is to claim that certain things are *not* explained—that is, certain things are fundamental. There are at least two kinds of things that dualists will say this about: phenomenal properties and physical-phenomenal correlations. Phenomenal properties are things like

---

requires counterfactual dependency, Humean 'constant conjunction,' or perhaps even probability-raising. Even the substance dualist can say that pains are reliably followed by stimulus-avoidance behavior, that the behavior counterfactually depends upon the pain, and so forth. If he chooses his theory of causation carefully, he can say that mental-physical causal interaction is entirely unproblematic—while treating it entirely on a par with purely physical causation (see Loeb 1981; Kim 2005; Bennett 2007 for related remarks).

[6] Or at least new-*ish*. Important precursors include Lycan 1981, Hill 1991, and McLaughlin 2001. See Kim 2005, chapter 5 for discussion.

what it's like to taste coffee, what it's like to feel pain, what it's like to see red. Physical-phenomenal correlations (or psychophysical correlations; I will use these terms interchangeably) are correlations between bodily states and the instantiation of these phenomenal properties. Perhaps such correlations hold across people or even across species; perhaps they only hold within a person over time. But there certainly seem to be some. Scientists do MRI scans, lesion studies, and so forth in order to figure out the 'neural correlates of consciousness.' More prosaically, orange juice tastes one way to people when they first get up, and another rather different way after they brush their teeth. Changes to the chemical environment in people's mouths have a very reliable and replicable effect on the way orange juice tastes, just as the ingestion of chemicals like ibuprofen has a reliable and replicable effect on the way a pain feels. So there are two kinds of things that dualists can say are fundamental: phenomenal properties and psychophysical correlations.

And now we get to what I take to be the crucial question. Just how many of these properties and correlations should the dualist say are fundamental? Is it *some* of them, or is it *all* of them? I claim that a minimally plausible dualism will only say that it is some, not all.

To see why, turn your mind to the view that says that *every single* phenomenal property and *every single* psychophysical correlation is fundamental. This is just an enormous number—a presumably infinite number!—of fundamental posits. The feel of a minor papercut is fundamental experiential property E_1; the feel of a slightly worse papercut is fundamental experiential property E_2 ... and so on and so forth. Similarly for the case of psychophysical correlations. Physical process P is reliably accompanied by a sweet taste. Quite similar physical process P^* is reliably accompanied by a slightly less sweet taste. Once again, the list goes on and on. It would be strange indeed if *each* such correlation had the status of fundamental law.

Certainly, the dualist need not say any such thing. Dualist slogans like 'consciousness is fundamental' can be taken as shorthand for the idea that *some* phenomenal properties, and *some* laws governing the correlations between the physical and the phenomenal, are fundamental.

Compare a purely physical case. Let us suppose that gravity is a fundamental force that figures in fundamental physical laws. This certainly does not entail that *every* fact or generalization about gravity is fundamental! No one thinks that generalizations about the behavior of objects with mass 1 kilogram in the Earth's gravitational field are fundamental, as well as generalizations about the behavior of objects with mass 2 kilograms in the

Earth's gravitational field, as well as generalizations about the behavior of objects with mass 3 kilograms in the Earth's gravitational field...oh, and generalizations about objects with mass 1 kilogram in the *moon's* gravitational field...and so on and so forth. Those principles are instead derived from more fundamental, more general laws.

A minimally plausible dualism will take a similar approach. There is no more reason to think that claims like "physical processes of type *P* are accompanied by flavor sensation of type *F*" are fundamental than there is to think that claims like "a 6 cm3 piece of lead weighs such-and-such on the moon" are. What the dualist should say is that there are some fundamental phenomenal properties and some fundamental laws governing how they are connected to the physical. There is a limited stock of fundamental phenomenal properties and psychophysical correlations or laws, which explain or ground the rest. Some correlations are fundamental law; the others are *derived*. In short, it is implausible for the dualist to fall silent about *all* phenomenal properties and *all* of the connections between the physical and the phenomenal. She will fall silent about some, but she owes us an explanation of others.

This is the more sophisticated appeal to simplicity that I referenced earlier. My claim is not that dualism loses to physicalism just because dualism has a bigger ontology. The claim is rather that a version of dualism loses to a different version of dualism because it has a *vastly* larger ontology that is not in any obvious way necessary.[7] Dualism is a theory about the world, and should be held to the same standards and aspire to the same theoretical virtues as any other theory about the world. Simplicity and elegance and unification matter. A version of dualism that postulates four fundamental psychophysical laws that explain all the rest of the correlations should, all things being equal, be preferred to a version of dualism that leaves all the correlations brute.

Now, I realize that the dualist can make the same reply as I offered earlier to the quick appeal to simplicity in favor of physicalism. She can dig in her heels, and say that there is no way whatsoever to systematize or explain experience: not only can it not be explained in physical terms, but it cannot be explained in *any* terms. There is just nothing to be said about what

---

[7] Note that this appeal to simplicity is consistent with my (2017, chapter 8) and Schaffer's (2015) view that the relevant theoretical virtue is simplicity in the fundamentals.

consciousness is or how it is connected to the physical. Every phenomenal property is fundamental, as is every psychophysical correlation.

Personally, I think such an attitude is bananas, and amounts to giving up completely. But I also recognize that someone who has this attitude will not be moved by that thought. So I will restrict the scope of my conclusion to those dualists who *do* see themselves as having something to say about the so-called "hard problem" of consciousness. For that is what is on the table: dualisms that try to explain consciousness and how it arises from the physical by appeal to a relatively small set of fundamental non-physical properties and laws. This amounts to trying to answer the hard problem, just not in fully physical terms.

This is David Chalmers' strategy. He agrees with everything I have just said (see particularly Chalmers 1996: 124–9; 1997: 399–400), and does not want to simply fall silent about all the psychophysical correlations. He does want to address the hard problem on which physicalism allegedly founders, and thinks that his dualism can help him answer it. He claims that the impossibility of providing a physical explanation of phenomenal consciousness does not mean that we should give up on the hard problem completely, or conclude that "conscious experience lies outside the domain of scientific theory altogether" (Chalmers 1995: 19). Those are not the right reactions. The right reaction, he says, is to look for a different kind of explanation of consciousness. In particular, the right reaction is to accept that answering the hard problem requires going beyond the physical. It requires an "extra ingredient" (Chalmers 1995: xx)—an ingredient that only a dualist can offer:

> Once we accept that materialism is false, it becomes clear that . . . we have to look for a "Y-factor," something *additional* to the physical facts that will help explain consciousness. We find such a Y-factor in the postulation of irreducible psychophysical laws. (Chalmers 1996: 245)

> A physical theory gives a theory of physical processes, and a psychophysical theory tells us how those processes give rise to experience. We know that experience depends on physical processes, but we also know that this dependence cannot be derived from physical laws alone. The new basic principles postulated by a nonreductive theory give us the extra ingredient that we need to build an explanatory bridge. . . . Nothing in this approach contradicts anything in the physical theory; we simply need to add further *bridging* principles to explain how consciousness arises from physical processes. (Chalmers 1995: 20)

The extra explanation-allowing ingredient, then, is a set of fundamental psychophysical laws. These laws are supposed to yield a substantive answer to the hard problem—an answer that no physicalist can provide.[8]

The picture thus far, then, is this. The dualist's project should be—and Chalmers' project indeed is—to provide a distinctively dualist explanation of phenomenal experience and the psychophysical correlations by appeal to a relatively small stock of fundamental phenomenal (or protophenomenal) properties and psychophysical laws. The goal is to use those to systematize, unify, and explain. As Chalmers (1996: 127) says, "the case of physics tells us that fundamental laws are typically simple and elegant; we should expect the same of the fundamental laws in a theory of consciousness." The fundamental psychophysical laws do not themselves link particular patterns of neural activity to easily recognized phenomenal states like a sensation of red, or the smell of dust. They are, instead, simple and general—more like F=ma or e=mc2—and are used to explain those correlations.

4. My Skepticism: Preliminaries

I am skeptical that the dualist can find anything here that will help. I do not think that she can systematize and unify the correlations without undermining her appeal to the explanatory gap. In Sections 5 and 6, I shall try to make this point in two rather different ways.

My first argument is a methodological one, and has to do with the very idea of the dualist engaging in empirical investigation to continue the search for explanation. The basic thought is that there is a tension in the very notion of a "naturalistic dualism"—not a contradiction, certainly, but an odd

---

[8] A quick clarification about how the appeal to fundamental laws or bridge principles is supposed to help. Clearly, Chalmers is not saying that he can get some explanatory mileage out of the claim that each macro-correlation is itself a fundamental law. I have just argued that it would be implausible to claim that each one is fundamental—but it would be far *more* implausible to think that doing so somehow explains why they hold! We cannot explain how and why a physical process-type P is accompanied by searing pain by citing a brute, fundamental law to the effect that P is accompanied by searing pain. That is not an explanation; that is just repeating the explanandum. Quite generally, one cannot *explain* a B*A connection by saying that there is a brute B*A connecting law. The macro-correlations are to be explained, not to do the explaining. So Chalmers' appeal to fundamental laws must involve a certain mismatch between the correlations in the *explanandum*, and the correlations in the laws that constitute the *explanans*. Since a correlation cannot be explained by claiming that it is itself a fundamental law, he needs to postulate some *other* fundamental laws to help do so.

tension that it would be a mistake to ignore. I will claim that it is odd for the dualist to think both that empirical work can help her systematize the teeming swarm of phenomenal properties and psychophysical correlations, and that the explanatory gap poses a real problem for physicalists.

My second argument arises from consideration of the shape and structure of the kinds of laws the dualist would offer. Even if we are careful to take seriously the dualist's *a priori* constraints on what sorts of thing might help, we either make no progress on the hard problem, or else wind up replacing the hard problem with a different problem that is equally hard.

Let me make one preliminary point before getting into either argument. I am about to begin fretting about who can offer what in the attempt to explain consciousness and the psychophysical correlations. It is important to bear in mind that *both* dualists and physicalists might want to postulate 'new'—that is, hitherto unrecognized—entities, properties, or laws to enable them to get somewhere with their explanatory burdens. It would be a mistake to think that only dualists can do so, that postulating anything new counts as the failure of physicalism. Physicalism is not the view that everything logically supervenes on, and can be explained in terms of, the properties, forces, entities, and laws understood by *current* physicists. Physicalism does not assume that current physics is finished. It is, of course, notoriously difficult to define 'physical', and consequently notoriously difficult to decide what sorts of additions to the stock of fundamental laws and entities are physicalistically acceptable.

Here is my guideline for deciding that question: if the addition either *is* conscious experience, or is needed *only* to make sense of conscious experience, physicalism fails. But if the addition is needed to make sense of *both* conscious experience *and* an array of other, paradigmatically physical, phenomena, then physicalism might well be true. For example, it is far from obviously a failure of physicalism to postulate a new fundamental force that explains, say, dark matter, gravity, the surface tension of liquids, *and* consciousness. Consequently, the mere prediction that *current* neuroscience, physics, etc. will not be able to explain consciousness—that something new will need to be discovered—is not itself a commitment to dualism. Commitment to dualism is only incurred when the newly postulated properties or laws have a certain nature. The dualist will take some sort of phenomenal or proto-phenomenal properties to be fundamental, and will postulate new fundamental laws that range over them. The physicalist will do no such thing.

5. The Methodological Argument

Consider the ways in which the dualist is going to search for the new fundamental laws. Here, my focus is simply on the search strategy, rather than any guessed specifics about what the laws might actually *be*. (My second argument will involve suggestions about what rough form the laws would have to take.) The dualist's idea seems to be that we should simply continue doing science, but with the appropriately open mind that comes from giving up the presumption that phenomenality can be explained in physical terms. Chalmers often talks this way. For example, he says that the "liberating force of taking consciousness as fundamental" is that "we no longer need to bash our head against the wall trying to reduce consciousness to something it is not; instead we can engage in the search for a constructive explanatory theory" (Chalmers 1997: 400). The dualist proclaims her dualism and then dives into scientific research to see what turns up.

I frankly do not see what is so liberating about dualism. I cannot see how it makes any difference at all to the course of empirical investigation. And since it does not, taking straightforward empirical investigation to help answer the hard problem undermines the appeal to the conceivability arguments to support dualism in the first place. The latter of those two claims is probably the more controversial one, but let me say something about each in turn.

Both the dualist and the physicalist have a long hard search ahead of them, and the difference between their long hard searches is opaque. The dualist and the physicalist have exactly the same research strategies at their disposal. Both will do a lot of serious neuroscience, and both will pay attention to introspective phenomenology in order to get a better understanding of 'phenomenal space.' Both will run labs, employ postdocs, and apply for NSF funding. Their antecedent commitments will not have any impact on what experiments are available to them, or on what they find. The physicalist research project and the dualist research project do not differ in their methodology or tools, but only in their predicted outcome. That is, the only real dispute is about what they will emerge with at the end of the day. When our intrepid researchers open their laboratory doors several hundred years hence, what will they announce? The physicalist bets that they will announce a solution to the hard problem that only relies upon roughly the sorts of laws, properties or entities that we need to make sense of the straightforwardly physical world. The dualist bets that they will announce a solution that takes consciousness as basic, and invokes new fundamental

psychophysical laws. That is the only difference between them. They disagree about the expected outcome of the very same course of scientific
investigation.

This puts the dualist in a rather precarious position. The dualist apparently agrees with the (type A) physicalist[9] both that we are currently
perplexed, and that at the end of science we will not be. But it is odd to
claim that no long hard search for a physicalist explanation of consciousness
can possibly succeed, yet keep faith in the long hard search for new fundamental laws that will enable a dualist to solve the hard problem. This is
particularly odd in light of the fact that it is the *very same long hard search*.
Indeed, it is hard to see how this faith in the march of science is consistent
with the dualist's appeal to the explanatory gap to support her view.

The dualist is making an *a priori* prediction about the outcome of
scientific research. The question is whether she is justified in doing so.
She, unsurprisingly, will claim that she is—she will claim that she has *a
priori* reason to think that the physicalist research program cannot succeed.
That is the point of the conceivability argument, and her appeal to the
explanatory gap more generally. But *my* point is that her reliance on those
arguments is rendered suspect by her subsequent embrace of empirical
investigation. If the dualist thinks that scientific research can uncover
hitherto unsuspected truths about the fundamental laws governing psychophysical connections, why should she not also think that it can uncover
hitherto unsuspected truths about the physical? That it can generate a
deeper understanding of our physicalist tools?

The dualist is endorsing a rather odd pair of propositions here. She is
simultaneously insisting that

the fact that we have no idea how to explain consciousness in physical terms
is a problem in principle, and there is no point in turning to science to
help us,

and that

the fact that we have no idea what the fundamental psychophysical laws are
is just temporary, and science will save the day.

---

[9] The type A physicalist thinks that any apparent explanatory gap between the physical and
the phenomenal is merely a function of our ignorance, and will be closed sometime in the
future. See Chalmers 2002: 251–2.

These claims are not straightforwardly incompatible with each other, but there is a real tension between them. Acceptance of the latter should undermine confidence in the former. The more you can see how research in the cognitive sciences can tell us how consciousness arises from the physical, the less secure you should be in your intuition that no purely physicalist story could ever work. All told, then, I suspect that the claim that anything explanatory can be found empirically conflicts with the dualist's reasons for being a dualist in the first place.

6. The Second Argument

My second argument for the claim that dualists cannot make progress on the hard problem is independent of the first. So set aside the methodological concern from the previous section, and suppose there is no tension between the empirical search for systematizing laws and the reliance upon the explanatory gap to dismiss physicalism. What should dualism look like? I begin by claiming that dualism must make some kind of appeal to proto-phenomenal properties—properties that are neither exactly physical nor phenomenal. I then consider two quite different ways of pursuing this appeal, and argue that neither helps at all. On the first, the hard problem simply does not go away; on the second, the hard problem is replaced with a different but equally hard problem.

The first stage of the argument, then, is to argue that the dualist is committed to some sort of protophenomenal properties—or, if that label has unwanted associations, perhaps 'phenomenal minima.'[10] Here is the idea. I have already argued that she should not claim that *every* phenomenal property is a fundamental property. The dualist should not claim that *what it's like to see red* is a fundamental property, and so is *what it's like to see crimson*, and so is *what it's like to see magenta . . .* Slogans like 'consciousness is fundamental' ought not be interpreted as meaning that every single phenomenal property and every single psychophysical correlation is funda-mental. Rather, the dualist should pursue the project of explaining some phenomenal properties and psychophysical correlations in terms of a more limited stock of fundamental properties and laws.

---

[10]   I owe the phrase to Ted Sider.

What might this limited stock of fundamentals look like? Well, it's not going to consist of some small set of familiar person-level phenomenal properties. For example, it would just be silly to claim that the only two fundamental phenomenal properties are *what it's like to see red* and *what it's like to taste a particular single malt scotch*. Those two do not exhaust the basic ingredients out of which the rich tapestry of conscious experience is woven! And although those particular examples are perhaps especially arbitrary, I do not see how any other small set of person-level experiences could exhaust the ingredients either. It is not the case that specific bits of person-level conscious experience build all the rest of person-level conscious experience.

The more promising move is for the dualist to claim that there are some unfamiliar, fundamental phenomenal or quasi-phenomenal properties out of which the familiar person-level ones are somehow built. There are common elements that combine and recombine in various ways to generate experience as we know it. Systematizing the relationship between the physical and the phenomenal is a matter of figuring out what those elements are, and what general laws govern their relations both to the physical and to each other. This is what I mean by 'phenomenal minima'. They might be properties of very small entities like carbon atoms, or they might be less-than-fully-phenomenal properties of larger entities like brains or persons. I will often speak in the former way, but I officially leave the matter open. In short: the dualist who shoulders the explanatory task I have set her is committed to postulating some sort of phenomenal minima.

From here, I can see two different ways for the story to unfold. The first is a kind of bridge-principle protophenomenalism. The second is a view that has been called various things, but the label that seems to have stuck is 'Russellian monism' (see Chalmers 1996: 153–5; 2002: 265–7; 2016b; Stoljar 2001). I shall look at each in turn.

On the first picture, the protophenomenal properties occupy in some sense an intervening level between the physical and the phenomenal. They constitute a kind of bridge that connects them. On this view, the new fundamental laws that enable a solution to the hard problem would not be directly between the physical and the phenomenal. They would instead be between the physical and the protophenomenal, and the protophenomenal and the phenomenal. That is, the correlations between the physical and the phenomenal would be given a two-stage explanation that makes reference to an intervening protophenomenal level. First, there are fundamental laws connecting properties like, say, *being a carbon atom* and special protophenomenal properties. Second, there are special fundamental laws of "mental chemistry" (Nagel 1979: 182; Coleman 2012) that govern the interactions among protophenomenal properties. Put enough carbon atoms together in the right sort of structure, and they will yield a pain.[11]

This picture has a certain appeal. You almost *can* see how the physical gives rise to consciousness; you almost *can* see how from certain arrangements of *carbon atoms* you get a pain. So, have we an answer to the puzzle? Have we a distinctively dualist explanation of how consciousness arises from the physical?

I say no. And the reason I say no is not, I think, what has come to be known as the 'combination problem' for panpsychism, though it is at least a cousin of sorts (recall that this chapter was originally written in 2005–6). The combination problem is originally due to William James, and comes in a variety of guises. One central variety is that "experiences don't sum," as Philip Goff (2006) puts it—that little fragments of phenomenality simply cannot by their nature combine into a 'larger' whole. Another central variety is that if experience *did* have some sort of quasi-mereological structure, we would notice—but our experiences seem simple and unitary. (See Coleman 2012 for these two versions; see Chalmers 2016a for even more versions. See also Stoljar 2006, Shani 2010, and Montero 2016 for more discussion; this list is far from exhaustive.) My concern is not that there is something special about phenomenal or protophenomenal properties that either prohibits them from combining or somehow would make their combinatorial structure manifest. As I said, I can kind of see the appeal of 'mental chemistry.' My concern is rather that I do not see how the hard problem can fail to rearise.

I claim that the bridging version of protophenomenalism faces a dilemma: either a version of the hard problem rearises between the protophenomenal and phenomenal, or else a version of the hard problem rearises between the physical and the protophenomenal. The crucial question is: just how phenomenal are these protophenomenal properties supposed to be?

First, suppose that they are not particularly phenomenal at all. This is a reasonable way to go, at least at first glance. After all, it seems sensible to deny that protophenomenal properties have any of the traditional marks of

---

[11] Note that on this approach, consciousness is not itself fundamental. It cannot be given a constitutive explanation in *physical* terms—so physicalism is false—but it *can* be given a constitutive explanation. Hence my earlier claim that the dualist would only *probably* say that consciousness is fundamental.

the mental. Here are three such marks, which are possessed by standard phenomenal properties like *feeling a searing pain*, or *having a visual impression as of a leafy green tree*. First, there it is something it is like to have them. Second, they are introspectible; we have a certain sort of privileged access to them. Third, that access is arguably incorrigible—although I can be wrong about whether I *do* see a tree, I cannot be wrong about whether I *seem* to see a tree. Dualists like to emphasize all three of these features. They are what make the mental so puzzling. And on this horn of the dilemma, we assume that protophenomenal properties have none of these features. They are not introspectible, incorrigibly or not, and there is nothing it is like to have them. But the more we make such apparently reasonable claims, the more the putatively protophenomenal properties look more physical than phenomenal, and the view starts looking more physicalist than dualist. If so, though, we now need a story about how consciousness arises from the *protophenomenal*. Now we need to know how certain kinds of fully phenomenal experience—what it's like to see red, what orange juice tastes like after brushing your teeth—arise from complex arrangements of properties that are not themselves fully phenomenal. The explanatory gap has not been closed; it has just been shunted into the space between the protophenomenal and the phenomenal. The hard problem rearises there.

We move to the second horn of the dilemma by deciding that that was all a mistake. Perhaps it is wrong to think of protophenomenal properties as being so similar to physical ones; perhaps they really *do* have the marks of the mental. Let us, then, consider the claim that protophenomenal properties *are* introspectible, that carbon atoms have privileged access into their protophenomenal states, and that there is something it is like to be a carbon atom. This move would indeed avoid the concern that we now need an account of how consciousness arises from the protophenomenal. However, it does so at a rather high cost. For one thing, the view is arguably committed to a strange near-panpsychism.[12] Even Thomas Nagel, who is tempted by protophenomenalism of roughly this variety—at least to the extent that it should be "added to the current list of mutually incompatible and hopelessly

---

[12] The view is not committed to full-blown *pan*psychism, unlike the next version of protophenomenalism to be discussed. For one thing, the view allows that there are fundamental physical particles that are not constituents of conscious beings, and which do not have protophenomenal properties. For another thing, bear in mind that the fundamental protophenomenal properties might be possessed only by large and complex physical systems—brains, for example. This, of course, makes them rather different than other fundamental properties, but that is only to be expected.

unacceptable solutions to the mind-body problem" (1979: 193)—resists the idea that "the components out of which a point of view is constructed would ... themselves have to have a point of view" (194). However, panpsychism is not my real complaint at the moment (I shall say more about it shortly). The important point for the moment is that this view, like the alternative, simply pushes the hard problem elsewhere. **If protophenomenal properties are so like phenomenal ones, well, then now we need a story about how the protophenomenal arises from the physical. We have lost out on the project of explaining personal-level fully phenomenal properties and correlations with less than fully phenomenal ones.**

Either way, then, the protophenomenalist has failed to address the hard problem. The more similar the protophenomenal properties are to phenomenal ones, the less headway can be made on the project of systematizing the correlations. And the more removed the protophenomenal properties are from phenomenal ones, the less point there is to postulating them at all. We still cannot see how human experience—genuine, full-blown consciousness—arises from complicated relations among such fragmentary shadows of phenomenality.

Indeed, there is a case to be made that this bridging version of protophenomenalism slides into a regress. To see it, consider the version that says that protophenomenal properties are quite different from ordinary phenomenal properties—the version on which they do not bear the marks of the mental. (A similar issue arises for the other version.) In order to bridge the gap between the protophenomenal and the truly phenomenal, maybe we should posit a *fourth* kind of property—protoprotophenomenal properties, or, better, protophenophenomenal properties. These occupy the intervening level between the protophenomenal and the phenomenal, and their connections between the two are governed by a limited set of fundamental protophenomenal–protophenophenomenal laws, and fundamental protophenophenomenal–phenomenal lawsfundamental. Lather, rinse, repeat. I am not fully convinced this regress argument works, but I nonetheless place it on the table for inspection. My main claim is the one from the previous paragraph: for bridging protophenomenalism, the hard problem rearises either between the physical and the protophenomenal, or between the protophenomenal and the phenomenal.

It is time to move away from the bridging version of protophenomenalism, and on to the second version: Russellian monism. On this view, the phenomenal minima do not occupy an intervening level between the physical and the fully phenomenal, but rather occupy physical properties themselves. Metaphorically speaking, they form the *core* of physical properties. More carefully, the idea is that there is independent motivation for the view that physical properties and entities can be characterized only relationally, by their causal-dispositional roles (Russell 1927). If such a view is correct, there is a pressing question about what intrinsic properties fill these causal-dispositional roles. One answer to this question is designed to also address the hard problem. If protophenomenal properties fill the causal-dispositional roles, two problems are solved at once. There are various ways to flesh out the details, but all that really matters for my purposes is the view's central claim—the world is qualitative *all the way down*.

Russellian monism avoids the dilemma that faced the bridge version of protophenomenalism; it does not simply push the hard problem elsewhere. Two features allow it to do this. First, the very nature of physical properties and entities is protophenomenal. Physical properties are relational, dispositional, "structural/dynamic" (Chalmers 2002: 265); intrinsic protophenomenal properties underlie them. This means that there is no gap between the physical and the protophenomenal in the first place, and Russellian monism dodges the second horn of the dilemma. Second, as long as the protophenomenal cores are taken to have the marks of the mental, or at least some approximation thereof, there may not be any particularly difficult question of how full-blooded phenomenal properties arise from them. So Russellian monism can dodge the first horn of the dilemma as well.

It is worth taking a moment to emphasize that the Russellian monist *must* claim that the protophenomenal properties are recognizably phenomenal. One reason is that just mentioned—the view would otherwise be impaled on the first horn of the dilemma. But the Russellian monist has a further reason, one that does not quite apply to the 'bridge' version of protophenomenalism. This further reason is that there would otherwise be very little reason not to count the view as a form of physicalism. After all, the view is that there are rock-bottom features of the world that account for the charge of electrons, the behavior of gases, the hardness of diamonds ... and consciousness. This is straightforwardly physicalist if those rock-bottom features are non-qualitative.

Recall my earlier remark that a good guideline for deciding whether or not an addition to our ontology counts as physical is the range of phenomena for which it accounts. If the additional feature either is consciousness, or explains nothing but consciousness, then that is probably sufficient for it not to be physical; if it explains clearly physical phenomena as well, then that is at least a *prima facie* reason to say that it is indeed physical. The Russellian monist's protophenomenal properties meet that *prima facie* guideline for counting as physical—they ground every physical property. However, if they also bear the marks of the mental, they meet the sufficient condition for *not* counting as physical. If the Russellian monist does not want to be a physicalist, then, he must say that protophenomenal properties are themselves recognizably phenomenal. (See Chalmers 2016b for discussion of whether Russellian monism counts as physicalist or not.)

As I have already suggested, this is not a particularly natural view. It is rather odd to claim that there is something it is like to be a carbon atom. However, it is hard to see how to do more than trade intuitions about this point. So let us set it aside, and suppose that there is, indeed, something it is like to be a carbon atom. I still do not like Russellian monism any more than I like the other version of protophenomenalism. It may solve the official hard problem, but only by generating a new problem that is just as hard.[13]

Start by noticing that the Russellian monist is committed to the following claims. There is no in principle difference between me and a carbon atom, or me and my socks. There are differences in organization, and complexity, and the like, but that is all. These are differences in degree, not kind; there is no unbridgeable chasm between me and my socks. But those, of course, are claims that any *physicalist* will endorse as well. The Russellian monist says that the world is mental all the way down. The physicalist says that it is physical all the way up. Both are forms of monism; both assimilate one of the allegedly different categories to the other.

Of course, the Russellian version of monism does get to say that there is no issue about how the qualitative arises from the nonqualitative, because the world is qualitative all the way down. But now the opposite problem arises! What shall he say about how the *non*qualitative arises from the qualitative? The physicalist says it is nonqualitative all the way up, and faces a question of how the qualitative gets into the picture. The Russellian monist says it is qualitative all the way down, and thus faces a question of how the nonqualitative gets into the picture. The difference between the physicalist and the Russellian monist is a reversal about what explains what: the physicalist wants to explain the mental in physical terms, and the

---

[13] It is tempting, but I think ill-advised, to try to raise another objection here—namely, that the Russellian monist has to deny that zombie worlds are conceivable, and thus has no reason not to be a physicalist. For a nice discussion of the Russellian monist's options, see Chalmers 2002: 266; 2016b: 28–9.

Russellian monist wants to explain the physical in mental terms. Yet the latter is just as tricky as the former, and to my knowledge no Russellian monist has ever even tried to say anything to alleviate the mystery.

After all, the Russellian monist not only claims that there is something it is like to be a carbon atom, but also that its phenomenal character is what *makes it be a carbon atom in the first place*. It is its intrinsic phenomenal or protophenomenal nature that is responsible for all of its causal powers, and that plays the dispositional role associated with being a carbon atom. Its intrinsic (proto)phenomenal nature grounds its disposition to bond in certain ways with hydrogen atoms and so forth, in the same way that possession of a particular crystalline structure grounds a glass's disposition to break if dropped (see, e.g., Chalmers 2002: 265). I have absolutely no idea how this is supposed to work, or why it is supposed to sound plausible, other than the fact that it would be convenient if it were true. So Russellian monism faces an inversion of the standard explanatory gap: I cannot see how to get the nonqualitative out of the qualitative in the way that Russellian monism requires. How can phenomenality be the right sort of thing to explain how negative charge works, the various ways that carbon atoms bond with oxygen, and the like? How would consciousness ground those causal powers?

So much, then, for Russellian monism. Postulating an intervening level of protophenomenal properties, à la the bridging version of the view, relocates the hard problem. Postulating an underlying level of protophenomenal properties, à la Russellian monism, turns the hard problem on its head for no good reason.

7. The Final Moral

Here, again, is the overall picture. I have argued that dualism does not avoid all explanatory burdens. It is very implausible for the dualist to go no further than postulating an enormous proliferation of fundamental properties and unsystematized fundamental psychophysical laws. Minimally plausible, scientifically respectable dualism will instead posit a limited number of fundamental phenomenal or protophenomenal properties, and a limited number of fundamental principles governing physical-phenomenal connections. Dualism will explain some aspects of conscious experience in terms of others, and will explain some particular physical-phenomenal correlations in terms of a few fundamental laws.

However, I have provided two more-or-less independent arguments against the claim that she can make any real progress here. First, I argued that there is a real tension between the dualist's faith in the empirical search for such laws and her deep skepticism about the physicalist's search for an explanation of consciousness in physical terms. The former should undermine the latter. Second, I looked at some possible forms her fundamental laws might take. Even though 'phenomenal minima' like protophenomenal properties might appear tailor-made for closing the explanatory gap, they do no such thing. The bridging version of the view cannot in principle give the dualist any explanatory purchase, and the Russellian monist version dismisses the hard problem at the expense of raising a new one. All told, then, matters look fairly bleak. Consciousness looks at least as mysterious to the dualist as to the physicalist; explanatory gaps remain.

Here is the dialectic as I see it. The dualist challenges physicalism by appeal to arguments like the zombie argument and the Mary argument. In the face of these challenges, the physicalist has a choice about how to respond: he can either cave or resist. And there is a real question, I think, about which of those responses is the correct one. This is an instance of a more general meta-philosophical issue. When should we stick to our guns and defend a view against an objection that is not obviously and straightforwardly fallacious? How stubborn should we be? I do not know how to answer that meta-philosophical question in full generality, or even whether there could be a general answer. But this chapter is intended as an argument for stubbornness in this particular case. Physicalists face challenges from the explanatory gap, yes, but dualists face their own versions. Since the same problems just get pushed elsewhere, we physicalists have motivation to resist. We should hold fast, and endorse one of the many ways of responding to the dualist's arguments.

So, admittedly, I do not know the physicalist solution to the hard problem. I am not sure how the physical facts explain the phenomenal facts. But I cannot see how denying that the physical facts explain the phenomenal facts makes life any easier. *Both* physicalists and dualists face versions of the explanatory gap, and retreating to dualism simply raises further questions that are just as hard as the ones physicalists face. *Dualism simply does not help*. It offers no advantage over physicalism.[14]

---

[14] This chapter has an unusual history. I initially wrote it in roughly 2005–6, and then I shelved it for *fourteen years*. There were reasons for that, though not very good reasons. I have revised it for clarity, and to make contact with some literature that has appeared since I first

References

Bennett, Karen. 2003. Why the exclusion problem seems intractable, and how, just maybe, to tract it. *Noûs* 37: 471–97.

Bennett, Karen. 2007. Mental causation. *Philosophy Compass* 2: 316–37.

Bennett, Karen. 2008. Exclusion again. In Jakob Hohwy and Jesper Kallestrup, eds., *Being Reduced*. Oxford: Oxford University Press, 280–305.

Block, Ned. 1995. On a confusion about a function of consciousness. *Behavioral and Brain Sciences* 18: 227–47.

Cameron, Ross. 2007. The contingency of composition. *Philosophical Studies* 16: 99–121.

Chalmers, David. 1995. Facing up to the problem of consciousness. Reprinted (1997) in Jonathan Shear, ed., *Explaining Consciousness: The Hard Problem*. Cambridge, MA: MIT Press, 9–32.

Chalmers, David. 1996. *The Conscious Mind*. Oxford: Oxford University Press.

Chalmers, David. 1997. Moving forward on the problem of consciousness. In Jonathan Shear, ed., *Explaining Consciousness: The Hard Problem*. Cambridge, MA: MIT Press, 379–422.

Chalmers, David. 2002. Consciousness and its place in nature. Reprinted (2002) in David Chalmers, ed., *Philosophy of Mind: Classical and Contemporary Readings*. New York: Oxford University Press, 247–72.

Chalmers, David. 2016a. The combination problem for panpsychism. In Godehard Bruntrup and Ludwig Jaskolla, eds., *Panpsychism: Contemporary Perspectives*. Oxford: Oxford University Press, 179–212.

Chalmers, David. 2016b. Panpsychism and panprotopsychism. In Godehard Bruntrup and Ludwig Jaskolla, eds., *Panpsychism: Contemporary Perspectives*. Oxford: Oxford University Press, 19–47.

wrote it. But I cannot claim that I have managed to bring in *all* of the relevant more recent literature, and I apologize to anyone whose work I should cite but do not.

In its earlier incarnation(s), it was presented at the NYU Mind and Language seminar, the Australasian Association of Philosophy conference, the Australian National University, Harvard University, Brown University, Columbia University, the University of Vermont, the University of California Davis, and the Metaphysics of Science workshop at Birmingham University. Thanks to everyone, particularly to the Corridor reading group, David Chalmers, Tyler Doggett, Derk Pereboom, Daniel Stoljar, and Ted Sider for extensive discussion. Thanks also to Selim Berker, Ned Block, Hartry Field, Kit Fine, Michael Glanzberg, Paul Griffiths, Thomas Nagel, Nick Shea, and Susanna Siegel for helpful comments. I'd particularly like to thank the unnamed person who got me started thinking about this chapter by remarking, "But I'm a dualist! I can say anything I want!"

Coleman, Sam. 2012. Mental chemistry: combination for dualists. *Dialectica* 66: 137–66.

Crane, Tim. 2001. The significance of emergence. In Carl Gillett and Barry Loewer, eds., *Physicalism and its Discontents*. Cambridge: Cambridge University Press, 207–24.

Descartes, René. 1641. Meditations on First Philosophy. Translated by Donald Cress (1993). Indianapolis: Hackett.

Dorr, Cian and Rosen, Gideon. 2002. Composition as a fiction. In Richard M. Gale, ed., *The Blackwell Guide to Metaphysics*. Oxford: Blackwell, 151–74.

Dowe, Phil. 2000. *Physical Causation*. Cambridge: Cambridge University Press.

Goff, Phillip. 2006. Experiences don't sum. *Journal of Consciousness Studies* 13.10–11: 53–61.

Hill, Christopher. 1991. *Sensations: A Defense of Type Materialism*. Cambridge: Cambridge University Press.

Jackson, Frank. 1982. Epiphenomenal qualia. *The Philosophical Quarterly* 32: 127–36.

Kim, Jaegwon. 1989. The myth of nonreductive physicalism. Reprinted (1993) in *Supervenience and Mind*. Cambridge: Cambridge University Press, 265–84.

Kim, Jaegwon. 1993. The nonreductivist's troubles with mental causation. Reprinted (1993) in *Supervenience and Mind*. Cambridge: Cambridge University Press, 336–57.

Kim, Jaegwon. 1998. *Mind in a Physical World*. Cambridge, MA: Bradford.

Kim, Jaegwon. 2005. *Physicalism, or Something Near Enough*. Princeton: Princeton University Press.

Kirk, Robert. 1974. Zombies vs. materialists. *Aristotelian Society Proceedings Supplement* 48: 135–52.

Kirk, Robert. 1996. Strict implication, supervenience, and physicalism. *Australasian Journal of Philosophy* 74: 244–56.

Kripke, Saul. 1980. *Naming and Necessity*. Cambridge, MA: Harvard University Press.

Levine, Joseph. 2001. *Purple Haze: The Puzzle of Consciousness*. Oxford: Oxford University Press.

Loeb, Louis. 1981. *From Descartes to Hume*. Ithaca: Cornell University Press.

Lycan, William. 1981. Psychological laws. *Philosophical Topics* 12: 9–38.

McLaughlin, Brian. 2001. In defense of new wave materialism: a response to Horgan and Tienson. In Carl Gillett and Barry Loewer, eds., *Physicalism and its Discontents*. Cambridge: Cambridge University Press, 208–21.

Merricks, Trenton. 2001. Objects and Persons. Oxford: Oxford University Press.

Montero, Barbara. 2016. What combination problem? In Godehard Bruntrup and Ludwig Jaskolla, eds., Panpsychism: Contemporary Perspectives. Oxford: Oxford University Press, 215–29.

Nagel, Thomas. 1974. What is it like to be a bat? Philosophical Review 83: 435–50.

Nagel, Thomas. 1979. Panpsychism. In Mortal Questions. Cambridge: Cambridge University Press, 181–95.

Papineau, David. 2001. The rise of physicalism. In Carl Gillett and Barry Loewer, eds., Physicalism and its Discontents. Cambridge: Cambridge University Press, 3–36.

Quine, W.V.O. 1948. On what there is. Review of Metaphysics 2: 21–38.

Russell, Bertrand. 1927. The Analysis of Matter. London: Kegan Paul.

Salmon, Wesley. 1984. Scientific Explanation and the Causal Structure of the World. Princeton: Princeton University Press.

Schaffer, Jonathan. 2015. What not to multiply without necessity. The Australasian Journal of Philosophy 93: 644–64.

Shani, Itay. 2010. Mind stuffed with red herrings: why William James' Critique of the mind-stuff theory does not substantiate a combination problem for panpsychism. Acta Analytica 25: 413–34.

Smart, J.J.C. 1959. Sensations and brain processes. Reprinted (2002) in David Chalmers, ed., Philosophy of Mind: Classical and Contemporary Readings. New York: Oxford University Press, 60–8.

Stoljar, Daniel. 2001. Two conceptions of the physical. Philosophy and Phenomenological Research 62: 253–81.

Stoljar, Daniel. 2006. Ignorance and Imagination: The Epistemic Origin of the Problem of Consciousness. Oxford: Oxford University Press.

van Inwagen, Peter. 1990. Material Beings. Ithaca: Cornell University Press.

9

On Characterizing Metaphysical Naturalism

Lok-Chi Chan

1. Introduction

Despite the fact that metaphysical naturalism (henceforth MN) and physicalism are widely discussed topics in, or even the metaphysical foundations of, many philosophical areas—e.g. the philosophy of mind, contemporary phenomenology, the philosophy of religion, metaethics, and the philosophy of science—there are several distinct and conflicting definitions of the two doctrines. The view that everything in the actual world is natural or physical requires the distinction between the metaphysically natural and non-natural, or the distinction between the physical and non-physical. It is commonly assumed (by both naturalists and non-naturalists) that tables, trees, and electrons are natural and physical and that disembodied minds, God, ghosts, and magic are non-natural and non-physical. However, there is disagreement about the explanation for this common assumption.[1]

Of the various proposed definitions of MN and physicalism, the *disciplinary characterization* (henceforth DC)[2] is the most popular. According to this characterization, the natural is defined with reference to whatever natural sciences posit; and the physical is defined with reference to whatever physical theories posit. This chapter is an attempt to offer a novel version of DC. With this in mind, it is important to note that the interest of this chapter is not whether or not MN (or physicalism) is true.

---

[1] I should note that metaphysical naturalism is not the same as *methodological* naturalism. Methodological naturalism is a doctrine according to which philosophy should be seen as an extension of science and should use similar methods. This chapter is concerned with *metaphysical* naturalism and considers it to be an independent doctrine. After all, there is a standard division between MN and methodological naturalism (see Devitt 1998, p. 46; De Caro & Macarthur 2010, p. 4; Papineau 2014, p. 116).

[2] This is Copp's (2012, p. 28) term.

Lok-Chi Chan, *On Characterizing Metaphysical Naturalism* In: *Oxford Studies in Philosophy of Mind Volume 1*. Edited by: Uriah Kriegel, Oxford University Press (2021). © Lok-Chi Chan. DOI: 10.1093/oso/9780198845850.003.0009

In what follows I first characterize DC as it has been understood and the main objections to it. I then examine a seminal version of DC that I call the *similarity approach* (SA), which is defended by Lewis (1983), Ravenscroft (1997), Braddon-Mitchell and Jackson (2007), and McPherson (2015). The approach is to allow an extension of current science, but that this extension be constrained by an adequate similarity to such science. I argue that while SA can avoid most of the main objections to DC, it has a fatal shortcoming. I then develop a novel version of DC using the strategy of SA that allows the extension of current science. I call this the *historical paths approach* (HPA). The idea is, very roughly, that MN can be defined with reference to the historical ideas that current scientific theories descend from. HPA can, I argue, avoid the fatal shortcoming of other implementations of SA. Finally, I show that a definition of MN developed from HPA is a useful definition and can provide a useful framework for the naturalization of the philosophy of mind and phenomenology (if possible).

2. The Disciplinary Characterization (DC)

Roughly, the DCs of MN and physicalism are:

DC (MN):   Every entity or property instantiated in the actual world is natural in the sense of being a posited entity or property of natural sciences or being exclusively constituted by those posited entities or properties.

DC (physicalism):   Every entity or property instantiated in the actual world is physical in the sense of being a posited entity or property of physics or being exclusively constituted by those posited entities or properties.[3]

---

[3] I use the term 'constitute' to mean the disjunction of a large inclusive family of ideas including constitution, reduction, realization, identity, and so forth, many of which are considered as rivals, and each of which, much like naturalism, is fairly imprecise and has distinct and conflicting conceptions (Melnyk 2003; Kim 2006). Such an ambiguity is unavoidable if we take into account the variety of metaphysical frameworks adopted by different naturalists, and if we want to avoid taking a stance in this internal dispute. While it is quite impossible to offer a comprehensive survey of these ideas here, I find it useful to follow Kim in using Smart's expression "nothing over and above" to capture the core idea and commonality of the family of ideas (Kim 2006, p. 275). Following Kim's interpretation, the idea is roughly that if Xs are nothing over and above Ys, then Ys are all we need for there to be Xs, and that no Xs can be considered as something in addition to Ys (Kim 2006, pp. 275–6).

There is also significant disagreement in metaphysics and philosophy of science concerning the nature of entities and properties. For our purposes, we may just take it that the entities here are the kind of thing that can be instantiated, and that the properties here are the kind of feature of such things that can be objectively conceived. But these are rough conceptions rather than

This chapter is concerned with MN, not physicalism. However, I take it that many arguments apply equally to both doctrines, so I will consider arguments by authors concerning the definition of physicalism.

DC is intuitively attractive to many, myself included. On the one hand, it appears to be consistent with most presumptions shared among philosophers about what MN should and should not be like. For one thing, as would be the case were DC true, we seem to determine whether or not something is natural by its relation to natural sciences. For another, it appears that DC matches well with widespread philosophical presumptions about the naturalness of particular entities or properties. Consider the paradigmatic cases that are often taken into consideration, such as tables, trees, Cartesian minds, God, and so on. All these cases can all be assigned their agreed upon categories by DC. Furthermore, the enlightenment materialists' and logical empiricists' attempts at a unified account of everything were found to be failures: the world is pluralistic and multifaceted, and thus cannot possibly be accounted for simply by appealing to certain metaphysical properties (e.g. those of 'matter' like spatiotemporality and solidity) or epistemic qualities (e.g. quantifiability and observability). Hence, while it is impossible to compare DC with other attractive approaches to characterizing MN here, DC seems to be more attractive than many of those which equate naturalness with a few metaphysical properties or epistemic qualities. This is because DC allows for a certain plurality of natural things, which is more in line with our current understanding of the world. The above considerations, then, provide us with sufficient reasons to develop DC to its fullest potential.

3. Problems Faced by DC

We have seen the intuitive pull of DC, but the approach also has several shortcomings. Only by being able to solve the problems, can a modified version of DC be successful. I will discuss them in turn.

---

formal definitions, and nothing in this chapter hangs on these particular conceptions. It is worth noting that some metaphysicians and philosophers of science believe that there are more fundamental and irreducible ontological categories such as capacities and activities, which can as well occur or be instantiated (for a nice survey, see Chen 2017). I see no reason why the DCs of MN and physicalism cannot expand to include such things, but for the sake of simplicity, I shall not take them into consideration.

3.1 Hempel's Dilemma

Hempel's dilemma was first formulated in Hempel (1969). If, on the one hand, MN is defined with reference to current science, then it is almost guaranteed to be incomplete and false, for it is almost certain that current science is an incomplete description of the world. If, on the other hand, MN is instead defined with reference to ideal science, then it is trivially true. That is, if ideal science is supposed to correctly describe everything (in the actual world), then MN is trivially true because everything (in the actual world) is automatically counted as natural.

3.2 The Problem of the Naturalistically Respectable in History

The second problem facing DC is whether historical ideas (or figures) can possibly be counted as being naturalistically respectable (Montero 2009). In history, many ideas (and theorists who believed in them) were typically considered naturalistically respectable. However, if we define MN with reference to current or ideal science, then most naturalistically respectable historical ideas must be counted as naturalistically unacceptable. For few ideas posit entities and properties that are also posits of current or ideal science (or are constituted by them). Hobbesian physics, for example, takes matter to be something like billiard balls: an object is describable only in terms of its spatiotemporal locations and motions; and it acquires a new motion only when another object is taking (and thereby pushing) it away from its current spatiotemporal location. But this view is rejected by contemporary physics. Unless a view like Hobbesian physics gets revived in ideal science, which seems unlikely, DC cannot count Hobbesian physics as naturalistically respectable.

3.3 The Problem of Naturalistically Unacceptable Scientific Theories

The third problem is the diversity of scientific theories. There are some current scientific theories that are presumably naturalistically unacceptable, but if MN is defined with reference to current scientific theories then these theories will be by definition naturalistically respectable. As Quine notes in his criticism of MN, "Quantum mechanics today, indeed, in its neoclassical or Copenhagen interpretation, has a distinctly mentalistic ring" (Quine 1995, p. 257). The Copenhagen interpretation includes the observer effect, according to which the way in which a measurement is made determines part of the results. The mentalistic interpretation of the Copenhagen interpretation goes further and suggests that the observer effect is best explained by the consciousness of the observer. If the mentalistic interpretation turns out to be a legitimate scientific theory, then current science is positing some mental properties at the quantum level of the world. Similarly, eminent neuroscientist John Eccles (1994), together with physicist Friedrich Beck, proposed a mind-body dualism which posits psychons, a kind of mental 'particle'. Both of these theories posit fundamentally mental properties that are in conflict with what many philosophers consider to be the standard understanding of MN (see, e.g. Kim 2003; Montero & Papineau 2016; Oppy 2018a).[4]

3.4 The Problem of the Scientifically Inaccessible

The fourth problem facing DC is the worry that there might be natural entities or properties that science cannot ever access due to, say, some sort of causal isolation or due to our cognitive limitations (Montero 2009). If there are things science cannot access, and if they are not constituted by things that are of scientifically accessible kinds, then DC cannot count them as natural. Defining the natural and non-natural solely with reference to the posited entities and properties of our theories is beside the point, for not all limitations of our knowledge or epistemic capability are relevant to the distinction between the natural and non-natural.

3.5 The Problem of Non-Actualized Properties and Worlds Containing Them

The fifth problem facing DC concerns whether so-called 'alien properties'— i.e. properties not actually instantiated—and worlds containing them can be counted as natural (Stoljar 2010). The worry is that, simply because our

---

[4] It is worth nothing that some philosophers argue that MN can tolerate some fundamentally mental properties (e.g. Chalmers 1996; Zhong 2016). See Section 4 for further discussion.

actual science cannot study other possible worlds and matters within them, (almost) all alien properties cannot possibly be natural, and MN will turn out to be false in (almost) every possible world that contains alien properties.[5] While our standard view suggests that some alien properties are natural and that MN is true in some worlds containing them, DC cannot allow this.

4. The Similarity Approach (SA)

Some suggest that a simple modification of DC can solve the problems above. The suggestion is to allow extensions of current science, but that this extension be constrained by an adequate similarity to such science (Lewis 1983; Ravenscroft 1997; Braddon-Mitchell & Jackson 2007; McPherson 2015). This is known as the similarity approach (SA). Even though I do not endorse the approach, I consider it to be fairly attractive, for it effectively solves four out of the aforementioned five problems. It leads to an extension of the inclusive range of DC, and thereby avoids the narrowness in the first horn of Hempel's dilemma (i.e. defining MN with reference to current scientific theories only). Future and historical scientific theories can be counted as naturalistically respectable through being adequately similar to current science. Alien properties and scientifically inaccessible properties can also be accounted for if they are likewise similar to some posited properties of current science. The problem of naturalistically unacceptable scientific theories is the only remaining problem, for MN is defined with reference to similarity to current science that by definition includes all current scientific theories, whether naturalistically respectable or not.

There is, however, a more fatal problem with SA, which I call the *dilemma of the right kind of similarity*. To have a level of similarity that acts as a boundary between the natural and non-natural, we need to have the right kind of similarity to act as the measure. The options are either (1) an overall similarity or (2) a similarity in a certain respect. However, on the one hand, (1) cannot work, for any boundary drawn by using overall similarity cannot work as the boundary we expect for MN. More specifically, it seems hopeless to expect that all presumably non-natural things are less similar to things in

---

[5] I add the qualification 'almost' because there are in fact exceptions. Due to mistakes, instrumental concerns, and so forth, some properties are posited by our scientific theories even though they exist only in worlds other than ours.

current science than presumably natural things in terms of overall similarity. I will discuss this in detail below. On the other hand, we might instead follow (2) and consider all presumptively natural things to be similar in some specific respect—such as being spatiotemporal or being governed by the laws of nature (to use Armstrong's 1978, p. 261 and McDowell's 1994, pp. 71–6 characterizations of naturalism as examples). Unfortunately, in this case the natural is, in effect, defined in terms of those specific respects, not in terms of similarity. Hence, if we were to accept this option, we are in effect accepting some other approach to characterizing MN and thus giving up SA (and, very possibly, DC too).

The concern is whether some presumably natural things are, with respect to overall similarity, less similar to the posited entities of current science than some presumably non-natural things. Consider the following analogy. Compare an ordinary cat, a cursed black cat, and some imaginary mythological animals like Yetis, Leviathans, and werewolves. It appears that, on the one hand, at least some versions of Yetis, Leviathans, and werewolves, namely those without magical properties, could be natural entities. On the other hand, the black cats as conceived by Medieval Europeans, which were cursed by the devil and were supposed to bring forth bad luck, are obviously non-natural entities. However, it appears that a conception of naturalness that appeals to mere overall similarity can hardly make sense of these categorizations. The cursed black cat is identical to an ordinary cat which is posited by natural sciences in every respect except the curse, but Yetis, Leviathans, werewolves, and the like are posited to have different physiologies from animals recognized by natural sciences.

While one may argue that a single curse makes a more significant dissimilarity than plenty of radical physiological differences, it is difficult to see why this is the case, unless we construe similarity in a specific respect that is not that of overall similarity. One may also argue that the cursed black cat, the werewolves, and the Yetis are *all* dissimilar to natural things, but that werewolves and Yetis can be counted as natural if they are exclusively constituted by natural things like physical particles. However, the notion of overall similarity used in this case to measure naturalness would be very narrow—too narrow for the purpose of SA which is to expand the inclusive range of naturalness.

It might be argued that in the case above the real issue is not overall similarity of entities but rather the overall similarity of properties. That is, the property of being cursed is radically different from ordinary biological and physiological properties. This might be true, but shifting the concern to properties does not resolve the problem. Consider the locational properties of strings and Hobbesian matter: it has been suggested that strings are not spatiotemporally located like Hobbesian matter but are instead instantiated in a non-local manner in eleven dimensions. While it appears that both of these locational properties are natural, the question remains as to the way in which we can say that their similarity is greater than, say, that between being vitalistic and being organic, or that between being karmic and (the ordinary sense of) being causal. I doubt that there is a satisfactory answer to this question. Since we are here comparing the degree of overall similarity of things that are dramatically different in nature, such a comparison risks committing a category mistake, or at the very least the relevant degrees are too vague to be compared unless we use a notion of specific similarity rather than overall similarity.

In the face of this problem, those who are sympathetic to SA and thus do not wish to repudiate it have two options. The first option is to accept that the inclusive range of MN is different from what most believe. After all, some philosophers argue for a revision of the inclusive range of naturalness. For example, it has been argued MN should tolerate some fundamentally mental properties.[6] Though this option is attractive, it is costly, for if we revise naturalness strictly according to degree of similarity, our presumptions concerning the naturalness or non-naturalness of many things (and the naturalistic respectability of many theories) might have to be radically revised. Furthermore, there is a certain unpredictability about the results the revision would produce. For instance, it might be the case that panpsychism and pantheism would need to be counted as naturalistically respectable, whereas Hobbesian physics and Newtonian physics would need to be counted as naturalistically unacceptable. If this turns out to be true, many discourses concerning MN in philosophy, for or against the doctrine, would have to be considered wrongheaded. This consequence may be too costly even for many of those who are sympathetic to the revisions.

The second option is to keep our assumptions about MN and the naturalness of things, and to develop or revise SA to bring forth a regimentation of its inclusive range which could be consistent with those assumptions. I believe that there is no non-radical way of development that can escape the dilemma of the right kind of similarity. My option is an intermediate proposal between repudiating SA and the second option: to *radically* revise

---

[6] See, e.g. Chalmers 1996; Zhong 2016. Note that these people do not deal with SA and its problems.

SA. More precisely, I will develop a novel version of DC with the same strategy that SA uses, whereby *extensions* of current science are allowed.

5. The Historical Paths Approach (HPA)

I call my approach the *historical paths approach* (HPA). HPA is based on a concept I use to replace the similarity relation used by SA, which is what I call the *historical paths* (HPs) of contemporary science.[7] HPs are the processes of modifying and developing scientific concepts over the course of history, along which scientific concepts are modified and finally developed into the versions in contemporary natural sciences. (Note that old paths that are disconnected from contemporary scientific concepts do *not* count as HPs.) Of course, the relevant 'concepts' here are theoretical contents and not methodological factors: for example, the concept <momentum> within Newtonian physics, the concept <positron> within contemporary particle physics, and the physicist's preference for mathematically quantifiable theoretical posits. What is suggested here assumes a distinction between concepts and theories, with the latter including Newtonian physics, the theory of relativity, string theory, the Darwinian theory of evolution, and so on; and HPs are about concepts, not theories. Although similar distinctions are seen in the works of many influential theorists, such as in Nagel 1961, Lewis 1972, Laudan 1977, Kuhn 1996, and Jackson 1998, and, not every philosopher will make such a distinction because those concepts themselves might be, as some theories of concepts suggest, small, component theories. I take no stance on this controversy; and I suggest that those who dislike the distinction can replace the notion of concepts here with the notion of small component theories which are components of bigger theories or theoretical frameworks. Some might wonder why I intend HPs to be about concepts but not theories. The motivation for my position is that only when HPs are about concepts can it resist the *problem of overinclusion*, which is the worry that HPs will be overly inclusive and thus useless. I will return to the problem in Section 5.2.

Let us return to the idea of HPs. Even though the concepts within Newtonian physics might be very different from those within string theory,

---

[7] In the case of physicalism, there might be some HPs of contemporary physics. Nonetheless, I will focus on MN and not assess whether or not an HPA to characterizing physicalism is attractive.

they have some substantive historical connections. For example, <momentum> is developed from <impetus> in medieval science; <gravity> in Einsteinian theory of relativity is developed from its counterpart in Newtonian physics, and it, in turn, has developed into <quantum gravity> in string theory. Of course, lots of scientific concepts have no older counterparts. For example, it is unclear that <positron> and <Higgs boson> have older counterparts. But they can be said to have been developed in close relation to concepts we already have, such as <electron> or <photon>, or the concept of physical particle in general. It is also important to note that we are talking about historical *paths*, not *a* historical path: there is more than one path, even within the same scientific discipline; and a single concept might be traced back to multiple paths. For instance, <light>, to which we now attribute the notion of wave-particle duality, can be traced back to its two counterparts in the particle theory and the wave theory, each of which can, in turn, be traced back to different paths.

On the other hand, some theoretical contents and methodologies in other scientific theories—such as Aristotelian teleology and some versions of vitalism—are (relatively more) disconnected from HPs, even though there may have been good reasons in the past for using these concepts. This is because many of the central concepts of those theories were wholly abandoned rather than modified and absorbed by new theories in a historical progression. For example, the concept of telos was abandoned rather than modified in physics. In other words, many of their central concepts fail to have descendants in current science.

If my hypothesis about the existence and nature of HPs is correct, then we may use the idea of HPs to formulate a definition of MN—call it the *historical paths definition* (HPD). The basic formulation is as follows:

HPD1:   Every entity or property instantiated in the actual world is natural in the sense of being a posited entity or property of some theoretical concept that is on some HP.[8]

Four remarks are in order. Firstly, not all scientific concepts posit entities or properties. What is important is that if an entity or property is natural, then there should be at least one concept that posits it. Secondly, the concepts of

---

[8] I omit here the clause in the original version of DC 'or being exclusively constituted by (i.e. being reducible to or realized by) those posits'. Since I am going to develop some fairly complex variants of HPD1, I purposefully set the clause aside to avoid unnecessary confusion.

some natural effects—by which I mean something like the causing of asphyxia by rail travel at high speed—might not be on the HPs. But these effects might be considered as the expected causal behaviours of some natural entities and thereby as natural. Thirdly, of course not all naturalistically respectable scientific concepts in history have descendants and are thereby on some HPs. I will get back to this problem in Section 7.

Fourthly, it is not impossible for there to be some very different HPs from the perspective of future science. For instance, it is possible to return to Aristotelian teleology, and a future scientist might therefore count our current scientific concepts to be ones that fail to have descendants. But this is not a problem. It would be problematic only if we assumed that our conception of MN ought to be modally and chronologically neutral in the sense that it leaves open which possible world the actual world is and when the present is, and could thereby account for counterfactual and future judgments. As we all have learned from Putnam and Kripke, not even natural kind terms like 'water' are modally and chronologically neutral: the meaning of the term 'water' depends on the empirically discovered fact that the watery stuff in the actual world is H2O, but this is not true for otherworld inhabitants, nor is it the way our ancestors understood the term. So we should be open to the possibility that future generations may have different conceptions of MN, just as the possibility they may discover that the watery stuff in the actual world is not H2O but something else.

At this point, my approach is yet to be completed—most problems facing DC are yet to be solved. However, before I further develop it, two problems must be addressed. They are (1) the *problem of disconnection* and (2) the *problem of overinclusion*. Only when these two problems are addressed, can the nature of HPs be made clear, and can we see a large part of how HPA can resist the worry motivating the dilemma of the right kind of similarity. Remember, the worry is there in the case of SA because no level of overall similarity can act as the required boundary which allows us to count things as natural or non-natural as we expect MN to do. Addressing these two problems allows us to see how the inclusive range of the HPs is shaped and can be used by MN as a boundary, which I believe to be more useful than the boundary drawn by SA.

5.1 The Problem of Disconnection

The problem of disconnection is the worry that HPs are not spread over substantial lengths of time. For instance, some followers of Kuhn's (1996) may claim that major developments in the history of science occur with paradigm shifts (i.e. with radical changes of the most fundamental assumptions within short periods of time). With these radical changes, it is unclear that there is any joining path because there might be too many disconnections between scientific theories.

An in-depth discussion of the philosophy and history of science (and of Kuhn's views) is outside the scope of this chapter, but let me outline my response briefly. It is difficult to see why the sceptic is correct. On the one hand, Kuhn's theory of paradigm shifts is very controversial and is not without alternatives (e.g. Laudan 1977). On the other hand, even granted that the theory is correct, it undermines only the view that concepts such as <gravity> and <space> are defined or understood in exactly the same ways before and after the paradigm shifts. However, this does not imply that there cannot be some kind of HP, on which old concepts are modified and absorbed by the new theories. In fact, Kuhn himself believes there are "borrowed elements" from the old paradigm, "both conceptual and manipulative", that are incorporated into the new ones (1996, p. 149). The examples he provides include <planet> and <space> (pp. 128, 149). It is true that he believes the borrowed elements are more radically revised than many believe: they form new relationships with other concepts in the new paradigms, and are, in addition, incommensurable with their older counterparts. But it is hard to see why this alone conflicts with the idea of HPs, for the idea does not commit itself to commensurability.

5.2 The Problem of Overinclusion

The other problem that follows is the problem of overinclusion. Some might, contrary to the adherents of the problem of disconnection, consider HPs to be overly inclusive and thus useless, since it is possible to understand our current science as descending from belief systems that are largely naturalistically unacceptable. For instance, some suggest that modern chemistry is a descendant of alchemy, which is full of magical concepts.

To respond to this objection, two conceptions have to be distinguished. Recall that HPs are about *concepts (or small, component theories)*, not *belief systems (or bigger theories)*. For example, HPs are not about whether alchemy as a belief system is the ancestor of modern chemistry but, rather, which particular concepts in alchemy are the ancestors of those in modern chemistry. In fact, as I have mentioned earlier, the problem of overinclusion is why I intend HPs to be about concepts—because HPs about theoretical frameworks, belief systems, or big theories cannot avoid being overly inclusive, but HPs about concepts can. Alchemy, as a discipline, is a belief system containing many concepts, including theoretical and methodological concepts about magic, classifications of chemicals, measurements, and so on. As history progressed, some of them were developed and absorbed by chemistry while others were eliminated or abandoned entirely. HPA has no problem taking some concepts in alchemy, such as its observations of chemical reactions, to be on the HPs, thereby taking them to be naturalistically respectable. Yet it notes that the theoretical concepts about magic within alchemy have been entirely abandoned and should therefore be considered naturalistically unacceptable. Put simply, only some but not all of the concepts within alchemy are on the HPs, and the presumptively naturalistically unacceptable ones are not on the HPs.

A worry is that, say, the alchemist's concept of gold and the vitalist's concept of muscle should not count as naturalistically respectable—the alchemist might believe that gold is a spiritual substance, and the vitalist certainly believed that muscles are powered by vital forces—but these concepts are doubtlessly on the HPs. The worry can be addressed by slightly modifying HPD1:

HPD2:   Every entity or property instantiated in the actual world is natural in the sense of being a posited entity or property of some theoretical concept(s) (1) that is on some HP and (2) every constituent concept of which (if any) is also on some HP.

The (2) clause is added to the definition as a condition of being naturalistically respectable. The idea of a constituent concept is as follows. There are complex concepts that are partially 'made up of' constituent concepts. For instance, <bachelor> is made up of <unmarried> and <male>. Let us apply HPD2 to the case of muscles powered by vital forces. While the vitalist believed that muscles are powered by vital forces, her concept of muscles may or may not be independent of her vitalist beliefs—for her concept of muscles might be based solely on, say, empirical observations and have nothing to do with her vitalism. If, on the one hand, Vitalist X's concept of muscles is not made up of vitalist concepts, then we may count the concept as naturalistically respectable and its posits as natural. If, on the other hand, Vitalist Y's concept of muscles is partially made up of her vitalist concepts, then even if the concept is on HP, we may count it as naturalistically unacceptable and its posited entity as non-natural. This strategy of analysing concepts allows us to count spiritual gold and muscles powered by vital forces as non-natural.

It might be objected that HPD2 is too strong. For instance, Isaac Newton was a theist. He certainly believed that everything was created by God, which we count as non-natural. Let us assume that he was so pious that whenever he formed a concept of a thing, he always bore in mind that it is a divine creation; call him the *pious Newton*. Does HPD2 imply that the pious Newton, and many other influential theist scientists like him, had no naturalistically respectable concepts of things at all, and that every posited entity of their concepts is not natural?

My answer is mixed. On the one hand, we can indeed say that the pious Newton's concepts of mass, gravity, and chairs are naturalistically unacceptable, and that every posited entity of his concepts is non-natural. This is not a significant problem, though, for what is important for us is not whether the pious *Newton's* concepts are naturalistically respectable, but whether some *Newtonian* concepts can be understood or interpreted in a naturalistically respectable way which is independent of his theism. Obviously, we do not need Newton's theism (or any other version of theism, for that matter) to understand, say, Newtonian mass and gravity. On the other hand, we can analyse the pious Newton's concepts in a more flexible way, and be more generous in granting naturalistic respectability. The strategy is to make use of counterfactual conditionals. Let us assume there is an idealized perfectly rational agent R sharing all beliefs of the pious Newton. It seems unlikely that, were R presented with compelling evidence that God does not exist, R would have abandoned his concepts of mass and chairs, or substantively or radically revised them. The reason is that R could have just slightly revised those concepts by removing the idea that they are created by God. Nothing concerning the general conceptions of what those entities or properties are like would have had to be modified.[9] With this in mind, we can take it that the pious Newton's concepts of mass, gravity, chairs, and tables are by and large naturalistically respectable, and that these concepts, understood in this way, can thereby posit natural entities and properties.

For the sake of clarity, and to avoid them becoming too complex and wordy, I shall not add the additional clause of HPD2 'and (2) every constituent concept of which (if any) is also on some HP' to the other variants of

---

[9] For a similar approach, see Lewis's (1972) theory of near-realization. Note that he is not dealing with the problem I am considering here.

HPD1 I am going to propose. Nonetheless, it is important to note that they can all be modified in the same way.

With the problem of disconnection and the problem of overinclusion solved, and the nature of HPs made clear, we see how the inclusive range of the HPs is shaped, and that the worry motivating the dilemma of the right kind of similarity dissolves. For cases like Hobbesian physics, even though they might not be that similar to current science, most if not all of their main concepts have been continuously modified and finally developed into those in current science. On the other hand, the concept of cases like fundamental mental properties, vital forces, karma, cursed animals, and the like are not on the HPs. Certainly, it can still be questioned whether the HPs can exclusively and exhaustively cover every natural entity or property that is posited in the history of science. The possibility that there are some other counterexamples cannot possibly be expunged. Nonetheless, as far as I am concerned there are no examples that cannot be handled by my developments of HPA below. The problem is, I believe, significantly less severe than it was in the case of SA.

6. Future Scientific Theories

I have offered HPD1 as the basic formulation of the historical paths definition, but it does not allow for future scientific theories to be counted as naturalistically respectable and it thus falls prey to Hempel's dilemma. This is because future theories are very likely to have new concepts that are not ancestors of current concepts. A modified version of HPD1 can solve this problem:

HPD3: Every entity or property instantiated in the actual world is natural in the sense of being a posited entity or property of some theoretical concept(s) that (i) is on some HP, or (ii) on some possible future path that is a reasonable extension of our current HPs.

Condition (i) is added to the definition as a sufficient but not necessary condition alternative to condition (ii). When presented with a concept, we form reasonable expectations of whether it could be a descendant of some our current scientific concepts developed via scientific advancement. For example, a physical particle that quarks are composed of is something we could expect to discover, and, in addition, we can treat its concept as a possible descendant of our current concept of physical particles.[10] On the contrary, a psychic universe described by some New Age theories is no such thing—while its concept was developed from its scientific counterpart, no future science is going to tell us its existence. Some might wonder whether the judgment concerning reasonable extensions here is a matter of similarity to current theories and hence a retreat to SA. I do not think so. At least, this is not merely a matter of similarity. Many other considerations can be invoked to bring forth a more sophisticated judgment than what mere similarity can provide: e.g. tendencies of what new discoveries are like, the scientific method in general (which includes principles such as the need for empirical observations or experiments, the preference for repeatability, and so on), theoretical virtues in general (such as simplicity, explanatory scope, and so forth), technological limitations, research strategies, and methodologies used by experts in different branches of science.[11]

Admittedly, the criteria of these judgments have to be fairly imprecise because they are based on abstract conceptions of what current science is like. The kind of judgment needed might be based on, say, what most reasonable laymen who are sufficiently informed about current science would accept as a possible science of a century later. These judgments are not the precise technical expectations a scientist would have with regard to possible discoveries based on current findings (say the expectation of a nanophysicist that silver might be used in the future as a conductor for a particular purpose). If the expectations are limited to precise technical expectations then revolutions in science cannot be accounted for. A set of expectations that is wider in scope is needed.

Some would be unsatisfied with the imprecision involved, but it is not a failing of the approach. As Ravenscroft argues in his defence of SA, on the

---

[10] No doubt, some possible future paths might be expected because of social or psychological factors, such as corruption in the scientific community, political upheaval, cultural influence, and the extinction of human beings, which most of us consider to be irrelevant to the discussion here. By the clause 'some possible future path that is expected through extending our current HPs', I only mean those HPs that are expected to develop because of unbiased and undisrupted scientific inquires, which are not intervened by the above factors. This move involves what Godfrey-Smith calls an "idealised simplification" (Godfrey-Smith 2014, p. 21; see also Musgrave 1981), in which a theorist deliberately imagines things to be simpler than they actually are, in order to construct a theory of significance.

[11] It is worth nothing that there is an asymmetry between HPs and possible future paths discussed here: it is a historical fact as to what HPs there are, but not all possible future paths will turn out to be true, and we often cannot tell which will and which will not. This is not a problem, however, for it is beneficial rather than detrimental to be inclusive of the possible future paths that will not turn out to be true. See the next paragraph for the reason for this.

one hand, what is most important is to be able to categorize most paradigmatic cases of the natural and non-natural; on the other hand, our conception of the natural is indeed imprecise and vague: if a characterization of the natural is committed to vagueness, the commitment might be an explanation of the vagueness within our conception of the natural, which is a virtue rather than a failing (Ravenscroft 1997, pp. 425–6). I think Ravenscroft is correct, at least when the two kinds of vagueness correspond to each other. The same can be said about HPD3. On the one hand, it is obvious that the kind of expectation HPD3 makes use of enables us to categorize most paradigmatic cases, such as the fundamentally mental, God, undiscovered particles, tables, and chairs, as we expect of MN. None of these falls in the marginal area between the natural and non-natural where vagueness is an issue. On the other hand, the naturalness (or naturalistic respectability) of some peculiar cases, such as qualia, free will, the self, and some of the posited entities of European phenomenology, is indeed difficult to determine;[12] and these cases also seem to be where the vagueness of the boundaries of HPD3 lies. Hence, the vagueness may be helpful in explaining why such uncertainties exist. I will discuss an additional advantage of this view in Section 9.

7. Naturalistically Unacceptable Scientific Theories

The next problem is that of naturalistically unacceptable scientific theories, according to which there are some current scientific theories that are presumably naturalistically unacceptable and which a standard DC would by definition count as naturalistically respectable. In response to this problem, one might argue that there is something like a *sudden divergence* from the general directions of the paths. That is, theories such as the mentalistic interpretation of the Copenhagen interpretation and Eccles's theory of psychons, by positing concepts such as the role of consciousness in the mechanics of fundamental physics, are not going along the general directions of gradual changes, towards which most concepts on the relevant paths are moving.

The idea of a sudden divergence is not ad hoc because it not only allows us to account for why some scientific theories are presumably naturalistically

---

[12] For a good overview of these debates, see Gallagher et al. (2015). For an example of the posited entities of European phenomenology whose naturalness is under debate, consider Merleau-Ponty's embodiment and embeddedness. For some contemporary contributions to the debate, see Varela, Thompson & Rosch 1991; Pollard 2014; Gallagher 2018.

unacceptable, but it is also useful in its own right, for it can (partially) explain the research directions of some scientists and philosophers. For example, some scientists are motivated to propose new interpretations of quantum mechanics that are alternatives to the Copenhagen interpretation in order to avoid its use of the (possibly mentalistic) observer effect. Consider the example of theoretical physicist Cramer, the proposer of the transactional interpretation. He writes:

> The knowledge interpretation's account of state vector collapse and nonlocality is internally consistent but is regarded by some (including the author) as subjective and intellectually unappealing. It is the source of much of the recent dissatisfaction with the Copenhagen interpretation. The author has proposed an alternative and more objective interpretation of the quantum mechanics formalism called the transactional interpretation. (Cramer 1988, p. 228)

In addition, some scientists and philosophers particularly expect and welcome such proposals (e.g. Price 1996). HPA offers a possible explanation of their motivation: they might, explicitly or tacitly, believe that the Copenhagen interpretation is a sudden divergence (though this belief is contestable) and thus want to avoid accepting it.[13] If this explanation is correct, then there can be a rational basis for this kind of motivation other than a mere intuitive discomfort about introducing the fundamentally mental. After all, it might be rational to have a conservative attitude. And since what I am describing here are probably *tacit* attitudes, this is compatible with the possibility that these theorists might have explicitly accepted some conceptions or characterizations of MN different than those developed by HPA.

8. The Alien and the Scientifically Inaccessible

We have seen how HPA survives objections from Hempel's dilemma, the problem of the naturalistically respectable in history, the problem of

---

[13] It is worth noting that I am not arguing that the observer effect in the Copenhagen interpretation is non-natural, nor that its concept is a sudden divergence. I am, in fact, inclined to think that the observer effect lies in the vague boundary area between the natural and non-natural. What I am suggesting is that those who (explicitly or tacitly) understand its concept as a sudden divergence might be rational to look for alternative interpretations; I am not arguing that their view is correct.

naturalistically unacceptable scientific theories, and even the dilemma of the right kind of similarity. What are left are three problems: the problem of the scientifically inaccessible, the problem of non-actualized properties and worlds containing them, and the problem concerning naturalistically respectable concepts in history that have no descendants. HPD3 cannot solve the former two problems because alien properties and scientifically inaccessible properties are not things we can discover in future science. Something similar can be said about cases like the concept <optical aether>: even though it is not logically impossible that we may rediscover the optical aether in future science, this is not expected by any sufficiently reasonable and informed person. But, again, a modification of the definition can solve the problems. The idea is to allow some variations of the natural things recognized by the previous formulations of HPD. The precise new formulation of HPD is as follows:

HPD4:   Every entity or property instantiated in the actual world is natural either (1) in the sense of being a posited entity or property of some theoretical concept that (i) is on some HP or (ii) on some possible future path that is a reasonable extension of our current HPs, or (2) in the sense of being a robust intradisciplinary recombination of the theoretical characters of some natural entities or properties identified by condition (1).[14]

Condition (2) is added to the definition as a sufficient but not necessary condition of naturalness. Let me first outline the theoretical characters concerned here, before I move on to the more complex idea of their robust intradisciplinary recombinations. By the term 'theoretical characters', I mean the framing of the intrinsic or relational characters of the relevant entity or property in a scientific theory or theoretical framework. There is substantial research in our best philosophy of science on such theoretical characters, and some major kinds of theoretical characters have been

---

[14]   Stoljar (2010, p. 88) argues against the use of cluster definitions of physicalism, where each of which consists of a cluster of independent, unrelated conditions. The worry is that it is arbitrary to consider various such conditions as a single doctrine when physicalism is expected to be a non-arbitrary and systematic metaphysical doctrine. This objection does not apply to HPD4, which consists of the disjunction of several conditions and is fairly complex. For condition (2) is a natural extension of condition (1) to deal with peculiar cases, but is not conceptually independent of it. Hence, despite the complexity of its definition, an MN characterized by HPD4 is a systematic metaphysical doctrine.

identified. For instance, some theoretical characters are surveyed in Craver and Tabery (2015):[15]

A. *Generation of phenomena*. The behaviour of the thing concerned as a whole, which can be classified into:
   1. *Production*. The thing concerned brings about some product.
   2. *Underlayer*. The thing concerned underlies the instantiation of something of another kind.
   3. *Maintenance*. The thing concerned holds some state of affairs or some range of states of affairs in place.
B. *Parts*. The parthood required of the composition of the thing concerned.
C. *Organization*. The organization of the parts of the thing concerned which is characteristic of it, and which can be classified into:
   1. *Spatial organization*. Location, size, shape, etc.
   2. *Temporal organization*. The order, rate, duration of the component activities.
D. *Levels*. The location of the thing concerned in the hierarchy of levels of things.
E. *Natural kinds*. The kinds of things to which the thing concerned belongs and whose members share a substantive, scientifically recognized similarity to each other.

This borrowed list is not meant to be exhaustive, but it sheds light on what theoretical characters there are.[16]

So far, so good. Let us get back to our discussion of HPD4. The additional condition (2) is not only about theoretical characters, but also about robust intradisciplinary recombinations of them. To have a recombination of

---

[15] It is worth noting that Craver and Tabery belong to the new mechanist school of philosophy of science, and thus their aim is to survey the characters of 'mechanisms', which they take to be the protagonist of particular special sciences. Nevertheless, I believe that those theoretical characters generalize to other posited entities and properties of natural sciences. It is also important to note that since I am taking the list of theoretical characters out of Craver and Tabery's new mechanist context, I have altered the descriptions of a few of them in order to make them more general.

[16] Not every reader will agree with my understanding of theoretical characters—for example, Lewis (1972, 2009) has a more monistic account of theoretical characters according to which these characters are largely about causal-nomological roles. This is not a problem, however, for HPD4 is neutral in this regard: such a reader could replace my conception of theoretical characters with her own; the definition is still useful. My conception is, after all, merely a recommended way of understanding theoretical characters; nothing hangs on it.

theoretical characters is to put them together in a new way. A toy example is that a unicorn is a recombination of a horse's theoretical characters and a horn, a parthood character shared by many horned animals such as rhinoceroses. The robustness here, then, concerns (1) the internal logical and conceptual consistency of the recombination and (2) its consistency with the theoretical frameworks in which we extract the relevant theoretical characters. (1) demands that the recombined thing cannot be a logically or conceptually impossible entity or property like a square circle; (2) demands that the recombined thing cannot be an incomplete entity or property according to the relevant theoretical frameworks: for example, no theoretical frameworks in animal studies can make sense of an animal without a physical body. An intradisciplinary recombination, then, is a recombination that makes use of theoretical characters merely from a single scientific discipline, such as physiology, molecular biology, or particle physics. A recombination of theoretical characters found in, say, cognitive science and particle physics (e.g. an electron that has emotions) does not count as an intradisciplinary recombination.

Let me elaborate on the application of HPD4 in light of a few examples which range from easy to difficult. We mentioned above the case of a unicorn, which is a recombination of the theoretical characters of a horse and some horned animals. It appears that it is a natural entity, unless it possesses some mysterious magical powers as described in some of the relevant folktales, for the relevant theoretical characters are all extracted from natural entities of some HPs, namely the horse and the horned animals. Similarly, a werewolf is a recombination of theoretical characters of human beings, wolves, and metamorphosis.[17] With the same approach, we can also deal with the case of the optical aether. Despite its being massless and transparent, the optical aether was believed to be a physical substance which is much like other physical substances posited by classical physics and which shares almost the same theoretical characters as them, such its being microphysical particles and its capacity to have and transmit motion. It is in fact in virtue of its possession of these theoretical characters that it was claimed to act as the medium of light waves, in the same way that water acts as the medium of water waves.

---

[17] Of course, an easier way of counting these animals as natural is, as mentioned in Section 6, to take into account the possibility that they are exclusively constituted by natural things like physical particles. Even so, I believe that consideration of naturalness at the level of special sciences is nonetheless useful in the methodological application of MN. See Section 9 for a related discussion.

HPD4 applies to properties as well. First, consider twin-mass, twin-charge, and twin-spin, which are considered by Stoljar (2010, p. 79) in his discussion of the problem of non-actualized properties. Suppose that an entity with twin-mass produces no gravitational forces but instead produces twin-gravitational forces. Twin-mass can nonetheless be counted as natural. For even though gravitational forces and twin-gravitational forces are different forces, they are identical in terms of their *format of operation*. Hence, twin-mass brings about a product that is *identical in format* to that of mass, and can be considered as a recombination of the theoretical characters of the latter. The same can be said about twin-charge and twin-spin. Consider, then, an example of a natural property that was posited by science in the past and whose concepts have no descendants left nowadays: levity. Scientists in history explained light substances like air and fire going upward by positing that such substance have levity in them. In addition, some chemists in history like Lavoisier believed a fluid called phlogiston left a body when it burned, and since things were heavier after burning—we now know this was due to oxidation—phlogiston was also believed to have levity. Levity can be considered as a negative version of weight (as understood in history), for it produces phenomena in a very similar manner to weight, albeit having a revised vector. In this light, it can also be considered as a recombination of the theoretical characters of weight.

Let me now show that the idea of robust intradisciplinary recombination in HPD4 does not lead to an overinclusion, namely the counting of presumptively non-natural things as natural. For our purposes here, I shall focus on the example of fundamental mental properties—which Kim, following Roy Wood Sellers, takes to be a crucial test case for characterizations of MN (Kim 2003, p. 96). The problem concerns how theoretical characters of things in, say, cognitive science are recombined: can the recombined thing be both mental and fundamental? I do not think so. Such recombinations can only be done in three ways, all of which are either unsuccessful or are not permitted by HPD4. Specifically, the recombination could involve (1) combining mental properties with fundamental physical things like electrons, (2) having ontological fundamentality as one of its theoretical characters, or (3) not having intrinsic characters concerning parthood. (1) is not permitted by HPD4 for the obvious reason that it involves interdisciplinary recombination, whereas HPD4 only allows for intradisciplinary recombination. (2) is not permitted for the same reason: it is not within the scope of cognitive science to posit ontological fundamentality; this theoretical character has to be found in particle physics. (3) will not be successful in making the recombined thing ontologically fundamental, for, on the one hand, not having intrinsic characters concerning parthood merely means that the descriptions of the thing concerned in the relevant theory(ies) 'bottom out' in the sense that descriptions of lower-level components come to an end. Such descriptive bottoming out does not imply ontological fundamentality, though it is compatible with it (Machamer, Darden & Craver 2000, pp. 13–14). On the other hand, it appears that the demand of robustness from contemporary cognitive science requires its posited things, bottoming out or not, to have some particular hierarchical characters. More specifically, its posited things should be located at some particular hierarchical level of things in the sense of constantly co-instantiating with some neurological processes, artificial intelligence, or the like, and being roughly compatible with the possibility that they be grounded in them.[18] This effectively eliminates the possibility of the recombined cognitive thing being ontologically fundamental.

9. The Usefulness of HPA

I believe that HPA is not only defensible as I have argued above, but also useful in several ways. Consider the way I handled the problem of naturalistically unacceptable scientific theories in Section 7 where I appealed to their sudden divergences. I argued that it not only allows us to account for the reason why some scientific theories are presumably naturalistically unacceptable, but that it is also useful in explaining the research directions of some scientists and philosophers who attempt to remain naturalistically respectable and, in addition, providing a rational basis for these directions.

There is another reason why HPA is useful. While the naturalness of some entities, properties, and states of affairs—such as qualia, free will, the self, some of the posited entities of European phenomenology, and the observer effect in the Copenhagen interpretation—is intensely debated, HPA offers us a useful framework to resolve these debates. HPA does not, as some other characterizations of MN do, offer answers to those debates by simply saying that those things are by definition natural or non-natural—which may imply that one group of philosophers (or scientists) are inexplicably

---

[18] Of course, cognitive science is not metaphysics, and thus the relationship between the relevant hierarchical levels are typically not restricted to particular metaphysical framings such as a reductionist one; they often are compatible with views like emergentism.

misguided.[19] Instead, following Ravenscroft's argument, HPA acknowledges that those debates are substantive and cannot be easily settled: the naturalness of those things is indeed difficult to determine, and might even be currently impossible to determine; for it is ambiguous whether they relate to the HPs in the way required by HPD4. This provides an elegant framework for different parties to settle their debates and reach some consensus: while we can all agree that some cases lie in the vague boundary area between the natural and non-natural, progress can be made by inquiring into the relevant scientific disciplines and thereby improving our ideas of their paths, which include our understanding of their historical paths and our expectations of their future paths. For instance, when two parties disagree about the naturalness of qualia or some of the posited entities of European phenomenology, an inquiry into recent neuroscience or cognitive science might change our view on what the historical and expected future paths of the discipline are like, and might thereby provide us with some clues as to how we can settle the debate (for examples of such projects see Hohwy & Frith 2004; Gallagher et al. 2015; Tononi & Koch 2015; Chan & Latham 2019). This provides a useful framework for the naturalization of the philosophy of mind and phenomenology.

10. Final Thoughts

I have proposed HPA by using the strategy of SA, which is to search for an extension of current science. I have argued that it can survive the main problems facing DC and the dilemma of the right kind of similarity facing SA, that it can explain some patterns of behaviour and intuitions of scientists, and that it can offer us a useful framework to resolve some philosophical debates. Braddon-Mitchell and Jackson (2007, pp. 34–5), two proponents of SA, remark that 'The vagueness in [SA] can perhaps be left to advances in philosophy and indeed in science itself to sort out.' I consider my proposal to be a development of SA because they share the same strategy, which is to search for an extension of current science. It is in this light a response to Braddon-Mitchell and Jackson's invitation.

---

[19] For a detailed discussion of this problem and the implications it has for philosophy and science, see Gallagher 2018.

Moreover, it provides a framework that allows other advances in philosophy and science to reduce the relevant vagueness in an easier way.[20]

One possible worry is that HPA is largely based on socio-historical but not metaphysical considerations, for it is somewhat a socio-historical issue as to which concepts are found on the HPs and which are not. This is counterintuitive and unsatisfactory. For when we use the term '*metaphysical naturalism*', we are usually trying to express a metaphysical notion, not a merely socio-historical notion.[21] But this would be a mistake. MN can be understood as a minimalist or parsimonious metaphysical framework. Its exclusive commitment to entities or properties posited by HP-related theoretical concepts is a pursuit of ontological economy, which is itself not an HP-related theoretical concept but a metaphysical commitment. To be more precise, every reasonable metaphysical framework has metaphysical commitments to entities and properties posited by HP-related theoretical concepts; the naturalist is a minimalist or parsimonious metaphysician who always restricts her metaphysical commitments to such entities and properties and is unwilling to have any additional commitments. By contrast, the non-naturalist goes beyond the minimalist restriction and has additional metaphysical commitments such as <God> and <the fundamentally mental>.[22] Some might find this solution unsatisfactory, for it can only count MN and not the *notion of the metaphysically natural* as a metaphysical notion: while the exclusive commitment to HP-related theoretical concepts is a metaphysical doctrine, HP-related theoretical concepts are still defined solely in socio-historical terms. But this is not so. Once the above idea of MN is accepted, then being natural is not only about adequately relating to HP, but also about playing certain roles in the minimalist metaphysician's ideology: the natural is the only kind of thing the minimalist metaphysician would posit. This is, again, a metaphysical issue.

One last point. This proposal of HPA is still incomplete, for the idea of HP is historical and there is certainly a problem of historical accuracy. No doubt, there might be historical facts that are in tension with the proposal

---

[20] Of course, as I noted in Section 5, there is still vagueness in my approach. But I have argued, following Ravenscroft, that the existence of vagueness in a characterization of MN is not necessarily a failing and might even be a virtue. What is important here is whether or not unwanted and problematic vagueness—such as that which leads to the dilemma of the right kind of similarity—is reduced; and if my arguments in this chapter are on point, it is.

[21] For a related argument, see McPherson 2015, pp. 124–8.

[22] For a more detailed and sophisticated discussion of the minimality of MN, see Oppy 2018b, pp. 34–6.

outlined in this chapter, for the history of science is far less linear, systematic, and unified than it may seem: there is no absolute guarantee that, say, all concepts of spirits and souls are not on the HPs. Of course, even if there are a few such cases on the HPs, they might be taken as insignificant noises that can be ignored when we construct a simplified, general theoretical model of what the HPs are like.[23] For example, the possibility that, say, a few spiritual concepts are on a few HPs should not be necessarily irreconcilable with a simplified, general model of HPs that takes them as some scientific developments that have got rid of spiritual concepts. But, again, any such model is yet to be verified.

This chapter is concerned with metaphysics—or, more precisely, the metaphysical foundation of the discourses in several philosophical areas, such as the philosophy of mind, contemporary phenomenology, the philosophy of religion, and metaethics—and not historical research. Its commitments to history are not claimed to be true in terms of a historical study, but rather should be seen as a hypothesis that is waiting to be assessed on the basis of empirical studies in the history and philosophy of science. A possible solution I favour is to see the concept of HP as a folk scientific concept or even a popular myth. According to the solution, what HP are should be assessed in terms of intuitions about the history of science, or what popular science tells us about the history of science, rather than real historical research. This might release the user of the doctrine of MN from the burden of requiring professional historical knowledge. After all, while such intuitions are perhaps historically wrong or inaccurate, they are indeed what many philosophers (and scientists) believe, and what motivate many of their research directions. In this respect, the real history of science might even be less important. Taking this into account, the intuition proposal might be useful and interesting enough for some disciplines like the philosophy of mind, contemporary phenomenology, the philosophy of religion, metaethics, metaphysics, the philosophy of language, and even for the philosophy of science, in which hard facts of science and its history are a serious concern—for scientists' beliefs and motivations are hard facts as such. I am leaving the question of whether the intuition proposal or the real history proposal is correct as an open question and a topic for future research.

[23] For detailed discussions of theoretical modelling, see Nagel 1961; Laudan 1977; Musgrave 1981; Godfrey-Smith 2014.

Acknowledgements

For useful discussions or comments, the author would like to acknowledge Eran Asoulin, John Bigelow, David Braddon-Mitchell, Belinda Calderone, Ruey-Lin Chen, Michael Duncan, Frank Jackson, Justine Kingsbury, Uriah Kriegel, Andrew James Latham, Erick Llamas, James Norton, Graham Oppy, Alex Sandgren, Simon Varey, Wai-hung Wong, Lei Zhong, and the philosophy of mind group at the Australian National University. The author is also grateful to Caleb Liang and Yi-Cheng Lin for their helpful administrative support to this research project. Special thanks are due to Belinda Rickard. This project is supported by a grant from the Ministry of Science and Technology of Taiwan (grant number: 108-2410-H-002-241-MY3).

References

Armstrong, D. 1978, 'Naturalism, materialism, and first philosophy', *Philosophia*, vol. 8, no. 2–3, pp. 261–76.

Braddon-Mitchell, D. & Jackson, F. 2007, *The Philosophy of Mind and Cognition*, 2nd edn, Malden: Blackwell.

Chalmers, D. 1996, *The Conscious Mind: In Search of a Fundamental Theory*, New York: Oxford University Press.

Chan, L.C. & Latham, A.J. 2019, 'Four meta-methods for the study of qualia', *Erkenntnis*, vol. 84, no. 1, pp. 145–67.

Chen, R.L. 2017, 'Mechanisms, capacities, and nomological machines: integrating Cartwright's account of nomological machines and Machamer, Darden and Craver's account of mechanisms', in H.K. Chao, S.T. Chen & J. Reiss (eds), *Philosophy of Science in Practice: Nancy Cartwright and the Nature of Scientific Reasoning*, New York: Springer.

Copp, D. 2012, 'Normativity and reasons: five arguments from Parfit against normative naturalism', in S. Nuccetelli & G. Seay (eds), *Ethical Naturalism: Current Debates*, Cambridge: Cambridge University Press, pp. 24–57.

Cramer, J. 1988, 'An overview of the transactional interpretation of quantum mechanics', *International Journal of Theoretical Physics*, vol. 27, no. 2, pp. 227–36.

Craver, C. & Tabery, J. 2015, 'Mechanisms in science', in E. Zalta (ed.), *Stanford Encyclopedia of Philosophy*. Retrieved 8 November 2020, https://plato.stanford.edu/entries/science-mechanisms/

De Caro, M. & Macarthur, D. 2010, 'Introduction: science, naturalism and the problem of normativity', in M. De Caro & D. Macarthur (eds), *Naturalism and Normativity*, New York: Columbia University Press, pp. 1–22.

Devitt, M. 1998, 'Naturalism and the a priori', *Philosophical Studies*, vol. 92, no. 1–2, pp. 45–65.

Eccles, J. 1994, *How the Self Controls Its Brain*, Berlin: Springer-Verlag.

Gallagher, S. 2018, 'Rethinking nature: phenomenology and a non-reductionist cognitive science', *Australasian Philosophical Review*, vol. 2, no. 2, pp. 125–37.

Gallagher, S., Janz, B., Reinerman-Jones, L., Bockelman, P. & Trempler, J. 2015, *A Neurophenomenology of Awe and Wonder: Towards a Non-Reductionist Cognitive Science*, London: Palgrave Macmillan.

Godfrey-Smith, P. 2014, *Philosophy of Biology*, Princeton: Princeton University Press.

Hempel, C.G. 1969, 'Reduction: ontological and linguistic facets', in S. Morgenbesser, P. Suppes & M. White (eds), *Philosophy, Science, and Method: Essays in Honor of Ernest Nagel*, New York: St. Martin's Press, pp. 179–99.

Hohwy, J. & Frith, C. 2004, 'Can neuroscience explain consciousness?', *Journal of Consciousness Studies*, vol. 11, no. 7–8, pp. 180–98.

Jackson, F. 1998, *From Metaphysics to Ethics: A Defence of Conceptual Analysis*, Oxford: Oxford University Press.

Kim, J. 2003, 'The American origins of philosophical naturalism', *Journal of Philosophical Research*, vol. 28, pp. 83–98.

Kim, J. 2006, *Philosophy of Mind*, 2nd edn, Boulder: Westview Press.

Kuhn, T. 1996, *The Structure of Scientific Revolutions*, 3rd edn, Chicago: University of Chicago Press.

Laudan, L. 1977, *Progress and Its Problems: Towards a Theory of Scientific Growth*, London: Routledge & Kegan Paul.

Lewis, D. 1972, 'Psychophysical and theoretical identifications', *Australasian Journal of Philosophy*, vol. 50, no. 3, pp. 249–58.

Lewis, D. 1983, 'New work for a theory of universals', *Australasian Journal of Philosophy*, vol. 61, no. 4, pp. 343–77.

Lewis, D. 2009, 'Ramseyan humility', in D. Braddon-Mitchell & R. Nola (eds), *Conceptual Analysis and Philosophical Naturalism*, Cambridge, MA: MIT Press, pp. 203–22.

McDowell, J. 1994, *Mind and World*, Cambridge, MA: Harvard University Press.

Machamer, K., Darden, L. & Craver, C. 2000, 'Thinking about mechanisms', *Philosophy of Science*, vol. 67, no. 1, pp. 1–25.

McPherson, T. 2015, 'What is at stake in debates among normative realists?', *Noûs*, vol. 49, no. 1, pp. 123–46.

Melnyk, A. 2003, *A Physicalist Manifesto: Thoroughly Modern Materialism*, Cambridge: Cambridge University Press.

Montero, B. 2009, 'What is the physical?', in A. Beckermann & B.P. McLaughlin (eds), *The Oxford Handbook of Philosophy of Mind*, New York: Oxford University Press, pp. 173–88.

Montero, B. & Papineau, D. 2016, 'Naturalism and physicalism', in K. Clark (ed.), *The Blackwell Companion to Naturalism*, Malden: Wiley-Blackwell, pp. 182–95.

Musgrave, A. 1981, '"Unreal assumptions" in economic theories: the F-twist untwist', *Kyklos*, vol. 34, no. 3, pp. 377–87.

Nagel, E. 1961, *The Structure of Science: Problems in the Logic of Scientific Explanation*, London: Routledge.

Oppy, G. 2018a, *Naturalism and Religion*, Abingdon: Routledge.

Oppy, G. 2018b, *Atheism and Agnosticism*, Cambridge: Cambridge University Press.

Papineau, D. 2014, 'The poverty of conceptual analysis', in M.C. Haug (ed.), *Philosophical Methodology: The Armchair or the Laboratory?*, Abingdon: Routledge, pp. 166–94.

Pollard, C. 2014, 'Merleau-Ponty and embodied cognitive science', *Discipline Filosofiche*, vol. 24, no. 2, pp. 67–90.

Price, H. 1996, *Time's Arrow and Archimedes' Point: New Directions for the Physics of Time*, Oxford: Oxford University Press.

Quine, W.V.O. 1995, 'Naturalism; or, living within one's means', *Dialectica*, vol. 49, pp. 251–63.

Ravenscroft, I. 1997, 'Physical properties', *Southern Journal of Philosophy*, vol. 35, no. 3, pp. 419–43.

Stoljar, D. 2010, *Physicalism*, New York: Routledge.

Tononi, G. & Koch, C. 2015, 'Consciousness: here, there and everywhere?', *Philosophical Transactions of the Royal Society B Biological Sciences*, vol. 370, no. 1668. https://royalsocietypublishing.org/doi/10.1098/rstb.2014.0167.

Varela, F., Thompson, E. & Rosch, E. 1991, *The Embodied Mind*, Cambridge, MA: MIT Press.

Zhong, L. 2016, 'Physicalism, psychism, and phenomenalism', *The Journal of Philosophy*, vol. 113, pp. 572–90.

III
CONTENT

10

Consciousness Meets Lewisian Interpretation Theory

A Multistage Account of Intentionality

Adam Pautz

All thinking has to start from acquaintance; but it succeeds in thinking about many things with which we have no acquaintance.

— Bertrand Russell

Acquaintance is a condition on the possibility of thought and justification.

— David Chalmers

Karl experiences a tomato of a round and somewhat bulgy shape. He believes that rabbits are getting into his garden. He worries that democracy is in trouble. He is confident that 68 plus 57 will always make 125.

In "Radical Interpretation" (1974), David Lewis asked: by what constraints, and to what extent, do the non-intentional facts about Karl determine such intentional facts? There are two popular approaches. First, the *reductive externalist program*. The austere physical facts about Karl are the only facts. Original intentionality reduces to informational-teleological relations between Karl's brain and the world. I will use "tracking relations" as neutral term for this kind of relations. Second, there is the totally different *phenomenal intentionality program*. According to it, the intentional contents of Karl's conscious experiences are determined by his internal brain states, not tracking relations to the environment. And his internal conscious experiences play a crucial role in pinning down the contents of his mental states.

I will argue against both approaches. I will agree with friends of phenomenal intentionality that reductive externalists neglect the role of our

Adam Pautz, *Consciousness Meets Lewisian Interpretation Theory: A Multistage Account of Intentionality* In: *Oxford Studies in Philosophy of Mind Volume 1*. Edited by: Uriah Kriegel, Oxford University Press (2021).

internally-determined conscious experiences in grounding intentionality. But I will fault them for not adequately explaining intentionality. They cannot just say "conscious experience explains it" and leave it at that. However, I will sketch an alternative multistage account incorporating ideas from both camps. In particular, by appealing to Lewisian ideas, we can explain how Karl's conscious experiences help to ground the contents of his other mental states. The result is a novel "consciousness first" approach to intentionality.

My plan is as follows. In Section 1 and Section 2, I will catalogue problems for the reductive externalist program and the phenomenal intentionality program. Along the way, I will lay down desiderata for a theory of intentionality. In Section 3, I will sketch my alternative multistage theory and show how it might satisfy those desiderata.

1. Problems with the Reductive Externalist Program

In Section 1.1 and Section 1.2, I catalogue problems for specific ideas within the reductive externalist program. In Section 1.3, I raise a more general problem. All the problems concern the connection between intentionality and conscious experience.

1.1 The Problem of Experiential Indeterminacy

My first problem for the reductive externalist program concerns how to determine Karl's sensory-perceptual experiences. I will assume intentionalism (Chalmers 2010, Dretske 1995, Horgan 2014, Tye 2019). Experiential phenomenology and intentionality are inseparable. The phenomenology of Karl's experiences is a matter of what perceptible properties he is conscious *of* (in other words, "experientially represents"). So determining his experiences is a special case of the problem of intentionality.

Roughly, a reductive externalist account of experiential intentionality goes as follows. The perceptible properties ("qualia") are response-independent physical properties (reflectance-types, chemical-types, etc.). The conscious-of relation is a complex tracking relation between subjects and such physical properties. For instance, for Karl to be conscious of the quality red (a certain reflectance-type), and have a "reddish" experience, is for Karl to undergo a subpersonal brain state that has the biological function of tracking (being produced by) the occurrence of red and that is poised to influence the cognitive system. The result is *reductive externalist intentionalism* about phenomenology (Dretske 1995, Tye 2019).

But indeterminacy worries undermine this view. Let me summarize two illustrations that I have developed in much greater detail elsewhere (Pautz 2017).

First, imagine that Karl and his kind evolved on *black-and-white earth*. On black-and-white earth, the following things are true. First, *surfaces* of all objects are either black or white—this is why I call it "black-and-white earth." Second, every object contains a smaller object. In particular, black outer objects contain red inner objects and white outer objects contain green inner objects. But the objects are impenetrable. Third, the color of the inner object and that of the outer object are causally yoked together by way of a natural, super-fast chemical process.

Now suppose Karl views a black object containing a red inner object (Figure 10.1, *left*). Does Karl have a "blackish" experience or a "reddish" experience? I intentionally described the example in physical terms, leaving open the character of his experience. Reductive externalists about phenomenology might say that Karl appropriately tracks, and thereby is conscious of ("experientially represents"), the outer black only. In that case, he has a blackish experience. Alternatively, reductive externalists might say that Karl appropriately tracks, and thereby is conscious of ("experientially represents"), the more distal *inner red*. On this account, although the outer black is part of the causal process, Karl isn't conscious of it—no more than he is conscious of his retinas or the light. It is just part of the causal process that enables him to be conscious of the inner red. In that case, he has a reddish experience. If the austere physical facts are all the facts, it's hard to see what could make one of these accounts determinately correct and the other incorrect.

My second example (Figure 10.1, *right*) is arrived at in two stages. First, *Harry* is on earth and *Sally* is on inverted earth. Harry looks at the sky. His

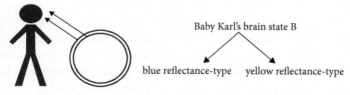

Figure 10.1 Black-and-white earth (left) and middle earth (right)

brain state B has the function of tracking the *blue* of the sky. So, according to reductive externalism about experience, B enables them to be conscious of the blue of the sky and to have an experience with a "bluish" phenomenology. On inverted earth, the sky is yellow. Even though the sky is yellow, it puts Sally into the same brain state B that Harry is in. In her population, this brain state B has the function of tracking *yellow*. So, according to reductive externalism, she is conscious of yellow and has a "yellowish" experience.

In the second stage, Harry and Sally leave their planets and wind up on *middle earth*. This is when Harry met Sally. Even though they evolved separately and belong to different species, they are able to have a baby, Karl. Baby Karl is born without eyes. But he does have a complete visual cortex. One day he undergoes brain state B and has a hallucinatory color experience.

On reductive externalism, does Baby Karl's have a bluish or a yellowish experience? Does his brain state B have a biological function of tracking *blue* or *yellow* (Figure 10.1, *left*)? There is no clear answer. In his dad Harry's population, B has a history of tracking blue. But, in his mom Sally's population, B has a history of tracking yellow.

Such cases make a dilemma for externalists (described in detail in Pautz 2017). One option is *radical experiential indeterminacy*. In the black-and-white earth case, as Karl views the object, it is determinate that he *either* has a blackish *or* a reddish experience, but it is indeterminate *which one*, because it is indeterminate whether he "experientially represents" the outer black reflectance or the inner red reflectance. Likewise, on middle earth, it is determinate that Karl either has a bluish or a yellowish hallucination, but it is indeterminate which one.

But, whatever we may think of radical indeterminacy in thought and language, radical indeterminacy in experiential character is incoherent.

Another option is *arbitrary identities*. Presumably, since relations are abundant, there is a tracking relation—call it tracking$_{17}$—that Karl on black-and-white earth bears to the outer black but not the inner red; and there is another tracking relation call it—tracking$_{18}$—that Karl bears to the inner red but not the outer black. Now, maybe it is just a "surd metaphysical fact" (Putnam 1981: 46–8) that the conscious-of ("experiential representation") relation is determinately identical with tracking$_{17}$ instead of tracking$_{18}$, so that it is determinate that Karl is consciously acquainted with the outer black rather than the inner red. And maybe this same tracking relation is one that Karl on Middle Earth bears to (say) yellow rather than blue when having his hallucination. So he has a yellowish experience rather a bluish one.

But the arbitrary identities view flouts the plausible idea that the conscious-of relation is a "stand out" relation. That is, when Karl is consciously acquainted with property P (e.g., a certain color), but not at all consciously acquainted with property P^*, there is a massive difference in his relation to P and P^*. The arbitrary identifies view flouts this because, while Karl stands in the tracking$_{17}$ relation the outer black (which on this view is identical with the relation of conscious acquaintance), he stands in the barely different tracking$_{18}$ relation to the inner red. On this option, then, there is no way in which the allegedly correct interpretation (viz., Karl is conscious of the outer black, and misses by a hair acquaintance with the inner red) "stands out" from the allegedly incorrect one (viz., Karl is conscious of the inner red, and the outer black is just part of the mediating causal process).

In short, the reductive externalist program has difficulty with

Experiential determinacy. There cannot be radical indeterminacy in the intentional contents of Karl's experiences. Moreover, the correct assignment of contents to his experiences and experience-based thoughts "stands out" (significantly differs) from alternative, incorrect interpretations.

1.2 Problems with the Inner Sentence Theory of Belief and Desire

Now suppose that Karl is a prelinguistic hominid with simple beliefs and desires. How might reductive externalists account for this?

Many reductive externalists accept Jerry Fodor's (1990, 2010) inner sentence approach ("the representational theory of the mind"). Here is the version I will focus on. First, although he lacks a language that he can experience, Karl has an "inner" subpersonal language that he cannot experience. The sentences of this inner language somehow get their contents (*that is red, that is round, there is a friend*) by way of tracking relations to external items. Once the content of an inner sentence is initially fixed, it tends to retain that content, even when it is temporarily severed from its normal connections to perceptual inputs and behavioral outputs. (This is required to explain false and irrational beliefs.) Second, there is a belief-box and a desire-box. The sufficient conditions for "box-inclusion" are functional. I will assume that *one* sufficient condition is this: *if* subpersonal inner sentences b_1, b_2,... and d_1, d_2,... typically interact to cause the actions which, according to $b_1, b_2, \ldots$, will satisfy $d_1, d_2, \ldots$, *then* inner sentences b_1, $b_2, \ldots$ are "in the belief-box" and inner sentences $d_1, d_2, \ldots$ are "in the desire-box." Call this *means-ends.* Finally, to believe that p is to have a subpersonal inner sentence in one's "belief-box" that means that p, and to desire that q is to have a subpersonal inner sentence is one's "desire-box" that means that q.

In my view, this popular reductive externalist approach to belief and desire misses some deep connections between Karl's beliefs and desires and his conscious experiences.

First, the inner sentence theory violates

Conscious-life constraint.   The beliefs and desires of individuals with conscious experiences cannot "radically change" if there is no change in *either* (i) their conscious experiences and *or* (ii) their dispositions to consciously act (including inner or outer speech dispositions, for individuals with language).

Here's an example showing why the inner sentence theory violates this. Karl the prelinguistic hominid is starving, and he is given vanilla ice-cream for the first time. He believes that this white stuff tastes *sweet and good* and wants this sweet, good-tasting stuff in his mouth. He devours it for five minutes. However, in the middle of his chow-down, while his experiences and behavior remain the same, his inner sentences are temporally scrambled. In particular, the subpersonal sentence "this tastes *horribly bitter and disgusting*" is tokened in his belief-box and "I will have this *specific bitter, disgusting stuff in my mouth*" is tokened in his desire-box. The inner sentence theory implies that, for this short ten-second interval, Karl suddenly, and for no reason, secretly acquired a new, irrational and totally false belief about the ice-cream (it tastes horribly bitter and disgusting) as well as a crazy desire (to have this specific disgusting stuff in your mouth). Call this *secret scrambling.* Against this, *throughout* Karl evidently believes it tastes *good* (not disgusting), and wants this *good* stuff in his mouth, even if these mental states are differently realized by different, intrinsically meaningless symbols at the hidden neural level.

The inner sentence theory also violates the following:

Constitutive experience-belief connection.   Experiences do not merely cause beliefs. They are *necessarily* apt to cause beliefs. That is, they are necessarily *compelling.* Necessarily, if Karl experiences clearly different colors, he is at least *disposed to* believe that they are different. If Karl is conscious of a red and round item, he *is disposed to* believe that such an item is present.

Necessarily, if Karl has a striking taste sensation, or a searing pain, he is disposed to believe he is in that state.[1]

The inner sentence theory violates this because it holds that Karl's conscious experience of a red and round thing is realized by a (iconic) neural representation in one area of his brain, while his belief that a red and round thing is there is realized by a (discursive, sentence-like) representation in another area of this brain. Further, the connection between the two is *utterly contingent*, and subject to radical and regular malfunction, like the connection between having joint pain and believing the weather will change, or between fire and a fire alarm. Against this, the experience-belief connection is stronger than that.

Finally, the inner sentence theory of belief and desire violates

Prelinguistic limits. (i) If Karl (like a prelinguistic hominid) lacks an *outer* language and is limited to having the usual range of human experiences, then there are rough limits on what he can believe and desire. He can have beliefs about perceptible properties, the kinds of things in his environment, other people, the near past and future, and so on. But he cannot believe propositions about specific large numbers, the laws of quantum mechanics, abstract philosophical doctrines, and so on. (ii) He can only form such sophisticated beliefs if he has an *outer* language.[2]

Prelinguistic limits is supported by pretheoretical reflection. Just try to describe possible circumstances where prelinguistic Karl clearly has such sophisticated beliefs: you cannot do it. It also fits the facts: humans came to have sophisticated beliefs only by inventing a sophisticated outer language. I will provide examples in Sections 3.2–3.4.

But prelinguistic limits is puzzling. What *explains* the necessary restriction on prelinguistic Karl's beliefs and desires? The inner sentence theory doesn't explain prelinguistic limits; in fact, it violates prelinguistic limits because it holds that Karl's beliefs and desires are fixed by his *inner* language,

---

[1] For defenses of a constitutive experience-belief connection, see Byrne 2018: section 6.2.10; Hawthorne 2006: 249–50; Lewis 1999: 6; Shoemaker 1996: ch. 3.

[2] For defenses of prelinguistic limits, see Bennett 1976: 96; Bermudez 2003: 150ff.; Blackburn 1984: 137–40; Dehaene 1999: ch. 4; Dennett 1987: 201; Hurford 2014: 124; Pinker and Jackendoff 2005: 206; Sacks 1989: ch. 2; Speaks 2010: 234ff.; Spelke 2003; and Wittgenstein 1953: 174ff. I note in passing that the individuals studied by Varley et al. 2005 who have aphasia but who are capable of mathematical thought are not a counterexample to prelinguistic limits because they can understand and accept mathematical sentences.

and in principle there are no limits on how sophisticated it might be. On the inner sentence theory, lacking an *outer* language should be no bar to having arbitrarily complex beliefs and desires.

For instance, pretend that Karl does indeed have something like an inner language. Suppose that Karl has a magical subpersonal detector that only does one thing: when there is a collection of exactly 167 things just behind his head (where he cannot see anything), it causes the symbol "167 things are behind me" to be tokened in his head. Suppose that this inner sentence then combines with sentences in his desire box to lead to rudimentary behavior (for instance, walking forward), so that it satisfies the means-end condition for being in the belief-box. The inner sentence model implies that on such occasions Karl *believes* that there are exactly 167 things behind him. Likewise, there is no reason why prelinguistic Karl could not have within his inner language terms that track *democracies* and *electrons* (Fodor 1990: 111). So, inner sentence theory implies that, when simple-minded Karl engages in other rudimentary behaviors, he might count as having beliefs about *democracies* or *electrons*.

But Karl the prelinguistic hominid evidently does not and (in the circumstances) cannot have such beliefs. For instance, he doesn't *believe* that there are exactly 167 things behind him—he has *no idea* what is behind him and no available way of thinking about large exact numbers.

1.3 A General Problem: Internalism about Experiential Intentionality

In any form, the reductive externalist program holds that all intentionality is grounded in "tracking" relations between the brain and the world. In their essay "The Intentionality of Phenomenology and the Phenomenology of Intentionality" (2002), Horgan and Tienson used an internalist thesis to argue against the reductive externalist program and for their alternative phenomenal intentionality program:

Internalism about experiential intentionality. The phenomenology of experience is not determined by tracking relations to the environment; it is internally determined. And much intentionality is inseparable from phenomenology.

Horgan and Tienson, like many others, hold experiential internalism to be "self-evident" from the armchair, not requiring argument (2002: n.23).

I disagree. However, decades of research in psychophysics and neuroscience support experiential internalism (Pautz 2010, 2019). What pains, smells, color qualities, and so on we experience are fixed by internal neural processing, not what external physical properties (types of damage, chemical-types, reflectance-types) our sensory systems have the function of tracking. And this does indeed rule out the reductive externalist program. Here are some illustrations.

First, consider a *coincidental variation case* (Pautz 2010). Karl and Twin Karl's sensory systems have the function of tracking the *same* types of damage, chemical-types, reflectance-types, and so on, but their internal sensory processing is very different. Given the empirically determined role of the brain, they have radically different experiences. Given intentionalism, their experiences, and their experience-based beliefs, *differ* in content. So standard tracking theories (Dretske 1995, Neander 2017, Tye 2019, Williams 2020) fail for experiential intentionality.

The *brain-in-the-void* (BIV) undermines all reductive externalist theories. Given experiential internalism, an accidental, life-long brain in the void (e.g., a "Blotzmann brain") undergoing all the same (actual and counterfactual) brain states as Karl would also have all the same experiences as Karl. Given intentionalism, the experiences of Karl-the-brain would have rich intentional contents, for instance *there is a round thing there*. And, although BIV-Karl doesn't have the same "wide" beliefs as Karl, it is common sense that BIV-Karl would share many beliefs with Karl—nearly all false in his case (Lewis 1994: 425). But BIV-Karl would not bear any tracking relations to external states of affairs—for instance, the state of affairs of there being a round thing before him (Pautz 2019).

2. Problems with the Phenomenal Intentionality Program

The reductive externalist program, then, fails to satisfy several plausible desiderata concerning links between intentionality and phenomenal experience. So let us turn to the phenomenal intentionality program.

Proponents of the phenomenal intentionality program typically accept "internalist intentionalism" about Karl's sensory-perceptual experiences (Chalmers 2010, Horgan 2014, Pautz 2010). The contents of Karl's experiences are determined by his brain states rather than by tracking relations to the environment. Unlike reductive externalism, this view satisfies internalism about experiential intentionality. For instance, BIV-Karl will share many of Karl's intentional states. And it may satisfy experiential determinacy. For example, on middle earth and black-and-white-earth, the contents of Karl's experiences, and so their phenomenal characters, are determinately pinned down by his brain states.

As for Karl's thoughts, friends of phenomenal intentionality accept the *cognitive experience theory*. Instead of explaining Karl's thoughts in terms of hidden inner sentences that track external states-of-affairs, they explain his thoughts in terms of special "cognitive experiences." Cognitive intentionality is "phenomenal intentionality" (Horgan and Tienson 2002).

In my view, the phenomenal intentionality program is along the right lines. In fact, I will incorporate their "internalist intentionalism" about sensory-perceptual experience into my own account in Section 3. More generally, I think that they are right to emphasize the role of conscious experience in determining intentionality. However, in this section, I will argue against their simple "cognitive experience theory" of thought. Here we need a more complex, multistage story (Section 3).

I will first describe the cognitive experience theory in greater detail (Section 2.1). Then I will argue that it violates some important desiderata on a theory of intentionality. It fails to adequately explain *thought content* (Section 2.2), the *holistic character of thought*, and *prelinguistic limits* (Section 2.3).

2.1 The Cognitive Experience Theory of Thought

In giving an account of how Karl has thoughts with certain contents, we must address well-known underdetermination worries due to Quine (1960) and Kripke (1982). For example, let the *quus$_g$-function* be an arithmetical function like the plus-function except that it gives weird results for some specific numbers too large for Karl to compute (e.g., some specific numbers in the googolplex range). Or suppose that extension of *friend** is like that of *friend* in nearly all worlds but that it has a somewhat twisted extension in very remote worlds (so that Karl's finite dispositions are neutral between *friend* and *friend**). How do the physical facts determine that Karl thinks that 68 plus 57 equals 125 rather than 68 *quus$_g$* 57 equals 125, or that Friedrich is a friend rather than a friend*?

The cognitive experience theory holds that Karl simply has special "cognitive experiences" that constitute his grasping the relevant contents. So the question "how do the physical facts determine that Karl grasps the relevant contents?" becomes the question "how do physical facts determine his cognitive experiences?" Here are some representative passages:

> Something is happening to you experientially as you read. Obviously, there is the visual or auditory experience [and] perhaps a rapid and silent process of forming acoustic mental images. But there is something else – a certain complex modification of the quality of one's course of experience, and not just of one's dispositional set. There is understanding-experience. [Its] existence is sometimes doubted, perhaps because it has no striking experiential feel in the way in which experience in any of the sensory modalities usually does.
>
> (Strawson 2010: 8)

> [Cognitive experience] makes it the case that I can think determinately about the number 2 although there is no relevant causal context. *Pfff!* This is the correct account of how it is that [such] content can be determinate in spite of all the problems raised for this idea by Kripke in his book *Wittgenstein on Rules and Private Language.* (Strawson 2010: 354)

> We have no explanation of how the systems of the brain that underlie or realize thought give rise to, or involve, conscious thought experience in the way in which they do. (Strawson 2010: 255, fn.54)

> Certain conscious states are intrinsically such as to ground thought or understanding. There is a conscious state which is intrinsically such as to ground the thought that two plus two equals four. (Goff 2012: 223)

> If consciousness is inside the head, then, in explaining [cognitive] phenomenology, we must confine ourselves to facts about what's going on inside the head; to what me and my brain in a vat twin have in common.
>
> (Goff 2012: 232)

> Physically and apart from phenomenology, there is no "one, determinate, right answer" to the question of what is the content of an intentional state. Content identity or determinacy is fixed phenomenally. For example, the what-it's-like of thinking "Lo, a rabbit" is different from the what-it's-like of thinking "Lo, a collection of undetached rabbit parts"
>
> (Graham, Horgan and Tienson 2007: 476)

> [My view] maintains that the intentional content of a thought is determined by its *intrinsic* phenomenal properties, *not its relational properties.* My teachers will be very disappointed in me. (Pitt 2004 fn.5, my italics)

> The part of what is thought that is fully determined by [cognitive] phenomenal character [is] a kind of thought content. (Siewert 2011: 264)

> If there is irreducible cognitive phenomenology, it individuates as finely as
> content.   (Kriegel 2015: 62)

In sum, the *cognitive experience theory* holds that, in addition to having sensory-perceptual experiences, Karl has special *cognitive experiences* with certain built-in contents. In fact, to have these experiences just is to grasp certain contents (see Pautz 2013: 209 and Chudnoff 2015: 135). These thought-contents are "narrow" because they are shared between Karl and his experiential duplicates. As for Karl's "wide" thought-contents (about particular individuals, natural kinds, etc.), they are derivative, a product of his narrow thought-contents and his relationships with external things. This view requires that Karl's phenomenal life is extremely rich. He has a special "democracy" cognitive phenomenology, and a special "plus-function" cognitive phenomenology, and so on. Such cognitive experiences are not reducible to sensory-perceptual experiences. For instance, suppose that Karl has a deaf twin who speaks *sign-language* instead of English, and that Karl and his twin are talking about arithmetic or the state of democracy. Then they have very different *sensory-perceptual experiences*. But, if cognitive experiences are irreducible, they presumably might have the very same *cognitive experiences*.

The cognitive experience theory has some initial appeal. And it may help to avoid a problem we pressed against the inner sentence theory. The inner sentence theory violates the conscious-life constraint on belief (Section 1.2). The cognitive experience theory might accommodate it by holding that to believe that *p* is to be disposed to the person-level cognitive experience of judging that *p* (Kriegel 2015, Smithies 2019). And maybe a similar story could be given for desire.

The cognitive experience theory is underdeveloped. What's the relationship between Karl's cognitive experiences and his physical-functional states? In the case of *sensory* experiences, two reductive theories have been tried. Behaviorists and functionalists identify sensory experiences with *functional-dispositional states*. Type-type identity theorists identify them with *categorical brain states*. Might either reductive theory work for *cognitive* experiences?

There is reason to think not. To illustrate, suppose that Karl has the cognitive experience with the built-in content that 68 plus 57 equals 125.

First, cognitive experience theorists would not reduce it to a functional-dispositional state involving his dispositions to use "68," "57," and "plus" in certain ways. For one thing, they hold that such dispositions *underdetermine* whether Karl thinks that 68 plus 57 equals 125 or 68 quus$_g$ 57 equals 125. So Karl's cognitive experience must be a "further state" that picks up the slack when it comes to fixing content. For another thing, Karl's cognitive experience is supposed to be a *categorical* state that *explains* Karl's dispositions to use language.

So perhaps Karl's cognitive experience that 68 plus 57 equals 125 is simply identical with his categorical brain state—type-type identity theory. But a simple Leibniz's law argument rules this out too. On the cognitive experience theory, it is part of the essence of this cognitive experience that it is true iff 68 plus 57 equals 125.[3] By contrast, this is *not* part of the essence of any brain state. For any brain state can be fully characterized in terms of *types of neurons* and the *times, directions*, and *intensities* at which they fire, without mentioning numbers or the plus-function. Therefore, the property of having a cognitive experience with certain built-in truth-conditions is distinct from (though it might be realized by) the property of undergoing a neural pattern.

So the cognitive experience theory naturally leads to *the further fact view* of thought. Some of Karl's thoughts, with their built-in contents, are not reducible in other terms. They are "further facts." This answers Quine and Kripkenstein. Of course, since everything depends on the physical, such facts *depend on* the physical facts about Karl (e.g., his brain states). But it's dependence without reduction. On a dualist version of the further fact view, the dependence is underwritten by contingent psychophysical laws. On a "physicalist" version, it is underwritten by metaphysically necessary "grounding laws" (more on this in the next subsection). I will assume that the cognitive experience theory is a further fact view.

Here is another question. On the cognitive experience theory, *some* thoughts and episodes of understanding are irreducible cognitive experiences. But which ones? Call this the *scope question*. Maybe it applies only to primitive thoughts with very simple contents closely related to perception (Mendelovici 2018). Then a different story is required for more sophisticated thoughts. But, in fact, proponents of the cognitive experience theory typically apply it to quite sophisticated thoughts: thinking that 68 plus 57 equals 125, that he's a friend, that democracy is in trouble, and so on. This "rich view" fits with the above quotations. It will be my target.

---

[3] This doesn't presuppose that this intentional state is a "relation to a proposition." So it is compatible with the nonrelational theory of intentionality defended by Prior (1968: 93ff.) and Kriegel (2011: ch. 3).

2.2 Against the Cognitive Experience Theory: Danglers

I don't think that there really are cognitive experiences with built-in phenomenal contents like 68 *plus* 57 *equals* 125 or *democracy is in trouble*. My first argument against the cognitive experience theory is that it leads to an incredible account of content.

For instance, on the cognitive experience theory, Karl's "cognitive experience" constitutes his thinking (and understanding the sentence as meaning) that 68 plus 57 equals 125 rather than that 68 quus$_g$ 57 equals 125. We saw in the previous section that Karl's cognitive experience must be *distinct from* his standard physical-functional states. Still, it is certainly somehow *dependent on* them: mental changes always depend on underlying purely physical changes. But which ones? One odd view would be that Karl's having the specific cognitive experience that 68 *plus* 57 equals 125 at this time, rather than some other cognitive experience, is somehow dependent on his set of *dispositions* to use "68," "57," and "plus" at that time. But, again, proponents of cognitive experience hold that such functional-dispositional states underdetermine content.

The only option remaining is the *brain-based explanation*: Karl's cognitive experiences depend on his *brain states*, even though they are distinct from those brain states. Strawson and Goff endorse something like it in the quotations at the beginning of Section 2.1.

The brain-based theory requires "intentional laws" linking brain states and thought-contents, for instance:

If Karl undergoes so-and-so brain state, then he has the cognitive experience that 68 plus 57 equals 125 (rather a cognitive experience that 68 quus$_g$ 57 equals 125).

If Karl undergoes such-and-such brain state, then he has the cognitive experience that someone is his friend (rather than a cognitive experience that someone is his friend*).

These special laws are what "solve" the underdetermination worries due to Quine and Kripkenstein. Given the rich variety of possible cognitive experiences, they must be extremely numerous. Given the further fact view, they are brute "necessary connections between distinct existences." On a dualist version, they are contingent (Graham, Horgan and Tienson 2007: 476). On a physicalist version, they are metaphysically necessary "grounding laws" (Rosen 2010: 132).

The brain-based theory is unorthodox. A standard explanation of why Karl thinks that 68 plus 57 equals 125, rather than that 68 quus$_g$ 57 equals 125, appeals to (i) how he's disposed to use certain (inner or outer) symbols together with (ii) considerations of "naturalness" (e.g., Lewis 1992). By contrast, the brain-based theory holds that Karl simply has a categorical cognitive experience with the built-in content *68 plus 57 equals 125*. And this in turn is directly explained by nothing but his *here-and-now brain state* (embedded in a network of such states) together with a special "intentional law."

Still, the brain-based theory is not unprecedented. John Searle has endorsed such a view:

> Intrinsic intentional phenomena are caused by neurophysiological processes going on in the brain, and they occur in and are realized in the structure of the brain [although] we do not know much about the details of how such things as neuron firings at synapses cause [intentional phenomena].   (Searle 1984: 5–6)

Although they neglect the issue, I have argued that friends of cognitive experiences (Kriegel, Siewert, Pitt, etc.) are led to the same theory, requiring special "intentional laws." But I will now argue that this theory is incredible, for a few reasons.

First, J.C. Smart (1959) objected to the complexity of brute "dangling laws" connecting brain states with distinct sensory-perceptual experiences. The brain-based cognitive experience theory is even more complex, requiring a slew of additional "danglers": special (nomic or grounding) laws connecting brain states with distinct cognitive experiences with certain built-in contents.

Second, these intentional laws will be arbitrary. What matters to experience are patterns of neural activity. But the connection between undergoing any pattern of neural activity and the thought ("cognitive experience") that 68 plus (rather than quus$_g$) 57 equals 125 is bound to be arbitrary.

Third, while some of Karl's thoughts have quite determinate contents, others have indeterminate contents. For instance, when Karl thinks that 68 plus 57 equals 125, the content is perfectly precise and determinate (at least if numbers are unique Platonic objects rather than set-theoretic constructions). By contrast, when he thinks democracy is in trouble, the content is quite indeterminate. We need to explain indeterminacy no less than determinacy. How can the brain-based cognitive experience theory explain it? One idea (suggested to me by Philip Goff) is that, while some brain states produce cognitive experiences that have built-in *determinate* contents, other brain states produce cognitive experiences with built-in *indeterminate* contents. To use Siewert's (2011: 264) language, "the part of what is thought that is fully determined by phenomenal character" is determinate in the one case, and indeterminate in the other. There is nothing more to say. However, I cannot accept that. Surely there is a more illuminating explanation—for example, one appealing to differences in "use plus naturalness" (see Section 3.4).

In sum, the cognitive experience theory leads to the brain-based theory of cognitive intentionality, but that theory is incredible. It violates a plausible desideratum:

Minimize danglers. In explaining the determinacy (and the indeterminacy) of Karl's thoughts, we should minimize brute "necessary connections" between Karl's physical states and his distinct intentional states.

2.3 Against the Cognitive Experience Theory: Holism

My next problem for the cognitive experience theory concerns the generally accepted thesis of *holism* about thought:

Holism. There are rough, metaphysically necessary connections between Karl's having a certain thought (e.g., the thought that there is a giant red cube there, the thought that someone is a bachelor, or the thought that 68 plus 57 equals 125) and other things, including perhaps: having the capacity for certain sensory-perceptual experiences, having certain inferential dispositions, having certain dispositions to try do certain things (given certain desires), having certain background linguistic or conceptual abilities, and so on.

Elsewhere, I posed a dilemma (Pautz 2010: 366 and 2013: 214ff.). Cognitive experience theorists can either reject or accept holism. Either way, I argued, they face serious problems.

In response, Philip Goff (2018) and Uriah Kriegel (2015) reject holism. Instead, they accept "atomism" or "modal independence" for cognitive experiences and so also for thoughts. By contrast, Michelle Montague (2019) and Charles Siewert (2016: section 6) accept holism. I want to look at their responses.

Let us start with *rejecting* holism. In fact, cognitive experience theorists are under pressure to take this horn. Typically, distinct existences are freely recombinable. So, if Karl's thoughts are really special experiential states that are distinct from all other mental states, and if they are not to be explained in terms of his language-use or dispositions, shouldn't they be modally independent from all these things, contrary to holism?

The problem with an atomistic cognitive experience theory is that it implies the possibility "thought scrambling" and "punctate minds." Let us take these in turn.

Thought Scrambling. Karl is a prelinguistic hominid who has a perceptual experience of a rock flying towards him which an enemy tribesman has thrown at him. On the cognitive experience theory, Karl presumably undergoes a *second*, quite different cognitive experience t_{26} which constitutes his *judging* that something is moving towards him. That is, there is a peculiar redundancy. Now suppose later he has an identical perceptual experience of another rock flying towards him (he's having a bad day). Given atomism, on this occasion, the cognitive experience t_{26} might be replaced by another cognitive experience t_{81} which constitutes judging *that there is nothing but a stationary giant cube sphere in front of me*. Still, everything else might be the same: he has nothing but a vivid, clear-as-day visual experience of a rock moving towards his head, he is afraid, he wants to avoid being hit, and he moves away as a result. There is also no change in his inner speech, since he is a prelinguistic hominid who lacks language and inner speech. Indeed, since cognitive experience is supposed to be subtle (otherwise it would be uncontroversial), Karl might not even *notice* that t_{26} has been replaced by t_{81}. Despite all this, proponents of an atomistic cognitive experience theory must say that, on the second occasion, when Karl has a vivid, clear-as-day experience of a giant rock headed towards him and so quickly moves away, he is "really" secretly judging *that there is nothing but a stationary giant red cube in front of me*.

Given atomism, the cognitive experience theory also implies that the following could happen. Karl is a modern human with language. Whenever he sees a female fox and says "That is a vixen," he "really" has the cognitive experience that it is a *bachelor*. But, because he is screwed up in another way, this causes him to have the cognitive experience that it is a fox and the cognitive experience that it is female. And if someone asks him what kind of thing he thinks is in front of him, he *points to* other female foxes around. So his visual experience, his speech, his inferential dispositions, his pointing behavior, and his behavioral dispositions are exactly as if they would be for someone who believes that it is a female fox. Still, an atomistic cognitive experience theory absurdly implies Karl has a deeply secret and super irrational belief that the perceived fox is a *bachelor*.

Or suppose that, on one solitary occasion, when Karl says "2 plus 2 equals 4," instead of having the cognitive experience that 68 plus 57 is 125, he has the different cognitive experience that 68 $quus_g$ 57 is 125. (Why couldn't there be such a cognitive experience?) However, suppose that there is no difference in his *other* "cognitive experiences," in his use of the mathematical term "plus" in any possible circumstances, and so on. On the cognitive experience ("further fact") theory, on this occasion Karl secretly thinks 68 $quus_g$ 57 is 125 rather than 68 plus 57 equals 125.

Goff (2018: 103–4) holds that these "thought scrambling" cases are indeed metaphysically possible. He says that the only reason we might think otherwise is that they are nomically impossible and difficult to imagine. I disagree. Thoughts cannot float free from everything else in this way. And I'm not really thinking that these cases are only nomically impossible and confusing this for metaphysical impossibility.[4]

How do we settle the issue? Here are a few points in my favor. First, you cannot conceive of such thought-scrambling from the first person. Second, the atomistic cognitive experience theory leads to an absurd form of skepticism. Suppose you say "68+57=125." Maybe you can know that you are having THIS cognitive experience; but how can you be so sure that THIS cognitive experience is one that determines a plus-content rather one that determines a $quus_g$-content, as in the above "scrambling" case? Third, if we follow Goff and take the permissive line that such cases are possible but just difficult to imagine, we are led to a general modal skepticism. For instance, why not say that round squares are possible but just difficult to imagine?

Punctate Minds. Suppose now that Karl is a disembodied brain-in-the-void (BIV). BIV only has the brain state sufficient for a single cognitive experience,

---

[4] Uriah Kriegel has suggested to me a response that goes beyond Goff's. In line with atomism, he accepts the metaphysical possibility of the "thought scrambling" cases described in the text. For instance, there is a possible case in which, thanks to the momentary insertion of an aberrant "cognitive experience," Karl the prelinguistic hominid, while experiencing a rock flying towards him, has a secret and causally isolated cognitive experience *that there is nothing but a giant red sphere before me*, which leaves absolutely no trace on the rest of his mental life (visual experiences, imagery, inner speech) or on his dispositions to act. But he adds that in such a case there is *also* a sense in which Karl believes the obvious—that there is a rock headed towards him—where that sense is given by something like the holistic "interpretation theory" I will propose in Section 3.2. This mixed view is interesting. But it still allows for atomistic "thought scrambling"—arbitrary thought insertions that leave no traces. And I find that impossible.

namely, the cognitive experience that allegedly constitutes thinking that 68 plus 57 equals 125. BIV just has a little experience-nugget. BIV has no other neural machinery. So BIV is not having, and indeed could not have, experiences of a number of things (e.g., two marbles or three musical notes). BIV also has no language or inner speech (including arithmetical language).

Goff (2018: 103–4) and Kriegel (2015: 54ff.) hold that such a punctate mind is possible, as required by their atomism. But I find it *a priori* impossible.[5] Here is a simple argument for my take (Pautz 2013: 213). To think that 68 plus 57 equals 125, you need concepts of *numbers*. And, to have concepts of numbers, you need to be at least *capable of having* experiences of a number of things (they could be non-veridical experiences or even imagistic experiences). But presumably Goff and Kriegel don't think that the cognitive experience that 68 plus 57 equals 125 is *itself* such an experience (e.g., it is not a visual image of 125 things). And, by stipulation, the BIV has *only* this single experience, and is not even *capable* of having any other experiences. So, it cannot have concepts like *68, 57, plus,* and *125*. Therefore, it cannot have such a thought.[6]

Let us then turn to the second option for friends of cognitive experiences. Instead of rejecting holism, they might try to accommodate it within their theory.

Montague (2019: 195–9) opts for this horn. On her view, thoughts are cognitive experiences that are wholly distinct from each other, from dispositions to try to act, and so on. Nevertheless, they are necessarily connected with each other, and with dispositions to try to act, and so on. So, like me, she thinks that the above-described "scrambling cases" are impossible. And maybe the bad-off BIV couldn't have a solitary cognitive experience that 68 plus 57 equals 125 because it doesn't satisfy certain complex pre-conditions

---

[5] The atomistic cognitive experience theory also makes a false empirical prediction. The theory says that the same cognitive experiences that we have—for instance, the cognitive experience that 68 plus 57 equals 125—could occur in splendid isolation in the absence of capacities for inner or outer speech (as happens in the BIV). But, presumably, since I'm in control of my thought, I'm in control of my cognitive experiences. So this view predicts that right now I could close my eyes and choose to have the isolated cognitive experience (and hence thought) that 68 plus 57 equals 125, in the *absence* of inner or outer speech ("68 plus 57 equals 125"). But I cannot do that.

[6] Kriegel (2015: 57) responds to this argument by retreating to a different case in which the punctate mind acquired arithmetical concepts by having had sensory-perceptual experiences of numbers of things *in the past*. But his atomism implies the possibility of the more extreme case described in the text in which a BIV system has a single arithmetical thought without *ever having had* experiences of numbers of things and indeed without even having the *capacity* for such experiences. And I argue that *this* case is impossible.

for having this experience, as Siewert (2016: section 6 and 1998: 285) suggests.

Now, Montague and Siewert are right to accept holism.[7] But they neglect to address a few arguments against combining holism with their cognitive experience theory.

First, the *missing explanation argument* (Pautz 2013: 215–16; Chudnoff 2015: 120). Given the cognitive experience theory, we cannot *explain* holism. We simply must say, as Montague and Siewert do, that, while some experiences (e.g., color experiences) are *not* necessarily connected with dispositions to act or infer in certain ways, other experiences ("cognitive experiences") *are* necessarily connected with rich dispositions of this kind. Moreover, all these specific necessary connections have no deeper explanation.[8] This is unexplanatory and complicated.

Second, Montague and Siewert's combination of the cognitive experience theory and holism faces the *argument from very distinct existences*. Take the thought 68 plus 57 makes 125. Given the cognitive experience theory, this is constituted by a special cognitive experience *E*. Further, *E* is not itself an (e.g., an imagistic) experience *N* of any number of things (much less 125 things). It is *totally different* from any experience of a number of things. Now, given a plausible form of holism, it's metaphysically necessary that, if a subject has a thought 68 plus 57 makes 125, they are capable of having experiences of numbers of things (otherwise the subject cannot have arithmetical concepts). Thus, the cognitive experience theory and holism imply the following: it's metaphysically necessary that, if a subject has a purely cognitive experience *E*, the subject must have had or be capable of having a totally different experience *N* of a number of things. But it is *a priori* implausible that there is a metaphysically necessary connection between such very different types of experiences. Holism sits poorly with the cognitive experience theory of thought.

Third, the *argument from prelinguistic limits*. In Section 1, we noted that Karl is only capable of a limited range of thought without language. Thought beyond that range requires having an outer language—a compositional system of representation. This is a holistic connection, broadly understood.

---

[7] Horgan and Tienson (2002: 526; and unpublished ms) also take the holist horn.

[8] *Pace* Chudnoff (2015: 121), the general thesis of phenomenal holism ("no two partial phenomenal states can be the same if they belong to different total phenomenal states") is logically two weak to entail and explain all the *specific* and *varied* holistic-inferential connections that must obtain between cognitive experiences ("there is a bachelor," "68 plus 57 equals 125"), other cognitive experiences, sensory experiences, and behavioral dispositions.

It cries out for explanation. We saw that the inner sentence theory of thought fails to explain it (Section 1.2). The cognitive experience theory also fails to explain it. In general, experience doesn't require language. So if thoughts are special experiences, shouldn't we be capable of any thought without language? For instance, couldn't a neuroscientist manipulate the brain states of prelinguistic Karl, so that he momentarily has the cognitive experience that 68 plus 57 equals 125, or the cognitive experiences you in fact have as you read the Declaration of Independence, without language being involved?

One response is that cognitive experience is "perceiving as," in particular, perceiving *a sentence as meaning that p*. So Karl cannot have the relevant cognitive experiences without language.

But there are two problems with this proposal. First, *some* thought is possible without language. Think of prelinguistic children, or Karl as a prelinguistic hominid (Section 1.2). So *some* limited range of cognitive experiences must be possible without language (Siewert 1998: 277–8). Therefore, the proposal needs revision: some cognitive experiences are possible without language, but for some reason *more sophisticated* cognitive experiences (advanced math, the Declaration of Independence, complex physics, etc.) essentially involve language. But this doesn't *explain* prelinguistic limits.

Second, if we have a cognitive experience with the complex content *that the sentence "68 plus 57 equals 125" means that 68 plus 57 equals 125*, we should in principle be able to have a cognitive experience with the *simpler* content *that 68 plus 57 equals 125*. (Compare: if you experience *that there is a red thing next to a green thing*, you can experience the simpler content *that there is a green thing*.) In that case, prelinguistic Karl should in principle be capable of having a cognitive experience in which he directly "grasps" this complex mathematical content without linguistic mediation, against prelinguistic limits.

2.4 Is Cognitive Experience Theory Supported by Introspection?

In sum, the cognitive experience leads to brute laws ("danglers") connecting Karl's brain states with sensible rather than twisted intentional contents (see Section 2.2). And it doesn't fit well with the basic "data" about thought, namely, holism and prelinguistic limits (see Section 2.3).

However, it might be replied that we are stuck with the cognitive experience theory because it is introspectively evident. For instance, suppose you read "2 plus 2 equals 4" or "democracy is in trouble." You understand what is said in a flash. Intuitively, no one could be in the same total phenomenal state as you without understanding the words as meaning that *2 plus 2 equals 4* and *democracy is in trouble*. The experiential state of grasping the meanings of these familiar words is the categorical ground of your disposition to provide certain answers to questions about their meaning and use. Since your sensory-experiential experiences are insufficient for grasping these contents, experiences of grasping them must be special, further experiences. If we didn't have such experiences, reading would be boring.

But there are two problems with the appeal to introspection. First, consider the following *continuum argument*. You read mathematical sentences of increasing complexity ("2 is greater than 1," "2+2=4," etc.). Eventually you get to ones involving very large numbers, imaginary numbers, more sophisticated mathematical functions, and so on. Let us stipulate that, by ordinary standards, you count as "understanding" all the sentences in the series: after all, you understand the constituent expressions, you understand the Arabic number notation, you understand the mathematical functions, and so on. That is, you are disposed to give correct answers (maybe with some effort) when asked to explain what they mean. Now, cognitive experience theorists hold that early in the sequence (e.g., "2 is greater than 1," "2+2=4") you have, over and above your sensory-perceptual experiences of the sentences and your dispositions to explain them, categorical cognitive experiences which consist in "grasping" or "seeing" the precise mathematical contents of the sentences. But, presumably, they will say that, eventually, when the sentences become longer and more abstract, you do *not* have such categorical cognitive experiences which consist in grasping the precise mathematical contents of the sentences. For surely your cognitive experiences are just not that rich and fine-grained. If these sentences had had slightly different meanings in English, your here-and-now experience of reading them would have been the same. In these more abstract cases, you only have sensory-perceptual experiences of the words and certain dispositions to use and explain them. (That is, their view of such cases resembles the view opponents of cognitive experiences like myself would apply to *all* sentences in the series, even the initial basic ones.) If so, there must be an answer to the "scope question" (see Section 2.1): *where* in the series of sentences did you stop having cognitive experiences in which you grasped the precise mathematical content of the sentence? No answer stands out as clearly correct (including "it's indeterminate but hereabouts"). This is very odd if we can know by introspection when our experiential state determines that we understand certain contents.

Second, I suggest that we can explain away the introspective appeal of the cognitive experience theory.

To see how, let us start with another case. Suppose you enter a room and see a few familiar friends. At first blush, you could not be in the same total experiential state and yet fail to know *who they are*. But, on second thought, this is not the case. In principle, you could have the very same total experiential state (with the same sense of familiarity) but without really having any idea who they are. The reason you might think otherwise is that in the actual situation information about who they are is *easily available*. You can easily open up a dossier of information about any one of them. So you might mistakenly think that all that information is somehow already "there," part of your total experience.

Likewise, when you read "democracy is in trouble," you could easily unpack what these words mean. I suggest that this explains away the appeal of cognitive experience theory. It explains why you might think that all that information is somehow already *there* and part of your experience. But this is an illusion. Seeing familiar words is like seeing old friends. And just as you could have the same total experience of your friends but not really know who they are, so you could have the same total experience of the words "democracy is in trouble" but not really know what they mean. Indeed, you might fail to understand them as meaning *anything at all* and have no idea how to use or define them. For you might have the same total experience of the words but utterly fail to satisfy the functional-dispositional requirements on understanding them as meaning anything (Chudnoff 2015: 147; Pautz 2013: 213; Putnam 1981: 4ff.). Of course, you typically "just know" in the moment that you understand the words as meaning something. But, contrary to the cognitive experience theory of thinking and understanding, your total *experience* in the moment itself doesn't entail that you understand them as meaning something.

3. Outline of a Multistage Theory of Intentionality

In the course of criticizing the reductive externalist program and the phenomenal intentionality program, I have laid out several desiderata. For instance, the contents of Karl's sensory-perceptual experiences are internally

Figure 10.2 A multistage theory of intentionality

determined. His beliefs and desires are connected to his conscious-life. We need to explain the determinacy (and indeterminacy) of thought-content. There are necessary limits to his prelinguistic thought and holistic constraints on his thoughts. Neither the reductive externalist program nor the phenomenal intentionality program adequately accommodates all these desiderata.

I will now outline a multistage theory of intentionality satisfying all the desiderata. Like friends of phenomenal intentionality, I will defend internalist intentionalism for Karl's sensory-perceptual experiences. And I will suggest that his conscious experiences play a crucial role in grounding determinate intentionality. But, like reductive externalists, I will suggest we need a real explanation of the contents of Karl's thoughts. We cannot just say "cognitive experiences do it." My explanation will co-opt some elements of David Lewis's account of Karl: his "interpretationism" about Karl's beliefs and desires (1974) and his appeal to "naturalness" (1992).

In outlining my theory, I will pretend that Karl's life spans human history. Diagrammatically, the theory goes as follows (Figure 10.2).

3.1 Stage One: Karl's Conscious Experiences with Thin Contents

My multistage theory begins with a view associated with the phenomenal intentionality program: an internalist and nonreductive form of intentionalism about Karl's sensory-perceptual experiences, as opposed to the reductive externalism form of intentionalism criticized in Section 1.

The quickest way to get a hold of this view is to compare it to the sense datum view defended by Russell in *The Problems of Philosophy* (1912). Suppose Karl views a tomato. On Russell's view, the physical tomato is intrinsically colorless. Karl's brain generates a reddish and round sense datum, and Karl bears a special relation of conscious acquaintance to this sense datum. The internalist form of intentionalism I favor is similar, but without sense data. It replaces sense data with states of affairs that may or may not obtain. Because of Karl's neural processing, Karl stands in a special, irreducible relation—the *conscious-of* relation—to the ostensible state of affairs of something being reddish and round. In illusion and hallucination, the state of affairs doesn't obtain. It seems to Karl that there is a sense datum but there really isn't one.

Here is a quick argument for this view (Pautz 2019). Given experiential internalism, BIV-Karl (see Section 1.3) might have the same tomato-like experience as Karl. Thus, BIV-Karl might be conscious of ("experientially represent") the (uninstantiated) property of being round. But BIV-Karl's brain state does not have the function of tracking (being produced by) that spatial property. Indeed, BIV-Karl bears no interesting physical relation whatever to the property. So the conscious-of relation (the "experiential representation relation") is not identical with any physical relation. As Ned Block (2019: 426) says, it appears that "we internalists should acknowledge an irreducible representation relation."

So the picture is one of grounding without reduction. Somehow, Karl's brain states ground his being conscious of various states of affairs, but the conscious-of relation is not reducible to any tracking or other physical relation. On a dualist version (Levine 2019), these "grounding" connections are contingent. On a physicalist version (Rosen 2010: 132), they are metaphysically necessary. I'm neutral here.

Internalist intentionalism is consistent with both "illusionism" about the traditional secondary qualities and also with "realism." On a realist version (McGinn 1996), physical things *acquired* colors-as-we-see-them when they came to habitually cause us to have experiences of those colors; the colors of things co-evolved with color experiences. On an illusionist form (Chalmers 2010, Horgan 2014, Pautz 2010), this is not so. Physical surfaces don't have colors-as-we-see them.

Karl also has experiences of acting. These, too, have built-in contents. These contents might have the form: *I'm making so-and-so happen* (Bayne and Levy 2006).

There is a debate about whether the built-in "phenomenal contents" of our experiences are "thin" or "rich." In Section 2, I denied that Karl has special "cognitive experiences" with built-in rich contents involving democracy and large exact numbers. For reasons I cannot go into here (but see Byrne and Siegel 2017), I also reject a "rich" view of Karl's sensory-perceptual experiences on which their phenomenal contents involve high-level properties like *being a tomato, being edible, expressing fear,* or *being wrong.* Rather, they only involve colors, shapes, movement, and gestalts (abstract complexes of shapes/sizes/colors). Likewise, the phenomenal contents of his *pains, pleasures,* and *emotional experiences* only concern bodily qualities.

Karl's conscious experiences are a source of reasons. On Pryor's "dogmatism" (2000), if Karl is conscious of ostensible state of affairs *p*, then he thereby has a basic *prima facie* reason to believe that *p*. Karl's experience-based reasons extend beyond the thin contents of his experiences. For instance, his history of experiences provides a reason to think all emeralds are green (rather than grue). Karl's conscious experiences are also a source of reasons for desire. For instance, if Karl has a severe pain, he has a basic reason to desire that it go away.

In sum, Karl starts with experiences with relatively thin contents. The next stages of my account propose "extension mechanisms" whereby Karl might move to beliefs, desires, and other intentional states with richer contents.

3.2 Stage Two: Karl's Beliefs/Desires within the Perceptual Circle

Imagine that Karl still lacks an outer language. Nevertheless, he has certain basic beliefs and desires. The second stage is a theory of them:

Best systems theory: If, given his history of *conscious experiences* and consequent *dispositions to act*, all the *best interpretations* assign to Karl the belief that *p* or the desire that *q*, *then* this grounds Karl having the belief that *p* or the desire that *q*.

To a first approximation, the best systems do the best job overall of maximizing Karl's rationality given his dispositions to act and his conscious experiences.

This account is inspired by Lewis's account in "Radical Interpretation" (1974). It is often called "interpretationist." But this term suggests instrumentalism. So I prefer "best systems theory."[9]

Let us consider an example. Return to the example where a rock is flying towards Karl and so he intentionally moves away (see Section 2.3).

---

[9] For further defense of development of this view, see also Braddon-Mitchell and Jackson 2007: ch. 11.

Infinitely-many perverse interpretations fit Karl's behavior. One of them is that he believes (despite experiencing otherwise) that the rock is moving *away*, that he wants to be hit on the head, and he believes that by moving away he will magically cause the rock to reverse direction and hit his head. What makes such perverse interpretations incorrect? This is an "underdetermination worry" not unlike those of Quine (1960) and Kripke (1982).

Lewis (e.g., 1986: 38ff.; 1994: 427ff.) provides an elegant solution. Given his experience of a rock headed towards him, Karl has a reason to believe that a rock is headed *towards* him. In addition, the desire to be hit on the head is unreasonable. So the above perverse interpretation gratuitously portrays Karl as massively departing from rationality. The interpretation that has Karl departing least from rationality assigns to him the belief that a rock is headed towards his head and a desire that it not hit his head. This is what singles it out as the *correct* interpretation. Call this the *reasons-based solution* to the underdetermination problem.

In general, if we are to avoid underdetermination, we cannot say that the best systems are just a matter of best "fitting the subject's behavior," as on behaviorism. Rather, we must define them as the systems that achieve an optimal balance of maximizing Karl's *substantive rationality* (responding to *experience-based reasons*) as well as his *structural rationality* (behaving so as to maximize expected utility, coherence, etc.). That is, prelinguistic Karl's beliefs and desires fixed jointly by his behavioral dispositions on the output side *and* by the reasons provided by his sensory-perceptual experiences on the input side.[10] Karl's conscious experiences (the first stage) are explanatorily (but not temporally) prior to his basic beliefs and desires.[11]

Since I am no skeptic, I think that Karl's experiences provide him with basic reasons to believe things that somewhat extend beyond the thin contents of his experiences; for instance, that all emeralds are blue (rather than grue). This explains how prelinguistic Karl can determinately believe such things.

When prelinguistic Karl's dispositions to act become regularly inharmonious with his history of experiences (e.g., he is mentally ill), the best systems

---

[10] This counts against Schwitzgebel's (2002: 269) claim that "what is for a subject to believe something does not require appeal beyond the subject's forward-looking [output-side] dispositions."

[11] If behavioral duplicates of Karl that work by huge input-output "look-up tables" ("blockheads," "marionettes") lack conscious experiences, my *consciousness-based* best systems theory can avoid the mistaken verdict that they have the same beliefs and desires as Karl. I can also appeal to the constraint proposed by Braddon-Mitchell and Jackson 2007: 120–2.

theory will assign him beliefs contrary to experiential evidence. The point is that correct interpretations minimize irrationality, not that they impute no irrationality.

The best systems theory is incomplete. It provides a recipe for determining prelinguistic Karl's beliefs and desires *given* a foundation: a rich set of facts involving his *conscious experiences*, his *actions*, and his *reasons*, all of which must be explanatory prior to his beliefs and desires. So best systems theorists must address the following three questions.

First, what determines Karl's *conscious experiences?* Given intentionalism about experience, this is a special case of the hard problem of intentionality. Call it the problem of *source intentionality*.

Second, what distinguishes Karl's *actions* (which are up for rationalization in terms of belief-desire) from his "mere bodily movements" (which are not)? Defining actions as movements that are nondeviantly caused by Karl's desires or beliefs would lead to *circularity*, since his desires and beliefs are precisely what the best systems theory is trying to explain.

Third, where do Karl's *reasons* come from? The best systems theory is up to its ears in normativity. It appeals to facts like "given so-and-so experiences, Karl has a *reason* to believe *p*," "so-and-so prior probabilities are rational," "Karl has a basic reason to desire so-and-so intrinsic values," "failing to maximizing expected utility is irrational," and so on. It is very difficult to provide a plausible (not list-like) reductive account of such notions.

These questions constitute the *source problem* for Lewis's best systems theory (Pautz 2013, Williams 2020). Different versions of the best systems theory result when we plug in different answers.

In Stage One, I advanced nonreductive internalist intentionalism about experience. When we plug this into the best systems theory, we obtain:

Nonreductive internalist best systems theory. The best systems theory combined with nonreductive internalist intentionalism about conscious experience (Chalmers 2010, Horgan 2014, Pautz 2010). A crucial source of intentionality is an irreducible relation of conscious acquaintance.

Therefore, in answer to the question of what determines Karl's conscious experiences, I hold with Russell (1912) that they involve an irreducible, internally-determined relation of conscious acquaintance with ostensible states of affairs. So, while Karl's beliefs and desires reduce to facts about his conscious experiences and dispositions to act, these facts cannot in turn be reduced to the austere physical facts about Karl.

In answer to the question of where prelinguistic Karl's reasons come from, I advocate dogmatism (Pryor 2000). Karl's reasons come from what ostensible states of affairs he is conscious of. And I am not especially concerned to reduce facts about reasons and rationality to something more basic.

In answer to the question of how to define Karl's actions, I suggest that they can be picked out prior to his beliefs and desires, thereby avoiding the above-mentioned circularity worry: they are the doings that he experientially represents himself as making happen (Bayne and Levy 2006).

Of course, the best systems theory comes in other forms. Lewis (1974, 1994) himself hoped for a fully reductive form of the best systems theory according to which *all* these facts about Karl ultimately reduce to the austere physical facts about him. But he never provided the details.[12] In this chapter, I'm assuming intentionalism about experience. The only well-developed reductive theories of experiential intentionality are externalist. So, reductive best systems theorists are led to

Reductive externalist best systems theory.   The best systems theory combined with externalist intentionalism about experience (Dretske 1995, Tye 2019). A crucial source of intentionality is a tracking relation between Karl's brain states and the world.

In his recent book *The Metaphysics of Representation* (2020), Williams defends a best systems theory along these lines. In particular, he favors a teleological tracking theory (Neander 2017). For instance, suppose Karl views a tomato. Karl is in a brain state that has the biological function of tracking a round thing with a red-reflectance. On Williams's view, this "tracking" fact constitutes his experientially representing that a round and red thing is there (2020: 185ff.). This is part of his evidence and constitutes his *reason* to believe that a round and red thing is before him (2020: 181ff.). Since he has this reason, the best (most-rationalizing) system assigns to him this belief, rather than some twisted belief.

My argument for nonreductive internalist best systems theory over Williams's reductive externalist best systems theory is simple. Williams's

---

[12] Indeed, Lewis's reductivism faces big problems. For instance, to avoid deviant interpretations of Karl's desires, he says the best systems will tend to assign "reasonable" desires congruent with "the system of intrinsic values" (1974: 336). But then Lewis (1989) reduces values to what Karl and his community would *desire to desire*. This is circular and still faces deviant interpretations.

theory is a form of the reductive externalist program. So it faces versions of the problems covered in Section 1. In particular, it violates the following two desiderata:

Internalism about experiential intentionality;

Experiential determinacy;

It is only nonreductive internalist best systems theory that accommodates these desiderata. Start with internalism about experiential intentionality. Research in psychophysics and neuroscience suggests that *BIV-Karl* could have all the same experiences as Karl, including the same tomato-like experience, even though his brain states don't have the function of tracking anything at all (see Section 1.3). Given that BIV-Karl has all the same experiences as Karl, it is obvious that he is *conscious of* ("experientially represents") the (uninstantiated) shape *round*, has a *reason* to believe that a round thing is there, and (mistakenly) *believes* that a round thing is there. But all this is inconsistent with Williams's reductive externalist best systems theory. What is required is a nonreductive internalist best systems theory (Pautz 2013, 2019).

Next, experiential determinacy. Given Williams's teleological tracking theory, it is arguably indeterminate whether, in the middle earth case, Baby Karl's brain state B earth represents blue or yellow (see Figure 10.1, *left*). If he also accepts externalist representationalism about phenomenal character (Dretske 1995, Tye 2019), he must say it is consequently indeterminate whether Baby Karl has a bluish or yellowish experience—which is incoherent.[13] By contrast, nonreductive internalist best systems theory avoids radical experiential indeterminacy. What color quality Baby Karl experientially represents is pinned down by his brain state.

Likewise, Williams's reductive externalist best systems theory lacks a plausible account of Karl on black-and-white earth (see Figure 10.1, *right*). In this case, Karl's visual system tracks$_{17}$ the black-reflectance of the outer object and also tracks$_{18}$ the red-reflectance of the inner object. Williams has

---

[13] Williams says that tracking-representational facts constitute Karl's *evidence* (2020: 181, 185). He doesn't explicitly accept the further claim of externalist intentionalism that they constitute the *phenomenal character* of his experiences. But since it is plausible that Karl's evidence and his phenomenal life are inseperable, he is under pressure to accept this further claim (Pautz forthcoming).

two options here. First, *indeterminacy*: it's indeterminate whether the experiential representation relation is identical with tracking$_{17}$ or tracking$_{18}$. So it is indeterminate whether he experientially represents black or red, and therefore indeterminate whether he has a reason to believe that a black thing is there or to believe that a red thing is there. The trouble with this option is that, given intentionalism, it implies indeterminacy concerning whether Karl has a blackish or reddish experience—which is incoherent. Second, *arbitrary identities*: it's just a brute fact that the experiential representation relation is identical with (say) the tracking$_{17}$ relation rather than with the intrinsically very similar tracking$_{18}$ relation. Therefore, his tracking$_{17}$ (representing$_{17}$) the outer black-reflectance is part of his evidence, and gives him a reason to believe that a black-reflectance object is there. But his tracking$_{18}$ (representing$_{18}$) the inner black-reflectance is *not* part of his evidence, and *doesn't* give him *any* reason to believe that a black-reflectance object is there. That is, tracking$_{17}$ (representing$_{17}$) has epistemic significance but tracking$_{18}$ (representing$_{18}$) has none at all, even though they are nearly identical. Accordingly, the best (most rationalizing) system assigns Karl the belief that a black-reflectance object is there, rather than that a red-reflectance object is there. But this is intolerably arbitrary. It requires the problematic idea that nearly identical relations can differ radically in their reason-grounding significance (Pautz 2017).

Only nonreductive internalist best systems handle this case without indeterminacy or arbitrariness. The austere physical facts are not the only facts. In addition to bearing the tracking$_{17}$ relation to the black-reflectance of the outer object and the tracking$_{18}$ relation to the red-reflectance of the inner object, Karl bears an internally-determined and irreducible relation of conscious acquaintance uniquely to a certain *sensible color*—say, the color red. This constitutes the determinate phenomenal character of his experience. The conscious-of relation is totally different from any tracking relation, and the sensible color *red* is totally different from any reflectance-type. So we accommodate the evident fact that in this situation Karl's relation to a certain color is totally different from his relation to anything else ("stands out"). And, because the conscious-of relation is totally different from both the tracking$_{17}$ relation and the tracking$_{18}$ relation, we can unproblematically hold that it possesses reason-grounding significance that these relations lack. So we have a more plausible account of how Karl uniquely has a reason to believe that a *red* object is there, and (given the best systems theory) determinately has this belief.

In general, like Russell (1912), I think that an irreducible conscious-of relation plays a crucial role in determining Karl's intentional states. Take a

superficial functional isomorph of prelinguistic Karl—Robot Karl—that fails
to stand in this relation to any states of affairs. For Robot Karl, the austere
physical facts are the only facts. Here there are bound to be many equally
good, coordinate "global interpretations" of the contents of Robot's Karl's
"perceptions," "evidence," "beliefs," "desires" (Pautz 2017). None "stands
out." The only reason why there is a (more or less) determinate, "stand-out"
interpretation in the case of the actual Karl (as there surely is) is that, unlike
Robot Karl, he bears an irreducible, stand-out relation of conscious
acquaintance to various ostensible states of affairs. It's *those* states of affairs
that his beliefs are determinately about.

The best systems theory of belief and desire can also accommodate the
desiderata violated by the inner sentence theory:

The conscious-life constraint;

The constitutive experience-belief connection;

Prelinguistic limits.

Start with the conscious-life constraint. We saw that the inner sentence
theory violates it, allowing for "secret scrambling" of Karl's beliefs and
desires while his conscious experiences and behavioral dispositions remain
the same. The reason is that it is an *inner-state* theory of belief and desire.
That is, in the first instance, it assigns contents (or content-plus-attitudes) to
individual subpersonal internal states (e.g., inner sentences), which may be
temporarily "secretly scrambled" while retaining those contents. By contrast,
my favored form of the best systems theory is *subject-based*: in the first
instance it assigns a whole system of beliefs and desires to a *subject-at-time*.
Moreover, it does so in a way that it only sensitive to the subject's *conscious
experiences* and consequent *dispositions to consciously act* at that time. So,
unlike the inner sentence theory, it rules out "secret scrambling" of Karl's
beliefs and desires and satisfies the conscious-life constraint.[14]

Next, the constitutive experience-belief connection. Experience is necessarily compelling. For instance, necessarily, if Karl has an experience of a
tomato, he is disposed to believe a red and round thing is there. The inner

[14] While I favor a *subject-based* version of the best systems theory of prelinguistic Karl's
beliefs and desires, Williams (2020: 11, 156) favors an *inner-state* version—in particular, one
which assigns contents to inner sentences in a Fodorian language-of-thought. I would argue that
such an inner-state theory violates the conscious-life constraint, the constitutive experience-
belief connection, and prelinguistic limits, for the same reasons given in Section 1.2. This is why
I favor a subject-based best systems theory.

sentence theory violates this (see Section 1.2). By contrast, the best systems theory accommodates it. Further, on this theory, it isn't a brute fact, but something that can be derived from more general truths. First, it is in the essence of experiences to *provide* reasons for belief. Second, it is in the essence of beliefs to be *responsive* to reasons. Therefore, in the absence of contrary behavioral dispositions, he automatically counts as believing the contents of his experiences.

Finally, I am especially impressed by how the best systems theory can explain prelinguistic limits. The basic idea: (i) experience-based, prelinguistic *reasons* are necessarily limited ("epistemic limits"); (ii) prelinguistic belief is constitutively connected to such reasons (the best systems theory); therefore, (iii) prelinguistic belief is necessarily limited.

For instance, suppose that prelinguistic Karl has before him a large pile of seashell beads that have small holes punched into them. He repeatedly places three shells on the ground, and then strings them together into a necklace. Since his experience gives him a reason to think that there are three shells on the ground, the best interpretation is that he believes that there are three shells, and he wants to make necklaces with three shells. So that is the correct interpretation.

However, there are limits. For example, suppose that Karl has a magical subpersonal mechanism that responds to a pile of exactly 167 shells, and causes him to vigorously wave his arms when and only when there is such a pile (similar to the example in Section 1.2). One interpretation is that he truly believes that there are 167 shells on the ground, and he wants to wave his arms when there are 167 shells. But there are many others: for instance, he mistakenly believes that there are 168 shells, and he wants to wave his arms when and only when there are 168 shells. Now here the reasons-based gambit for selecting a unique correct interpretation doesn't work. For, while Karl can have an experience-based reason to believe that there are three rather than two or four shells there, his experience just doesn't provide a reason to believe that there are 167 rather than 168 (such precise numerosity facts are not perceptually manifest). So, no specific large-number interpretation can ever stand out as "best" or "most rationalizing." Thus, by connecting beliefs to reasons, the best systems theory *explains* the otherwise puzzling fact that, without an outer language, Karl is necessarily unable to have beliefs about specific large numbers. It explains why, beyond small numbers, his numerical beliefs are *necessarily* only approximate.

More generally, prelinguistic Karl has experience-based reasons to believe things *within a certain range*. Let us call this the *perceptual circle* (PC). As noted above, this range extends somewhat beyond the thin contents of Karl's sensory-perceptual experiences—but not too far. (So a better name might be "prelinguistic circle.") They include beliefs about small numbers, the sensible properties of things, Rosch's basic level categories (Fodor 2010: 29), basic spatial and temporal relations, the recent past and near future, generalizations (all emeralds are green), emotional states, basic kinship relations, and types of actions. But prelinguistic Karl can never have experience-based reasons for beliefs far outside this perceptual circle: for instance, beliefs about large exact numbers, very abstract kinds (e.g., democratic socialism), the laws of quantum mechanics, distant objects and people, and so on. For his experiences have quite thin contents, concerning only shapes, colors, movements, propensities of movement, sounds, smells, tastes, bodily states—that's it (see Section 3.1). And the "gap" between this meager input and such outside-the-perceptual circle matters is just too great (even with the help of *a priori* connecting principles). So there can never be a unique best (most rationalizing) system that attributes to prelinguistic Karl such a belief. That is why, on the best systems theory, prelinguistic Karl can never determinately count as having such a belief, no matter what he does. I know of no alternative proposal about the nature of belief and desire that explains prelinguistic limits.

This concludes my argument for nonreductive internalist best systems theory. However, given prelinguistic limits, the best systems theory cannot be the whole story. How might Karl eventually form outside-the-perceptual-circle beliefs about the laws of quantum mechanics and the like? Here I will suggest a different story appealing to outer language. Accordingly, Stage Three is an explanation of linguistic meaning (Section 3.3). Then Stage Four (Section 3.4) is an account of how Karl can believe outside-the-perceptual-circle contents by accepting outer language sentences expressing those contents.

3.3 Stage Three: An Anchored Use Theory of Linguistic Meaning

Imagine, then, that Karl and his tribe invent a language, which eventually comes to resemble modern English.

What fixes the meanings of sentences and expressions of the language? I favor an *anchored use theory*. Briefly, the meanings of some initial, basic expressions were *mentalistically anchored*. This is congruent with a broadly "head-first" approach to meaning (Bennett 1976; Lewis 1975). But mentalistic anchoring only goes so far. For outside-the-perceptual-circle terms, a different story is required. Let us take these points in turn.

As I said, prelinguistic Karl can have a certain limited stock of beliefs involving matters within the perceptual circle. Since such beliefs are explanatory prior to linguistic meaning, they can be used to help explain the meanings of an initial stock of basic expressions. For instance, perhaps "is red" initially came to mean *is red* by virtue of being conventionally associated with the belief that something is red (Bennett 1976, Lewis 1975). So we have:

Mentalistic anchoring.   The limited prelinguistic beliefs of Karl and others helped explain the meanings of an initial stock of basic expressions referring to within-the-perceptual-circle matters. Initially, mental content was prior to linguistic meaning.

This initial stock of mentalistically anchored terms might have included expressions referring to the following:

> small exact numbers
> sensible properties
> Rosch's basic level categories
> basic spatial and temporal relations
> emotional states
> basic kinship relations
> types of actions

However, given prelinguistic limits, mentalistic anchoring cannot help fix the meanings of expressions outside this list, such as "167," "googolplex," "democracy," "neutrino." For instance, we cannot say that "there are 167 shells in the pile" inherits its content from the explanatorily prior belief that there are 167 shells in the pile. For this would arguably imply that Karl could believe this exact-number content without any outer language. And above I argued that this is not the case.[15]

---

[15] For discussion, see Avramides 1989: 113ff.; Bennett 1976: 96; Blackburn 1984: 137–40; and Lewis 1975: 27. I think that prelinguistic limits undermines Lewis's (1975, 1992) two-stage mentalistic approach (taken up by Williams 2020: 149ff.) on which the contents of *all* uttered sentences are inherited from explanatorily prior beliefs with those contents and then the contents of the all unuttered sentences can be extrapolated. Mentalistic anchoring only applies to a much more meager set of basic, initial expressions. For the rest of language, we need a

Therefore, we must supplement mentalistic anchoring with

Non-mentalistic use theory.   For any outside-the-perceptual-circle sentence which means that p, the correct account of this cannot invoke an explanatorily prior capacity to believe that p, because Karl's community lacks such an explanatorily prior capacity. Rather, it typically appeals to ideal regularities of use.

In my view, such outside-the-perceptual-circle expressions include expressions for:

abstract kinds
larger exact numbers
certain natural kinds
theoretical entities
certain normative properties
distant objects

In sum, the anchored use theory is a mixed view consisting of mentalistic anchoring and a non-mentalistic use theory. Thought initially breathed life into language, helping to inject a modicum of determinacy. Then language took on a life of its own. Expressions came to mean things that Karl could not think about without the help of language.

But how does the non-mentalistic use theory work? Like Horwich (2005), I favor metasemantic pluralism. Typically, ideal regularities of use determine meanings, but they differ for different types of expressions. Let me give some examples.[16]

Abstract expressions. Here I mean "semantically stable" expressions for abstract properties and kinds, such as "agent," "philosopher," "knows," "game," and "democracy." For these expressions, I favor a kind of anchored-hierarchical use theory. Karl and others in his community started with an initial stock of within-the-perceptual-circle expressions O_1, O_2, O_3

---

separate, non-mentalistic use-theory. The result is a messier, more disjunctive story. But I think it is truer to the facts.

[16] A big part of Horwich's own program is his rejection of standard "truth-referentialism" (truth and reference crucial to explaining meaning). But I would prefer to combine his use theory with truth-referentialism and a standard compositional meaning theory. See Horwich 2005: 44ff. for discussion.

... They are the "original" or "old" expressions. Their meanings were mentalistically anchored, and they referred to the types and properties listed above. They enabled Karl's linguistic community to grasp scenarios within the perceptual circle. So, they could then introduce new expressions A_1, A_2, A_3 ... governed by certain ideal regularities of the form:

If $[O_1, O_2, \dots]$, accept sentence $[\dots A_n \dots]$

If $[O_1, O_2, \dots]$, reject sentence $[\dots A_n \dots]$

Once A_1, A_2, A_3 ... acquired meanings in this way, they are able to iterate the process, and introduce new words B_1, B_2, B_3 governed by new ideal regularities of use:

If $[A_1, A_2, A_3 \dots]$, accept sentence $[\dots B_n \dots]$

If $[A_1, A_2, A_3 \dots]$, reject sentence $[\dots B_n \dots]$

Finally, they reach very abstract expressions, such as "game," "democracy," and "supervenience." In this way, expressions of Karl's language come to be associated with very abstract properties that would be outside of his cognitive reach without language.

These ideal regularities of usage are determined by the dispositions of Karl and others to use the expressions A_1, A_2, A_3 ... in response to experienced scenarios and to *correct* each other's usage. Because their dispositions can be in "error" and only cover finitely many cases, there is a gap between them and the ideal regularities. To close the gap, we must appropriate another Lewisian idea: naturalness as a kind of external constraint (Chalmers MSa: 10).

This anchored-hierarchical picture does not require that the "new" expressions are easily definable in expressions of the "old" expressions (think of "game"). Nor does it require that the original, mentalistically anchored expressions are rich enough to form an analytic scrutability-base for all truths.[17]

---

[17] Chalmers's (MSb) defends *anchored inferentialism*. Unlike my own view, his view does presuppose a scrutability thesis. There are other differences. Chalmers applies his theory to "mental concepts" and holds that mental content is always prior to linguistic content, while I give priority to outer language for all outside-the-perceptual-circle content. In addition, Chalmers seeks a uniform theory for all non-basic concepts, while I think (following Horwich 2005) that we must settle for a messy, pluralistic approach.

Mathematical expressions. As I said, the conscious-based best systems theory explains how prelinguistic Karl could have determinate beliefs about small exact numbers. He might also have beliefs about the *next number.* Then his community invented a system of number words. The meanings of the first few number-words could be directly mentalistically anchored. For the rest, speakers had the intention that the *next* number-word in the counting sequence refers to the *next number* (Dehaene 1999, Spelke 2003). In this way, some number-words came to refer to larger exact numbers, like 10. This enabled them to have the intentions required for setting up the Arabic numeral system.

Once they can think of large exact numbers in this way, they were able to introduce the "+" symbol. Even though their dispositions are finite and "error-prone," the simplest or most "natural" ideal rule for this expression is: accept instances of "$x+y=z$" iff z stands for the number which is equal to x *plus y.* This solves the plus-quus problem (Chalmers MSa: 10).

Logical constants. Once the contents of sentences are fixed, we can enter into certain inferential practices ("entry rules and exit rules") with them. And this can fix the semantic values of the logical constants (e.g., Williams 2020: 38ff.).

Certain natural kind terms. When prelinguistic Karl quenched his thirst, it was perhaps indeterminate whether he wanted to drink *water* (the natural kind) or the *watery stuff* (the surface kind). Then his community came up with a term, "water," that specifically refers to the natural kind rather than the surface kind. This enabled him to have beliefs specifically about the natural kind. Maybe the meaning of "water" is constituted by the fact that the ideal law for its usage is: accept "x is water" iff x has the underlying nature of the stuff in our seas, rivers, lakes, and rain (Horwich 2005: 27).

Theoretical expressions. Perhaps the meaning of "neutrino" is fixed by our underived acceptance of "If there is a type of particles that plays the neutrino-role, then there are neutrinos" (Horwich 2005: 27).

This completes my sketch of a *non-mentalist use theory* for outside-the-perceptual-circle expressions of outer language. My discussion has been short on detail. I have only given a "picture." But everyone needs such a theory. Those who favor an inner sentence theory of belief need a non-mentalistic use theory for expressions of the language of thought, where "use" is understood broadly to include asymmetric dependence (Fodor 1990), conceptual role (Williams 2020), and so on. I rejected the inner sentence theory (see Section 1.2). Instead, I think that the explanation starts with expressions of *outer* language. But, no matter where we start, we are all in the same boat: we all need a non-mentalistic use theory of how our representations came to latch onto some outside-the-perceptual-circle contents rather than others.

3.4 Stage Four: Language Extends Belief beyond the Perceptual Circle

In Stage Three, we saw that, since the beliefs of prelinguistic Karl cannot extend beyond the perceptual circle, there must be a theory (a "use" theory) of how sentences of his language came to mean outside-of-the-perceptual-circle contents *which doesn't appeal to an explanatorily prior ability to believe those contents*. Given this, Stage Four suggests that Karl comes to believe outside-the-perceptual-circle contents by understanding and accepting sentences expressing those contents. In general, language gives Karl a new way of believing:

The outer sentence theory of belief. If Karl understands and accepts an outer sentence s that means that p in his community, then this grounds his believing that p.[18]

So Karl has two ways of believing something. One way is given by the best systems theory introduced in Stage Two (Section 3.2). Call beliefs grounded in this way *language-independent beliefs*. The other is given by the outer sentence theory. Call beliefs grounded in this way *language-mediated beliefs*. The result is:

Pluralism about belief: To believe that p is to satisfy either (i) the best systems condition *or* (ii) the outer sentence condition for believing that p.[19]

Now we have an explanation of outside-the-perceptual-circle belief as well as inside-the-perceptual circle belief. Karl believes inside-the-perceptual-circle contents by satisfying the best systems condition. In fact, once he has language, he can also believe the same (or similar) contents by accepting

---

[18] In some cases s can also be associated with a different content p^* (a "primary intension") in Karl's idiolect on the basis of his individual, idiosyncratic (and often not well-defined) use-dispositions (Chalmers MSb).

[19] Bermudez (2003: 66, 150ff.), Dennett (1987: 19, 201, 207, 233), and Speaks (2010: 234ff.) defend other forms of pluralism about belief.

sentences that express those contents. For instance, Karl believes that Friedrich is his friend in a language-independent way; given his experience-based reasons and behavioral dispositions, all the best interpretations assign to him this belief. He believes a similar content in a language-mediated way as well: he understands and accepts "Friedrich is my friend." As for outside-the-perceptual-circle contents, Karl has only one way of believing them: by understanding and accepting sentences that express them. The ideal use regularities for the expressions in Karl's community associate them with increasingly abstract properties and kinds lying farther and farther outside the perceptual circle. By accepting sentences employing those expressions, Karl believes contents he couldn't believe without the help of an outer language (e.g., there are 167 shells there, the laws of quantum mechanics). The capacity for outside-the-perceptual-circle belief (Stage Four) evolved simultaneously with outside-the-perceptual-circle linguistic meaning (Stage Three).[20]

Typically, Karl's language-independent and language-mediated beliefs align, as when he believes that Friedrich is his friend. But sometimes they do not. For example, suppose that Karl hallucinates a human face and acts as if he is afraid. But he knows that he is hallucinating and so accepts "there is no face there." Does he believe that there is a face there or does he believe that there is no face? We feel pulled in different directions (Byrne 2018: 146). I think that the right thing to say is that he believes that there is a face there in a language-independent way and he believes that there is no face there in a language-mediated way. Likewise, when a student in a fraternity initiation trick is threatened with a red-hot poker but in fact is touched on his back with a piece of ice, and then says "That's hot!," his language-mediated belief is mistaken but his language-independent belief about his experiential state is correct (Lewis 1999).

Karl's language-independent beliefs, as given by the best systems theory, are rationally constrained. As for his language-mediated beliefs, there is more latitude here. For instance, if Karl acquires Cotard's syndrome, he might believe that he is dead, by understanding and accepting (in some

---

[20] In Section 3.2, I defended "epistemic limits": Karl's *experience-based* reasons are limited to *within-the-perceptual-circle* matters (e.g., *there are three shells*). I suggested that this, together with the best systems (reasons-responsive) theory of belief, explains why his prelinguistic beliefs are likewise limited. In that case, we need a different story about the source of his reasons for his more sophisticated, language-mediated *outside-the-perceptual-circle* beliefs (e.g., *there are 1,067 shells*). I accept *epistemic pluralism*. There is more than one source of good epistemic standing. Karl's *outside-the-perceptual-circle* beliefs can be "justified" or "reasonable" in the sense that they are reliably formed, or have a high probability given what he knows in a certain way.

minimal sense) the sentence "I'm dead." In this way, my pluralist theory allows for irrational belief (*pace* Smithies 2019: 150).

The argument for pluralism (or "disjunctivism") about believing is simple. For *prelinguistic* Karl's beliefs, there is a strong case for a subject-based best systems theory. It satisfies the desiderata that the inner sentence theory violates (Section 3.2). But, as we saw, this theory will only work for Karl's within-the-perceptual-circle beliefs. So, for Karl's outside-the-perceptual-circle beliefs, we need a different theory. Here the outer sentence theory fills the bill. The resulting pluralist theory explains why some thought is possible without an outer language but other forms of thought require an outer language. And, unlike the inner sentence theory of belief, it *remains in line with the conscious-life constraint*, because it only appeals to Karl's conscious experiences and dispositions to consciously act—now including his dispositions to "accept" *outer* sentences.

The pluralist theory says that one way of believing that p is by *understanding* and *accepting* a sentence meaning that p. How can these relations be explained?

Take *understanding* first. I think that no general and simple analysis is possible. The conditions on understanding an expression differ for different types of expressions. For instance, the conditions required for understanding logical expressions differ from the conditions for understanding moral expressions. For some expressions (e.g., "democracy"), counting as understanding them might typically require understanding some other, more basic expressions. The conditions on understanding are never hard and fast. Understanding *admits of degree*. That is why there is no clear answer to the question of whether a 6-year-old who says "daddy is a physicist" really thinks that daddy is a *physicist*.[21]

Even though conscious experience has only thin content (see Section 3.1), it anchors all understanding. A robot with no experiences doesn't really understand any words, even if there is a sense in which the robot's words play similar inferential roles to our words. For instance, to understand "167," you need to know what a number is. And that requires having the capacity to have experiences of numbers of things. This is another respect in which consciousness is essential to my account.

---

[21] By contrast, since whether you have a certain cognitive experience with built-in content p is presumably a binary, nongraded matter, the cognitive experience theory has the implausible implication that there is a form of understanding or grasping that it is "on–off" and doesn't admit of degree. See Bourget 2015 for an interesting discussion.

Now turn to *accepting*. Since the outer sentence theory proposes that believing an outside-the-perceptual-circle content p is to be explained in terms of accepting a sentence that means that p, I cannot on pain of circularity say that accepting a sentence that means that p is to be explained in terms of believing that p. The outer sentence theory requires that acceptance is characterizable in belief-independent terms, since it is used to explain how Karl believes outside-the-perceptual-circle contents. (Similarly, since the *inner* sentence theory (Fodor 1990) explains believing that p in terms of accepting*—that is, having in one's belief-box—an inner sentence that means that p, it requires a belief-independent account of this.) I have no general analysis up my sleeve. As with understanding a sentence, I think that the conditions on accepting a sentence differ for different types of sentences. Often accepting a sentence involves a disposition to use the sentence in reasoning and planning. Although I have no belief-independent account of accepting a sentence up my sleeve, I am confident that accepting is indeed prior to believing when it comes to outside-the-perceptual-circle matters, so that such an account must be possible in principle.

I have proposed a pluralist theory of the state of believing. What about the activity of thinking? Karl can also count as thinking that p in multiple ways. For instance, he can engage in spatial thinking using mental imagery. However, Karl's outside-the-perceptual-circle thinking is generally realized by "inner speech," understood as a quasi-perceptual process representing outer speech (Byrne 2018: 198ff.; Carruthers 1996: ch. 2). In these cases, the content of Karl's thought is just the content (in the context) of the imagined sentence, or a sentence he would take to elucidate it. Since the content of the sentence (e.g., "all the beers are in the fridge," "democracy is in trouble") is bound to be indeterminate and incomplete in various ways, so is the content of Karl's thought.

The resulting pluralist view of belief and thought is superior to the cognitive experience theory of thought that goes with the standard phenomenal intentionality program. We saw in Section 2 that the cognitive experience theory fails to adequately accommodate the following desiderata:

Minimize danglers
Holism
Prelinguistic limits

By contrast, my pluralist theory of thought nicely accommodates these ideas. First, the pluralist theory minimizes danglers. To explain how Karl believes sensible contents rather than deviant contents, it needs no special "intentional laws."

For example, return to Stage Two in which Karl lacks an outer language. He might believe that someone is a friend, rather than a friend*. How so? The cognitive experience theory appeals to a special cognitive experience with the built-in content *he is my friend*, together with a special brute intentional law linking this experience to his brain state (Section 2.2). By contrast, my pluralist theory requires no such special intentional law. For such language-independent beliefs, I accept the *best systems theory*. Karl's history of experiences gives him a stronger reason to believe that the person is a friend (more natural) than to believe that the person is a friend* (less natural). Compare: his experiences give him a stronger reason to believe that emeralds are blue (more natural) than to believe that they are all grue (less natural). The best systems (reasons-based) theory uses this generally accepted epistemic fact to explain why Karl believes that the person is a friend, rather than a friend*.[22]

Recall that we must explain indeterminacy as well as determinacy (Section 2.2). For instance, in Stage Four, when Karl thinks that 68 plus 57 equals 15, the content of his thought is perfectly precise and determinate. By contrast, when he thinks democracy is in trouble, the content of his thought is quite indeterminate. We saw that cognitive experience theorists can only say "some brain states produce cognitive experience with determinate contents while other brain states produce cognitive experiences with indeterminate contents." By contrast, my pluralist account provides a real explanation. In the case of such outside-the-perceptual thoughts, I accept the outer sentence theory. Karl doesn't grasp any such contents merely by having certain "cognitive" experiences. Rather, he grasps the contents only by understanding and accepting the sentences—"68 plus 57 equals 125" and "democracy is in trouble"—which mean those contents. This in turn involves use-dispositions and not just his experience at the time (Section 2.4). Our use of mathematical expressions is highly constrained, and here there is a very "natural" and simple use-rule that fits use, namely

---

[22] See, e.g., Lewis 1986: 38ff. and 1994: 427ff. Lewis is often associated with a toy "use plus naturalness" theory, which uses "naturalness" as a *basic* constraint (and which gives priority to language). In fact, in the case of mental content, he explicitly *derives* his "naturalness constraint" from his more general best systems or "reasons-based" theory of mental content (Pautz 2013: 222; Williams 2020: 62). Some objections to the toy theory do not apply to Lewis's actual view (Dorr 2019: section 4.7; Pautz 2013: 221–2).

the "plus" rule (Chalmers MSa: 10).[23] By contrast, our use of "is a democracy" is less constrained, and here there are many equally natural ideal laws of use that fit our use dispositions, corresponding to different precisifications of "democracy." That explains the difference in content-determinacy without special intentional laws.

Next, holism. Karl's thoughts are holistically bound up with other things—attempts to do things, other thoughts, sensory-perceptual experiences, language-use, and so on. The cognitive experience of thought can accommodate this only by positing a slew of brute and implausible necessary connections between Karl's "cognitive experiences" and these other things (Section 2.3). By contrast, because my pluralist theory eliminates cognitive experiences, it avoids the need to posit such special, brute necessary connections. In effect, it reduces thoughts with rich contents to complex holistic conditions involving actual and potential sensory-perceptual experiences with thin contents. Holism is a trivial consequence.

Finally, prelinguistic limits. We saw that the cognitive experience theory makes prelinguistic limits totally mysterious. By contrast, my pluralist ("disjunctivist") theory elegantly explains it. The best systems theory uses "epistemic limits" to explain why prelinguistic Karl's thoughts are necessarily limited and why the limits are what they are (Section 3.2). The only *other* way of having thoughts is given by the outer sentence theory. That is why Karl's thoughts beyond these limits are necessarily language-mediated.

3.5 Credo: Thin Experience Reductivism

Let *thin experience reductivism* be the claim that all the mental facts about Karl—including all the intentional facts—reduce to (i) facts about actual and potential sensory-perceptual-emotional experiences with *thin* contents ("thin experiences") and (ii) the functional-behavioral facts about him (including his linguistic dispositions and "wide" functional facts involving

---

[23] Horgan and Graham (2010: 328–9) object that an external naturalness constraint would need to be an *extra* "brute fact." (Philip Goff also pressed this objection in discussion.) But all of us *already* believe that *plus* is more natural than $quus_g$. So the plus-interpretation "stands out"—and this is the core intuition. Thus, in fact, the naturalness-based solution to underdetermination doesn't require belief of anything "extra" beyond what we already accept. Indeed, it is rather Horgan and Graham's *own* solution that requires something extra: a special intentional law (dangler) linking Karl's brain state to his alleged "cognitive experience" that 68 plus (rather than $quus_g$) 57 equals 125 (as we saw in Section 2.2).

his relation to his environment). On this view, the only experiences that must be mentioned in the reductive base for Karl's mental life are his experiences with thin contents. Let the *further fact view* be any view on thin experience reductivism fails. The cognitive experience theory of thought (Section 2.1) is an example.

My multistage theory starts with Karl's thin experiences. So it is congruent with thin experience reductivism. Since supplying specific reductive analyses is difficult, any such specific form of thin experience reductivism will be controversial. However, we can offer two general arguments that *some* form of thin experience reductivism is right.

First, the *argument from small steps*. To illustrate, consider mathematical thought. In Stage One, Karl certainly starts off with only thin experiences. So *initially* thin experience reductivism is true. For instance, he repeatedly places three shells on the ground, and then strings them together into a necklace. This is *sufficient* for his judgement *that there are three shells there*. A further fact—for instance, a mysterious "cognitive experience"—is not required. Next, suppose that he learns a body-based "language" in which he points to different parts of his body (starting with the fingers) to indicate different numbers. He points at a pile of shells and then points at his big toe, thereby communicating the thought *there are 29 shells in the pile* (Dehaene 1997: 93–5). Intuitively, all this might only involve Karl having "thin experiences" of parts of his body. It needn't involve his having, at some specific moment, a totally novel "cognitive experience" with the built-in content *there are 29 shells in the pile*. Finally, suppose that he gradually learns a base-ten number system and different function-names ("plus," "minus," etc.). One day he thinks *68 plus 57 equals 125*. Again, intuitively, at no single step in this process does Karl need to have a wholly novel *kind* of *experience*—a "cognitive" experience—with a built-in rich content *68 plus 57 equals 125*. Intuitively, it's enough that he has thin experiences of new symbols and gradually becomes increasingly competent in using them. The result: merely Karl's thin experiences and increasingly sophisticated linguistic behavior can constitute his thinking *there are three shells*, *there are 29 shells*, and *68 plus 57 equals 125*.

Second, a more elaborate *supervenience argument*, which will proceed in two steps. First, thin experience *supervenience* is plausible. Second, thin experience supervenience supports thin experience *reductivism*.

First, thin experience supervenience is supported by reflection on *duplication cases*. Suppose that on different occasions Karl has various mental states. He has an experience of a rock flying towards him and moves out of the way. He believes that a rock is flying towards him. He says "68 plus 57 is 125" and believes that 68 plus 57 is 125. He gets a paycheck and says, while pointing to his financial institution across the street, "I'm bringing this check to the bank," meaning that he is bringing his check to that financial institution. He is happy-go-lucky and says "the future looks bright" and believes that the future looks bright. Now consider *Twin Karl*, a *thin experience duplicate* of Karl. He (i) has all the sensory-perceptual-emotional experiences with *thin* phenomenal contents as Karl and (ii) is like Karl as regards all functional-behavioral facts.

Given the Karl and Twin Karl are *inner–outer* duplicates in all these respects, could their beliefs, thoughts, and desires nevertheless radically differ? For instance, could Twin Karl "really" secretly believe the *negations* of everything Karl believes, despite having all the same thin experiences, saying all the same things, and having all the same dispositions as Karl? Or, when he has the same vivid experience of rock flying towards him, could Twin Karl differ from Karl in secretly and irrationally thinking that the rock is moving *away* (Section 3.2), even though he ducks, says it is headed towards him, and so on? When he says "68 plus 57 is 125," could he differ from Karl in "really" thinking 68 $quus_g$ 57 is 125, even though he does sums the same way as Karl under all possible conditions? When he gets his paycheck and says, while pointing to his financial institution across the street, "I'm bringing this to the bank," could he differ from Karl in that he "really" means he is bringing it to an *embankment*, even though (like Karl) all his verbal and behavioral dispositions are appropriate to the financial-institution interpretation (Siewert 1998: 279ff.)? Could he "really" secretly think the future looks dark, even though all his thin-experiences, speech, and dispositions are happy-go-lucky? I do not find such radical variation between Twin Karl and Karl to be clearly conceivable. This supports thin experience *supervenience*.

It might be said that, although Twin Karl's thoughts could not radically *differ from* Karl's, it is conceivable that he should be a "cognitive zombie" who *lacks* all thought, contrary to thin experience supervenience. For instance, Terry Horgan (2013: 243–4) says that Twin Karl might be a mere perfect "symbol manipulator" who doesn't really *understand* any English sentences. If Twin Karl might be a complete thin-experiential-cum-functional duplicate of Karl and yet lack understanding, then states of understanding must be elusive "further facts"—for instance, special "cognitive experiences."

But this is not clearly conceivable. To see this, start with rudimentary contents, as in the sequence argument above. Here Horgan's claim is very implausible. For instance, it is quite clear that, just by virtue of having the same sensory-perceptual experience of three shells on the ground and the same behavioral dispositions as Karl, Twin Karl will also perfectly well understand the content *there are three shells there*. Further, as we go up the conceptual ladder in small steps, at each point, changes in thin experiences and linguistic competence are intuitively enough for changes in thought and understanding. So Twin Karl must think and understand the same things as Karl.

Thin experience supervenience, then, is plausible. The next step of the argument says that thin experience supervenience supports thin experience *reductivism* over the further fact view. After all, if some thoughts and states of understanding were really "further facts" or extra "cognitive experiences" (Kriegel, Siewert, Goff), we would expect they *could* radically differ between Karl and Twin Karl in the above-mentioned ways, while holding everything else fixed, contrary to thin experience supervenience. But we saw this is inconceivable. By contrast, thin experience reductivism offers a simple explanation of thin experience supervenience.

Here is an analogy (Lewis 1994: 413). Take a black-and-white pixel-screen. The gestalt properties of the screen (*containing a square, containing a happy-face*) *supervene on* the arrangement of black and white pixels. This suggests that they *reduce* to such arrangements.

Because of the "hard problem of consciousness," Karl's conscious experiences with thin contents are mysterious. But, if we accept thin experience reductivism rather than the further fact view, then we can rest assured that Karl's other mental states with "richer" contents (e.g., the thought that 68 plus 57 equals 125) pose no *additional* profound mystery. To explain them, we don't need to posit dangling "intentional linking laws" (Section 2.2). For, although it's hard to supply the details, we know that they *somehow* reduce to patterns in Karl's actual and possible thin experiences and relations to the world, just as gestalt features of the screen reduce to patterns of black and white.

4. Conclusion

I have argued that both the reductive externalist program and the phenomenal intentionality program miss out on certain desiderata on an adequate theory of intentionality (Sections 1–2). Then I sketched a multistage theory of intentionality that does satisfy them (Section 3). Maybe it is along the right lines.[24]

References

Avramides, A. 1989. *Meaning and Mind*. Cambridge, MA: MIT Press.

Bayne, T. and N. Levy. 2006. The Feeling of Doing: Deconstructing the Phenomenology of Agency. In N. Sebanz and W. Prinz, eds., *Disorders of Volition*. Cambridge, MA: MIT Press, 49–68.

Bennett, J. 1976. *Linguistic Behavior*. Cambridge: Cambridge University Press.

Bermudez, J. 2003. *Thinking Without Words*. Oxford: Oxford University Press.

Blackburn, S. 1984. *Spreading the Word*. Oxford: Oxford University Press.

Block, N. 2019. Arguments Pro and Con on Adam Pautz's External Directedness Principle. In A. Pautz and D. Stoljar, eds., *Blockheads! Essays on Ned Block's Philosophy of Mind and Consciousness*. Cambridge, MA: MIT Press, 421–6.

Bourget, D. 2015. The Role of Consciousness in Grasping and Understanding. *Philosophy and Phenomenological Research* 95: 285–318.

Braddon-Mitchell, D. and F. Jackson. 2007. *Philosophy of Mind and Cognition*. Oxford: Blackwell.

Byrne, A. 2018. *Transparency and Self-Knowledge*. Oxford: Oxford University Press.

Byrne, A. and S. Siegel. 2017. Rich or Thin? In B. Nanay, ed., *Current Controversies in Philosophy of Perception*. London: Routledge, 59–80.

Carruthers, P. 1996. *Language, Thought and Consciousness*. Cambridge: Cambridge University Press.

Chalmers, D. 2010. *The Character of Consciousness*. Oxford: Oxford University Press.

Chalmers, D. MSa. Reference Magnetism and the Grounds of Intentionality. Available at http://consc.net/books/ctw/excursus20.pdf.

Chalmers, D. MSb. Inferentialism and Analyticity. Available at http://consc.net/books/ctw/excursus19.pdf.

[24] Earlier versions of this chapter were presented at Rice University, the University of Cambridge, the University of Leeds, and the Institut Jean Nicod. Thanks to the audiences on those occasions for helpful feedback. I am also grateful to Jacob Beck, David Chalmers, Jim van Cleve, and Robbie Williams for comments on an early draft. Thanks especially to Uriah Kriegel for detailed and very helpful comments on the penultimate draft.

Chudnoff, E. 2015. *Cognitive Phenomenology*. London and New York: Routledge.

Dehaene, S. 1999. *The Number Sense*. Oxford: Oxford University Press.

Dennett, D. 1987. *The Intentional Stance*. Cambridge, MA: MIT Press.

Dorr, C. 2019. Natural Properties. *The Stanford Encyclopedia of Philosophy*. Available at https://plato.stanford.edu/archives/fall2019/entries/natural-properties/.

Dretske, F. 1995. *Naturalizing the Mind*. Cambridge, MA: MIT Press.

Fodor, J. 1990. *A Theory of Content and Other Essays*, Cambridge, MA: MIT Press.

Fodor, J. 2010. *LOT 2: The Language of Thought Revisited*. Oxford: Oxford University Press.

Goff, P. 2012. Does Mary Know I Experience Plus rather than Quus? *Philosophical Studies* 160: 223–35.

Goff, P. 2018. Conscious Thought and the Cognitive Fine-Tuning Problem. *Philosophical Quarterly* 68: 98–122.

Graham, G., T. Horgan and J. Tienson. 2007. Consciousness and Intentionality. In M. Velmans and S. Schneider, eds. *The Blackwell Companion to Consciousness*. Malden, MA: Blackwell, 468–84.

Hawthorne, J. 2006. *Metaphysical Essays*. Oxford: Oxford University Press.

Horgan, T. 2013. Original Intentionality is Phenomenal Intentionality. *The Monist* 96: 232–51.

Horgan, T. 2014. Phenomenal Intentionality and Secondary Qualities: The Quixotic Case of Color. In B. Brogaard, ed., *Does Perception Have Content?* Oxford: Oxford University Press, 329–50.

Horgan, T. and G. Graham. 2010. Phenomenal Intentionality and Content Determinacy. In R. Shantz, ed., *Prospects for Meaning*. Amsterdam: de Gruyter, 321–44.

Horgan, T. and J. Tienson. 2002. The Intentionality of Phenomenology and the Phenomenology of Intentionality. In D. Chalmers, ed., *Philosophy of Mind: Classical and Contemporary Readings*. Oxford: Oxford University Press, 520–33.

Horgan, T. and J. Tienson. Unpublished. Phenomenal Intentionality and Phenomenal Holism.

Horwich, P. 2005. *Reflections on Meaning*. Oxford: Oxford University Press.

Hurford, J. 2014. *The Origins of Language*. Oxford: Oxford University Press.

Kriegel, U. 2011. *The Sources of Intentionality*. Oxford: Oxford University Press.

Kriegel, U. 2015. *The Varieties of Consciousness*. Oxford: Oxford University Press.

Kripke, S. 1982. *Wittgenstein on Rules and Private Language*. Cambridge, MA: Harvard University Press.

Levine, J. 2019. On the Meta-Problem. *Journal of Consciousness Studies* 26: 148–59.

Lewis, D. 1974. Radical Interpretation. *Synthese* 21: 331–44.

Lewis, D. 1975. Languages and Language. In K. Gunderson, ed., *Minnesota Studies in the Philosophy of Science*, Volume VII. Minneapolis: University of Minnesota Press, 3–35.

Lewis, D. 1986. *On the Plurality of Worlds*. Oxford: Blackwell.

Lewis, D. 1989. Dispositional Theories of Value. *Proceedings of the Aristotelian Society* 63: 113–37.

Lewis, D. 1992. Meaning Without Use. *Australasian Journal of Philosophy* 70: 106–10.

Lewis, D. 1994. Reduction of Mind. In S. Guttenplan, ed., *A Companion to Philosophy of Mind*. Oxford: Blackwell, 412–31.

Lewis, D. 1999. Letter to Timothy Williamson. Available at http://www.projects.socialsciences.manchester.ac.uk/lewis/letter-of-the-month-november2018/.

McGinn, C. 1996. Another Look at Color. *Journal of Philosophy* 93: 537–53.

Mendelovici, A. 2018. *The Phenomenal Basis of Intentionality*. Oxford: Oxford University Press.

Montague, M. 2019. Cognitive Phenomenology, Sensory Phenomenology, and Rationality. In A. Sullivan, ed., *Sensations, Thoughts, Language: Essays in Honor of Brian Loar*. London: Routledge, chapter 8.

Neander, K. 2017. *A Mark of the Mental: In Defense of Informational Teleosemantics*. Cambridge, MA: MIT Press.

Pautz, A. 2010. Do Theories of Consciousness Rest on a Mistake? *Philosophical Issues* 20: 333–67.

Pautz, A. 2013. Does Phenomenology Ground Mental Content? In U. Kriegel, ed., *Phenomenal Intentionality*. Oxford: Oxford University Press, 194–234.

Pautz, A. 2017. The Significance Argument for the Irreducibility of Consciousness. *Philosophical Perspectives* 31: 349–407.

Pautz, A. 2019. How Can Brains in Vats Experience a Spatial World? A Puzzle for Internalists In A. Pautz and D. Stoljar, eds., *Blockheads! Essays on Ned Block's Philosophy of Mind and Consciousness*. Cambridge, MA: MIT Press. 379–420.

Pautz, A. forthcoming. Review of Williams' *The Metaphysics of Representation*. *Mind*.

Pinker, S. and R. Jackendoff. 2005. The Faculty of Language: What's Special about It? *Cognition* 95: 201–36.

Pitt, D. 2004. The Phenomenology of Cognition. *Philosophy and Phenomenological Research* 69: 1–36.

Prior, A.N. 1968. Intentionality and Intensionality. *Proceedings of the Aristotelian Society*, Supplementary Volumes, 42: 73–106.

Pryor, J. 2000. The Skeptic and the Dogmatist. *Noûs* 34: 517–49.

Putnam, H. 1981. *Reason, Truth and History*. Cambridge: Cambridge University Press.

Quine, W. 1960. *Word and Object*. Cambridge, MA: MIT Press.

Rosen, G. 2010. Metaphysical Dependence: Grounding and Reduction. In R. Hale and A. Hoffman, eds., *Modality: Metaphysics, Logic, and Epistemology*. Oxford: Oxford University Press, 109–36.

Russell, B. 1912. *The Problems of Philosophy*. London: Williams and Norgate.

Sacks, O. 1989. *Seeing Voices*. Berkeley: University of California Press.

Schwitzgebel, E. 2002. A Phenomenal-Dispositional Account of Belief. *Noûs* 36: 249–75.

Searle, J. 1984. Intentionality and its Place in Nature. *Synthese* 61: 3–16.

Shoemaker, S. 1996. *The First-Person Perspective and Other Essays*. Cambridge: Cambridge University Press.

Siewert, C. 1998. *The Significance of Consciousness*. Princeton, NJ: Princeton University Press.

Siewert, C. 2011. Phenomenal Thought. In T. Bayne and M. Montague, eds., *Cognitive Phenomenology*. Oxford: Oxford University Press, 231–67.

Siewert, C. 2016. Consciousness and Intentionality. The Stanford Encyclopedia of Philosophy. Available at https://plato.stanford.edu/entries/consciousness-intentionality/

Smart, J.C. 1959. Sensations and Brain Processes. *Philosophical Review* 68: 141–56.

Smithies, D. 2019. *The Epistemic Role of Consciousness*. Oxford: Oxford University Press.

Speaks, J. 2010. Explaining the Disquotational Principle. *Canadian Journal of Philosophy* 40: 211–38.

Spelke, E. 2003. What Makes Us Smart? Core Knowledge and Natural Language. In D. Getner and S. Goldin-Meadow, eds., *Language in Mind: Advances in the Study of Language and Thought*. Cambridge, MA: MIT Press, 277–311.

Strawson, G. 2010. *Mental Reality*, 2nd edn. Cambridge, MA: MIT Press.

Tye, M. 2019. Homunculi Heads and Silicon Chips: The Importance of History to Phenomenology. In A. Pautz and D. Stoljar, eds., *Blockheads! Essays on Ned Block's Philosophy of Mind and Consciousness*. Cambridge, MA: MIT Press, 545–70.

Varley, R., N. Klessinger, C. Romanowski, and M. Siegal. 2005. Agrammatic but Numerate. *Proceedings of the National Academy of Sciences of the United States of America* 102: 3519–24.

Williams, J.R.G. 2020. *The Metaphysics of Representation*. Oxford: Oxford University Press.

Wittgenstein, L. 1953. *Philosophical Investigations*. Oxford: Blackwell.

11

On Being Internally the Same

Matthew Parrott and Anil Gomes

1. Introduction

There are many disagreements among philosophers about the nature of the mind. One which has shaped the landscape of contemporary philosophy of mind is the debate between internalism and externalism about the nature of mental states. This debate focused initially on mental states with content but has since extended into many other areas, including the nature of causal psychological explanations, the epistemic status of self-knowledge, and the proper scientific methodology for cognitive psychology. Yet despite the widespread influence of these two doctrines, it is not clear what substantive philosophical issue divides internalists and externalists. That is, when internalists and externalists disagree, what are they disagreeing about?

Standard formulations of internalism and externalism formulate the theses in metaphysical terms, often using supervenience claims (Brown, 2009; Lau & Deutsch, 2016). There is nothing mistaken or incoherent about adopting such formulations. But we will suggest in this chapter that they are to be rejected. We will instead sketch the outlines of an alternative epistemic formulation of internalism and externalism according to which internalism and externalism are doctrines about the extent to which an agent's mental states can vary independently of the capacity for introspective discrimination. We aim to show that this epistemic formulation can avoid certain objections, and that it improves in key ways on the metaphysical formulations we discuss in the first part of the chapter. We shall also argue that the epistemic formulation marks a substantive distinction, one which is important for philosophical theorizing about the nature of the mind.

To make things more precise, we borrow our terminology and initial set-up from Williamson (2000), with slight emendations. Let a *case* be a possible total state of a system, consisting of an agent at a time paired with the external environment. *Conditions* are specified by 'that' clauses and obtain

Matthew Parrott and Anil Gomes, *On Being Internally the Same* In: *Oxford Studies in Philosophy of Mind Volume 1.* Edited by: Uriah Kriegel, Oxford University Press (2021). © Matthew Parrott and Anil Gomes. DOI: 10.1093/oso/9780198845850.003.0011

or fail to obtain in each case. A case α is *internally like* a case β if and only if the agent in α is internally the same as the agent in β. We leave open for the moment what has to be the case for two agents to be internally the same. A condition C is *narrow* if and only if for all cases α and β, if α is *internally like* β, then C obtains in α if and only if C obtains in β. A state S is *narrow* if and only if the condition that one is in S is narrow; otherwise S is broad. Internalism about a set of mental states is the claim that those states are narrow; externalism is the denial of internalism.

Using this framework we can distinguish different accounts of the internalism/externalism distinction in terms of the requirements which have to hold in order for two agents to be internally the same. Differing accounts of what it is for two agents to be internally the same will have different consequences for which mental states count as narrow. And even when differing accounts of internal sameness happen to agree on which states count as narrow, they will present us with different ways of understanding the distinction between internalism and externalism.

This suggests two ways in which we can compare and contrast competing accounts of internal sameness. First, we can examine which states an account classifies as narrow and assess whether this partition is theoretically fruitful. Some accounts of internal sameness will yield a partition that is theoretically unproductive or ad hoc. Second, we can consider which account of internal sameness presents the most philosophically illuminating way of understanding the distinction between internalism and externalism. The aim here is not to elucidate existing debates in the literature, but instead to hone in on a philosophical issue which is the best candidate for a substantive point of disagreement between internalists and externalists.

To see how this second criterion can be applied, consider a longstanding debate between groups of neighbours about whether to install speed humps on Princes Street. At one level, this debate can be correctly characterized as obtaining between those who are in favour of the installation of speed humps, and those who are against it. But reflection on other cases—speed humps which are ineffective; making Princes Street into a one-way street; other traffic-calming measures—can help us to see that the debate is more perspicuously characterized as between those who think commuting efficiency poses an acceptable risk to child safety, and those who disagree. That is to say, although the neighbourhood disagreement superficially concerns the presence of speed humps, it is more fundamentally about the relative values of child safety and ease of commuting. This is the substantive point of disagreement between the groups of residents. We will apply similar considerations to competing formulations of internal sameness.

Since the terms 'internalism' and 'externalism' are terms of art, there is no simple way to apply these two tests, and we cannot decide which account of internal sameness to accept based on which best corresponds to pre-theoretic notions. Instead, we need to assess each account in turn and consider whether its formulation of internal sameness provides a theoretically appropriate partition of views, and whether it captures a substantive issue underlying philosophical disputes between internalists and externalists.

In this chapter, we shall consider five accounts of internal sameness. The first three are *metaphysical accounts* in that they take two agents to be internally the same in virtue of some metaphysical truth about the agents. They are familiar from standard presentations of internalism and externalism. According to the *physical account*, two agents are internally the same if and only if the total internal physical states of the agents are the same. According to the *functional account*, two agents are internally the same if and only if the total internal functional states of the agents are the same. And, according to the *phenomenal account*, two agents are internally the same if and only if the total phenomenal states of the agents are the same.

Each of these accounts provides a clear formulation of internal sameness. To that extent, they are unproblematic. Nevertheless, we shall argue that they fail when matched against the two tests noted above. In some cases, the grouping of states which the account classifies as narrow looks theoretically ad hoc. And in some cases, the resulting distinction does not seem to identify a substantive philosophical issue which distinguishes internalists and externalists.

What are the options if we reject these metaphysical accounts? In the second part of the chapter we will investigate the prospects for endorsing an *epistemic account* of internal sameness. Epistemic accounts take two agents to be internally the same in virtue of some epistemic fact about the agents. According to the epistemic accounts that we shall consider, two agents are internally the same if and only if the total states of the agents are *introspectively indiscriminable*. We will argue that objections raised to epistemic accounts apply only to those formulated in terms of a *personal* conception of indiscriminability. This leaves open that a notion of impersonal indiscriminability can be used to formulate an account of internal sameness which is both theoretically productive and tracks a fundamental issue in philosophy of mind that is at the centre of the dispute between internalists and externalists. On the resulting view, the question of whether to endorse internalism or externalism turns out to be a question about the extent to which our mental lives are constrained by our capacities to introspectively discriminate our perspective on the world from certain alternative kinds of perspectives. We end the chapter by suggesting that this might be a question which clarifies why debates about internalism and externalism matter for our theoretical endeavours.

Here's the structure of the chapter. In Section 2, we'll summarize the standard twin-earth argument for externalism. In Sections 3 and 4, we'll consider three *metaphysical* accounts of internal sameness: a *physical* account, a *functional* account, and a *phenomenal* account. We shall argue that each account has problematic consequences insofar as either it entails an unconvincing partition of philosophical theories, or it fails to characterize a substantive issue of concern in the internalism and externalism dispute.

In the second part of the chapter, we turn to *epistemic* accounts. In Section 5, we suggest that an account of internal sameness which makes use of an *impersonal* notion of introspective indiscriminability can avoid some of the standard problems raised against epistemic accounts. In Section 6 we consider an objection to the impersonal account which concerns the grounding of epistemic facts. Finally, in Section 7, we suggest that this epistemic account captures an important distinction within the philosophy of mind.

2. Externalism

Externalism is often motivated by the idea that propositional attitudes are individuated by their contents, and that the contents ascribed to propositional attitudes depend on features of an agent's environment. This form of argument for externalism traces back to the work of Hilary Putnam (1975, 1981) and Tyler Burge (1979, 1982), and it is with externalism so understood that we'll be concerned in this essay.[1]

---

[1] Instead of the terms 'internalism' and 'externalism', Burge prefers to use the terms 'individualism' and 'anti-individualism', but he regards the two sets of terms as interchangeable (Burge, 2007). In his earlier writings, Burge seems to take the term 'individualism' primarily to designate a view that denies 'essential reference to the social context' of an individual (1979, pp. 132–3). In later work, he describes 'individualism' as denying constitutive relations between a person's mental states and her physical *or* social environment (1986b, p. 221, our emphasis),

Consider the state of thinking that water quenches thirst. Externalists hold that this state is broad, which is to say that it does not follow from the fact that two agents are internally the same that they are both thinking that water quenches thirst. A standard externalist argument for this conclusion proceeds as follows: consider a world which is the same as ours in all respects except that it contains not water, but a colourless, odourless liquid with the same appearance but with a different chemical structure. Call this *twin-water*. In this counterfactual world, there is a twin-version of you who is *internally the same* as you. When you use the term 'water', you refer to H_2O, but when your twin uses the term 'water', she refers to XYZ. Thus, the thought that you express by a sentence of the form 'water quenches thirst' is true because water quenches thirst, whereas the thought that your twin expresses by a sentence of the form 'water quenches thirst' is true because *twin-water* quenches thirst. Since the truth-conditions for the thoughts differ, the mental states themselves differ: you and your twin are thinking different thoughts. It follows that the state of thinking that water quenches thirst is broad.

This is a standard version of twin-earth reasoning. It has been an enormously influential form of argument in the philosophy of mind, and many philosophers share the judgement that twin-earth reasoning picks out something philosophically interesting. Even philosophers who are not persuaded by this form of argument take their disagreement about how to evaluate twin-earth cases as a substantive disagreement about the conditions

and Burge himself reports that 'by the mid-1980s' he came to consistently use the term 'individualism' to apply to 'any view that takes the nature of mental states to depend entirely on physical factors in the individual or psychological resources cognitively available to the individual' (2007, p. 153). This may suggest that Burge takes 'individualism' to be a doctrine about the relation of mental states to some metaphysical facts about the physical environment, along the lines of some of the metaphysical formulations that we canvass below. However, Burge has also emphasized how various historical versions of 'individualism' are typically motivated by epistemological considerations, and he sometimes uses the notion of a subject's 'discriminative abilities' in formulating his main argument against 'individualism' in a way which may suggest an epistemic formulation of individualism and anti-individualism along the lines that we propose later in this chapter (Burge, 1986a). This doesn't seem to us to be an equivocation. Throughout his work, Burge is primarily concerned with defending the specific externalist doctrine that an individual's mental states are 'constitutively what they are partly by virtue of relations between the individual in those states and a wider reality' (2007, p. 3). To defend this thesis, however, Burge does not need a single precise conception of individualism; rather, he can simply appeal to our intuitions about conditions that are obviously part of 'wider reality'. Since there are very different sorts of 'individualist' theories found throughout the history of philosophy, and his work aims to refute all of them, Burge often intentionally characterizes 'individualism' in very broad terms. Thus, we can think of Burge's anti-individualism as denying the disjunction of all the accounts of internalism presented in this chapter.

for thinking that p. This suggests that our intuitions about twin-earth cases are sensitive to whatever differences between earth and twin-earth are relevant for individuating states of thinking that p.

In what follows, we shall assume that twin-earth reasoning is coherent, which means that it relies upon a substantive and intelligible notion of internal sameness holding between you and your twin.

3. Physical and Functional Accounts

So how should we understand the notion of internal sameness in the above argument? The classical presentation of externalism takes it that two agents are internally the same if and only if the total internal physical states of the agents are the same (cf. Burge, 1986b, p. 6; Crane, 1991; Fodor, 1987; Gertler, 2012; McLaughlin & Tye, 1998). Call this the *physical account*.

Although the physical account remains popular in orthodox presentations of externalism and internalism, it faces difficulties. The first is that it appears to misclassify certain forms of dualism as externalist. According to the physical account, any dualist theory which endorses the claim that it is possible for states of thinking that p to vary independently of physical states is thereby committed to thinking that all states of thinking that p are broad. Such views allow that two agents who are in the same total internal physical state can differ as to whether they are thinking that p, because whether or not one is thinking that p is not determined by one's total internal physical state. So, they allow some cases which are internally alike, but which differ as to whether the agent is thinking that p. Therefore, on the physical account, these dualist theories have the consequence that all states of thinking that p are broad.[2]

Is this a serious problem for the physical account? It is often assumed that all dualist theories are internalist, but we do not make this assumption. Rather, our claim is that *this* form of dualism should be classified as internalist. For even though it holds that states of thinking that p vary independently of an agent's total internal physical state, those states of thinking do not depend on anything obviously *external* to the agent. From a theoretical perspective, it looks odd to group these dualist theories with the externalist theories of Putnam and Burge.

---

[2] Several philosophers have recognized this as a problem for the physical account. See, for instance, Burge (1986a), Farkas (2003), and Gertler (2012).

The second problem for the physical account is more delicate. As we saw, Putnam's original motivation for externalism focused on the reference of 'water'. However, the standard way of presenting this argument for externalism fails. For the physical account claims that two agents are internally the same if and only if the total internal physical states of the agents are the same. And philosophers standardly assume that an agent's *skin* demarcates a natural boundary for the total physical state of an agent (Davies, 1993, 1998; cf. Gertler, 2012). But if we define our counterfactual world as qualitatively identical to the actual world except for the fact that every instance of water is an instance of *twin*-water, then you and the twin-version of you are *not* internally the same. You are partly composed of water, so, if your twin is composed of *twin*-water, it is false that there is an agent in the counterfactual world who is internally the same as you. If we find Putnam's twin-earth reasoning compelling, it suggests that his argument does not really require that agents be internally the same if and only if they are in the same *total* physical states.[3]

Can we amend the physical account to overcome these problems? In debates about the metaphysics of the mind, the recognition that individuals can differ physically whilst remaining mentally the same prompted the development of functional accounts of the mental (Armstrong, 1968; Lewis, 1972; Putnam, 1967). A natural response to the second worry is to claim that although the agents are not 'molecule for molecule' physical duplicates, still they share all the same internal *functional* properties, and this suffices for internal sameness. This recommends adopting a *functional account* of internal sameness. According to the functional account, two agents are internally the same if and only if the total internal functional states of the agents are the same. Assuming, again, that we can use an agent's *skin* to demarcate a natural boundary for the total functional state of an agent, Putnam's initial case involves agents who are functionally the same.

But the functionalist account faces the same problem as the physical account when it comes to partitioning philosophical theories. In the same way that a dualist may take states of thinking that *p* to vary independently of the physical state of the agent, so too might a dualist take states of thinking that *p* to vary independently of the *functional* profile of the agent, such that there are cases in which two agents are in the same total internal functional

---

[3] Farkas (2003) uses a twin-earth case involving differences in the bacterium responsible for meningitis to suggest that twin-earth reasoning is insensitive to the physical sameness of the agents involved.

state but differ as to whether they are thinking that p. The functional account is committed to the claim that these forms of dualism treat states of thinking that p as broad. Again, this seems to us to be a theoretically unhelpful classification.

If one is sceptical as to whether there are possible views on which states of thinking vary independently of the functional profile of agents, we can broaden our discussion to mental states more generally. Consider those who think that phenomenal states—those states for which there is something it is like to be in them—vary independently of the functional profile of agents (Block, 1978). These views hold that there are cases in which two agents are in the same total internal functional state but differ as to whether they are in the same phenomenal state. The functional account of internal sameness is committed to classifying these types of views as externalist. Once again, this seems to us to be an unhelpful classification.

4. The Phenomenal Account

In recognition of some of the concerns in the previous section, Farkas proposes that two agents are internally the same if and only if they are in the same phenomenal states. She claims that you and your twin counterpart are subjectively the same, where this means that 'things appear (look, taste, smell, sound) the same for [you]; or the world is (and has always been) the same from [your] subjective viewpoint' (2008, p. 83). Call this the *phenomenal account*: two agents are internally the same if and only if the total phenomenal states of the agents are the same.

Farkas's account makes sense of the emphasis placed in Putnam's original argument on the fact that twin-earth is a place where everything *appears* the same to the subject. On Farkas's view this is not a coincidence: in keeping appearances fixed, we fix the phenomenal properties of a subject's experiences: 'when I say that things appear the same (colour, shape, or otherwise), this amounts to saying that the experiences of things looking in this way for some subjects have a common phenomenal property' (2008, p. 89). Thus, according to the phenomenal account, the thesis of externalism is the denial of the claim that the phenomenal properties of mental states determine the content of those mental states.

Does the phenomenal account improve on the physical and functional accounts? It seems to fare better with cases which raised problems for physical and functional accounts. The forms of dualism we considered are plausibly cases in which the agents are in the same internal phenomenal states. And in Putnam's initial twin-earth case, although the agents are not in the same physical state, it is natural to think they are in the same internal phenomenal states, and that this explains why internalists and externalists are inclined to treat them as internally alike.

But there is a concern, which Farkas recognizes, parallel to the problem we raised for physical and functional accounts. To recap, the problem was that each of these views misclassifies certain forms of dualism as holding that all states of thinking that p are broad. Similarly, the problem for the phenomenal account is that it forces us to classify certain views about phenomenal character as internalist, when it seems like they ought to count as externalist. We take this to count against the phenomenal account.

Consider strong representationalist views which take the phenomenal character of an experience to be identical to its representational content. These views hold that the state of having phenomenal property P is identical to some state of representing p (Tye, 1995). Can this view be combined with the view that states of representing p are broad? On the face of it there is nothing to prevent them from being combined, and a number of authors have endorsed this combination (e.g. Dretske, 1996; Lycan, 2001). Following Dretske, we can call this combination of views *phenomenal externalism*. Phenomenal externalists not only deny that the agents in the twin-earth cases are in the same representational state—since they take states of representing p to be broad—but they also deny that the agents in the twin-earth cases are in the same *phenomenal* state.

An example will help illustrate the view. Take the visual experience of a glass of water. According to the phenomenal externalist, the phenomenal properties of your visual experience are just representational properties. Say those representational properties are the ones involved in the state of representing that there is a glass of water in front of you. Then the phenomenal character of your visual experience must be characterized in terms of what it is like to see *water* in front of you. Your twin is not representing a glass of *water* in front of her; she is representing a glass of *twin*-water. So the phenomenal character of *her* visual experience can only be characterized in terms of what it is like to see *twin*-water in front of her. The content involved in the state of representing determines the phenomenal character of the agent's experience.

Phenomenal externalism looks like a coherent view. But the phenomenal account of internal sameness has an odd implication for this view: namely that all states of representing p which are identical to states exemplifying phenomenal property P are trivially narrow. More precisely, the phenomenal account holds that a state S is narrow if and only if, for all cases α and β, if the agent in α is in the same phenomenal state as the agent in β, then the condition that one is in S obtains in α if and only if the condition that one is in S obtains in β. But phenomenal externalism claims that states of having phenomenal property P are identical to states of representing p. It follows from this that representational states which are identical to phenomenal states are trivially narrow. So, the phenomenal externalist cannot hold that all states of representing p are broad. This is an odd implication.

The problem ramifies when we broaden our focus to mental states more generally. Certain naïve realist views in the philosophy of perception hold that an agent's perceptual experience is partially constituted by the objects of which she is perceptually aware (Brewer, 2011; Campbell, 2002; Martin, 2004). These types of views look like they should count as externalist, since they hold not just that the *content* of our mental states depends on features of the external environment, but that certain kinds of phenomenally conscious mental episodes depend on features of the external environment. But these views are also classified as internalist by the phenomenal account. The reasoning is the same as above: since the phenomenal character of a perceptual experience is constituted by the objects perceived, all perceptual experiences with the same phenomenal character are relations to the same objects. Thus, any cases in which agents are in the same phenomenal state are trivially cases in which agents are in the state of perceiving a certain object. The phenomenal account strangely classifies naïve realist views as holding that states of perceiving are narrow.

Farkas acknowledges this problem for the phenomenal account, but we do not think she fully recognizes its force. Farkas's response is not that these views *should* be classified as internalist, but that there is no better account of internal sameness. For, she suggests, the only other option is to characterize the internal sameness relation in epistemic terms—and this, she thinks, won't work. The remainder of this chapter evaluates the epistemic option.

5. Epistemic Accounts and Indiscriminability

Farkas notes that a natural option for a phenomenal externalist is to characterize the sense in which you and your twin are internally the same in epistemic terms: your twin's case is, in some sense, *indiscriminable* from yours. This suggests that we can use the notion of indiscriminability to fix the notion of internal sameness.

The central idea is that two agents are internally the same if and only if the total states of the agents are *introspectively indiscriminable*. Following Williamson (1990, p. 7), we can think of discrimination as the process of activating knowledge that two things are distinct. Thus, two states are introspectively indiscriminable if and only if an agent is not in a position to know through introspection that the states are distinct. The qualifier 'through introspection' is important, since disciminability is sensitive to *modes of presentation*. Two objects which are indiscriminable under one mode of presentation may be discriminable under another (Williamson, 1990, pp. 14–20). So, states that are indiscriminable through introspective reflection may well be discriminable in other ways. Indiscriminability is thus to be understood as the impossibility of activating knowledge that two things are distinct, and *introspective* indiscriminability as the impossibility of activating knowledge that two things are distinct on the basis of introspection.

This epistemic account has all the benefits of the phenomenal account, since if two agents are in the same phenomenal state, then neither is in a position to know through introspection that the states are distinct. So, any two cases which are internally the same according to the phenomenal account are internally the same according to the epistemic account. But the epistemic account is wider in scope than the phenomenal account, since it allows for cases where states are introspectively indiscriminable but not phenomenally identical. This is the source of the epistemic account's advantage over the phenomenal account, but also the source of its difficulties.

It is a source of advantage because this feature of the epistemic account allows it to correctly classify phenomenal externalism *as* externalist. On the phenomenal externalist view, the state of your representing that *water* is in front of you is not identical to your twin's state of representing that *twin*-water is in front of her, because the contents of those states are determined by a relation which each of you stand in to your environment. It follows that your conscious experience of a glass of water is not identical to your twin's conscious experience of a glass of *twin*-water. It is this difference in phenomenal character which presented problems for the phenomenal account.

But the epistemic account has no problem here, for phenomenal states which are intrinsically quite different may nevertheless be indiscriminable (cf. Fish, 2008). So, even though the phenomenal externalist view entails that there is a difference in phenomenal character across twin-earth cases, one might nevertheless think that these states are introspectively indiscriminable, since neither you nor your twin is in a position to discriminate the conscious experience of water from the conscious experience of *twin*-water. (How could you be, since they look the same?) If this is the case, then the epistemic account correctly classifies phenomenal externalism as a form of externalism.

This advantage turns on the thought that the states in these cases are introspectively indiscriminable despite having different phenomenal characters. Making good on this claim requires us to say more about the notion of introspective indiscriminability. We said above that two states are introspectively indiscriminable if and only if an agent is not in a position to know through introspection that the states are distinct. Suppose that one thought that knowing something through introspection involved the presence of an introspective state which represents some aspect of the state which one introspects.[4] Then one might also hold that an agent is not in a position to know through introspection that two mental states are distinct iff she is in the same introspective state with regard to both of those states. On this way of cashing out the notion of introspective indiscriminability, the impossibility of discrimination is explained not by the sameness of the introspected phenomenal states, but by the sameness of the introspective states which target the qualities of those states.

But this way of explicating the notion of introspective indiscriminability leads to problems similar to those faced by the phenomenal account of internal sameness, for it forces us to classify certain views about introspection as internalist, when it seems like they ought to count as externalist. Consider a view of introspection which takes states of introspective awareness to depend on the mental states which they represent. One example is those accounts of phenomenal introspection which take qualities of introspected phenomenal states to be embedded within, or otherwise partly constitutive of, the states of introspective awareness which underlie our knowledge of our own phenomenal states (Chalmers, 2003, p. 235; Gertler, 2001, p. 307). Can these views of introspection be combined with phenomenal externalism about the phenomenal properties of mental states? Call such a combination *introspective externalism*.[5] Introspective externalism holds that introspective states depend on the states which they represent, and that states exemplifying phenomenal properties are identical to representational states, which are themselves broad. Introspective externalists deny that agents in the twin-earth cases are in the same representational state; they deny that agents in the twin-earth cases are in the same phenomenal state; and, most importantly, they deny that agents in twin-earth cases are in the same *introspective* state.

Introspective externalism looks like a coherent view. But, if the epistemic account of internal sameness understood introspective indiscriminability in terms of sameness of introspective state, then we would have a recurrence of the problem which was raised above for the phenomenal account: since all states of representing p which are identical to states exemplifying phenomenal property P are trivially narrow, any two cases in which agents are in the same introspective state are also trivially narrow. The type of introspective externalist view under consideration therefore comes out as internalist. This classification seems to us to be mistaken, and we think it would be a problem for the epistemic account if it had this result. However, the lesson is not that we should reject the epistemic account but that we should not understand introspective indiscriminability in terms of sameness of introspective state.

How, then, should we understand introspective indiscriminability? We introduced introspective indiscriminability as the impossibility of activating knowledge on the basis of introspection that two things are distinct.[6] The kind of discrimination in play here isn't one which involves holding up two particulars and comparing them. For instance, when one introspects one does not simultaneously apprehend both one's current thought that water quenches thirst and the thought of one's twin-counterpart that twin-water quenches thirst, as one might do when discriminating two apples or two colours. Rather we take introspective indiscriminability to involve an agent not being in a position to know through introspection that her current mental state is distinct from the type of mental state her twin exemplifies. In other words, it is not possible for an agent to know through introspection

---

[6] There is a trivial sense of discriminability in which an agent can know of any particular with which she is consciously acquainted that is not any other thing. But this is not the sense that figures in the epistemic account. If I'm consciously acquainted with Batman, then I can discriminate him from any other distinct individual. But this is compatible with my not knowing that he is distinct from Clark Kent. It is this latter sense of discrimination—discrimination of an item from some relevant comparison class—which is in play in our account.

that her current thought is not one of the *twin-water* thoughts.[7] This impossibility is perfectly compatible with an agent and her counterpart being in different introspective states.

Our picture here is one on which internal sameness is explicated fully in terms of the epistemic capacities of possible agents. Someone who is thinking about water is not in a position to know through introspection that her current thought is not among the class of thoughts we demarcate by considering the counterfactual twin-earth case. It is worth noting that this need not have sceptical implications for an agent's self-knowledge. Someone who is not in a position to know through introspection that her current thought is not a twin-water thought may still be in a position to know that she is thinking about water, either because knowing that one is thinking about water does not require one to rule out that one is not thinking about twin-water (Falvey & Owens, 1994; Gibbons, 1996; Sainsbury, 1997; Williamson, 2000, ch. 5), or because she can rule out that she is not thinking about twin-water, albeit not solely on the basis of introspection.[8]

On this conception of internal sameness, it is perfectly possible for agents to be unable to discriminate introspective states which are actually rather different, just as we saw earlier that it might be possible for agents to be unable to discriminate phenomenal states which are actually different. Thus, one can allow introspective states to be partially constituted by the introspected states which they represent, and hold that some of those introspected states depend on aspects of the environment, whilst recognizing that agents are unable to discriminate those introspective states from the differently constituted states of their twin-earth counterparts. Introspective externalism is correctly classified by the epistemic account as a form of externalism.

---

[7] It isn't clear that the predicate 'is one of the Fs' expresses the relation of identity. In plural logic it is standardly thought of as a primitive logical relation that holds between a singular term and a plural term (Linnebo, 2017). Nevertheless, once we understand 'discriminability' in Williamson's terms of activating knowledge, then the central claim of the epistemic account is that it is not possible for an agent to know through introspection that a is not one of the Fs (i.e. that her current mental state is not one of the twin-water thoughts). We take no stand on how to correctly interpret the logical form of the content of the agent's knowledge. Failures of discrimination are just failures to know something.

[8] This latter option might be pursued by someone who thinks that an agent can rule out the possibility that she is thinking about twin-water on the basis of her knowledge that she is thinking about water, and the knowledge that this is incompatible with thinking about twin-water. McKinsey (1991) suggests that this raises additional questions about the range of a priori knowledge; we won't consider this issue in this chapter.

So far, so good. But Farkas levels several objections to accounts which characterize internal sameness in terms of introspective indisciminability. In each case, the charge is that the epistemic account is committed to treating pairs of cases as internally the same which we are not inclined to treat as such.

The first form of the objection concerns cases in which the agents involved are non-human animals such as cats that lack the capacity to introspectively discriminate their experiences (cf. Siegel, 2008). Since *any* pair of cases would be introspectively indiscriminable to cats, it would follow that *any* pair of cases is internally the same. This is too liberal a conception of internal sameness.

Farkas's second objection is that many states are introspectively indis-criminable from each other in virtue of the fact that the agent lacks sufficient knowledge of what they are like. Consider an agent who can't tell the difference between a female house finch and a female Cassin's finch: her perceptual experiences of these birds would be introspectively indistinguish-able, but Farkas thinks that we shouldn't treat these cases as internally the same. This objection could possibly be avoided if we rule out cases that a subject cannot discriminate simply because of ignorance. We are not bird enthusiasts and so neither of us can discriminate an experience of a female house finch from one of a female Cassin's finch. But that does not make them introspectively indiscriminable to us. If we spent some time learning about finches, we'd be able to tell the two apart.

Farkas's third objection holds that this response won't work in general, because there will ultimately be certain pairs of mental states that one is not able to discriminate because of natural limitations on one's discriminatory capacities. Farkas focuses on limitations of memory and makes her point with the following example: 'When I have the taste of one wine, the experience is present in all its completely determinate phenomenal specifi-city, to the exclusion of all others; but, as soon as the experience is gone, the details immediately fade from reflective consciousness, and what we retain in memory for comparative purposes is less specific' (2008, p. 113). The worry here is that because Farkas's own discriminatory capacities are limited by the capacity of her memory, small differences in the phenomenal character of her experiences of different wines will not be discriminable. In that case, however, it will be possible that certain pairs of introspectively indiscriminable mental states will nevertheless be phenomenally distinct. And Farkas believes it is a mistake to think that two different conscious experiences, of two different wines, are internally alike simply because the

330 MATTHEW PARROTT AND ANIL GOMES

subject of these experiences cannot remember fine-grained phenomenal information.

It is this last concern which really gets to the heart of Farkas's objection to the epistemic account. The problem is that there seem to be pairs of cases which an agent cannot discriminate, not because these experiences are internally the same, but because the agent's discriminatory capacities are limited. That limitation may be temporary, as in the case of ignorance, or more permanent, as in the case of the natural limitations of memory, and at its extreme it may involve the lack of a discriminatory capacity at all, as in the case of non-human animals. In each case, the problem is the same: certain limitations in an agent's discriminatory capacities seem to result in the epistemic account classifying pairs of cases as internally the same which should not be so counted. The epistemic account has too liberal a conception of internal sameness.

This is an important objection. But we do not think that it applies to all forms of an epistemic account. It demonstrates that a plausible epistemic account should not characterize introspective indiscriminability in terms of the psychological capacities of specific agents. Let's call such an account a *personal* conception of introspective indiscriminability. Such a conception holds that if there is some particular agent that cannot introspectively discriminate between two states, then these two states are introspectively indiscriminable for that agent. But, as Farkas's objections show, the personal conception is too liberal. When considering whether certain types of mental states are internally the same, our interest is not with whether some particular person has a good memory, or has some specific level of introspective acuity. If the personal conception were the only way to explicate the epistemic account, then we agree that it would be in trouble.

But, setting aside questions about whether some particular agent is able to discriminate two states, we might also be concerned about whether it is possible for introspective reflection to discriminate two mental states. Following Martin (2006), we shall call this more demanding notion an *impersonal* conception of introspective indiscriminability. Whereas the *personal* conception holds that the conscious states of two agents are *introspectively indiscriminable* just in case *those* agents are unable to know through introspection that their states are distinct, the *impersonal* conception of introspective indiscriminablity prescinds from any reference to actual persons. Instead, it holds that the states of two agents are *introspectively indiscriminable* if and only if it is not possible to know through introspection that the states are distinct. The impossibility here is unrestricted. It is a claim about the limitations of introspection itself rather than any particular agent's exercise of that capacity (cf. Soteriou, 2016, ch. 3).

The impersonal conception of introspective indiscriminability can avoid Farkas's worries about cats, the ignorant, and folks who have deficits or limitations on their discriminative capacities. Contrary to what Farkas suggests, it is possible for some agent to introspectively discriminate distinct experiences had by a cat, even though that cat herself cannot do so. And it is possible for some agent to introspectively discriminate the experience of a female house finch from the experience of a female Cassin's finch, even though we cannot. And it is possible for some agent to introspectively discriminate distinct experiences of wine, even if Farkas cannot.

We suggest, then, that Farkas's objections to an *epistemic* account of internal sameness apply only to one which characterizes the notion in terms of a *personal* conception of introspective indiscriminability. This suggests that the objections can be avoided if we use an *impersonal* conception. Therefore, we propose the following epistemic account of internal sameness: a state S is narrow if and only if, for all cases α and β, if the total state of the agent in α is impersonally introspectively indiscriminable from the total state of the agent in β, then the condition that one is in S obtains in α if and only if the condition that one is in S obtains in β.

This proposal improves on the metaphysical accounts we considered earlier. It provides us with the most theoretically appropriate grouping of views, explaining the sense in which the type of dualist views we considered earlier are internalist and why phenomenal externalism is externalist. It also identifies a substantive fault line in the philosophy of mind, a dispute about whether one's mental states can vary independently of certain introspective capacities. This is an issue worth caring about.[9]

---

[9] One additional point in support: at the end of 'The Meaning of "Meaning"', Putnam makes clear that the entities which populate twin-earth can be thought of as *epistemic counterparts* of the entities which populate our earth (Putnam, 1975, pp. 242–3; cf. Putnam, 1990, pp. 55–6). This supports the claim we have made in this section: the fundamental relation which holds between you and your twin is an *epistemic* relation. Putnam notes that the phrase 'epistemic counterpart' comes from Kripke, and many who have followed Kripke have supposed that an object on twin-earth is an epistemic counterpart of an object on earth because on twin-earth I would have—as Kripke puts it—'the same sensory evidence that I in fact have' (Kripke, 1980, p. 142; cf. Sawyer, 1999, p. 361). But the previous discussion of phenomenal externalism and naïve realism shows why this further step is unwarranted: two cases can involve epistemic counterparts even when one's sensory evidence is different in the two. The characterization of twin-earth as an epistemic counterpart of the earth motivates a formulation of internal sameness in terms of introspective indiscriminability.

In the next section, we consider an objection to the epistemic account; in the final section, we argue that formulating the notion of internal sameness in epistemic terms can better capture the significance of the dispute between internalism and externalism when thinking about the nature of the mind.

6. Grounding Introspective Indiscriminability

The epistemic account under consideration holds that two agents are internally the same because the mental states of those agents are introspectively indiscriminable. As we saw, the phenomenal account also has this consequence. However, unlike the epistemic account, the phenomenal account is in a position to explain why the mental states of two agents are introspectively indiscriminable, namely because those states share the same phenomenal properties. So, although the phenomenal account faces some obstacles, it might seem like a positive feature of the account is that it at least is in a position to explain why two states are introspectively indiscriminable.

In contrast, the epistemic account looks to have *no* explanation of why the states in question are introspectively indiscriminable, at least so long as any explanation is to turn on features of the objects of introspection. It may be true that you cannot know through introspection that your current thought is not one of the *twin*-water thoughts, but, for the epistemic account, this is not *because* of some feature or property of your thought. This would not be problematic if we were operating with a personal notion, since we could at least then explain why two states could not be discriminated by appealing to facts about the psychological capacities of agents. But once we adopt an *impersonal* conception of indiscriminability, it is less clear what sort of explanation we can give of why two states cannot be discriminated.[10]

Consider an analogy with visual indiscriminability. Suppose that we wanted to fabricate a bunch of replica apples. If we had a sufficient level of skill, and designed the right equipment, we might succeed in producing schmapples, perfect replicas that are visually indiscriminable from genuine

---

[10] This worry seems to lie behind one of Brie Gertler's objections to an epistemic account. Gertler presents a dilemma for the externalist who must decide whether a difference in an agent's intensional contents 'must be' introspectively discriminable. If the externalist takes the second horn of the dilemma, Gertler complains that since a difference in intensional content would not suffice for introspective discriminability, it is unclear what could possibly ground or explain the introspective discriminability of two thoughts. She concludes that 'the only feature that could ground subjective distinguishability seems to be phenomenal character' (Gertler, 2012, p. 62).

apples. Suppose further that not only can we not visually distinguish them, but that no possible visual system can discriminate schmapples from apples. They are impersonally visually indiscriminable. A very natural thought is that schmapples must have roughly the same size, shape, and colour of real apples and, moreover, it is *because* of this that they are impersonally visually indiscriminable. The fact that schmapples are *impersonally* visually indiscriminable from apples looks to be explained by the fact that they share certain basic visible properties with apples. If schmapples had nothing in common with genuine apples, it would be very hard to grasp why no possible visual system could distinguish the two.

The challenge for the epistemic account is thus either to provide a plausible, non-question-begging, explanation of why the mental states of two different agents cannot be discriminated, or to make plausible the idea that no such explanation is required. In the case of vision, we are able to explain why two distinct objects are impersonally indiscriminable by appeal to a common appearance. This puts pressure on the first horn. But the second horn looks to involve a mysterious ungrounded epistemic capacity.

This is a serious objection. Nevertheless, there may be ways in which a defender of the account could mitigate its force. One option is for the epistemic account to reject the claim that facts about the introspective indiscriminability of two mental states must ultimately be explained. This would be a way of taking the fact that two mental states are impersonally introspectively indiscriminable to be basic. Although this would be in the spirit of the epistemic account, some will object to the postulation of mysterious ungrounded epistemic facts.

More plausibly, the epistemic account could reject the idea that our explanation of visual indiscriminability should be used as a model for explaining impersonal introspective indiscriminability. Our capacity for visual discrimination has certain impersonal limits, and, as we have seen, these can partly be explained by facts about visible appearances. But if we apply this model to our capacity for introspective discrimination, then we would have to think that the limits of that capacity are similarly to be explained in terms of the appearances of introspectable mental states. This looks to assume that we should treat our introspective relation to our own mental states on the model of perceptual awareness of objects in our environment. And there are reasons to resist that assumption.[11]

[11] See Martin (2006) for a development of this line of thought, and Shoemaker (1994) for influential objections to a perceptual model of introspection.

Once we set aside the analogy with visual discrimination, we can see that it is possible that limitations on the capacity for introspection discrimination should not be explained in terms of any features of the objects of introspection, but in terms of the nature of that capacity itself. In other words, it is the capacity of introspective discrimination, impersonally conceived, that is limited in terms of what it is able to discriminate. And an explanation of those limits need only appeal to the character of introspection itself, rather than to the character of the objects over which it ranges.[12]

7. Indiscriminability and the Nature of the Mind

Let us assess the balance sheet. We have argued that the epistemic account provides a more plausible grouping of views as internalist and externalist since it has the resources to explain why phenomenal externalism counts as externalist and why certain dualist views count as internalist. But we recognize that this incurs the burden of explaining why it is that two mental states are impersonally introspectively indiscriminable. In this final section we shall suggest that the epistemic account has the further advantage of capturing a substantive philosophical issue which figures centrally in debates about the nature of the mind. On the epistemic formulation of internal sameness, internalism says that two agents who are in introspectively indiscriminable mental states are in the same mental state; externalists deny this. So, adopting the epistemic formulation allows us to see how certain debates about the nature of the mind can be usefully characterized as concerning the relation between an agent's mental states and the capacity for introspective discrimination.

We will motivate this thought with reference to the perspective that the epistemic formulation gives us on what many take to be a paradigm of internalism, namely the position put forward, even if not endorsed, in Descartes's First Meditation.[13] The basic structure of the First Meditation

---

[12] One might worry that this line of response involves 'idealization' of the capacity for introspective discrimination. But bear in mind that an impersonal conception of introspective indiscriminability quantifies over possible agents. So, if two mental states are impersonally introspectively indiscriminable, then they cannot be discriminated by any possible agent. It is not unreasonable to think of this as a general feature of the capacity for introspective discrimination, but it is not an idealization.

[13] Internalism about the mind is often attributed to Descartes (Burge, 1986b, p. 117; Crane, 1991; Farkas, 2008; McDowell, 1986), but it is now recognized that this attribution is complicated by Descartes's appeal in the Third Meditation to the principle that 'in order for a given

involves an attempt to challenge the foundations of the meditator's knowledge, first through consideration of doubt occasioned by recognition that the meditator might be dreaming, and then by consideration of the possibility of being misled by an evil demon. One natural way to read this as presenting a form of internalism is by taking the evil demon scenario as providing a test for narrowness: the states which would be present in both your case and the counterfactual evil-demon scenario are *narrow*. The First Meditation presents a form of internalism to the extent that it shows that all and only mental states are so present. (Farkas makes this explicit; see her 2008, pp. 19–24).

This suggests that we can draw upon different accounts of internal sameness in thinking about how to best understand the position presented in the First Meditation. This is a difficult scholarly issue, which we won't pretend to resolve here, but we believe a couple of points are worth making. First, it is very implausible to think that Descartes is attempting to identify some *physical* states which would be present in both the ordinary and evil demon cases. The meditator has, after all, already been led to doubt that she has hands or a body (AT 7:19–20; CSM 2:13). So it is implausible to think the evil demon scenario is one in which you are in the same total physical state as you are in the normal case. Nor does Descartes focus on any behavioural commonalities between the two cases, of the sort which would help identify a functional state obtaining in both cases.

More plausible is the idea that the evil demon scenario is one in which one's perspective on the world remains the same even whilst the nature of the world is radically different. But how should we understand this notion of a 'perspective on the world'? Farkas's suggestion is, in effect, that it involves the presence of phenomenal properties.[14] But there are reasons to think this

idea to contain such and such objective reality, it must…derive it from some cause which contains at least as much formal reality as there is objective reality in the idea' (AT VII:40–1; CSM II:28–9), a principle which, on the face of it, looks to involve the rejection of internalism for some mental states. But even if we should be careful about the attribution of internalism to Descartes given his overall commitments, it is still widely assumed that at least the First Meditation presents a classical internalist scenario—even if it is one that Descartes will later take himself to show is not ultimately coherent (Burge, 2007, pp. 420–1).

[14] Farkas argues that those states which obtain in both the normal and the evil demon scenarios are those to which the agent has privileged access, in effect delimiting the features in question on the basis of how they can be known (2008, pp. 19–24). But she also argues that all and only those states to which an agent has privileged access are phenomenal states: states with phenomenal properties (2008, pp. 130–3). So the initial epistemic delimitation of the states in question is grounded in some metaphysical facts about the nature of those states, such that it is those states with phenomenal properties which obtain in both normal and evil demon cases.

is unsatisfactory. First, it sits uncomfortably with the text. The progression in the First Meditation does not involve a winnowing away of features about which one can be mistaken, until one is left with a realm of the phenomenal.[15] This is particularly clear in the comparison between painting and thinking, which structures the move from the consideration of dreaming to the evil demon scenario. In this passage, Descartes doesn't build on the dreaming scenario by noting that it involves a set of phenomenal states about which one cannot be mistaken. Instead, he points out that experiencing and thinking might involve the jumbling up of simpler universal things. This would be curious if his aim was to identify a certain realm (the phenomenal) about which one couldn't be deceived.

Secondly, although it is common to present the First Meditation as involving the identification of an impregnable phenomenal realm, this reading sits uncomfortably with Descartes's insistence on God's omnipotence. God is free to make it not true that all the radii of the circle are equal (AT 1:152–3; CSMK III:25–6), or that 1 and 2 are not 3 (AT 5:224; CSMK III:358–9). This omnipotence would seem to preclude there being a set of phenomenal states about which the meditator simply cannot be deceived.[16]

How, then, should we understand the thought that the evil demon scenario is one in which one's perspective on the world remains the same? The epistemic account offers a nice suggestion: the evil demon scenario is introspectively indiscriminable from one's actual case. Descartes tells us of the dreaming scenario that, 'there are never any sure signs by means of which being awake can be distinguished from being asleep' (AT 7:19; CSM II:13); and, in the discussion of the evil demon scenario, he places great weight on the possibility that it might be an imperfection in oneself which underlies one's inability to rule out that alternative. The First Meditation thus provides a way of making vivid that certain cases are introspectively indiscriminable from one's own, and the Second Meditation onwards can be seen as an attempt to isolate what can be salvaged from that observation. If this is right, then to the extent that we think of the First Meditation as a paradigm of internalism, it is because it presents a series of cases which are introspectively indiscriminable from one's own. And the internalist thought is that *those* cases are ones in which agents are in the same mental states.

[15] Rorty (1980) and Williams (1986) sometimes present the first *Meditation* in this way.
[16] For a summary of some of the complications in Descartes's account of the metaphysics of modality, see Cunning (2014).

Why is this relevant? Many debates in the philosophy of mind are viewed as debates in the metaphysics of mind, as if the relation between the mental and the physical were the only substantive issues of interest or concern. We think the interest and significance of the First Meditation is obscured when one reads it as making a point about the metaphysics of mind. Similarly, we think the interest and significance of twin-earth reasoning and the internalism/externalism distinction are similarly obscured when one understands them as marking a distinction in the metaphysics of mind. The First Meditation encourages us to think about the relation between certain introspective capacities and the nature of mentality itself. The case of twin-earth does likewise. Both present the possibility of cases which are introspectively indiscriminable from one's current case. On the epistemic account, the internalist and externalist disagree about the implications this has for an agent's mental states. That is, they disagree about whether limitations on the capacity for introspective discrimination fix or determine an agent's mental states. This is a dispute which is worth marking.[17]

References

Armstrong, D. M. (1968). *A Materialist Theory of the Mind*. London: Routledge.

Block, N. (1978). Troubles with functionalism. *Minnesota Studies in the Philosophy of Science*, 9, 261–325.

Brewer, B. (2011). *Perception and Its Objects*. Oxford: Oxford University Press.

Brown, J. (2009). Semantic externalism and self-knowledge. In A. Beckermann & B. P. McLaughlin (eds), *The Oxford Handbook of Philosophy of Mind* (pp. 767–80). Oxford: Oxford University Press.

Burge, T. (1979). Individualism and the mental. *Midwest Studies in Philosophy*, 4(1), 73–122.

Burge, T. (1982). Other bodies. In A. Woodfield (ed.), *Thought and Object*. Oxford: Oxford University Press.

Burge, T. (1986a). Cartesian error and the objectivity of perception. In P. Pettit & J. McDowell (eds), *Subject, Thought, and Context*. Oxford: Clarendon Press.

Burge, T. (1986b). Individualism and psychology. *Philosophical Review*, 95 (January), 3–45.

[17] Our thanks to Tim Bayne, Bill Brewer, Will Davies, Nick Jones, Uriah Kriegel, Guy Longworth, Matthew Soteriou, and an anonymous referee for discussion and comments. Versions of this material were presented at Cardiff University, Monash University, and the University of Warwick: our thanks to all the participants for their comments.

Burge, T. (2007). *Foundations of Mind*. Oxford: Oxford University Press.

Campbell, J. (2002). *Reference and Consciousness*. Oxford: Oxford University Press.

Chalmers, D. (2003). The content and epistemology of phenomenal belief. In Q. Smith & A. Jokic (eds), *Consciousness: New Philosophical Perspectives* (pp. 220–72). Oxford: Oxford University Press.

Crane, T. (1991). All the difference in the world. *Philosophical Quarterly, 41* (January), 1–25.

Cunning, D. (2014). Descartes' modal metaphysics. In E. N. Zalta (ed.), *Stanford Encyclopedia of Philosophy* (Spring 2014 edition), https://plato.stanford.edu/entries/descartes-modal/.

Davies, M. (1993). Aims and claims of externalist arguments. *Philosophical Issues, 4*, 227–49.

Davies, M. (1998). Externalism, architecturalism, and epistemic warrant. In C. Macdonald, B. Smith, & C. Wright (eds), *Knowing Our Own Minds: Essays in Self-Knowledge* (pp. 321–63). Oxford: Oxford University Press.

Dretske, F. (1996). Phenomenal externalism, or if meanings ain't in the head, where are qualia? *Philosophical Issues, 7*, 143–58.

Falvey, K. & Owens, J. (1994). Externalism, self-knowledge, and skepticism. *Philosophical Review, 103*(1), 107–37.

Farkas, K. (2003). What is externalism? *Philosophical Studies, 112*(3), 187–208.

Farkas, K. (2008). *The Subject's Point of View* (Vol. 69). Oxford: Oxford University Press.

Fish, W. C. (2008). Disjunctivism, indistinguishability, and the nature of hallucination. In A. Haddock & F. Macpherson (eds), *Disjunctivism: Perception, Action, Knowledge* (pp. 144–67). Oxford: Oxford University Press.

Fodor, J. A. (1987). *Psychosemantics: The Problem of Meaning in the Philosophy of Mind*. Cambridge, MA: MIT Press.

Gertler, B. (2001). Introspecting Phenomenal States. *Philosophy and Phenomenological Research, 63*(2), 305–28. doi:10.1111/j.1933–1592.2001.tb00105.x.

Gertler, B. (2012). Understanding the internalism-externalism debate: what is the boundary of the thinker? *Philosophical Perspectives, 26*(1), 51–75.

Gibbons, J. (1996). Externalism and knowledge of content. *Philosophical Review, 105*(3), 287–310.

Kripke, S. A. (1980). *Naming and Necessity*. Cambridge, MA: Harvard University Press.

Lau, J. & Deutsch, M. (2016). Externalism about mental content. In E. N. Zalta (ed.), *Stanford Encyclopedia of Philosophy* (Winter 2016 edition), https://plato.stanford.edu/entries/content-externalism.

Lewis, D. (1972). Psychophysical and theoretical identifications. *Australasian Journal of Philosophy*, 50(3), 249–58.

Linnebo, Ø. (2017). Plural quantification. In E. N. Zalta (ed.), *Stanford Encyclopedia of Philosophy* (Summer 2017 edition), https://plato.stanford.edu/entries/plural-quant/.

Lycan, W. G. (2001). The case for phenomenal externalism. *Philosophical Perspectives*, 15(s15), 17–35.

McDowell, J. (1986). Singular thought and the extent of 'inner space'. In J. McDowell & P. Pettit (eds), *Subject, Thought, and Context*. Oxford: Clarendon Press.

McKinsey, M. (1991). Anti-individualism and privileged access. *Analysis, 51* (January), 9–16.

McLaughlin, B. P. & Tye, M. (1998). Externalism, twin earth, and self-knowledge. In C. Macdonald, P. K. Smith, & C. Wright (eds), *Knowing Our Own Minds: Essays in Self-Knowledge* (pp. 285–320). Oxford: Oxford University Press.

Martin, M. G. F. (2004). The limits of self-awareness. *Philosophical Studies, 120* (1–3), 37–89.

Martin, M. G. F. (2006). On being alienated. In T. S. Gendler & J. Hawthorne (eds), *Perceptual Experience* (pp. 354–410). Oxford: Oxford University Press.

Putnam, H. (1967). The nature of mental states. Reprinted in B. Beakley & P. Ludlow (eds), *The Philosophy of Mind: Classical Problems, Contemporary Issues* (pp. 51–8). Cambridge, MA: MIT Press, 1992.

Putnam, H. (1975). The meaning of 'meaning'. *Minnesota Studies in the Philosophy of Science, 7*, 131–93.

Putnam, H. (1981). *Reason, Truth, and History*. Cambridge: Cambridge University Press.

Putnam, H. (1990). Is water necessarily H2O? In J. Conant (ed.), *Realism with a Human Face* (pp. 54–79). Cambridge, MA: Harvard University Press.

Rorty, R. (1980). *Philosophy and the Mirror of Nature*. Princeton, NJ: Princeton University Press.

Sainsbury, R. M. (1997). Easy possibilities. *Philosophy and Phenomenological Research, 57*(4), 907–19.

Sawyer, S. (1999). An externalist account of introspective knowledge. *Pacific Philosophical Quarterly, 4*(4), 358–78.

Shoemaker, S. (1994). Self-knowledge and inner sense 1: the object perception model. *Philosophy and Phenomenological Research*, 54(2), 249–69. doi:10.2307/2108488.

Siegel, S. (2008). The epistemic conception of hallucination. In A. Haddock & F. Macpherson (eds), *Disjunctivism: Perception, Action and Knowledge* (pp. 205–24). Oxford: Oxford University Press.

Soteriou, M. (2016). *Disjunctivism*. London: Routledge.

Tye, M. (1995). *Ten Problems of Consciousness: A Representational Theory of the Phenomenal Mind* (Vol. 282). Cambridge, MA: MIT Press.

Williams, M. (1986). Descartes and the metaphysics of doubt. In A. O. Rorty (ed.), *Essays on Descartes' Meditations* (pp. 117–40). Berkeley: University of California Press.

Williamson, T. (1990). *Identity and Discrimination*. Oxford: Blackwell.

Williamson, T. (2000). *Knowledge and its Limits*. Oxford: Oxford University Press.

12

Relational Imperativism about Affective Valence

Antti Kauppinen

It's easy enough to imagine a lion chasing a young antelope on the savannah. Given the failure rate of lion attacks, it is potentially a matter of life and death for both. Their hearts racing, the animals strain their muscles to the utmost, sending dust in the sky and tremors underground. It's much harder to imagine what goes through an ungulate mind, but let's try. Insofar as the antelope has conscious experience, it may well be dominated by fear. Of late, it has become common to think that such affective experiences have the feel they do in virtue of having evaluative content, so that what gives fear its negative feel is that it is as if it is telling the antelope "This is bad" or maybe "Being chased by the lion is bad for you!" In this chapter, I'll defend an alternative answer, according to which the phenomenologically distinctive content of the fear is something much closer to "Run, motherf*cker, run!!"

Let's start by clarifying what is at issue. It is widely, though not quite universally, agreed that there is something it is like to have conscious experience—that conscious experience has a *phenomenal character*. What I will focus on here is the phenomenal character of *affective experiences*— algedonic states or aspects, emotions, and moods—which can at least typically be characterized as positive or negative. In other words, affective experiences have *valence*: they feel good or bad. The question I'm going to address, then, is the following: in virtue of what do affective experiences have valenced phenomenal character? As the savannah story suggests, the answer I'll defend will appeal to *imperatival* content, extending views proposed by Colin Klein and Manolo Martinez in the context of debates about pain and unpleasantness.

My argument will proceed as follows. I'll begin by looking at the functional role of valence—what it does and what it doesn't do. I contend that the key role of valence is explaining and rationalizing inherent motivation,

Antti Kauppinen, *Relational Imperativism about Affective Valence* In: *Oxford Studies in Philosophy of Mind Volume 1*.
Edited by: Uriah Kriegel, Oxford University Press (2021). © Antti Kauppinen.
DOI: 10.1093/oso/9780198845850.003.0012

but not as currency in deliberation. Here, I focus on two competing intentionalist explanations of valence, evaluativism and imperativism. On the face of it, evaluativists, who hold that affects have valence in virtue of representing something as good or bad, have an advantage when it comes to explaining how valenced experiences rationalize action and judgment, but I raise some doubts about that. Imperativists, in turn, have an edge when it comes to explaining how valenced experiences motivate, but extant views face deep challenges when it comes to other aspects of valence.

In Section 2, I turn to developing a new, generalized version of first-order imperativism that I call relational imperativism. Roughly, I argue that valenced experiences have two kinds of interrelated content. Their *indicative* content represents a state of affairs or an object that matters to the subject in the light of a background concern. Their *imperative* content consists of a command that is subjectively authoritative in virtue of linking up with the background concern, and that tells the subject to see to it that the sort of thing represented by the indicative content either will or won't obtain in the future. I argue that this account provides a suitably nuanced picture of how valenced experience motivates, and a plausible characterization of its phenomenal feel.

The final section addresses some important objections that have been raised in the literature against imperativism. The first important challenge concerns the datum that valenced experiences not only motivate but also rationalize. My response appeals to the well-known psychological mechanism of projection or objectification: when we experience being authoritatively commanded to do something about something, it predictably changes the way things practically appear to us. When the antelope fears the lion, the lion appears to it as something *to-be-fled-from*. I claim that such *affective practical seemings* resulting from imperative content suffice to make sense of how valenced experiences rationalize. The second key challenge concerns the explanation of *intensity* of affect in terms of commands. Klein and Martinez have presented a sophisticated model that appeals to a kind of inbuilt priority ranking among imperatives. I propose a simpler account of intensity in terms of the level of opportunity cost that imperative contents tell us to bear in order to satisfy them. Third, I address what I'll label the Shooting the Officer Objection: why should we want to get rid of experiences like pains, if their negative phenomenal character consists of our being told to see to it that some bodily condition goes away? What's so bad about being told to make the future different from the present? I argue that just as parallel objections to evaluativism, this objection amounts to begging the question when it comes to the badness of negative experiences. I also maintain that the unpleasantness of an experience doesn't in itself motivate us to get rid of the experience, which we can see if we consider world-directed emotions like grief. Instead, what motivates and rationalizes, say, taking painkillers is being (contingently) attitudinally displeased with feeling bad.

1. The Debate about Valence: From Evaluativism to Imperativism

1.1 The Concept of Valence

Let us begin by taking a closer look at the motivational role of valence. If I take pleasure in eating ice cream, I tend to be motivated to eat more ice cream, even if prior to tasting it, I had no such desire. If I'm grateful to Sandy for lending me her bike when I needed it, I tend to be motivated, at least to some extent, to help her in turn, even if I had no such motivation before. Note that you could be motivated to return a favour just because you think it's the right thing to do, without feeling grateful—but your feeling of gratitude seems to suffice on its own for motivation, at least potentially. If I'm tranquil, I tend to be motivated, if that's the right word, to let things be as they are instead of rearranging them somehow, even if I hankered for something different before.

What these reflections suggest is that *valenced phenomenal character is potentially motivating by itself*. I don't claim that this is obvious—there is more to gratitude, for example, than its phenomenal aspect, and some might argue that it is the non-phenomenal aspects that account for motivation. But insofar as introspection can be relied on here, it appears to be precisely the *feeling* of gratitude that guides me towards reciprocating, or the toothache that finally gets me to call the dentist. It would be rash to conclude that valenced affects necessarily motivate—indeed, I'll argue that they don't. But when they do, they do not merely channel pre-existing desires. I'll use the term "inherent motivation" for this phenomenon (the more common term "intrinsic" suggests necessity). Because of its inherently motivating character, it is unsurprising that it is common to identify valence with pleasantness or unpleasantness of an experience—after all, pleasures and pains seem to be inherently motivating, and motivational hedonists like Bentham even hold that they're the *only* inherent motives. But while I think that positive feelings feel good, I don't believe that valence just *is* pleasantness or unpleasantness, because such identification would suggest that anger, say, inherently motivates *in virtue of* its unpleasantness, which I don't think is true. Moreover, it's not conceptually confused to think of valence as consisting of evaluating something as good or bad, even if one does not think that such evaluations are necessarily pleasant or unpleasant. So instead of pleasantness or unpleasantness of experience, I'll take as my primary explanandum inherently motivating phenomenal character.

Valence does not just motivate action, however—it also *rationalizes* it, at least subjectively. The way I would describe it is that when you have a valenced affective experience, it appears to you that you have a reason to act or should act in a certain way, or at least the experience presents something in a favourable or unfavourable light. If you're grateful to Sandy, it makes at least some sense to you to return the favour. Your toothache doesn't just get you to call the dentist, but also presents the condition of your tooth in an unfavourable light.

It's worth highlighting that I will not treat it as part of the explanandum the surprisingly common view that valence serves as *common currency in deliberation* (e.g. Levy and Glimcher 2012, Carruthers 2018), that is, as something that commensurates the value of different options. Here is how Luca Barlassina illustrates the alleged deliberative role of valence: "To decide whether to go to the movies or to a restaurant, you can imagine either activity and use the elicited valences ('this seems more pleasant than this') to guide your choice" (forthcoming, 2). But it does not do justice to the phenomenology of deliberation to assume that we make our choices on the basis of how we feel about our options, not to mention how much pleasure or displeasure we anticipate getting from them. While such considerations do play a role in *some* decisions (possibly including the kind of leisure choices Barlassina mentions), deliberation also, and centrally, involves beliefs about what is right or good, and is crucially shaped by our prior plans and commitments. If there's a common currency to deliberation, it's *utility*, and that's just because "utility" is a catch-all term for how our preferences rank our options, whatever they're based on.

1.2 Evaluativism and Its Discontents

How, then, can we account for valence? For reasons of space, I'll have to set aside views that hold there's nothing to explain (e.g. Smuts 2011) and externalist views that appeal to attitudes either towards our experiences or the world (e.g. Heathwood 2007, Jacobson 2019). Instead, I'll just focus on two competing *intentionalist* views, which link phenomenal character with the *intentional content* of an experience. Intentionalist views are internalist but not brute, since they offer a further explanation of valenced phenomenology. According to what I'll call *Phenomenal-to-Intentional Reductionism*, experiences have their phenomenal character in virtue of their intentional content, which in turn can be naturalistically explained (e.g. Tye 1995). A minority tradition subscribes to *Intentional-to-Phenomenal Reductionism*, according to which it's instead phenomenal character that explains intentional content of at least some experiences (e.g. Mendelovici 2018). To be neutral, I'll just assume *Phenomenal-Intentional Parallelism*: the phenomenal character of an experience *matches* its intentional content—same intentional content entails same phenomenal character (at least in those respects that matter here), and vice versa.

The most common form of intentionalism is *representationalism*, according to which mental states have the phenomenal content they do in virtue of their representational content. When it comes to affective phenomenal character, it is not plausible that the representational content in question simply concerns how things are. One reason to think so is that affective character can vary independently of such representations—for example, two people might have pain states that represent the same kind of bodily disturbance while nevertheless experiencing pain of different intensity (Pautz 2010). The standard representationalist answer is to say that affective states also have an additional, *evaluative* representational content, such that variations in character and intensity of affect are explained by variations in the type and degree of represented value—for example, one pain feels worse than another because it evaluates my bodily condition as worse (Cutter and Tye 2011). Here are a few representative evaluativist claims:

A subject's being in unpleasant pain consists in his (i) undergoing an experience (the pain) that represents a disturbance of a certain sort, and (ii) that same experience additionally representing the disturbance as bad for him in the bodily sense.   (Bain 2012)

The valence component of affective states like pain and pleasure is a nonconceptual representation of badness or goodness.   (Carruthers 2018)

An emotion has negative valence because it contains a perceptual experience of a negative thick value.   (Teroni 2020)

Evaluativism is currently the most popular internalist account of valence. Maybe the best case for it appeals to the role of valence in not only motivating but also rationalizing action (Helm 2002, Bain 2012). I'll reconstruct it as follows:

1. The phenomenal character of an experience matches its intentional content.
2. The intentional content of valenced affects (e.g. pain) rationalizes world-directed actions and judgments about value.
3. The intentional content of valenced affects only rationalizes world directed-actions and judgments about value if they have world-directed representational content, which they represent as good or bad (in a particular way).
4. So, valenced affects represent something as good or bad (stronger: affects have valence in virtue of representing something as good or bad).

Premise 2 calls attention to the fact that an affective experience like feeling pain in your ankle not only motivates but also rationalizes an action that changes your ankle-directed behaviour, such as not putting weight on it. What's more, such experiences also seem to rationalize judging that the damage in your ankle is bad for you, much in the same way as perceptual experiences rationalize perceptual beliefs. Premise 3 then claims that experiences can only play these roles if their contents are evaluative. Suppose that your pain presents the damage in your ankle as bad. This experienced badness rationalizes behaviour that reduces it—by your lights, you have a reason to reduce the damage. It is a further question whether these evaluative contents are conceptual or non-conceptual, where conceptual contents are those linked with linguistic capacities or general recognitive skills (e.g. Evans 1982). The mainstream view is that they are non-conceptual (e.g. Tappolet 2016, Carruthers 2018, Mitchell 2020 [2018]). One key argument for this claim appeals to fineness of grain: just like our colour experience plausibly discriminates between more shades than we have concepts for, our affective experiences discriminate between more ways of being valuable than our concepts do. As Jonathan Mitchell (2020 [2018]) maintains, someone with a crude aesthetic conceptual repertoire could nevertheless experience different paintings as beautiful in different ways while lacking even the ability for even demonstrative re-identification of the represented property.[1] It is a tricky question just how non-conceptual contents can rationalize beliefs that do have conceptual contents (indeed, Mitchell thinks they don't), but presumably the answer will be of the same sort as in the case of ordinary perception.[2]

In spite of its popularity, I have serious doubts about evaluativism, however. First, evaluativists rightly emphasize that one need not possess *concepts* of specific kinds of goodness or badness to have valenced experiences, and that possessing such concepts does not suffice to capture the fine grain of valenced experiences. Even individuals who do have such concepts represent something as good or bad in a different, non-conceptual way when they have affective experiences. But what exactly are we talking about when we talk about non-conceptual representation of goodness or badness? What makes a non-conceptual representation one of *goodness*, in some sense? How do we non-conceptually represent one thing as *better* than another? It is hard to find arguments for this in the literature. It won't suffice to say, for example, that the subject is disposed to form evaluative beliefs in response to valenced experiences, since that wouldn't explain how the valenced experiences themselves represent their objects evaluatively (you might be disposed to think blue things are good without your experience of blueness representing its object as good). Nor does it suffice if the experiences somehow track what is actually good or bad for the subject (which is the line that Cutter and Tye 2011 try out)—an experience might co-vary with what's good without its object appearing *as* good *to the subject*. My suspicion is that when we spell out what non-conceptual representation of value amounts to, we end up with a view that is *not* fundamentally an evaluativist one (as I'll argue in Section 3).[3]

Another worry is an old but good Humean one: how is it that (non-conceptual) representations of goodness or badness are inherently motivating in the way that valence is supposed to be? After all, the standard

---

[1] Mitchell's main argument for non-conceptualism is based on first-exposure affective experiences, such as one's first encounter with the sublime, which according to him feature evaluations that are not cognitively significant and which the subject herself consequently can't understand.

[2] Carruthers also suggests that "only states with nonconceptual content are phenomenally conscious" (2018, 664), so insofar as valenced affects are phenomenally conscious, their content must be nonconceptual. I'm agnostic on this point.

[3] Julien Deonna and Fabrice Teroni (2015) have recently developed an alternative evaluativist approach, according to which affective valence is accounted for by embodied evaluative *attitudes* towards non-evaluative contents. From my perspective, the key challenge to this type of view is making sense of the rationalizing role of affective experiences, since it is most naturally explained by appeal to their content.

view in philosophical psychology has it that representational states are not inherently motivating—their job is to tell us how things are, not provide the push (or guidance) in one direction or another (Anscombe 1957). Simply stipulating that they're part of an affective state or have non-conceptual content is no argument to the contrary. There are, to be sure, some who hold that *evaluative* representations can directly motivate. But this is a highly contentious claim, and again raises the question of whether what makes representations specifically evaluative is that they contain a non-cognitive component (e.g. Gibbard 2003, Ridge 2014).

1.3 Varieties of Imperativism

While the considerations I just mentioned are far from decisive, they do give us a good reason to look for an alternative to evaluativism. The leading intentionalist alternative is *imperativism*. To understand it, let's start with the difference between "The door is open" and "Open the door!" The traditional line is that the sentences have the same content but different force attached to them. But recently many have argued that we need to distinguish a difference in *content* here. Here's how Luca Barlassina and Max Hayward (2019, 6) characterize it:

Indicative Content:

(i)   Has the function of carrying information, for example, that p is the case;

(ii) Has truth conditions: it is true if p is the case and false if not;

(iii) The audience correctly uptakes it by forming a belief.

Imperative Content

(i)   Has the function of directing its addressee to do something, for example, to F;

(ii) Has satisfaction conditions: it is satisfied if and only if the addressee Fs;

(iii) The addressee correctly uptakes it by forming a motivation.

Various kinds of argument have been offered for the existence of imperative content (rather than just imperatival force attaching to propositional content). For example, Ruth Millikan argues that the proper function of some content-types, 'imperative intentional icons', is to produce certain effects, and that their content is the "last item of the series of things it is supposed to map onto and to produce" (1984, 100). Hector-Neri Castañeda (1975) holds that some utterances express 'practitions' instead of propositions, where practitions are thought contents that link an agent and action in a practical way (see also Chrisman 2016). Peter Hanks argues in a similar fashion that 'predicative propositions' and 'imperative propositions' involve combining properties with objects in different ways, which allows for distinguishing between indirect reports like "Jones told Smith that Smith will go to the store" and "Jones told Smith to go to the store" (2007, 150).

For the purposes of this chapter, I will henceforth simply assume that there are imperative contents and not just imperatival force, without committing to any of the above ways of cashing out this idea. This assumption opens up the possibility of an alternative intentionalist strategy: perhaps affective experiences feel the way they do in virtue of their imperatival content.

Why be an imperativist? Colin Klein (2015) begins with homeostatic sensations like thirst, hunger, and itching, which have as their biological function restoring some sort of bodily balance. They plausibly don't do this by informing us about the source of the imbalanced condition so as to inform potential deliberation. Rather, they function like a fire alarm does: they insistently tell us what to do—Drink! Eat! Scratch!—hogging our attention and interrupting other projects. Still, they're not mere reflexes: thirst isn't a stimulus to which you automatically respond to by drinking. In order to play just this kind of functional role, Klein argues, homeostatic sensations must have imperatival content and consequently a corresponding nagging phenomenal character. And he holds that much the same goes for pains, whose imperatival content gives them their *sensory* phenomenology.

Importantly for my purposes today, imperativism has also been proposed as an account of *valence*. The main argument for it appeals to the motivational role of valence:

1. The phenomenal character of an experience matches its intentional content.
2. Valenced phenomenal character is inherently motivating—when we take the experience at face value, we're motivated to act.
3. For taking an experience at face value to motivate us to act, the intentional content of the experience must be imperatival rather than indicative.

4. So, valenced phenomenal character consists (at least partly) in having imperatival content (stronger: affects have valence in virtue of their content containing a command).

Premises 1 and 2 are both widely accepted. For premise 3, imperativists rely on the sort of Humean considerations that I mentioned in criticizing evaluativism. For a content to be such that it directly motivates us when accepted or taken up, it must have satisfaction-conditions rather than truth-conditions. If we accept this, the 'pushy' phenomenology of valenced affects requires them to have imperatival content, possibly in addition to other kinds of content.

A number of different versions of imperativism have been proposed, in particular in the context of theories of pain. I'll introduce them by considering what they say about a situation in which you're in pain because you've twisted your ankle. According to *first-order imperativism about valence* defended by Manolo Martínez (2011), the pain sensation that you feel has two kinds of content. First, its *indicative* content says something like "There's damage to your ankle". Having this kind of content, according to him, accounts for the sensory phenomenal character of your ankle pain. Second, the sensation has *imperatival* content, which says something like "See to it that the damage in your ankle goes away!", and accounts for the negative affective valence of pain. This is a first-order view, because the valence-generating imperative is directed towards a non-mental state of affairs.

First-order imperativism has been subjected to various criticisms. Evaluativists, naturally enough, complain that it can't account for the reason-giving force of pain (Bain 2011), or variations in intensity (Cutter and Tye 2011). I'll come back to these points in Section 3. But it's worth noting that first-order views also face criticism within the imperativist camp. In particular, Luca Barlassina and Max Hayward level a number of charges against it. First, they hold that it is not sufficient for negative valence that experience contains a first-order imperative (2019, 10). For example, thirst tells us to drink, but mild thirst isn't unpleasant. I don't think this is a serious problem, however—saying that mild thirst is mildly unpleasant is not much of a bullet to bite. Second, however, Barlassina and Hayward hold that there can be valence without a world-directed imperative. Depression is unpleasant, but, they claim, according to best theories, it's characteristic of depression that "world-directed urges have disappeared" (2019, 10). And third, they claim that first-order internalist views haven't spelled out how to distinguish between imperatives that give rise to negative valence and those associated with positive valence. They point out that it won't do to say that negative imperative content "directs its addressee to stay clear from, or to avoid, or to get less of, something in the non-mental world" (2019, 11)—after all, agonizing hunger motivates us to get more food. One could say that hunger tells us to stop having an empty stomach—but, Barlassina and Hayward note, we need a principled basis for distinguishing between sensations whose contents are characterized by "Stop having an empty stomach!" and "Eat something!" Finally, they maintain that first-order imperativism can't explain why we should get rid of, say, unpleasant pain rather than damage, if the imperative concerns the latter. I'll address the last three problems at various points below, since my own view will be close to Martinez.

Higher-order imperativism, defended by Colin Klein, would avoid these problems. According to it, the unpleasantness of pain is instead "constituted by a second-order imperative directed toward the first-order sensation" (2015, 186). Here the content of the imperative can be glossed as "Don't have that sensation!" This type of view makes sense of the fact that the unpleasantness of pain motivates us to take painkillers, even though we know perfectly well that they won't help with damage to our ankle, for example. But it also has serious costs—for example, it's not plausible that a neutral sensation becomes unpleasant in virtue of a command to get rid of it, nor is it plausible that a command to get rid of a sensation is itself unpleasant (2015, 16–19). To avoid these issues, Barlassina and Hayward advocate instead what they call *reflexive imperativism*, according to which, roughly, the imperatives involved in unpleasant experiences tell us to get rid of the experience they're a part of, while other experiences are pleasant in virtue of containing imperatives to pursue more of the very same experience. I'll come back to this view in Section 3, but to foreshadow a little, its key weakness is that it is forced to give a strained explanation of the world-directed intentionality of affective experiences, unlike first-order imperativism.

2. Generalizing Imperativism about Valence

In this section, I'll begin to develop a generalized version of imperativism about valence that is intended to apply to all kinds of affective state. Put in its crudest terms, the view is that an experience has negative valence when it simultaneously presents things as being in a certain way and commands us to ensure that they won't be that kind of way.[4] Here is a more precise statement:

Relational Imperativism

An experience has positive (negative) valence for S when it has (a) indicative content p that represents an actual or possible state of affairs that bears on a (possibly novel) background concern of S and (b) subjectively authoritative imperatival content telling S to see to it that states of affairs relevantly like p will (won't) obtain in the future by engaging in some behaviour characteristic of the affect type.

I will argue that this kind of intentional content accounts for the inherently motivating phenomenal character of valenced affects, and respond to objections to it (mostly) in Section 3.

But first, I'll spell out my thesis in more detail. I'll illustrate it with the help of four kinds of negative affect:

- (e_1)   Pain: My ankle hurts.
- (e_2)   Sensory displeasure: I have the unpleasant experience of having bitten a rotten apple.
- (e_3)   Attitudinal displeasure: I'm displeased that Sweden beat Finland.
- (e_4)   Fear: I'm afraid of a bear in front of me on the path.

(I'll come back to moods and positive affects later.) Let's begin with the indicative content. It's become common to think that the felt aspect of fear is itself a *feeling towards* the bear, for example (Goldie 2000). The natural way to cash this out is to say that the affective experience itself has this state of affairs as its indicative content. It's part of the affective experience that things appear to you to be in a certain way—even if you don't believe they are that way (say, in the case of phantom pain in a limb you know you don't have). In the cases above, the appearances might be as follows:

- (a_1)   Pain: My ankle is damaged.

---

[4] Relational imperativism is thus parallel to those externalist views that hold that unpleasant experiences consist in a relational state of taking things to be in a certain way and intrinsically wanting them not to be that way (Jacobson 2019) and, in a different way, relational expressivist views about normative belief (Toppinen 2013, Schroeder 2013).

(a₂)   Sensory displeasure: There's a rotten taste in my mouth.

(a₃)   Attitudinal displeasure: Sweden beat Finland.

(a₄)   Fear: There's a bear poised to do something I really wouldn't like to me.

Note that some of these appearances concern the world, and some concern mental contents. In particular, sensory displeasures represent sensations (naturally enough). In each case, you could have the feeling even if the appearance isn't veridical.

In the case of valenced affective experience, the state of affairs represented by the experience must *matter* to the subject. Bearing in mind that it is at least conceptually possible for many sorts of creatures to have valenced experiences, it is best to construe the relevant sense of mattering as thinly as possible. I'll thus say that the indicative content engages with some *background concern* of the subject. By background concern I mean an open-ended standing desire in the broadest sense. It could be the biological drive to survive or avoid bodily damage, or it could be a fan's dispositional desire for her team to win, or endorsement of a moral standard. In my examples, the relevant concerns might be expressed as follows:

(bc₁)   Pain: May there be no bodily damage to me!

(bc₂)   Sensory displeasure: May I not have the taste of spoiled food in my mouth!

(bc₃)   Attitudinal displeasure: May the Finnish team do well!

(bc₄)   Fear: May I not get hurt!

The role of such background concerns in affect is most obvious when they differ among people—for most people in the world, it's neither here nor there whether Sweden beats Finland or not, so they have no affective response to such news. Because of such facts, psychologists working on emotion tend to emphasize the importance of usually automatic and non-conscious *appraisal* of goal-relevance for the generation of affect (e.g. Frijda 1986). Some, like Robert Roberts (2003) even hold that negative valence consists in appraisal of something as frustrating one's concerns, but this goes too far. First, non-conscious appraisal is not sufficient to account for valenced *phenomenal* character. This is not to say we can't have, say, negative emotions without realizing it—but insofar as such emotions are occurrent, they shape the horizon of our experience while escaping our attention, similar to the way stress functions (Haybron 2008). And it's not plausible that negative valence consists in consciously appraising something *as* concern-frustrating, as Deonna and Teroni (2020) observe. Second, *prior* concern or appraisal is not necessary for valence. Sometimes our (non-valenced) experiences explain why we have the concerns we do. For example, a first-time experience with spicy food may immediately yield a novel liking. I'll return to this soon when discussing subjective authority.

The second and distinctive kind of content for imperativism is the first-order, world-directed imperative. Recall here Martinez's characterization of the imperative in pain as "Don't have this bodily disturbance!" For the general case, it's too narrow to specify the target of the imperative as the indicated state of affairs itself—after all, it might well be an unrepeatable event that will in any case not occur again. It's thus better to cash out the imperative as "See to it that *the sort of thing* indicated in this experience won't obtain in the future!", where what counts as "the sort of thing" depends on the context. Note that contrary to Barlassina and Hayward's characterization of first-order views, the imperative doesn't just tell us to get less of *something*, but specifically refers to the indicative content of the experience. In their example of agonizing hunger, the indicative content is that we lack nourishment, and the imperative content tells us to see to it that we won't lack nourishment any more, even if we have to sacrifice a lot of other things. There's nothing arbitrary about this *relational* structure giving the experience negative valence.

Before giving examples, I want to emphasize, first, that the claim isn't that something verbalized along these lines is going through the subject's head. Rather, the formulation is meant to capture the satisfaction conditions of an experiential content that is itself non-conceptual in the sense that it doesn't require possessing a concept of the future, not to mention the concept of being indicated in experience, among others. Stipulating such contents is needed to capture the dynamics of experience and action—in the very simplest case, feeling bad in a certain way tends to motivate a certain type of action, which tends to make the bad feeling go away if successful. They should also make sense of the bodily action readiness characteristically associated with many valenced experiences. Second, my verbal character-ization is meant to give the *form* of the first-order imperative central to negatively valenced experience. On my view, many particular negative affects tell us to achieve this type of outcome in a particular way—after all, fear doesn't feel bad in the same way as anger, and motivates different behaviour when taken at face value. So I would suggest that pain tells you to see to it that the sort of bodily damage indicated by the experience won't obtain in the future *by protecting the damaged body part*, and fear tells you to see to it that the sort of state of affairs indicated in its content won't obtain *by seeking safety*. The specific actions they motivate may depend on the context and the agent's background beliefs.

An important aspect relational imperativism is the *authority* of the imperative for the subject. Pain or fear is more like a boss telling you what to do than like a passer-by making a request. What could be the source of such subjective and practical authority? Not, for example, that it would be unpleasant if we didn't do as commanded, since that assumes what we're trying to explain (Bain 2011). Fortunately, there is a candidate at hand: the background concern. When fear tells you to run away, it speaks *in the name of* your background concern to stay alive and unharmed. Less metaphorically, the suggestion is that our motivational and affective systems interact, so that only affects that link up in the right way with background motivation have valenced character (which is not to say affects that don't do so lack phenomenology altogether). As I noted above, this is compatible with experiences *generating* the motivation. It could be that the first time you taste spicy food, the key content of your experience can be verbalized as "There's a fiery sensation in my mouth; let me see to it that I have more sensations like this!" If this experience engages your motivational system, say by generating a (possibly short-lived) liking for this sort of thing, your experience will have positive valence, even if you didn't have a *pre-existing* concern that was satisfied by spicy sensations.[5]

One reason to adopt this model is that it makes good sense of the curious phenomenon of *pain asymbolia*, where people with certain sort of brain damage report feeling pain in response to certain stimuli, but lack any motivation to avoid it and deny that it's unpleasant. Nor do they act to avoid threats to their bodily integrity. Both Colin Klein (2015) and David Bain (2014) have proposed that pain asymbolia is best explained in terms of absent concern for the condition of one's body. Bain argues convincingly that what happens in such cases is that the lack of concern alters the phenomenal character of pain such that it is no longer unpleasant for the subject. He claims that imperativism can't explain "why not caring about one's bodily integrity should prevent pain's imperative content". Evaluativism, for its part, holds that if I lack concern for my body, I won't find the damage

---

[5] You might have a standing desire to eat food that tastes good, to be sure—but that couldn't explain why spicy food *tastes good* for you.

indicated by pain as bad for me, so it isn't unpleasant. However, if valenced character is linked with subjective authority of imperatives, which requires a background concern, imperativism also predicts that the asymbolics' pain is not unpleasant for them in virtue of the absent concern for their bodily integrity. It is, in fact, much more natural to link background concern with the authority of imperatives than lack of evaluation—if evaluation is straight representation, why would not caring about whether something happens entail that I don't think that it is *bad* for me? What would stop me from thinking "That's bad for me, but I don't care about it"? The imperativist account thus seems actually superior to the evaluativist one on this score.

With these considerations in mind, here's what the imperatival content of my examples might look like:

(i₁)   Pain: See to it that your ankle isn't damaged by protecting it!

(i₂)   Sensory displeasure: See to it that you will not have this sort of sensation in the future by avoiding what caused it!

(i₃)   Attitudinal displeasure: See to it that Sweden won't beat Finland in the future!

(i₄)   Fear: See to it that there won't be a bear poised to do to you something you really wouldn't like by seeking safety!

It is important here that it doesn't follow from an affect telling you to act in a certain kind of way that you will be motivated to act like that—your desires, plans, and beliefs might prevent the *conative uptake* of the imperative. Feelings don't necessarily motivate, even if the motivation is non-instrumental when it's there. And when there is conative uptake, the specific direction it takes depends on the subject's background beliefs—whether you rub the ankle that hurts or lift it in the air depends on what you think will help protect it. This is why it's a mistake to identify imperatival content with 'urges', if they're understood as motivational states. This is crucial for understanding attitudinal displeasure in imperativist terms, since it is often not possible to do anything about what displeases us (or what we regret or grieve). Knowing this, we may not be motivated to do anything either—though in some cases, we engage in a kind of magical thinking and are motivated to, say, yell at the TV as if it changed the way our team plays. This is all perfectly consistent with the displeasure telling us to change the way things are—indeed, the felt inability to respond to an experienced command does nothing to make us feel better.

So, the view holds that fear, for example, has a negatively valenced character in virtue of (a_4) *There's a bear poised to do something I really wouldn't like to me* and (i_4) *See to it that there won't be a bear poised to do something you really wouldn't like to you by seeking safety!*, when the latter has authority in virtue of (bc_4) *May I not get hurt!*, which (a_4) is appraised to (possibly) frustrate the way things are going. Before assessing the account, let's take a look at some positive affects as well. They pose a prima facie challenge for imperativism, since it has often been observed that positive emotions are typically less directly linked to specific actions than negative ones. Still, positive emotions do tell us to do something. The best way to cash it out seems to me to be along the lines of "Explore further possibilities for realizing or relishing this sort of thing in the future!" This type of content fits well with the broaden-and-build evolutionary rationale suggested by Barbara Fredrickson (2001) for positive emotion. In the ordinary case, positive feelings result from its seeming to us that things are going our way, so it's no surprise they don't call for taking things in a different direction. Rather, they tell us to let things be (and indeed prevent them from changing) and look around for more of the same at one or another level of abstraction. I've also included relishing in the content of the imperative, since sometimes further world-directed action directed at realizing the state of affairs is superfluous or impossible, but we can still engage in *mental action* of seeking ways to appreciate the situation in further ways.

Here's how some paradigm positive feelings look like from this perspective. Start with *sensory pleasure*. Suppose you bite into a ripe persimmon. The intentional content of your experience might be "There's a sweet taste on your tongue; explore further possibilities for this kind of taste in your mouth and attend to its characteristics!" (More generally, sensory pleasures call for more of the same sort of sensation by way of same sort of stimulation.) A paradigm *attitudinal pleasure* might be taken in your favourite team winning. Its content would be along the lines of "Your team won; [explore further possibilities for this kind of thing, and] attend to this fact!" As in attitudinal displeasure, the action directive in such cases is typically idle, since you neither can nor need do anything about the fact that pleases you. But you can pause and contemplate what happened, and perhaps bring it to the attention of others. *Joy* can be quite similar, though perhaps more intense, and calls for more energetic exploration of similar possibilities. And *interest* informs you that its object has so far aroused and satisfied a desire to know, and tells you to explore it further.

So far, I've set aside an important kinds of valenced experience, moods like (occurrent) anxiety, irritability, depression, tranquillity, and elation. (Note that while we sometimes use these terms for dispositional conditions, they clearly can also denote modes of consciousness.) They pose a prima facie challenge to first-order imperativism, since like positive emotions, they don't seem directly linked to action. Indeed, in some moods action doesn't seem possible, as in a kind of depression, and in others it doesn't seem necessary, as in tranquillity. Nevertheless, I think the present account has sufficient resources to explain what's going on. Say that I'm anxious about my coming move. The experience involves associating the move with some unspecific threats. It's negative in virtue of telling me to get rid of those unspecific threats. Since I don't know what to do about unspecific threats, I can't respond to such an imperative with specific motivation (if not with motivation to cancel the move altogether, which is not available if anxiety is more general). I can respond with bodily action readiness to fight or flee whatever comes my way, however, which is a typical sign of anxiety. In the case of some sorts of depression, to be sure, even such action readiness (as well as motivation) can be absent. Insofar as it is not simply a state of suppressed affect, it could be because depression represents us as pointlessly trying to do things that are not worth it, whatever we do, and tells us to see to it that we don't engage in further pointless activity. On the positive side, tranquillity has as its indicative content something like the thought that things are going all right without my interference. Applying the relational formula, the mood's imperative content tells me to see to it that this will be the case in the future and to engage in the mental action of appreciating the way they are right now. This, again, seems to have just the right motivational consequences: according to it, conative uptake of tranquillity motivates us not to mess up anything by interfering with it and to contemplate the niceness of our situation, so we hang back and smile.

Having filled in some details of relational imperativism, we're now in a position to tentatively evaluate it. Does imperatival content of the kind defended account for the phenomenal character of valenced affects? Some find it in general hard to believe that any imperatives would explain valence. Others think it is evident that they do—Martínez (2015b) says that "This is what disgust feels like: it feels like being compelled not to get polluted by disease-causing substances." Here introspection may yield different answers. This is a difficult question to adjudicate, since the rules of the game are not at all clear. That's why I have focused instead on the functional role of valenced character. And here generalized imperativism does seem to provide a plausible, nuanced picture of how both positive and negative affects are inherently if contingently motivating. If, say, interest tells you to explore its object (or the sort of thing its object is) further, it's easy to see why yielding to your interest in, say, a Lego set gets you to play with it and be on the lookout for more Lego sets, and consequently endlessly talk to your parents about getting new Lego sets. Sensory displeasure all on its own tends to motivate you to avoid the kind of food—or sound or texture—that caused it, if you conatively assent to what it tells you. And pain, among other things, gets us to avoid stepping on a hurt ankle. So, generalized imperativism seems to do a good job when it comes to how valence motivates us to engage with the world. But there are, of course, serious challenges to it, as we'll see next.

3. Objections and Replies

3.1 Objection 1: Imperativism Can't Explain How Affects Rationalize

One might grant that relational imperativism does a good job of explaining the motivational role of valence, but what about *rationalizing* action and judgment? One of the main arguments for evaluativism was that it can explain this—as Bain (2012) puts it, "unpleasant pains rationalise avoidance behaviour in virtue of presenting certain bodily states as bad". Carruthers suggests that felt badness is an element of the phenomenology of emotions in particular:

> When a bear looms out of the bushes while one is hiking (causing fear) it is the threatening aspect of the bear (its size, its claws) that seems bad. All of one's focus when afraid is generally outward-directed, targeted on the object of one's fear. [...] Negative valence represents the presence of the bear (or its threatening aspect) as bad.   (2018, 664–5)

Is there any way for imperativists to make sense of the rationalizing role of affects and their presentational phenomenology? I think so. The first step of the argument is reformulating the target in a way that doesn't beg any questions in favour of evaluativism. Consider, first, how Christine Korsgaard characterizes animal experience:

> We might suppose that when an antelope flees from a lion, she is afraid.
> But she need not think about the fact that she is afraid... Perhaps she just
> sees the lion as a danger, as a thing that is *to-be-fled*.
>
> (2018, my emphasis)

For Korsgaard, affective experiences involve what she calls *teleological perception* of our environment. Such perceptions suffice to rationalize flight just as well—or actually better—than a generic perception of badness (after all, it's a deliberation-inviting open question what to do with something bad). In emphasizing teleology in connection with emotions, Korsgaard joins up with a long tradition. Consider Sartre's description of pity or sympathy:

> I feel pity for Peter and I come to his aid. For my consciousness, one thing
> alone exists at that moment: Peter-having-to-be-aided. This quality of
> 'having-to-be-aided' is to be found in Peter.   (2004 [1936], 10)

I'm going to label the sort of appearance that Korsgaard and Sartre talk about an *affective practical seeming*. It is a species of non-doxastic appearance: it can affectively seem to us that things are in a certain way even if we don't have a corresponding belief (and even if we have an opposing one). This kind of seeming is what imperativists must explain to explain how valence rationalizes. Why is it that when we're afraid of something, it appears to us as something to be fled? To be precise, the datum isn't that affective practical seemings are somehow inherent in valence; rather, it suffices if imperativists can explain why experiences with imperatival content predictably give rise to affective practical seemings. This is important, because such seemings clearly couldn't *consist* in imperatives—they have a mind-to-world direction of fit.

What I want to argue is that relational imperativism offers a natural explanation of affective practical seemings, so that we don't need to be evaluativists to account for them. The story is simple and appeals to a widely recognized psychological mechanism of *projection*. The *locus classicus* for this kind of line is Hume's famous observation: "taste has a productive faculty, and gilding and staining all natural objects with the colours, borrowed from internal sentiment, raises in a manner a new creation." J.L. Mackie (1977) develops the view further, arguing that we have a tendency to see commands issued by socially accepted norms or purported divine authority as inhering in actions themselves, and Simon Blackburn

(1993) explains why projecting our attitudes in this manner serves useful purposes. For example, instead of focusing on what someone told me to do, I can focus on whether the thing itself really is to be done.

I argued above that when we have a valenced affective experience, it is as if we're being authoritatively told or invited to do something. If there is a psychological mechanism of projection, as there seems to be, it is predictable that such demands change the way our situation appears to us. For a parallel, consider the situation when an officer tells a private to load his gun. Directly, the order just concerns the action. But we can also ask how a horizon of practical possibilities with respect to the gun looks like to the private who accepts this order. The gun will appear to him as something *to-be-loaded* when he thinks about what to do. Similarly, then, if my fear has an indicative content (e.g. "that bear might attack me") that bears on my concern (e.g. for personal safety), and related authoritative imperative content (e.g. "see to it that sort of situation in which the bear might attack me won't obtain by fleeing it"), it will appear to me teleologically as something that summons me to leave the scene—as something *to-be-fled-from*, at a certain cost to other things I care about.

Suppose that imperativism can explain why valenced experiences (at least tend to) include affective seemings. The rest of the rationalization story is quickly told. As I look at the bear, it appears to me as something to-be-fled, and so as something I have reason to flee. From my perspective, this suffices to rationalize flight, or at least give rational support to the action, even if it is outweighed by other considerations. It is perhaps more interesting that this story also makes possible a kind of *reconciliation with evaluativist views*. After all, recall my worry about what it is to non-conceptually represent something as bad or good. Now we have a good candidate answer: perhaps it just consists in representing it as summoning less or more of the same sort of thing—something non-conceptually appears as bad to a certain degree in the light of an objectified imperative, if you will, saying that it is to be avoided at such-and-such cost. In that case, my view is compatible with some evaluativist accounts—but gives a further analysis of their central content.[6] This seems to me like a good further argument in favour of relational imperativism over evaluativism.

---

[6] This claim is obviously parallel to the claims that expressivists like Blackburn (1998) and Gibbard (2003) make regarding non-naturalism. There is a lot more to say on this point, but space will not allow me to do it here.

3.2 Objection 2: Imperativism Can't Make Sense of the Intensity of Valence

One standard objection to imperativism is that it can't capture the *intensity* of affective valence, the fact that some pains or fears feel worse than others (Cutter and Tye 2011). The argument is simple:

1. Some pains, fears, and hopes are more intense than others—intensity is a core feature of valenced phenomenal character.
2. Commands can't be more or less intense (even if they can be, e.g. more or less polite).
3. So, there is no way to explain intensity in terms of commands.
4. So, imperativism can't account for valenced phenomenal character.

Klein and Martinez (2019) have offered a model for rejecting premise 2. Their solution begins by stipulating that the content of an imperative isn't just its satisfaction conditions, but also includes a ranking of all possible worlds. They propose that like the Cold War era Autovon telephone system, whose calls included a signal indicating their relative priority (so that, for example, Flash calls rank their connection as more important than Routine calls, and Routine calls rank their connection as less important than Flash calls), pain commands, too, rank their satisfaction relative to each other. In the simplest case, imperative *i* is more forceful than imperative *j* when not only the ranking function of *i* ranks the worlds in which *i* is satisfied over those in which *j* is satisfied, but so does *j*'s ranking function—*j*, as it were, yields to *i*. (For a more sophisticated model, see Martínez 2015a.) Correspondingly, a more intense affect issues a more forceful command in this sense: "So, for example, one pain is more intense than another just in case their world-rankings agree that one should tend to the body part involved in the first pain at the expense of the one in the second."

My worry about this attempt is that this only works for very special cases, in which imperatives make mutual reference to one another (or third ones, as in their more sophisticated model). It is highly implausible that this would be a necessary condition for experienced imperatives, which very simple creatures can experience, after all. Fortunately, there seems to be a simpler imperativist account of intensity available. In their informal description of intensity, Klein and Martinez (2019, 15) refer to a difference in opportunity cost that one is willing to bear for more or less intense pain. What I want to propose is that that we can make use of the same notion in defining the force of a command. In simplest terms, one command is more forceful than another when it requires us to bear a greater opportunity cost to carry it out. Compare these three military orders:

(1) Hold the line!
(2) Hold the line at any cost!
(3) Hold the line at the cost of some but not nearly all of our soldiers dying!

All of these commands have the same satisfaction conditions: they are satisfied when the soldiers hold the line. But (2) is more forceful than (1), since (1) implicitly allows some leeway—it leaves open that there's some costs too large to bear to hold the line. Taken literally, (2) ranks all the worlds in which the imperative is satisfied higher than any of the worlds in which it is not satisfied, regardless of consequences for anything else. In reality, even orders like (2) express commands that are not absolute, so that there are some costs whose avoidance is in the spirit of the command even if it's not in the letter, such as destruction of all humanity. In rational armies, it's mutually understood that (1) expresses something like (3). Exactly which ranking function it expresses—which losses go too far—is a matter of context.

The difference between (2) and (3) comes out in the way they rank the following possibilities (for example):

(w_1) The soldiers hold the line & some soldiers die or are wounded (up to -5 utils).

(w_2) The soldiers hold the line & all soldiers die in the course of doing so (-10 utils).

(w_3) The soldiers don't hold the line & all soldiers escape damage (0 utils).

Assuming that each command tacitly also contains "Sacrifice as little as possible!", (2) ranks the possibilities as $w_1 > w_2 > w_3$. (3), in turn, imposes a ranking of $w_1 > w_3 > w_2$. In other words, (2) tells the addressee to hold the line even at the cost of -10 utils rather than fail to do so, in spite of the upside of there being no damage. (3) tells the address to hold the line at the cost of up to -5 utils rather than escape with no damage (or, for that matter, escape with minor damage), but it also ranks escaping to live to fight another day higher than everyone dying. Thus, (2) is more forceful than (3), because it demands to bear a higher opportunity cost for complying than (3) does. Here is a general formulation of the thesis:

Forcefulness of Imperatives
Imperative i is more forceful than imperative j iff i ranks worlds in which i is satisfied and the addressee loses up to u utils higher than worlds in which i is not satisfied and the addressee doesn't lose up to u utils, while j ranks worlds in which j is satisfied and the addressee loses up to v utils higher than worlds in j is not satisfied and the addressee doesn't lose up to v utils, and $u>v$.

Again, the contrast with Klein and Martinez's (2019) view is that my model doesn't assume that the ranking conditions of imperatives make reference to other imperatives, but just that imperatives at least implicitly tell us to bear some level of opportunity cost.

With the account of comparative forcefulness of imperatives in hand, accounting for the intensity of affect is straightforward: the more forceful the imperative, the more intense the affect. For example, the more forceful the order to explore more possibilities for the same sort of thing, the more positive the valence of the affect is. So, a more intense joy, for example, tells you to sacrifice more of other good things to explore more possibilities for the sort of thing indicated in its content than a less intense one.

3.3 Objection 3: Shooting the Officer

My version of imperativism, like first-order imperativism in general, holds that affects have valence in virtue of telling us to do something about our situation. But, a well-known objection goes, how could first-order imperatives explain how they also motivate and rationalize action that aims to do something about our experience itself? For example, why take painkillers? We do, after all, have reason to get rid of even non-veridical pains, like pain felt for a phantom limb, or pain caused by something that doesn't in any way damage us (Bain 2011).

This objection is evidently parallel to what is known as the Shooting the Messenger Objection to evaluativism. As Hilla Jacobson puts that objection in the context of pain, "If we endorse the suggestion that the first-order con-attitude which is constitutive of pain is cognitive, we are committed to a picture according to which each time we take a pain killer, we behave like the ruler who killed the messenger who brought him bad news" (2013, 519). If unpleasant pain just tells us that something is bad for us, it isn't clear why it would itself be bad, or why we'd have reason to get rid of it. Since imperativism holds that pain is more like an officer than like a messenger, I'll label the corresponding challenge the Shooting the Officer objection:

Shooting the Officer

1. According to relational imperativism, negative valence is constituted by a command to see to it that the indicated content won't obtain.
2. There is nothing non-instrumentally bad about being commanded to see to it that the sort of thing indicated in one's experience won't obtain, and no reason to get out of the state of being so commanded.
3. So, relational imperativism can't explain why we have reason to get rid of negative affective states by, e.g. taking painkillers.

My response to this objection takes the same form as Bain's response to Shooting the Messenger. The core problem with the argument is that the second premise begs the question against imperativism (as well as evaluativism). After all, suppose that imperativism is right. In that case, pain's unpleasantness just is a matter of having a certain sort of relational imperative content. Therefore, if unpleasantness is intrinsically bad for you, being commanded to see to it that the sort of thing indicated in one's experience won't obtain is intrinsically bad for you. Bain (2019) calls his corresponding case for evaluativism the "Leibniz's Law Argument". I see no reason why an imperativist couldn't use exactly the same line. Thus, the reason why unpleasant pain is bad, and why there's a reason to get rid of it, is that it is unpleasant.

There is, to be sure, a further problem for relational imperativism. Even if it is as a matter of fact non-instrumentally bad for you to undergo an unpleasant experience, that doesn't suffice to rationalize wanting to get rid of it, unless you also conceive of it *as* bad. Indeed, so far we still lack an explanation for why we even *want* to get rid of unpleasantness, as opposed to damage or danger or loss. This is indeed a challenge for first-order views. Barlassina and Hayward formulate the putative explanandum instructively by claiming that affective experiences have a *reflexive* motivational force: "The mental state which affective phenomenal character motivates us for or against is the very same mental state that has affective phenomenal character" (2019, 5). This is a key motivation for their own reflexive imperativism, according to which unpleasant sensations basically tell us to get rid of *themselves*, or more precisely the experience they're a part of, saying "Less of me!"

I think the right response begins by denying reflexive motivation. It's not the case, for example, that an unpleasant experience U motivates us to avoid or get rid of U itself, or even a state like U. Take a world-directed emotion like grief. It is surely a negative affective state. But it doesn't intrinsically motivate us to take grief-killers. What we wish for in the first instance is for the world to be different—for the loved one we lost to come back to us, and not just as a means to make ourselves feel good. Normally, of course, we don't think we can do anything, but people who believe in communion with the dead are sometimes motivated by grief to take part in seances. For a more mundane case, fear will again suffice—it tells us to flee, not to take a pill that gets rid of itself, even if one becomes available.[7] It may be less obvious that not even sensory pleasures or displeasures motivate us to pursue or avoid pleasures or displeasures. But that's the case nevertheless: the pleasure of eating a perfect strawberry doesn't motivate me to pursue more *pleasure*, but to *taste more strawberries*, that is, to seek more of the pleasing sensation.

This is not to say that we don't want to avoid unpleasant experiences. We surely do—but that's different from saying that unpleasantness itself tells us to get rid of itself. After all, we desire to avoid unpleasantness even when our experience is currently pleasant. It's rather a background concern that we (contingently) have (cf. Cutter and Tye 2014, who also offer a plausible evolutionary explanation). And it helps explain why we sometimes do have unpleasantness-directed motivation. Suppose I'm undergoing an unpleasant experience, such as a toothache. The toothache itself tells me to get my tooth fixed (and indeed motivates me to find a dentist). But I'm in addition also *attitudinally displeased* by the fact that I'm undergoing this unpleasant experience. As above, this attitudinal displeasure involves an indicative content, *I'm undergoing an unpleasant experience*, which I appraise as frustrating my background concern *Let me not undergo unpleasant experiences!* This background concern lends authority to the imperatival content *See to it that you won't be undergoing an unpleasant experience like this in the future!* (Note that unlike higher-order imperativism, the present account can avail itself of this direction of explanation, because we're not now trying

---

[7] For Barlassina and Hayward, valenced affects motivate us to pursue worldly aims as a *means* of improving our hedonic state, which serves as reward or punishment (Barlassina and Hayward 2019, 28). If that were the case, we should be motivated to take a pill that gets rid of fear if we believed it to be more effective means than fleeing the danger.

to explain unpleasantness, but motivation to get rid of it.) Conatively taking up *this* second imperative, then, explains my motivation to take painkillers. And because the unpleasantness of the experience will also appear to me as to-be-avoided as a result of projecting the authoritative imperative, it also subjectively rationalizes taking painkillers.

On this story, then, it's being displeased with the unpleasantness of pain that explains and rationalizes taking painkillers, not the unpleasantness itself. It's worth noting that though pretty much everyone has the background concern to avoid unpleasantness, we're not always displeased to undergo unpleasant experiences. This is the case with grief and fear (at least as long as it's felt to be functional). Even pain can belong in this category, say for athletes who want to push themselves Bradford 2020. Unlike reflexive imperativism, relational imperativism then predicts, correctly, that we lack inherent motivation to get rid of the experience (as opposed to changing the world).

4. Conclusion

It is not an unappealing idea that what it is to be conscious of something as valuable in a particular way is to experience it as inviting or calling for pursuit or engagement or exploration or consumption, depending on its nature. I've argued that the motivational and rational role of such experiences gets neatly explained, if we take them to involve both a representation of how things are now and a related subjectively authoritative command, which also account for the teleological appearances. Valenced affective experiences are in this sense primitive modes of consciousness of apparent value, and quite possibly crucial building blocks for conceptually articulated evaluative thought.[8]

References

Anscombe, G. E. M. (1957). *Intention*. Harvard University Press.

Bain, David (2011). The imperative view of pain. *Journal of Consciousness Studies* 18 (9–10): 164–85.

---

[8] The stimulus for writing this chapter came from some remarks made by David Bain in a conversation regarding my earlier and now superseded work on related issues (Kauppinen 2020). I'm also grateful to Uriah Kriegel, Lilian O'Brien, and Fabrice Teroni for written comments on earlier drafts, and Andrew Lee for some sharp challenges.

Bain, David (2012). What makes pains unpleasant? *Philosophical Studies* 166 (1): 69–89.

Bain, David (2014). Pains that don't hurt. *Australasian Journal of Philosophy* 92 (2): 305–20.

Bain, David (2019). Why take painkillers? *Noûs* 2017 (2): 462–90.

Barlassina, Luca (forthcoming). Beyond good and bad: reflexive imperativism, not evaluativism, explains valence. Thought.

Barlassina, Luca & Hayward, Max Khan (2019). More of me! Less of me!: reflexive imperativism about affective phenomenal character. *Mind* 128 (512): 1013–44.

Blackburn, Simon (1993). *Essays in Quasi-Realism*. Oxford University Press.

Blackburn, Simon (1998). *Ruling Passions*. Clarendon Press.

Bradford, Gwen (2020). The badness of pain. *Utilitas* 32 (2): 236–52.

Carruthers, Peter (2018). Valence and value. *Philosophy and Phenomenological Research* 97 (3): 658–80.

Castañeda, Hector-Neri (1975). *Thinking and Doing: The Philosophical Foundations of Institutions*. D. Reidel Pub. Co.

Chrisman, Matthew (2016). *The Meaning of 'Ought': Beyond Descriptivism and Expressivism in Metaethics*. Oxford University Press.

Cutter, Brian & Tye, Michael (2011). Tracking representationalism and the painfulness of pain. *Philosophical Issues* 21 (1): 90–109.

Cutter, Brian & Tye, Michael (2014). Pains and reasons: why it is rational to kill the messenger. *Philosophical Quarterly* 64 (256): 423–33.

Deonna, Julien & Teroni, Fabrice (2015). Emotions as attitudes. *dialectica* 69 (3): 293–311.

Deonna, Julien & Teroni, Fabrice (2020). Emotional experience: affective consciousness and its role in emotion theory. In U. Kriegel (ed.), *The Oxford Handbook of the Philosophy of Consciousness*, 102–23. Oxford University Press.

Evans, Gareth (1982). *The Varieties of Reference*. Oxford University Press.

Fredrickson Barbara L. (2001). The role of positive emotions in positive psychology. The broaden-and-build theory of positive emotions. The American Psychologist 56 (3): 218–226.

Frijda, Nico H. (1986). *The Emotions*. Cambridge University Press.

Gibbard, Allan (2003). *Thinking How to Live*. Harvard University Press.

Goldie, Peter (2000). *The Emotions: A Philosophical Exploration*. Oxford University Press.

Hanks, Peter W. (2007). The content–force distinction. *Philosophical Studies* 134 (2): 141–64.

Haybron, Daniel M. (2008). *The Pursuit of Unhappiness: The Elusive Psychology of Well-Being*. Oxford University Press.

Heathwood, Chris (2007). The reduction of sensory pleasure to desire. *Philosophical Studies* 133 (1): 23–44.

Helm, Bennett W. (2002). Felt evaluations: a theory of pleasure and pain. *American Philosophical Quarterly* 39 (1): 13–30.

Jacobson, Hilla (2013). Killing the messenger: representationalism and the painfulness of pain. *Philosophical Quarterly* 63 (252): 509–19.

Jacobson, Hilla (2019). Not only a messenger: towards an attitudinal-representational theory of pain. *Philosophy and Phenomenological Research* 99 (2): 382–408.

Kauppinen, Antti (2020). The world according to suffering. In D. Bain, M. Brady, and J. Corns (eds), *The Philosophy of Suffering*, 19–36. Routledge.

Klein, Colin (2015). *What the Body Commands: The Imperative Theory of Pain*. MIT Press.

Klein, Colin & Martínez, Manolo (2019). Imperativism and pain intensity. In David Bain, Michael Brady, & Jennifer Corns (eds), *The Philosophy of Pain: Unpleasantness, Emotion, and Deviance*, 13–26. Routledge.

Korsgaard, Christine M. (2018). *Fellow Creatures: Our Obligations to the Other Animals*. Oxford University Press.

Levy, Dino J. & Glimcher, Paul W. (2012). The root of all value: a neural common currency for choice. *Current Opinion in Neurobiology* 22 (6): 1027–38.

Mackie, John L. (1977). *Ethics, Inventing Right and Wrong*. Penguin Books.

Martínez, Manolo (2011). Imperative content and the painfulness of pain. *Phenomenology and the Cognitive Sciences* 10 (1): 67–90.

Martínez, Manolo (2015a). Pains as reasons. *Philosophical Studies* 172 (9): 2261–74.

Martínez, Manolo (2015b). Disgusting smells. *Journal of Consciousness Studies* 22 (5–6): 191–200.

Mendelovici, Angela (2018). *The Phenomenal Basis of Intentionality*. Oxford University Press.

Millikan, Ruth G. (1984). *Language, Thought, and Other Biological Categories*. MIT Press.

Mitchell, Jonathan (2020) [2018]. On the non-conceptual content of affective-evaluative experience. *Synthese* 197: 3087–111.

Pautz, Adam (2010). Do theories of consciousness rest on a mistake? *Philosophical Issues* 20 (1): 333–67.

Ridge, Michael (2014). *Impassioned Belief.* Oxford University Press.

Roberts, Robert C. (2003). *Emotions: An Essay in Aid of Moral Psychology.* Cambridge University Press.

Sartre, Jean-Paul (2004) [1936]. *The Transcendence of the Ego: A Sketch for a Phenomenological Description.* Routledge.

Schroeder, Mark (2013). Tempered expressivism. In Russ Shafer-Landau (ed.), Oxford Studies in Metaethics, Volume 8, 283–314. Oxford University Press.

Smuts, Aaron (2011). The feels good theory of pleasure. *Philosophical Studies* 155 (2): 241–65.

Tappolet, Christine (2016). *Emotions, Value, and Agency.* Oxford University Press.

Teroni, Fabrice (2020). Valence, bodily (dis)pleasures and emotions. In David Bain, Michael Brady, & Jennifer Corns (eds), *Philosophy of Suffering*, 103–22. Routledge.

Toppinen, T. (2013). Believing in expressivism. In Russ Shafer-Landau (ed.), *Oxford Studies in Metaethics, Volume 8*, 252–82. Oxford University Press.

Tye, M. (1995). *Ten Problems of Consciousness: A Representational Theory of the Phenomenal Mind.* MIT Press.

IV
HISTORY OF PHILOSOPHY
OF MIND

13

From Known to Knower

Affinity Arguments for the Mind's
Incorporeality in the Islamic World

Peter Adamson

In his *magnum opus*, the *Platonic Theology*, the Renaissance philosopher
Marsilio Ficino provides an avalanche of arguments for the incorporeality of
soul. One of them is, he says, "an argument of the Arabic Platonists
(*Platonicorum Arabum sententia*)."[1] The gist of it is that what we grasp
with the mind, or intellect, is a "universal form," also called "intelligible form
or species." If the mind were in the body and thus an extended and divisible
entity, then the mind's object would also have to be extended and divisible.
But such an intelligible form cannot be extended or divisible. Therefore, the
human mind is immaterial. Ficino's source is not far to seek. The "Arabic
Platonist" in question is Avicenna (Ibn Sīnā, d. 1037), who presented this
argument in his *Healing* (*al-Shifā'*). This is shown by the development of
Ficino's proof, which like Avicenna's goes on to rule out the possibility that
the intelligible form is in the mind the way a point is in a line. The goal here
is to answer a potential counterexample in which something indivisible does
reside in something divisible.

To the obvious objection that the mind can know about corporeal things,
not only about universal intelligibles, Avicenna would respond that this is
not, strictly speaking, true. Of course humans have the capacity to grasp
bodily things, things that are particular rather than universal. But it is not in
virtue of having a mind (in Arabic *'aql*, corresponding to Greek νοῦς and
Latin *intellectus*) that we do this. Rather, we possess other capacities like
sensation, imagination, and memory, which we use to deal with corporeal
and particular things. In Avicenna's view, the mind depends on these

---

[1] For the translation quoted here and the Latin text, see Allen and Hankins 2001–6, vol. 2,
book 8, ch. 4.

Peter Adamson, *From Known to Knower: Affinity Arguments for the Mind's Incorporeality in the Islamic World* In:
Oxford Studies in Philosophy of Mind Volume 1. Edited by: Uriah Kriegel, Oxford University Press (2021).
© Peter Adamson. DOI: 10.1093/oso/9780198845850.003.0013

inferior powers in order to do its work, but it only arrives at properly intellectual knowledge by freeing the object of its thought from "extraneous" features that tie the object to body and make it particular instead of universal.

He illustrates this with an example in another of his most important treatises, *Pointers and Reminders* (*al-Ishārāt wa-l-tanbīhāt*):[2]

> A thing is an object of sense-perception when it is observed. Then, it becomes an object of the imagination after it is absent, by having its form represented inwardly, as when you see Zayd, for instance, but then when he is absent from you, you imagine him. Then he is an object of intellect (*maʿqūl*) when on the basis of Zayd, for instance, the idea (*maʿnā*) of human is conceptualized, which also exists for other [humans]. When he is an object of sense-perception, he is covered up with things extraneous to his essence (*māhiyya*) which, when eliminated, have no impact on the core (*kunh*) of his essence, for instance location, position, quality, size, as they are now. If one supposed them to be exchanged for others, this would have no impact on the true nature (*ḥaqīqa*) of the essence of his humanity... The interior imagination (*al-khayāl al-bāṭin*) imagines it together with those accidents, being unable to abstract it from them absolutely... As for the intellect, it is able to abstract the essence that was surrounded by extraneous attachments that render it individual.

In this concise presentation of his epistemology, Avicenna explains that we first grasp particular objects like Zayd through sensation. We might, for instance, see Zayd standing in the market wearing a white shirt. Subsequently we can use the imagination (*al-mutakhayyila*) to, as we might put it, "call Zayd to mind." But in fact mind has nothing to do with it, according to Avicenna. When we *imagine* Zayd we are still entertaining the idea of a particular man, even if we change some of the specifics that accidentally occur to him, like if we now picture him standing in a forest wearing a black shirt. The mind or intellect, by contrast, uses "abstraction (*tajrīd*)" to get at the essential nature of Zayd, which is simply humanity. This is an intelligible object that is universal, as all humans share one and the same essence.

---

[2] For the Arabic, see Dunyā 1957–60. Translations in Goichon 1951, Inati 2014. The passage is at *Ishārāt* 3.8, 367–70 in the Dunyā edition. This and all other translations in the chapter are my own unless otherwise noted.

Nearly every aspect of this account is a matter of controversy among scholars of Avicenna's thought.[3] Fortunately though, the main point we need for what follows is not contentious. This is that the mind only grasps abstracted, universal objects like humanity as opposed to cognitive content that is tied inextricably to particular objects, whether these be actual or possible. This has a number of consequences for Avicenna's philosophy more generally. For instance, it underlies his notorious claim that God, being purely immaterial and intellectual, does not know particulars as such. As I have argued elsewhere, this is hardly surprising since humans do not *know* particulars as such either, at least not if we are talking about intellectual knowledge.[4] As already explained, we use embodied capacities like sensation and imagination to do that.

Another implication is teased out in the argument mentioned by Ficino. To establish that the human soul is an immaterial substance, Avicenna works backwards from the object of intellectual knowledge to the subject of that knowledge. Since we know that the object is abstract in character, we must assume that the mind in which this object resides is incorporeal. For, if the power by which the object is grasped were a bodily one, then it would "individualize" the known object in knowing it. The intuition here is a fairly straightforward one. Physical things like a red apple instantiate quiddities like appleness and redness in a particular way. So if we want the mind to have genuinely universal thoughts, the mind had better not be a physical thing.

While the details are distinctive to Avicenna, the general strategy is not. To the contrary, philosophers in the Islamic world frequently had recourse to what I will call "affinity arguments," in which the nature of the knower is assumed to correspond to the nature of the known. Thus the incorporeality of the mind is established on the basis of the incorporeality of its object. For the sake of context and comparison, I will look briefly at a few other examples below before returning to Avicenna and the criticisms faced by his version of the affinity argument in post-Avicennan philosophy. These criticisms exemplify the fact that later philosophy in the Islamic world, despite being generally unknown in the European and North American philosophical circles, sometimes comes closer to capturing modern-day

---

[3] Particular controversy concerns the role of abstraction and how our dependence on sensation fits with Avicenna's notorious invocation of an "active intellect" in his epistemology. On this, see, for instance, Hasse 2001, McGinnis 2007, D'Ancona 2008, Gutas 2012.

[4] See Adamson 2005. For subsequent studies of this issue, see, e.g., Nusseibeh 2009, Benevich 2019, Zadyousefi 2019.

intuitions than did the more Aristotelian philosophical tradition that preceded it. Indeed, we should admit here at the outset that the fundamental assumption of the affinity arguments will probably strike most readers as having little intuitive appeal. Why would we need to think that the mind must somehow be similar to its object in nature? Yet as we're about to see, this very assumption was a persistent one, with roots in antiquity and widespread acceptance for one and a half millenia of philosophy. It is thus instructive to see why so many philosophers endorsed it, as if it were just obvious, and to learn how that intuition was questioned and ultimately rejected—something that seems to have happened in the Eastern Islamic world before it happened in Europe.

1. Affinity Arguments

As some readers will already have guessed, my use of the phrase "affinity argument" alludes to a passage in Plato's *Phaedo*. This passage would not have been a direct inspiration for Avicenna, but it does begin a tradition of arguing in this way for the soul's incorporeality. Plato has Socrates set out a distinction between "two kinds of beings, the visible and the invisible (δύο εἴδη τῶν ὄντων, τὸ μὲν ὁρατόν, τὸ δὲ ἀιδές)" (79a6–7). To which of these kinds, asks Socrates, should the soul be assigned? To the invisible, of course, firstly on the straightforward grounds that we can't see it with our eyes, and secondly on the more contentious grounds that:

> When the soul investigates by itself it passages into the realm of what is pure, ever existing, immortal and unchanging, and being akin (συγγενής) to this, it always stays with it whenever it is by itself and can do so; it ceases to stray and remains in the same state as it is in touch with things of the same kind, and its experience then is what is called wisdom (φρόνησις).[5]

Since the soul is "more like and more akin (ὁμοιότερον καὶ συγγενέστερον)" (79e1) to unchanging and divine things, it will itself be indestructible like they are. Of course the goal of the proof is to show that the soul is immortal, but towards that end Socrates seeks to establish that it is incorporeal. This is

---

[5] *Phaedo* 79d1–7, trans. G.M.A. Grube.

to rule out the possibility that the soul is a physical substance, perhaps a subtle one that could blow away with the wind upon death (78d).

In Aristotle's *De anima* we get a rather different argument intended to show that the mind does not use a bodily organ. Aristotle does not here argue, as Plato had done, that the mind must be a non-physical entity because it knows non-physical things. Instead, he argues that if the mind were "mixed with the body ($\mu\epsilon\mu\hat{\iota}\chi\theta\alpha\iota\ \tau\hat{\omega}\ \sigma\acute{\omega}\mu\alpha\tau\iota$)" (429a25), the properties of its organ would block it from coming to know those properties. The idea is that if the mind's organ were, for instance, hot, then the mind would already be actually hot. But it should begin by being only potentially hot, because it is in the nature of the mind to be only potentially, not actually, all things before it thinks about them (429a24). As I say, this is not the same as the affinity argument we found in Plato. One might even be tempted describe it as a *dis*-affinity argument, since the gist is that the mind must be unlike its object: in itself it cannot already have the properties of its object.

It would, however, be more accurate to say that Aristotle here appeals to the idea of *merely potential affinity* between the mind and its objects.[6] Aristotle in fact goes so far as to say that the mind actually "becomes the various things ($\H{\epsilon}\kappa\alpha\sigma\tau\alpha\ \gamma\acute{\epsilon}\nu\eta\tau\alpha\iota$)" it thinks once it knows them in actuality (*De anima* 429b6–7). That claim could be said to fill a gap in Plato's affinity argument. The intuition invoked by Plato was a widespread one in pre-Aristotelian philosophy, as Aristotle himself notes: "like knows like ($\gamma\iota\nu\acute{\omega}\sigma\kappa\epsilon\sigma\theta\alpha\iota\ \tau\hat{\omega}\ \acute{o}\mu o\acute{\iota}\omega\ \tau\grave{o}\ \H{o}\mu o\iota o\nu$)" (*De anima* 404b17–18). Thus both Empedocles and Plato himself, in the *Timaeus*, held that the soul must be made up of the same elements as the things known by soul, as otherwise it would impossible for soul to know them.[7] Aristotle takes himself to have improved on these accounts by explaining why, and in what sense, soul must have an affinity to the things it knows. It must be sufficiently like them that it can actually become them.

As we'll see, this idea will still be central in affinity arguments given by thinkers of the Islamic world. So, too, will be the contrast between particulars and universals, another Aristotelian innovation. One context in which Aristotle invokes this new distinction is in the epistemology laid out in the

---

[6] A further argument is that the consideration of that which is "intensely intelligible ($\sigma\varphi\acute{o}\delta\rho\alpha\ \nu o\eta\tau\acute{o}\nu$)" makes the mind more acute thereafter, whereas experiencing intense sensible objects, like colors or smells, has the reverse effect (429b1–4). Avicenna uses this in the same chapter as his affinity argument, *Soul* 5.2, at 219 in the 1959 Rahman edition.

[7] See, further, Diels 1879, 499, and 502 for the application of the idea to thinking ($\varphi\rho o\nu\epsilon$an) as well as sense-perception. For commentary on this evidence, see Sedley 1992.

Posterior Analytics. There Aristotle laid down that knowledge in the strict and proper sense—the sense presumably involved when we use the intellect—concerns what is eternal and what is universal, the latter being ungraspable by sensation (see *Posterior Analytics* 1.8, 75b21–26; 1.31, 87b28–35).[8]

One could easily write a paper, or even a book, about the echoes of these ideas in later ancient philosophers, who were much concerned to fuse the accounts of the *De anima* and *Posterior Analytics* into a single theory and then harmonize the results with the epistemology of Plato. But as this chapter concerns the Islamic world, let us skip ahead to uses of the affinity argument among prominent *falāsifa*, that is, devotees of Hellenic philosophy who were the heirs of that syncretic, late ancient project. The first *faylasūf* was al-Kindī (d. after 870), who lived in ninth-century Iraq and was closely linked to the caliphal family there. In an epistle *On the Intellect*, he makes the Aristotelian point that "when [the soul] unites with the intellectual form, it and the intellectual form are not distinct . . . when the intellectual form unites with it, it and the intellect are one and the same thing, subject and object of intellection."[9] But he also echoes the presuppositions of the Platonic affinity argument when he says that forms "are of two types," one material and sensible, the other immaterial and grasped by intellect.[10] The clear implication is that the soul, or at least its intellective aspect, is also immaterial. This is not drawn out explicitly in *On Intellect* but the point is made elsewhere in the Kindian corpus.[11]

---

[8] For these constraints, see the classic paper, Burnyeat 1981. For the reception of this aspect of Aristotle's epistemology in the Islamic world, see Adamson 2007a.

[9] *On the Intellect* §5; all translations of al-Kindī are taken from Adamson and Pormann 2012.

[10] *On the Intellect* §3.

[11] As, for instance, at *On Recollection* §VII.1 ("intellect and soul are both incorporeal . . . the soul is one of the forms of the intellect"), *That there are Incorporeal Substances* §6 ("the soul is the intellectual form"), and *On Sleep and Dream* §VIII.4. Plato's affinity argument is also recalled in the following passage at *Discourse on the Soul* §II.3: "When this soul . . . is separated from the body, it knows all that is in the world, and nothing can hide anything from it. This is indicated by a quotation from Plato where he says that many virtuous ancient philosophers had freed themselves from the world, and no longer attached any importance to sensory things. After they had withdrawn from [this world] by contemplating and investigating the true nature of things, knowledge about the invisible was revealed to them." Note here especially the reference to invisible objects of cognition. See also *On Sleep and Dream* §VII.3: "the soul is the place of all sensible and intellectual things . . . Plato said this because all things that are known are either sensible or intelligible, and the soul has the ability to perceive both the intelligibles and the sensibles. He used to say that the soul senses, i.e., that it perceives the objects of sensation in their essence, and that it engages in intellection, i.e., that it perceives the objects of intellection in their essence."

Al-Fārābī (d. 950) also wrote an epistle *On the Intellect*, which gets us closer to Avicenna's version of the affinity argument. Like Avicenna after him, he uses the idea of abstracting forms from sensible objects, forms which then become immaterial intelligibles for the intellect:

> Before they become intelligibles in actuality, the intelligibles in potentiality are forms in parcels of matter (*mawādd*) that are outside the soul, but when they become intelligibles in actuality, then as such their existence is not the one they have as forms in parcels of matter.[12]

He goes on to explain that features accidental to the known object itself, like place, time, position, and "corporeal qualities (*kayfiyyāt jismāniyya*)" are removed from the object once it is made actually intelligible, that is, once it is actually in the mind. This strongly suggests that the intellect is incorporeal, but al-Fārābī does not draw that inference yet. It is only later in the treatise that he elaborates on Aristotle's point that the intellect has no bodily organ:

> For its subsistence, [the intellect] has no need that the body serve as matter for it, nor does it need, for any of its actions, to turn to help from an action of a psychological power in the body, nor to use any bodily organ at all.[13]

Strictly speaking this goes only for the "acquired intellect," which is al-Fārābī's designation for the human mind when it is considering the intelligibles it has already learned through the process of abstraction. For the initial abstraction of an object of knowledge on the basis of external sensible things, the mind does of course depend on the body, since it could not do this without sensory organs.

We might say that here al-Fārābī gives us the premises needed for an affinity argument in favor of the intellect's incorporeality, and also states the conclusion, without explicitly using the premises to establish that conclusion. For this we can again jump ahead chronologically, to a thinker who is actually later than Avicenna but still in sympathy with the older, more faithfully Aristotelian approach of al-Fārābī. This is Averroes (Ibn Rushd, d. 1198), known in the Latin tradition as "the Commentator" for his extensive and painstaking exegesis of Aristotle—a project he carried out

---

[12] Bouyges 1948, 16. See also the partial translation of the letter in Hyman and Walsh 1983, 215–21.
[13] *Risāla fī-l ʿAql*, 31–2.

even as thinkers of the Islamic heartlands in the East were losing interest in philosophy translated from Greek, and focusing their attention on Avicenna instead.[14] Averroes' most notorious teaching was that there is a single potential or "material" intellect shared by all humankind.[15] This doctrine was much debated in Latin medieval and Renaissance philosophy and has been the subject of a prodigious amount of nuanced scholarship in more recent times.[16] Here I would simply like to point out that it is, among other things, an application of the affinity argument.

Indeed, in the relevant section of his *Long Commentary on the De Anima*, Averroes pulls together many the ideas we have just surveyed to reach his surprising result about the unity of the intellect.[17] He is much impressed by the aforementioned proof in which Aristotle sought to establish that the mind needs no bodily organ. In its boundless capacity to receive *all* forms, the mind is like prime matter, the pure potentiality that underlies physical objects. The difference is that, whereas matter takes on form so as to become some *particular* thing, the mind becomes something *universal*. As Avicenna reasoned, the mind would render its objects particular if it were material or bodily:

> Prime matter receives diverse forms, that is, individual and particular forms, while this [nature, *sc.* the material intellect] receives universal forms. From which it is apparent that this nature is not a determinate particular (*aliquid hoc*), nor a body, nor a bodily power. For if it were so, then it would receive forms inasmuch as they are diverse and particular.
>
> (388)

What he means by "diverse forms (*formas diversas*)," I take it, is multiple forms of the same species, like the distinct forms of humanity in Zayd, ʿAmr, and Socrates. It is matter that differentiates these humans who share the

---

[14] For an attempt to place this endeavor in its historical context, see Di Giovanni 2018.

[15] Here one should be aware that the designation "material" for this kind of intellect is metaphorical: as we'll see Averroes say, it is like matter in that it can take on all forms, but it is not actually made up of matter. Thus, apparent paradox notwithstanding, Averroes would say that the material intellect is immaterial.

[16] See, for instance, Davidson 1992; Taylor 1998 and 2013; Black 1999; Wirmer 2008, 287–409.

[17] The *Long Commentary* is lost in Arabic apart from fragments, but extant in Latin. Cited by page number from the edition in Crawford 1953. For an English translation, with very helpful introduction, see Taylor 2009, from which I quote with occasional alterations.

same nature. The mind, by contrast, receives the form as a universal through the abstractive process already described by al-Fārābī.

But unlike al-Fārābī and Avicenna, Averroes thinks that there is only one potentiality for this reception of the universal intelligible, which is shared in common by all humans. For, if the mind is potentially its object of knowledge and knows only when it becomes that object, then the mind must have a character that matches that object. Since the object is unique and universal—there is only one intelligible form of humanity, for instance—the potential mind, too, must be unique and universal. That there is, indeed, only one universal form is proven by pointing to the fact that when one person teaches another about a universal idea, the teacher and student must be grasping exactly the same thing (412). Of course the teacher's *experience* of understanding this thing is not the same as the student's, but this is because the teacher experiences the intellective activity as connected to the use of forms in her own imagination, which are different from those in the student's imagination (405–6). That difference is made possible by the fact that, unlike intellect, imagination *is* a bodily power, seated in the brain. So long as a material subject for the cognition is in play, we are always dealing with particular and not universal forms. So if the classroom topic is the nature of humanity, for instance, the teacher will be drawing on her sense-experiences and memories of humans, the student on his. But the understanding of universal humanity is one and the same for both of them, indeed for everyone who understands it.

As Averroes notes, the affinity argument had been used by predecessors like al-Fārābī and Avicenna to prove the uniqueness of the so-called "agent intellect," a superhuman mind that somehow interacts with the human mind to facilitate our understanding of universal intelligibles (the notoriously abstruse source text is Aristotle, *De anima* 3.5). This permanently actual source of understanding is identical with all the intelligible forms. Since there is only one set of such forms, there can be only one agent intellect. Thus Averroes' innovation is really just to extend this same reasoning to the "material" intellect, that is, the human capacity for understanding. He says with some asperity that it is simply inconsistent to assert the unity of the agent intellect, but not the material intellect, given that the use of the affinity argument is entirely parallel:

> The marvel is how they all concede this demonstration to be true with reference to the agent intellect, but don't agree when it comes to demonstrating the material intellect, even though the cases are entirely similar, so

that what one admits in one cases should be admitted in the other too. We are able to know that the material intellect must be unmixed on the basis of judgment and apprehension. For, because we make a universal judgment in virtue of it concerning things that are infinite in number...the consequence is that it is an unmixed power.[18]   (441–2)

"Unmixed," that is, with body. It is an immaterial capacity, not possessed by one human at a time but a single capacity common to all humans, in keeping with the universality of the objects towards which the capacity is directed.

This line of argument faces an obvious objection: why can't I have a particular idea, one that is in my mind and not yours, but that is an idea *about* something universal? That would allow a mismatch between subject and object, thus undermining the use of an affinity argument. The objection sounds plausible. Think, for instance, of the way that a particular word uttered, or written on a piece of paper, can have a universal meaning. Why not say that the same can happen with an idea in the mind? But when medieval critics of Averroes made just this point it did not convince his adherents. An excellent example can be found in another Italian Renaissance thinker, Agostino Nifo, who unlike the aforementioned Marsilio Ficino was a staunch proponent of Averroes. In a treatise on the intellect, he raised as an objection against the Commentator that the intellect knows universals through "species," what we might nowadays call "representations." In fact Nifo uses this latter term himself when he states the objection: the species "are singular in their existence, but universal by virtue of their signification, designation, and representation (*in significando ac annuendo repraesentandoque*)."[19]

Against this Nifo simply reasserts Averroes' position, including the analogy drawn between the potential intellect and prime matter:

The potential intellect is the matter of the intelligibles, as prime matter is the matter of sensible [forms], differing only by virtue of [their] universal and particular modes of reception, as Averroes said.[20]

---

[18] On the idea that the material intellect can grasp an infinity of things in a simple act of intellection that has universal force, see Bouyges 1930, 579, translated at van den Burgh 1954, 358.

[19] Translation from Engel 2015, 502, citing Spruit 2011, 444.

[20] Translation from Engel 2015, citing Spruit 2011, 521. As Engel points out, Nifo later goes on to distance himself from this position and accept the *species* theory, but it is not clear how sincere this is on his part.

For Nifo the intellect can "immediately access (*immediate attingunt*)" the universal intelligibles only by *becoming* those intelligibles, as Aristotle had said. Averroes had already suggested an argument against distinguishing the intellect from its object, namely that it would lead to a regress whereby the intellect would need a further act of intellection to grasp the second object (the representation) by which it is trying to grasp its primary object, and so on (435). And crucially, at least from Averroes' point of view, this non-representational account has Aristotle on its side, since we read in the *De anima* that when we understand something, "the understanding in actuality is the same as the thing (τὸ δ' αὐτό ἐστιν ἡ κατ' ἐνέργειαν ἐπιστήμη τῷ πράγματι)" (431a1).

2. Avicenna and his Critics

Let us now return to the argument of Avicenna mentioned in Ficino's *Platonic Theology*. As already mentioned, it is found in the treatise on soul within Avicenna's enormous *Healing*.[21] Avicenna's approach differs from what we have seen in al-Kindī, al-Fārābī, and Averroes in that he focuses on the idea of indivisibility.[22] It is above all in being indivisible that the mind has an affinity to its objects. If the mind's activity were realized in the body or a bodily organ then its object would be divided along with the bodily seat of that activity. As Avicenna puts it, the object would "become imaginative, not intelligible" (212.5). Admittedly, intelligible objects are in a sense divisible. For instance, a species can be "divided" into its genus and differentia (e.g., *human* into *animal* and *rational*). But this is not the sort of divisibility we find in the body, because body is subject to *indefinite* division. If, as with the body, one could divide an intelligible into parts and then divide again, and again, without limit, then we would violate a finding of logic, namely that "the essential genera and differences for a thing are not potentially infinite" (212.14–15). Rather, the intelligible object must be grasped as "a certain unity that is undivided" (215.17.18).[23]

---

[21] For the Arabic text, see Rahman 1959, §§5.2, 210–14. I am grateful to Tommaso Alpina for making available to me his draft translation of this chapter.

[22] Cf., Aristotle's observation, at *De Anima* 430a26, that intellection cannot err when it is concerns "indivisible" things (τῶν ἀδιαιρέτων νόησις).

[23] Cf., *Ishārāt* 407.5–408.3: "there are intelligibles that are one in actuality, and grasped intellectually insofar as they are one. So they are grasped intellectually only insofar as they are undivided. Therefore it cannot be inscribed in something that is spatially (*bi-waḍʿ*) divided, but every body, and every power in a body, is divided."

This gives us the premises necessary for Avicenna's own affinity argument, which is set out most succinctly in the following passage:

> 214.1–5: If it is impossible that the intelligible form be divided, or inhere at the indivisible extreme of magnitudes [that is, in an unextended point], but it doubtless has some recipient in us, then clearly we may conclude that the subject (*maḥall*) of the intelligibles is a substance that is not a body (*jawhar lā bi-jism*), nor is what we have that attains them a power in a body. For otherwise, whatever applies to divisible bodies would apply to [that power], with the various absurdities following from this. Instead, what we have that attains the intelligible form is a non-bodily substance. (*jawhar ghayr jismānī*)

The things that "apply" or "attach" (*yalḥaqu*) to bodies include features like position, place, and quantity—the same features that, according to al-Fārābī, needed to be separated from the intelligible object in the process of abstraction. Avicenna is in full agreement with this, also speaking of the known object as an "abstracted form (*ṣūra mujarrada*)" (214.9) and affirming that this form, once suitably freed from its bodily accoutrements, has no place, position, or division and can therefore no longer reside in a body (214.17).

Avicenna adds a further version of the affinity argument. This is one we have not yet seen, though like Averroes' analogy between the mind and prime matter, it is clearly inspired by Aristotle's argument that the mind must by nature already be all knowable things potentially. The things the mind can know, Avicenna says, are indefinite or infinite. But no body can have infinite potentiality:

> 216.5–10: Something that is potentially capable of infinite things cannot be a body, or a power in a body...So it is completely impossible for the essence that conceptualizes the intelligibles to subsist in a body, and its activity is not carried out in a body or through a body. Let no one say that this is also true of imaginative things, for this is wrong. The animal power never imagines anything to which infinity may apply.

Here Avicenna stays true to his strict division between intellection and our other cognitive faculties, which are seated in the body and are directed towards sensible particulars. Though these lower functions make intellection possible for us, they are of a fundamentally different order, as shown by the fact that attention to sensible particulars distracts us from using the intellect (220.12–14; 223.5–8).

The dividing line between intellect and lower cognitive faculties is simultaneously a dividing line between humans and non-human animals. This point is already implied by Avicenna's ascribing the lower faculties to the "animal power (al-quwwa al-ḥayawāniyya)" in the passage just quoted. Avicenna builds on earlier accounts from the medical and philosophical traditions to develop the idea that humans have five "internal senses" seated in the brain, most of them shared with animals.[24] With this theory, Avicenna implicitly recognizes the narrow scope of intellection as he has defined it: the rational soul, or mind, is concerned only with universal intelligibles and how they interrelate. When you experience having breakfast, remember later in the day what you had for breakfast, imagine how breakfast might be improved, or plan what to have for breakfast tomorrow, none of this is an exercise of the human intellect. For, in each case, you are concerning yourself with particulars, either actual ones you have encountered or possible ones you are only envisioning. By the same token, it turns out that animals are not missing out on much by lacking intellect. They cannot engage in abstract consideration of universals, but apart from that the higher animals, at least, share most of our mental life.

One commonality between humans and animals is a faculty Avicenna was the first to identify: wahm. The term is usually rendered in English as "estimation," following the medieval Latin translation aestimatio. But this is misleading, as the power has nothing to do with estimating. It is, rather, a capacity seated in the brain, with which humans and animals can perceive features (ma'ānī) that are ungraspable for the five external senses. Avicenna's famous example, repeated by many later thinkers in both the Islamic and Latin Christian world (it even turns up in Descartes), is that a sheep can perceive that a wolf is hostile, which is why it flees the wolf. This cannot be explained with reference to external senses like vision and hearing, since hostility is not a property that is visible, audible, etc.

It is noteworthy that, when explaining the function of wahm, Avicenna stresses that it concerns itself with particular sensible things (al-maḥsūsāt al-juz'iyya).[25] And one can see why Avicenna is at pains to restrict wahm and

---

[24] For an early study, see Wolfson 1935. More recent discussions include Black 1993 and 2000, and Pormann 2013.

[25] al-Ishārāt, 379.2, and see Rahman 1959, 43.10 and 166.5 for the restriction of wahm to maḥsūsāt, that is, things that are also perceptible to the external senses. Both passages give the example of the sheep and wolf.

the other internal senses to particulars. His use of the affinity argument to establish the mind's incorporeality requires a correspondence between the subject and object of cognition. Just as we have an incorporeal power for grasping objects abstracted from bodily things, so corporeal cognitive powers should perceive bodies and their properties. If he were to admit that non-human animals can grasp genuinely "abstract" ideas—that is, universals—then he would either have to say that a corporeal power can grasp such ideas, or that animals have non-corporeal cognitive powers just like we do. Neither is acceptable to him. The former concession would undermine his affinity argument, the latter his sharp contrast between humans and animals.

Yet these features grasped by the *wahm*, which Avicenna calls *ma'ānī*, do sound dangerously close to the universals grasped by intellect.[26] For one thing, is a wolf's hostility to a sheep really "divided" the way that, say, the wolf's gray color is divided in the parts of its coat? One of Avicenna's later critics, the Mu'tazilite theologian Ibn al-Malāḥimī (d. 1141), thought not. In a lengthy critique of Avicenna's affinity argument, he wrote:

> As for [your premise] that whatever inheres in a divisible thing is itself divisible, this is hardly a primary axiom. For someone might deny this, saying that what inheres (*ḥāll*) is like an attribute (*ṣifa*) and inheres in the subject (*maḥall*). So nothing prevents that what has the attribute be divisible, even as the attribute or inhering property is unified, insofar as it is an attribute. Don't you realize that you yourselves say the power of *wahm* perceives properties (*ma'ānī*), and among such properties are some that are one, like the hostility of the wolf for the sheep?[27]

Then, too, we might ask, are animals really bound to particulars in their perception? Avicenna insists that the sheep can grasp only the hostility of *this* wolf and not of wolves in general. But he himself mentions phenomena that seem to cast doubt on that supposition, for instance that dogs that have been beaten with sticks have a fear of sticks.[28] Avicenna thinks he can explain this by appealing to the functions of imagination, memory, and

---

[26] For this point in the context of the Latin reception of Avicenna, see Oelze 2018, 53.

[27] Ansari and Madelung 2008, 161.20–5 (see further Madelung 2012). The same point is made, again alluding to the wolf and sheep example, by another critic named Sharaf al-Dīn al-Mas'ūdī (d. before 1204). See Shihadeh 2016, 244. My thanks to Michael Noble for his assistance in locating these and other relevant passages in post-Avicennan philosophy.

[28] Rahman, *Avicenna's De anima*, 185.3.

wahm, but it could easily seem that the dog is reaching a universal conclusion about all sticks based on its "experience (*tajriba*)" of one stick, just as we come to understand that all humans are rational based on our experience of individual humans.

Again, this point was noticed in post-Avicennan philosophy, in this case by the great theologian-philosopher Fakhr al-Dīn al-Rāzī (d. 1210). In a passage where he is questioning the need to postulate a distinct faculty called *wahm*, he wonders whether it is really reasonable to contrast *wahm* to intellect:

> One might argue: if the power of *wahm* perceives the hostility of some given individual, then it may perceive hostility not insofar as it belongs to that given individual, or insofar as it does. But in the first case, the *wahm* would have perceived universal hostility, but then the *wahm* would be the same as intellect, for it is intellect that perceives universals.[29]

Elsewhere, he asserts the potential objection more explicitly:

> True, what exists outside the mind [e.g., hostility] is something particular, and in something particular, namely a certain wolf. But the scope (*qadar*) by which I know it is something universal, just as, when someone knows that there is one man in this house, what he knows is something universal (*kāna ma'lūmuhu amran kulliyyan*). For "man who is in this house" can be said interchangeably of numerous [men], even though this man is in himself particular, and this house too is in itself particular.[30]

Elsewhere, he observes that judgments like "this is an enemy," which are available to *wahm*, are no less indivisible than the sort of universal, intellectual judgments reserved by Avicenna to the intellect.[31]

These lines of attack were anticipated by Avicenna's most famous critic, al-Ghazālī (d. 1111). In his *Incoherence of the Philosophers* (*Tahāfut al-falāsifa*) he presented a whole battery of arguments against the Avicennan version of the affinity argument.[32] Following a presentation of the cognitive faculties recognized by Avicenna, including *wahm*, al-Ghazālī undertakes to

---

[29] al-Baghdādī 1990, vol. 2, 342.11–343.1. The refutation then continues by saying that in the second case, the *wahm* would need to perceive the given individual to grasp that it is hostile, but then *wahm* is just the same as sensation.

[30] Najafzādeh 2005, vol. 2, 258.5–8.   [31] al-Saqqā 1987, vol. 7, 65.

[32] Cited by section number from Marmura 1997.

refute Avcienna's claim to have proved that the soul is a "substance that subsists through itself" (§18.12). He then presents the affinity argument that moves from the indivisibility of intelligibles to the indivisibility of their "subject (*maḥall*)" namely the intellect or rational soul. Two responses are considered. First, that *wahm*, which Avicenna considers to be a power seated in the body, is able to grasp properties that are indivisible. After all, it's not as if hostility has parts that could exist independently of one another (§§18.17 and 19). In general, there is more than one way that "features (*awṣāf*)" relate to their subjects. So even if color is divided along with the body in which it resides, perhaps knowledge is undivided while being in a divisible body, just like the indivisible hostility in the divisible wolf (§18.22).[33]

Al-Ghazālī's second response reveals a further potential weakness in Avicenna's argument, and may also indicate how al-Ghazālī himself, and other theologians who responded to Avicenna, conceived of the subject in which knowledge inheres. Here his point is that there is more than one way to be indivisible. When Avicenna argued that the mind is indivisible, this amounted to much the same thing as Plato saying it is "invisible." Both affinity arguments try to place the mind outside the physical realm entirely. But what if there are material objects that are indivisible, that is, the atoms standardly postulated in the physical theories of Islamic theologians? Al-Ghazālī puts the point like this: "how do you refute someone who says that the subject of knowledge is an individual substance that occupies space (*jawhar fard mutaḥayyiz*), and is indivisible? This is familiar from the school of the theologians (*madhhab al-mutakallimīn*)" (§18.16). As the last remark indicates, it was standard among authors of Islamic theology (*kalām*) to hold that bodies are not indefinitely divisible, as the Aristotelians claimed. Rather, they are made up of atoms, which are bearers of "accidents (*aʿrāḍ*)" like rest and motion. Classically, the *kalām* tradition assumes that it is God who associates the accidental features with the atoms.

In *kalām*, an atom is strictly speaking not a "body," as it is assumed that a certain number of atoms must join to make the smallest possible body. So in fact al-Ghazālī could even agree with Avicenna's claim that "what we have that attains the intelligible form is a non-bodily substance." Actually the feature of atoms recognized in *kalām* that most clearly distinguishes them from the sort of substance Avicenna had in mind is, as al-Ghazālī says, that they are "space-occupying." So his point is that if all the affinity argument

[33] The same point is made by al-Masʿūdī at Shihadeh 2016, 244.

shows is that the bearer of knowledge is indivisible, then a space-occupying, but indivisible and hence not "bodily," substance would satisfy this criterion. Like al-Ghazālī's point about *wahm*, this criticism can be found in other post-Avicennan thinkers who responded to Avicenna's argument. Commenting on the version found in Avicenna's *Pointers*, al-Rāzī says with typical perspicacity:

> What was sought in this section was a proof that an instance of knowledge is incapable of division; and every space-occupying thing is divisible; therefore the subject for instances of knowledge (*maḥall al-'ulūm*) is something that is not space-occupying, nor does it subsist through what is space-occupying. So if we affirm an indivisible space-occupying [thing], then the argument fails.[34]

What these responses to Avicenna ignore, though, is that the same chapter of the *Healing* where we find the affinity argument from indivisibility also includes an argument against atomism. So, in fact, Avicenna anticipated this escape from his argument. All the criticisms of al-Ghazālī and al-Rāzī show is that his affinity argument will only be as strong as the refutation of atomism that accompanies it.[35]

Or perhaps these criticisms do show something else, by calling our attention to a pitfall threatening affinity arguments concerning the mind, by undermining the central intuition that drove these arguments over so many centuries. The various versions of the argument have in common that they ascribe to the knowing mind some feature or features thought to belong to the mind's object of knowledge: invisibility, incorporeality, indivisibility, and so on. But it is far from clear that the mind has to have *all* the properties possessed by its object, in order to know that object. Why not suppose that a "space-occupying" indivisible thing can grasp a "non-space-occupying" indivisible thing; or that if the power of *wahm*, which is seated in a body, grasps the indivisible property of hostility, that the mind can do the same thing while being a bodily power? Once we start thinking along these lines, we might give up on the idea that the mind needs any sort of affinity to its objects. It may only need a suitable *relation* to those objects, and we know that things of radically different kinds can bear relationships to one

---

[34] *Sharḥ al-Ishārāt*, 286.14–16.   [35] See, further, Lettinck 1999, McGinnis 2013.

another.[36] And, as it happens, conceiving of knowledge as a relation is another traditional idea in Islamic theology. Putting this together with the other *kalām* idea that the mind (or "heart," as they often put it) is atomic in character, we have the makings of a radically un-Aristotelian philosophy of mind according to which a space-occupying yet indivisible subject knows simply by acquiring a relation to whatever it knows.[37]

The Aristotelian response would seem obvious. As Aristotle himself stated, when the mind knows it actually *becomes* its object. And if the subject and object of knowledge are identical, then of course we have to admit that they share all the same properties, because of the indiscernibility of identicals (a far less contentious principle than the identity of indiscernibles). But doesn't taking this claim to its logical extreme land us with a theory like that of Averroes? As we saw, he argued that since the known object is singular and universal, the knower too (the "material intellect") is singular and universal. This is a conclusion Avicenna would like to avoid. On his view, one person's intellective grasp of a form is distinct from another person's grasp of that same form. But how can this be if its object is universal, and it has all its object's properties?

The answer is that Avicenna does not accept that the mind "becomes its object," at least not in the straightforward sense that would make subject and object indiscernible:

> To be sure, the forms of things do inhere in the soul, adorning and ornamenting it, and the soul is like a place for them, through the intermediary of the material intellect. But if the soul were actually to *become* the form of one of the existents... it would follow that the soul would then have no potentiality to receive any other form or anything else. But in fact [the soul] does receive another form different from that form. Again, if this other form is not different from the first form, that would be strange indeed, for [soul's] receiving and not receiving would be one and the same. But if they are different, then without doubt – if it is the intelligible form – [the soul] has become different from itself. Or, none of this is the

---

[36] An obvious example in the medieval context would be that God, who is as different from His creatures as anything can be, still bears relations to those creatures, such as the relation of being their Creator.

[37] Such a view is suggested, for instance, by al-Masʿūdī at Shihadeh 2016, 242–3, who in responding to Avicenna's affinity argument agrees that the knower does not take on an "attribute" in such a way as to divide it, like body divides color or heat, but just knows because there is a relation (*iḍ fa*) between knower and known—the relation, too, he points out, is indivisible.

case, but instead the soul is intellecting, "intellect" meaning the potential by which it engages in intellection, or meaning the forms of these intelligibles in themselves. And because they are in the soul they are intelligible. But the intellect, the intellecting and the intelligible are not one and the same thing in our souls.[38]

In this dense passage Avicenna makes the rather convincing point that the mind cannot become strictly identical to its object, since that object would not seem to have the power to grasp other objects, whereas the mind retains that power. For instance, the universal idea of humanity does not have the ability to think about the universal idea of horse. Rather, the mind receives a given form by becoming its *subject*, rather than becoming the same as that form.

If we look back at the affinity argument stated earlier in this same work, we will see that there Avicenna was also clear that the mind is a subject (*maḥall*) for its object and not strictly identical with the object. His argument, then, was not that the mind must be undivided if it is to *become* an undivided idea, but that the mind must be undivided if it is to be a suitable "place" or "seat" for the idea.[39] This is a much narrower claim than what we found in Plato at the beginning of the tradition of affinity arguments. Avicenna's affinity argument in the *Healing* does not invoke a general intuition that the mind is somehow "like" its objects, nor does he, like Averroes, believe that there needs to be full identity between the subject and object of thought. He only needs to persuade us, using the analogy to properties like color, that forms are "like" their subjects in respect of (in-) divisibility. As we've seen, critics like al-Ghazālī and al-Rāzī understood this and duly focused their attention on whether an indivisible thing can in fact inhere in a divisible subject. Hence their interest in *wahm*, which seems to be precisely such a case.

In the passage cited from Avicenna's *Pointers* at the beginning of this chapter, Avicenna makes a stronger claim. The abstracted form needs to be not just indivisible, but divested of all "extraneous attachments that render it individual," if it is to be intelligible. It will need to lack "location, position,

---

[38] Rahman, *Avicenna's De Anima*, §5.6, 240.6–19. I have also discussed this passage in the appendix of Adamson 2007b.

[39] The locution "place of forms," which appears in the passage just cited from Avicenna, is taken from Aristotle, *De anima* 429a27–8 who approves of the phrase, apparently used in Plato's circle but not found as such in any Platonic dialogue. On the late ancient reception of the passage, see Steel 2016.

quality, and size" for example. I take it that these features are also shared by the mind, and by the same reasoning used in the affinity argument from the *Healing*. If the mind had a location, for instance, then a form inhering in it would have a spatial location, as the red of an apple is located where the apple is located. Again, the mind must lack the features that "individualize" bodies. It can grasp an incorporeal object only by being an incorporeal subject. But if the object of knowledge is universal, not individual, doesn't this mean that the subject of thought, too, must be universal? That would after all land us with the Averroist theory of the unicity of intellect. Avicenna's answer comes in another part of the *Healing*, the section on *Metaphysics*:

> The way in which this form is a trait (*hay'a*) in a particular soul is that it is an individual instance of knowledge or conceptualization (*aḥad askhhāṣ al-ʿulūm aw al-taṣawwurāt*) . . . In different respects, it is universal and particular.[40]

As he goes on to explain, the idea is particular insofar as it is something inhering in one particular mind, but universal insofar as it relates to the many particulars of which it is an idea. I have an idea of humanity, for instance, which relates to all humans. But it is my idea and mine alone.

This is reminiscent of the representationalist objection to Averroes' unicity theory, which we saw Nifo rejecting out of hand. And indeed, Avicenna will speak about the "representation (*mithāl*) of a thing's true nature (*ḥaqīqa*) being inscribed in the essence (*dhāt*) of the perceiver."[41] Whether his epistemology should, in general, be described as "representationalist" is a difficult question I will not delve into here. Instead, I will conclude by noting that Avicenna's view is surprisingly congenial to the *kalām* way of understanding the mind. Using a piece of *kalām* terminology, *maḥall*, he exploits the difference between a "subject" and its inhering property to avoid asserting identity between the mind and its object. He also explains the universality of the mind in terms of a relation, albeit that this is a relation between the intelligible form and many particulars, rather than a relation directly between the mind and the many particulars.[42] This

---

[40] Marmura 2005, §5.2.6.   [41] *Ishārāt* 3.7, 359 in the Dunyā edition.

[42] Thus al-Masʿūdī, at Shihadeh 2016, presents the Avicennan position as follows: "the intellectual power's perception of the things it perceives is a contact (*mulāqā*) between the intellectual power and the forms of the intelligible true realities (*ṣuwar al-ḥaqāʾiq al-maʿqūla*)" (210.9–10). He then rejects this, writing: "in fact, investigation and inquiry show that the true

may of course be a sign that Avicenna was influenced by *kalām*. But if so, his later critics felt that the influence did not run deep enough. In their eyes, he failed to rule out an atomic conception of the mind, and invoked an intelligible form that seemed to be a superfluous holdover from Aristotelianism. It would be simpler just to explain knowledge as an unmediated relation between knower and known—two relata that need not, after all, have anything special in common.[43]

References

Primary Sources

P. Adamson and P.E. Pormann (trans.), *The Philosophical Works of al-Kindī* (Karachi: 2012).

M.J.B. Allen (trans.) and J. Hankins (ed.), *Marsilio Ficino: Platonic Theology*, 6 vols. (Cambridge, MA: 2001–6).

H. Ansari and W. Madelung (eds.), *Rukn al-Dīn Ibn al-Malāḥimī: Tuḥfat al-mutakallimīn* (Tehran: 2008).

M.M. al-Baghdādī (ed.), *Fakhr al-Dīn al-Rāzī: al-Mabāḥith al-mashriqiyya fī ʿilm al-ilāhiyyāt wa-l-ṭabīʿiyyāt*, 2 vols. (Beirut: 1990).

M. Bouyges (ed.), *Averroes: Tahafot al-Tahafot* (Beirut: 1930).

M. Bouyges (ed.), *al-Fārābī: Risāla fī-l ʿAql* (Beirut: 1948).

F.S. Crawford (ed.), *Averrois Cordubensis Commentarium magnum in Aristotelis De anima libros* (Cambridge, MA: 1953).

---

reality of perception is something other than contact. Rather, it is a relational state (*ḥola iḍāfiyya*) of the perceiver to the thing that is perceived" (212.10–12). Al-Rāzī declares himself open to two versions of the relational view—between the mind and its own form, or between the mind and the known object, at *Sharḥ al-Ishārāt* vol. 2, 226–9.11: "according to us, the truth is that perception isn't best understood as being just the occurrence of that form [in the intellect]; rather it means a state of relation (*ḥela nisbiyya*), between either the intellectual power and the essence of the form that exists in the intellect, or between the power and the thing established in extramental reality."

[43] This research was supported by funding from the European Research Council (ERC) under the European Union's Horizon 2020 research and innovation programme (grant agreement No. 786762), and by the DFG under the aegis of the project Heirs of Avicenna: Philosophy in the Islamic East from the 12th to the 13th Century. I am very grateful for stimulating discussion, and help finding relevant texts, from researchers attached to both projects, especially Tommaso Alpina for passages in Avicenna, and Fedor Benevich, Michael Noble, and Sarah Virgi for passages in post-Avicennan philosophy in the East.

H. Diels (ed.), *Theophrasti Fragmentum De sensibus*, in *Doxographi Graeci* (Berlin: 1879).

S. Dunyā (ed.), *Ibn Sīnā: al-Ishārāt wa-l-tanbīhāt*, 4 vols. (Cairo: 1957–60).

A.E. Goichon (trans.), *Avicenne, Livre des directives et remarques* (Paris: 1951).

A. Hyman and J.J. Walsh (eds.), *Philosophy in the Middle Ages* (Indianapolis: 1983).

S. Inati, *Ibn Sina's Remarks and Admonitions: Physics and Metaphysics* (New York: 2014).

M.E. Marmura (ed. and trans.), *al-Ghazālī: The Incoherence of the Philosophers* (Provo: 1997).

M.E. Marmura (ed. and trans.), *Avicenna: The Metaphysics of the Healing* (Provo: 2005).

ʿA.R. Najafzādeh (ed.), *Fakhr al-Dīn al-Rāzī: Sharḥ al-Ishārāt wa-l-tanbīhāt*, 2 vols. (Tehran: 2005).

F. Rahman, *Avicenna's De Anima* (London: 1959).

A.Ḥ. al-Saqqā (ed.), *Fakhr al-Dīn al-Rāzī: al-Maṭālib al-ʿāliya min al-ʿilm al-ilāhī*, 9 vols. (Beirut: 1987).

A. Shihadeh (ed.), *Doubts on Avicenna: A Study and Edition of Sharaf al-Dīn al-Masʿūdī's Commentary on the Ishārāt* (Leiden: 2016).

A. Spruit (ed.), *Agostino Nifo: De intellectu* (Leiden: 2011).

R.C. Taylor (ed.), *Averroes (Ibn Rushd) of Cordoba: Long Commentary on the De Anima of Aristotle* (New Haven: 2009).

S. van den Burgh, *Tahafut al-Tahafut (The Incoherence of the Incoherence)* (Cambridge: 1954).

Secondary Sources

P. Adamson, "On Knowledge of Particulars," *Proceedings of the Aristotelian Society* 105 (2005), 273–94.

P. Adamson, "Knowledge of Universals and Particulars in the Baghdad School," *Documenti e Studi sulla Tradizione Filosofica Medievale* 18 (2007a), 141–64.

P. Adamson, "*Porphyrius Arabus* on Nature and Art: 463F Smith in Context," in G. Karamanolis and A. Sheppard (eds.), *Studies on Porphyry* (London: Institute of Classical Studies, 2007b), 141–63.

F. Benevich, "God's Knowledge of Particulars: Avicenna, *Kalām*, and The Post-Avicennian Synthesis," *Recherches de Théologie et Philosophie Médiévales* 76 (2019), 1–47.

M.F. Burnyeat, "Aristotle on Understanding Knowledge," in E. Berti (ed.), *Aristotle on Science: The Posterior Analytics* (Padua: 1981), 97–139.

D.L. Black, "Estimation in Avicenna: The Logical and Psychological Dimensions," *Dialogue* 32 (1993), 219–58.

D.L. Black, "Conjunction and the Identity of Knower and Known in Averroes," *American Catholic Philosophical Quarterly* 73 (1999), 159–84.

D.L. Black, "Imagination and Estimation: Arabic Paradigms and Western Transformations," *Topoi* 19 (2000), 59–70.

C. D'Ancona, "Degrees of Abstraction in Avicenna. How to Combine Aristotle's *De anima* and the *Enneads*," in S. Knuuttila and P. Kärkkäinen (eds.), *Theories of Perception in Medieval and Early Modern Philosophy* (Berlin: 2008), 47–71.

H.A. Davidson, *Alfarabi, Avicenna and Averroes on Intellect* (Oxford: 1992).

M. Di Giovanni, "Averroes, Philosopher of Islam," in P. Adamson and M. Di Giovanni (eds.), *Interpreting Averroes: Critical Essays* (Cambridge: 2018), 1–26.

M. Engel, "Elijah Del Medigo and Agostino Nifo on Intelligible Species," *Documenti e studi sulla tradizione filosofica medievale* 26 (2015), 495–516.

D. Gutas, "The Empiricism of Avicenna," *Oriens* 40 (2012), 391–436.

D.N. Hasse, "Avicenna on Abstraction," in R. Wisnovksy (ed.), *Aspects of Avicenna* (Princeton: 2001), 39–72.

P. Lettinck, "Ibn Sīnā on Atomism," *al-Shajarah* 4 (1999), 1–51.

J. McGinnis, "Making Abstraction Less Abstract: The Logical, Psychological, and Metaphysical Dimensions of Avicenna's Theory of Abstraction," *Proceedings of the American Catholic Philosophical Association* 80 (2007), 169–83.

J. McGinnis, "Avicenna's Natural Philosophy," in P. Adamson (ed.), *Interpreting Avicenna: Critical Essays* (Cambridge: 2013), 71–90.

W. Madelung, "Ibn al-Malāḥimī on the Human Soul," *The Muslim World* 102 (2012), 426–32.

S. Nusseibeh, "Avicenna: Providence and God's Knowledge of Particulars," in Y.T. Langermann (ed.), *Avicenna and His Legacy: A Golden Age of Science and Philosophy* (Turnhout: 2009), 275–88.

A. Oelze, *Animal Rationality: Later Medieval Theories 1250–1350* (Leiden: 2018).

P.E. Pormann, "Avicenna on Medical Practice, Epistemology, and the Physiology of the Inner Senses," in P. Adamson (ed.), *Interpreting Avicenna: Critical Essays* (Cambridge: 2013), 91–108.

D.N. Sedley, "Empedocles' Theory of Vision and Theophrastus' *De sensibus*," in W.W. Fortenbaugh and D. Gutas (eds.), *Theophrastus: His Psychological, Doxographical and Scientific Writings* (New Brunswick: 1992), 20–31.

C. Steel, "Soul and Matter as the Place of Forms: Neoplatonic Interpretations of Aristotle, *De anima* III 4, 429a27–9," in J. Halfwassen et al. (eds.), *Soul and Matter in Neoplatonism* (Heidelberg: 2016), 233–57.

R.C. Taylor, "Averroes on Psychology and the Principles of Metaphysics," Journal of the History of Philosophy 36 (1998), 507–23.

R.C. Taylor, "Themistius and the Development of Averroes' Noetics," in R.L. Friedman and J.-M. Counet (eds.), *Medieval Perspectives on Aristotle's De Anima* (Louvain: 2013), 1–38.

D. Wirmer, "Nachwort: Einführung in die Psychologie des Averroes," in D. Wirmer, *Über den Intellekt: Auszüge aus seinen drei Kommentaren zu Aristoteles' De anima* (Freiburg: 2008), 287–409.

H.A. Wolfson, "The Internal Senses in Latin, Arabic and Hebrew Philosophical Texts," *Harvard Theological Review* 28 (1935), 69–133.

A. Zadyousefi, "Does God Know that the Flower in My Hand Is Red? Avicenna and the Problem of God's Perceptual Knowledge," *Sophia* 58 (2019), 1–37.

Index

For the benefit of digital users, indexed terms that span two pages (e.g., 52–53) may, on occasion, appear on only one of those pages.